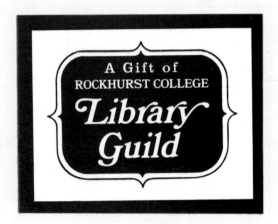

ACCOUNTING
INFORMATION SYSTEMS

ACCOUNTING
INFORMATION SYSTEMS

GEORGE H. BODNAR
The George Washington University

ALLYN AND BACON, INC.
Boston London Sydney Toronto

Cover: Louise Nevelson. *Transparent Sculpture VI*. (1967–68). Plexiglas. 19 X 20 X 8 inches. Collection of Whitney Museum of American Art. Gift of the Howard and Jean Lipman Foundation, Inc.

Library of Congress Cataloging in Publication Data

Bodnar, George H
  Accounting information systems.

  Bibliography: p.
  Includes index.
  1. Accounting—Data processing. 2. Information storage and retrieval systems—Accounting. I. Title.
HF5679.B59   657'.028'54   79-21008
ISBN 0-205-06884-7

CONTENTS

PREFACE

OBJECTIVE

The objective of this text is to assist the reader in acquiring the skills and expertise expected and required of a contemporary accounting systems analyst or auditor. The book itself aspires to fill a need for a text that gives the accounting systems course an identity in a subject matter that is particularly relevant to professional accounting systems work.

The book is intended for a one semester course in accounting information systems for advanced undergraduate- or graduate-level accounting majors and for others interested in the subject matter. Introductory financial and managerial accounting courses are a necessary prerequisite, and it is desirable but not essential that the reader possess some knowledge of a computer programming language. The book may serve as a supplement to advanced undergraduate or graduate courses on information systems because of its emphasis on accounting applications and controls.

SUBJECT MATTER

As a professional topic and field of study, the subject of accounting information systems has experienced dramatic change over the last decade. The now common addition of the term *information* to the more traditional phrase *accounting systems* signifies the dramatic changes and enhanced system capabilities that have resulted from the widespread application of computerized data processing technology.

Computer technology has altered the nature of accounting systems, and thus has altered the qualifications required of an accounting systems analyst or auditor. The design or audit of an accounting information system must consider the data processing technology employed by the system. The data processing configuration of an accounting information system is an important factor in the role the system occupies in an organization's internal control system. Contemporary technology complicates professional internal control considerations and at the same time introduces powerful capabilities to provide useful information relevant to a wide range of organizational decision-making needs and requirements. Expertise in systems techniques such as flowcharting and scheduling, a familiarity with contemporary data processing technology, and an in-depth understanding of internal control considerations are essential to an accountant's performance of traditional duties relating to the design and audit of accounting information systems.

Concurrent with the systems design and auditing changes wrought by data processing technology, significant change has occurred in the professional environment of accounting information systems. With the passage of the Foreign Corrupt Practices Act by Congress in 1977, adequacy of accounting records and internal control became a matter of law. Even before this law, the internal audit function had grown steadily in professional stature and responsibility, which the above act will predictably enhance. The Institute of Internal Auditors now has over 16,000 members in 85 countries. These professionals subscribe to a code of ethics, take part in programs of certification and continuing education, and adhere to a set of standards for the professional practice of internal auditing. Concurrent with this trend toward professionalization of the internal auditor, other trends—the establishment of audit committees by organizations, an increasing concern for white-collar crime and computer-related crime by the federal government and society at large, an increased dependence in organizations of all sizes on computer technology for basic accounting and informational needs, and notably a trend toward having internal audit managers report to a vice-presidential or higher level in the organization—suggest the increased professional responsibilities and social importance associated with contemporary accounting information systems.

This textbook was initiated with the view that an in-depth treatment of internal control and the related accounting procedures is central to an accounting systems course. Existing texts on accounting information systems either closely parallel numerous computer/management information systems texts in their coverage, or else they tend to dwell on a single case study conversion of a manual to a computer-based system. Both of these approaches tend to duplicate the academic content of other disciplines to the exclusion of topics more relevant to professional accounting systems work. This is obviously true of computer/management information system texts. This situation exists at a time when "systems" are ubiquitous in the accounting profession; at the same time, the once traditional topic of procedures is disappearing from auditing texts by necessity as SEC and AICPA pronouncements, statistical sampling, ethics, and other topics demand coverage in the auditing course.

ORGANIZATION

This text is different from existing texts on accounting information systems in both selection and organization of topics. The discussion of computer topics focuses on the processing of accounting data in a variety of systems-batch, real-time/on-line, and integrated (for example, POS System) systems—and provides an in-depth discussion of the related internal control considerations.

Topics more relevant to management information systems courses—such as the computer acquisition process, hardware features, programming languages, and the use of computers in nonaccounting-based applications —are presented in overview fashion.

Traditional material on internal control in application systems is presented as distinct chapters early in the text (Chapters 3, 4, and 5). Subsequent chapters initially discuss accounting technology in manual systems (Chapters 6 and 7), gradually moving toward computer-based systems (Chapters 8 and 9). A separate discussion of computer data processing procedures and controls (Chapter 10) precedes the discussion of computer-based application system illustrations (Chapters 11 and 12). The concluding chapters are topical extensions of material particularly relevant to contemporary accounting systems analysis and design: software/data management (13), distributed processing (14), system development (15), and project management (16). The discussion of computer topics, particularly in these later chapters, is oriented towards the needs of the accounting professional.

ASSIGNMENT OF CHAPTERS

The gradual progression from manual systems to computer systems is based on the view that students must understand manual system principles in order fully to understand computer-based systems. The text is designed to be studied sequentially; however, the modular nature of the topical organization allows the instructor to alter the flow of topics to fit his own needs and the background of students in the course.

Chapter 1 provides an overview of the subject area and the nature of professional systems work. Chapter 2 presents essential systems terminology and techniques (including flowcharts). Chapters 3, 4, and 5 present a "technology-free" discussion of accounting application systems, emphasizing internal control considerations in systems design. This sequence exposes the student to the nature of accounting applications prior to an examination of technological considerations in systems design. Some instructors may choose to assign Chapter 16 immediately after Chapter 2 to increase the emphasis given to systems techniques and to introduce contemporary value of information/decision-making concepts early in the course. Chapter 6 might be assigned immediately after Chapter 3 as several of the professional problems contained in Chapters 4 and 5 assume a knowledge of the technology discussed in Chapter 6.

Chapter 6 discusses double-entry accounting in the context of manual, one-write, and bookkeeping machine systems. Chapter 7 provides a transition to computer systems with a discussion of coding systems and an overview of electromechanical card-oriented systems. Chapter 8 discusses principles of computer data processing, emphasizing the coding of accounting data for computer processing. Chapter 9 discusses file processing techniques and data management, subjects which are relevant to the design of computer-based application systems.

The instructor's use of Chapters 6 through 9 should be dependent on the computer background of the students and the instructor's preference for covering traditional system topics. Chapters 6 and 7 are highly problem-oriented in addition to providing a useful framework for understanding computer systems.

Chapter 10 presents an overview of computer processing procedures and an in-depth discussion of application controls in a computer environment. The presentation of controls concentrates on user-oriented data controls—the focal point of most internal control evaluations. Chapters 11 and 12 present a variety of computer-based application systems. Each application system discussed is illustrated with one or more flowchart.

Chapter 13 discusses software and data management concepts. Chapter 14 provides detail on minicomputers and distributive processing. Chapter 15 is an overview of the systems development process, emphasizing the importance of "systems auditability." Chapter 16 discusses value of information (information economics) concepts and project scheduling and management techniques.

PROBLEM MATERIAL

The text contains numerous problem and discussion questions. Each chapter is followed by a set of review questions for student or classroom use and also a series of discussion questions or problems intended for written assignment and/or class discussion. The text contains several problems that are of a term project nature; many of the problems are adapted from professional examinations (CPA, CMA, CIA).

A more detailed discussion of problem material and class assignments is contained in the instructor/solutions manual that is available with this text.

ACKNOWLEDGEMENTS

I am indebted to Professor Anthony J. Mastro, Chairman of the Department of Accounting at the George Washington University, for his encouragement and perseverance as this material was developed and used as lecture notes over several years.

I wish to thank Professor Ronald J. Teichman of the Pennsylvania State University for his detailed and careful reviews of earlier drafts. The overall organization and content of this text was significantly enhanced through Professor Teichman's suggestions.

I also wish to acknowledge the reviews of Professor J. Hal Reneau, of Arizona State University, and others.

I am indebted to the following organizations for their permission to reprint or adapt material subject to their copyrights:

The American Institute of Certified Public Accountants
The Institute of Internal Auditors, Inc.
The Institute of Management Accounting of the National Association
    of Accountants (for use of problem materials from past CMA exams)
NCR Corporation
Burroughs Corporation
Safeguard Business Systems, Inc.

ACCOUNTING
INFORMATION SYSTEMS

ACCOUNTING INFORMATION SYSTEMS: AN OVERVIEW

1

The title of this chapter contains the words *accounting*, *information*, and *systems*. Accounting is an activity that identifies, collects, processes, reports, and analyzes economic data. Information is useful data, and a system is a collection of resources designed to achieve certain objectives. An accounting information system (henceforth to be abbreviated "AIS") is a collection of resources, such as people and equipment, designed to transform economic data into useful information. This information is made available to a wide variety of users to assist in the planning and control of the activities of an organization.

Data is useful only if it satisfies a need. The concept of information as useful data implies that AIS has utility only in satisfying user needs. Such needs may be personal, like the necessity to keep one's own checkbook in balance; or they may be organizational, as in the general need for a business to assess periodically the profitability of its various activities. This text focuses on AIS as it relates to organizations.

In contemporary business theory, organizations are viewed as a collection of decision-making positions. Organizations exist to pursue goals or objectives. As a system, every organization accepts inputs and transforms them into outputs that take the form of products and services. A manufacturing firm transforms raw material, labor, and other inputs into tangible items such as furniture that are subsequently sold in pursuit of the goal of profit. A university accepts a variety of inputs such as faculty labor and student time and transforms these inputs into a variety of outputs in pursuit of broad goals such as education and the promotion of knowledge. A manufacturing firm is easier to define as a system as its inputs, outputs, and transformation processes are much more measurable or observable than those of a university system. Conceptually, all organizational systems seek goals or objectives through a process of resource allocation. Resource allocation is accomplished through the processes of managerial decision making. Information has economic value to the extent that it facilitates resource allocation decisions, thus assisting a system in its pursuit of goals.

ACCOUNTING INFORMATION SYSTEMS AND BUSINESS ORGANIZATIONS

Contemporary accounting theory and practice views accounting as a viable information system that fulfills the needs of its users, both those external and internal to the firm, for information pertaining to the resource allocation processes of an organization.

The purpose of an AIS is to provide economic data to a variety of decision makers according to their needs and entitlement to the information. The subfunctions of accounting include data collection, processing and control, summarization, distribution, and interpretation.

The users of accounting data can be partitioned into two broad groups: external and internal. External users include stockholders, investors creditors, governmental agencies, customers and vendors, competitors, labor unions, and the public interest at large.

External users receive and depend on a variety of outputs from an organization's AIS. Many of these outputs are of a routine nature. Accounts payable transactions with suppliers, for example, require outputs such as purchase orders and checks from an organization's AIS. Customers receive bills and make payments, which are processed by the AIS. Employees receive paychecks and other payroll-related data; stockholders receive dividend checks and routine information concerning execution of stock transactions.

The information needs of external users are wide and varied. The publication of general-purpose financial statements, such as a balance sheet and income statement, and other nonroutine outputs assist in meeting these needs. Stockholders, investors at large, creditors, and other external users utilize a firm's general-purpose financial statements to evaluate past performance, predict future performance, and gain other insights into an organization.

Internal users comprise managers, who require different information depending on their level in an organization or on the particular function they perform. Figure 1.1 represents a schematic diagram of the different levels of managerial interest in an AIS. Figure 1.1 is intended to emphasize that there are different information needs and demands at different levels in an organization. For example, top management is generally concerned with long-run, as opposed to daily, planning and control. Accounting reports to top management consist largely of aggregated and summarized items such as total sales. Lower-level managers receive information more relevant to the particular subunit they operate, such as the

FIGURE 1.1.   Pyramid of Information Levels in an Organization

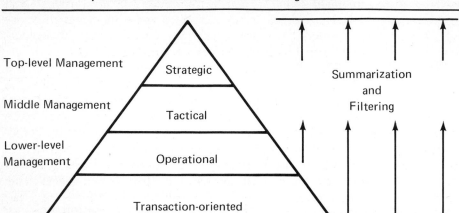

total sales of department A. Personnel in the lower levels of an organization, such as clerks processing payroll or sales transaction data, have constant interaction with the detail, transactional data itself.

Transaction Processing Cycles

Historically, a manual-based accounting system was often the only formal information network in a business organization. This is still often true in a new or small organization. It has long been impossible in our society to organize any financial activity and to survive without some form of accounting system. Tax laws typically are a prime motivator in this area. By necessity and historical precedent, certain features are common to AIS:

1.   they are financially oriented;
2.   most of the data-producing sources are recurring transactions to the organization; and
3.   the data records are chiefly historical in nature.

Accounting has been closely associated in the past with transaction processing systems. Although usually financial in nature, most transactions also generate statistical data that is of interest to management. A transaction is an event of interest. The receipt of a sales order or a notice of the arrival of goods from a supplier is an example of a business transaction. Figure 1.1 showed the transaction processing subsystem as the base of the management information pyramid. AIS are designed and implemented not only to produce the ledger balances from which financial statements are prepared but also to produce a wide variety of management and operational information in nonaccounting terms.

The initial task of an AIS is the recognition of transactions that should be processed by the system. A postulate of accounting theory states that all economic events that involve an organization in exchanges of a financial nature with other entities should be reflected in the organization's financial statements. An AIS routinely processes these monetary transactions as well as other transactions pertaining to economic events that are internal to an organization. Examples of internal economic events that may be processed by an AIS include the transfer of assets from inventory to a production process, depreciation calculations, and adjustments to customer invoices and other documents. It is important to recognize that AIS also process transactions concerning events that are not directly reflected in those ledger balances that are the basis of financial statements. Customer address changes and employee pay rate changes are examples of important AIS-processed transactions that do not directly affect an organization's financial statements.

Although no two organizations are identical, most organizations experience similar types of economic events. These events generate transactions that may be grouped according to four common cycles of business activity:

1. revenue cycle—events related to the distribution of goods and services to other entities and the collection of related payments;
2. expenditure cycle—events related to the acquisition of goods and services from other entities and the settlement of related obligations;
3. production cycle—events related to the transformation of resources into goods and services;
4. finance cycle—events related to the acquisition and management of capital funds.

A transaction processing cycle consists of one or more application systems. An application system processes logically related transactions. Each organization defines its own unique application systems. An organization's revenue cycle might commonly include application systems concerned with customer order entry, billing, accounts receivable, and sales reporting. An expenditure cycle might commonly include application systems concerned with vendor selection and requisitioning, purchasing, accounts payable, and payroll. A production cycle would include application systems concerned with production control and reporting, product costing, and property accounting. An organization's finance cycle might include application systems concerned with cash management and control, debt management, and the administration of employee benefit plans.

The concept of transaction processing cycles provides a framework for analyzing an organization's AIS. Although no two organizations may include the same application systems within a given transaction processing cycle, the cycle concept provides a basis for categorizing the flow of economic events that are common to all organizations.

The cycle concept emphasizes the similarities within the AIS of organizations of different sizes and different industries. The concept of transaction processing cycles has gained currency within the auditing profession in recent years:

> . . . cycles provide a common basis for discussing what happens in an entity, how to control what happens, and how economic events can impact several different segments of the organization at the same time. [Arthur Andersen & Co., 1978; p. 33.]

> An understanding of internal accounting controls requires a reasonably detailed description of the various accounting systems. To facilitate description, transactions are placed in natural groupings—called transaction cycles. Transaction cycles are described to show the flow of each type of transaction through the various functions of the business. [Touche Ross & Co., 1978; p. 7.]

Transaction cycles offer a systematic framework for the analysis and design of AIS in that there is a similar objective for each of the various cycles. This objective is to serve as an integral part of an organization's internal control system.

ACCOUNTING INFORMATION SYSTEMS AND INTERNAL CONTROL

Perhaps the most important aspect of an AIS is the role it plays in an organization's internal control system. The term *internal control* suggests actions taken within an organization to assist in regulating and directing the activities of the organization.

Most information needed by management to control finances and the progress of operations comes from the accounting records. One of management's major responsibilities is stewardship. Management must protect the resources of an organization against possible losses ranging from such causes as embezzlement to careless use of supplies or productive materials, unwarranted extension of credit, failure to purchase from the lowest-cost supplier, inefficient workers, and outright theft.

Control is necessary to assure that management policies and directives are properly adhered to. Management is far removed from the scene of operations in a large organization, and personal supervision of employees is an impossibility. As a substitute, management must rely on various control techniques to implement its decisions and goals and to regulate the activities for which it has the ultimate responsibility. Control is necessary over a wide range of activities, such as the maintenance of adequate but not excessive inventory quantities, the consumption of supplies in production and administration, and the payment of bills within allowed discount periods. Good internal control is a key factor in the effective management of an organization.

Basic Elements of Internal Control

An internal control system is best described as an organizational plan to protect assets, insure the reliability of accounting information, and promote operational efficiency. Ideally it would protect the company against fraud, waste, and theft on the part of both internal and external elements. Aside from this, an internal control system should facilitate the tracking of errors of omission and comission, thereby simplifying audit procedures.

An internal control system should allow for the establishment of responsibilities within an organization. For every task or job function there should be a person responsible for its proper execution. The reason is twofold: responsibilities must be clearly assigned in order to delineate problem areas and direct attention to these areas; and, once employees have a clear understanding of the scope of their responsibilities, they tend to work harder toward controlling these responsibilities.

A system of internal control also calls for the maintenance of adequate records in an effort to control asset management and analyze the assignment of responsibility. Good documentation means that records should be maintained by all parties involved in a transaction. Accordingly, all records should allow cross-referencing from one area of responsibility to another. Along this same line, responsibilities for related transactions should be divided. In the process, one area of responsibility will provide a check on the other and vice versa. The people responsible for the custody of assets should not be the same as those responsible for the recording of the assets in the books of record. Employees are less likely to misappropriate or waste assets if they realize that others are recording their use. This does not mean that work should be duplicated, although in many cases some duplication is unavoidable. Ideally, a task can be so divided as to allow job functions to pose a natural check on each other.

For example, the inventory records maintained by an inventory application system establish accountability over goods in a store. Periodic physical inventory counts will reveal shortages that may occur or errors that may creep into the records, and the knowledge that the results of their activities will be compared gives both the stock clerks and the inventory clerk an incentive to carry out their work with care. The stock clerks will watch the accuracy of receiving room counts as goods are transferred to their custody, as the receiving records will be the basis for charging the inventory records for the goods for which the stock clerks must account.

Segregation of Accounting Functions

Of primary importance from an internal control viewpoint is the segregation of duties so that no department or individual controls the accounting records relating to its own operation.

A common violation of this principle occurs when an organization delegates both accounting and financial responsibilities to the same individual or department. As both the accounting and finance functions are primarily concerned with monetary elements, "logical" thinking tends to place both responsibilities under one person. Handling the financing function of a business is just as much an operating responsibility as handling the manufacturing or sales function. Recognizing this fact suggests the need for a segregation of the accounting and finance functions.

A common approach is to delegate the accounting function to a controller or similar office and the finance function to a treasurer. Typically the controller and treasurer are top-management officials, functioning on an equal plane with other executives who report directly to the president of an organization. The organization chart in Figure 1.2 illustrates such an arrangement.

The accounting function involves several subfunctions. In a small business, the controller is likely to handle these other activities himself, but in a large concern, the duties are ordinarily delegated to staff assistants or department heads.

Figure 1.2 shows several normal staff functions that commonly report to the controller. The budgeting function involves the preparation of operating budgets, capital expenditure budgets, and the related forecasts and analyses used by management in planning and controlling the operations of the organization. The internal audit function is now common in large organizations. A growing recognition of the necessity for good internal control and also of the complexities of an adequate system of internal control in a large organization has led to the development of internal auditing as a control over all other internal controls. The internal audit function is charged with monitoring and assessing compliance to

FIGURE 1.2. Organization Chart

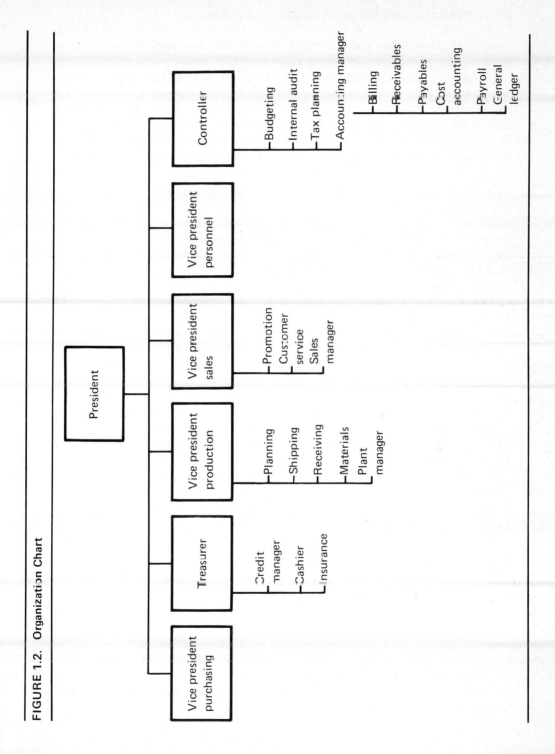

company procedures and policies and also with the execution of certain control functions such as performing periodic bank reconciliations. The tax planning function concerns the administration of tax reporting and the analysis of transactions that have significant tax consequences for the organization. The accounting manager supervises the routine operating functions of the accounting department.

The internal audit function has historically been subject to the authority of the controller or other chief accounting officer, as shown in Figure 1.2. The Securities and Exchange Commission and other professional groups as well have questioned this organizational placement of the internal audit function, urging instead that internal auditing have more independence by being administratively responsible to top management. A recent survey showed that 76 percent of the sample companies had internal audit managers report to a vice-presidential level or higher, as compared to 40 percent in 1963. The SEC might require this type of organizational structure in the future.

The treasurer's responsibilities concern the finances of the business. He arranges to obtain the funds necessary to finance the cost of operations and is charged with securing any required funds under the best terms commensurate with the needs of the business. In addition, the treasurer is responsible for the custody and handling of the liquid assets of the business-cash, receivables, and investments. Records establishing accountability over these assets are maintained under the controller in order to obtain the desired segregation of accounting and operations. Under the treasurer is the credit manager, charged with responsibility for credit and collections, but the original charge to accounts receivable and the accounting for receivables are both handled by the accounting department. Cash collections on these receivables are placed in the custody of a cashier, who is also responsible to the treasurer. Accountability over the cashier is established through the accounts receivable records and the general ledger record of cash. The credit to receivables that relieves the credit manager of responsibility when cash is received on an account is offset by the debit to cash that charges the cashier with the collected funds.

THE PRODUCTION OF ACCOUNTING INFORMATION

The production of useful information is constrained by the environment of an AIS and the cost/benefit structure inherent to users' decisions. Information is presented in an uncertain environment. The uncertainty of the environment in which information is developed and presented means that estimates and judgments must be made. No information system can ignore the practicality of presenting information. If information costs more to provide than it is worth to the user, it is not practical to provide this information.

From an organization's viewpoint, one might draw a distinction between two broad classes of accounting information: that which is mandatory or required and that which is discretionary. Various governmental agencies, private agencies, and legislation set statutory requirements for record keeping and reports. Reports, for example, are required for federal and state income taxes, social security taxes, to the Securities Exchange Commission, Federal Trade Commission, and the like. These reports are mandatory. In addition, certain basic accounting functions are essential to normal business activity. Payroll and accounts receivable are prime examples. These functions must be performed in any organization if the organization is to survive.

Other accounting information is discretionary. Budgetary systems, responsibility accounting systems, and specific reports for internal management are examples of discretionary information. Conceptually, information should be required to satisfy a cost/benefit criterion. While this criterion theoretically applies to all the outputs of an AIS, the point is that the typical organization does not have control or discretion over all of its information requirements. In meeting mandatory information requirements, the primary consideration is to minimize costs while meeting minimum standards of reliability and usefulness. When the provision of information is discretionary, the primary consideration is that the benefit obtained exceed the costs of production.

Data Processing Functions

The term *data processing* refers to transforming or processing descriptive items (data) about certain events into information. The terms *data* and *information* are often loosely equated. Figure 1.3 diagrams the data

---

FIGURE 1.3. Data Processing Cycle

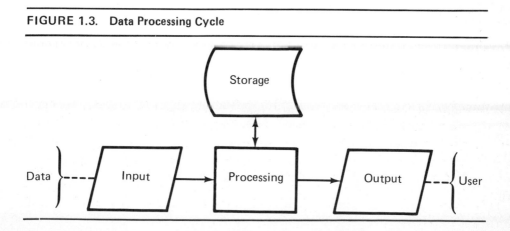

processing cycle. Data comprises any set of characters or symbols that is accepted as input by a data processing system. Data is input to a data processing system, and this system processes data into outputs. These outputs are information if they are meaningful to the user. Thus information implies both processing and meaningfulness to the user. For example, a phone call is data, whereas the number of phone calls per day is information if this figure is meaningful to the user. A sales transaction is data, whereas the daily total sales figure is information to the sales manager.

All data processing, whether done by hand or electronic methods, involves certain basic procedures. These procedures may occur in different sequences, and not all processing involves the same set of procedures. The initial step in data processing is the *originating or input stage*. Data pertaining to relevant events (transactions) must be captured (recorded) in a form that facilitates further processing. The original recording medium (for example, a sales slip) is often termed a *source document*. Fundamental to automatic data processing is the *coding* or *classification* of data items for further processing. Source documents may be *batched:* that is, further processing is delayed until a number of documents are accumulated. Finally, most input items should be subject to *verification:* that is, a check to insure that the original recording of data was correctly performed.

Processing includes the operations that transform data into outputs. Processing may require the following procedures. *Sorting* is the arrangement of data in some arbitrary, predetermined sequence. Sorting falls generally into two types: sorting to sequence for transcription to other records or for filing purposes and sorting to obtain a distribution, as by product, by territory, or by type of expense. *Calculating* pertains to arithmetic manipulation of input data. The calculation of net pay is an example. The calculating step is an important one, often involving a good deal of effort if done manually. *Summarizing* is the reduction or aggregation of data to a more concise or usable form. A myriad of individual sales transactions are summarized as "total sales." *Storage* is the placement of data into files for future reference. Some data may be input to storage, but never reach the output stage. The forms in which data may be stored vary considerably, as does the length of time that some data must be stored. Common storage methods are ordinary paper, magnetic media, microfilm, and punched paper media.

While the input and processing steps are a means to an end, the *output* or *communication* stage is the end in itself. The output stage involves *reporting*, which is the formal distribution of processed data. Reporting usually requires *retrieval*, recovering stored data from storage, and often *reproducing*, copying or duplicating data from one medium to another.

FIGURE 1.4. Data Processing Techniques

Processing Methods	Origination Input	Classifying	Sorting	Calculating	Summarization	Storing	Retrieving	Reproduction	Output
Manual methods	Handwriting Written records	Hand posting Pegboards	Pegboards Keysort cards	Manual	Pegboards Worksheets	Paper files	Manual	Carbon paper	Written reports
Manual with machine assistance	Typewriter Cash register	Cash register	Mechanical sorters	Adding machines Calculators Accounting machines		Mechanized filing and retrieval systems Microfilm		Duplicators Copying machines	Documents prepared by machine
Electronic methods	Magnetic and optical readers Point of sale devices	Computer				Magnetic media Computer output Microfilm	Function of system design	Multiple copies from printer	Printed, visual, or voice

13

Communication is a broader term than reporting; it refers to the transfer of data from one point to another in usable form. *Transportation* relates to the physical movement of data within the system. Finally, *issuances* refer to documents such as checks, statements, W-2 forms, and so on, that are used externally or in other data processing operations.

The above has identified basic steps in data processing. The means of performing these steps vary according to whether manual or electronic processing methods are used. Generally, manual methods are efficient for small-volume tasks and electronic methods for high-volume tasks. This generalization is not straightforward; many businesses use various combinations of these methods. Figure 1.4 illustrates several basic data processing steps and methods of accomplishing each within a manual or electronic system.

The Technology of AIS

An AIS utilizes both human and capital resources. The production of physical goods (such as food or automobiles) has become increasingly automated. Automation usually increases productivity; rising salary levels

FIGURE 1.5. Unit Cost/Volume Relationships in Data Processing

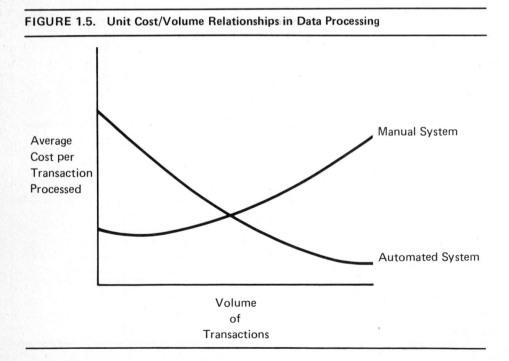

can often stimulate automation. These factors are at play in the production of information as well as physical goods. Automation generally requires large initial capital costs, which makes low volume comparatively expensive relative to manual methods. We can, however, envision a crossover point (Figure 1.5) where automation's lower variable cost per unit (increased productivity) recovers the initial capital costs when compared to a manual system on an average cost basis. It should be noted that computer costs on a unit or similar basis have fallen dramatically over the past decade. The price history of electronic hand calculators illustrates this fact. At the same time, labor costs have constantly increased.

A completely manual system ("pen and ink") utilizes people exclusively. People are flexible, possess judgment, and can adapt to changing circumstances. These advantages are offset by certain disadvantages: people are slow and unreliable (compared to machines). Like machines, people can make errors of omission. For example, a clerk may forget a procedural step or add a series of numbers incorrectly; similarly, a machine may malfunction and generate the same errors. However, unlike machines, people may commit errors of commission. A person may purposely omit a procedure or enter an erroneous number on a document. Such behavior is generally not ascribed to a machine itself. Fraud and other errors of commission are generally much more difficult to deal with than errors of omission.

Most manual systems utilize various types of office machinery. Common examples are typewriters, calculators, cash registers, and duplicating machinery. Such devices perform various data processing functions. A cash register, for example, records and may summarize sales transactions. A typewriter serves to increase the speed and legibility of transcription. Such machines require constant interaction with people, don't significantly undermine the advantages of people, and enhance their disadvantages. Office machinery itself has undergone dramatic changes in the last decade; most of these changes incorporate computer technology. Typewriters, for example, are now part of "word processing" systems. Cash registers are frequently "point of sale" terminals or recorders.

Automated data processing systems include capital components. Earlier automated systems were electromechanical. Based on the punched card, these systems utilized electromechanical devices to perform data processing functions. These mechanical devices minimized human contact in the operation they performed (for example, sorting cards with a mechanical card sorter), but still required human involvement between processing steps. Such systems increase the speed and reliability of processing but reduce flexibility. They require a degree of formalization that demands extensive and careful design prior to implementation.

Dramatic cost reductions in computer technology have made electromechanical systems obsolete. Such systems are only briefly highlighted in this text. Electronic data processing systems (EDP) amplify the considerations just mentioned. Compared to electromechanical systems, EDP offer increased speed and minimized human involvement between data processing steps; this amplifies the degree of formalization required in such systems and creates a need for extensive analysis and design.

Management Information Systems (MIS)

A concept of considerable interest to contemporary organization theory is that of a management information system (MIS). Adding the word *management* to information systems implies that the systems are designed to provide information relevant to the management of the entire organization. An MIS also provides information relevant to external users. As a concept in contemporary organization theory, however, the MIS implies a "total" information system, one that provides a wide variety of information above and beyond that which has historically been associated with the accounting information system within an organization.

The concept of an MIS is inclusive of accounting information systems. Most MISs have several subsystems, of which an AIS is generally the largest and most formalized. Other MIS subsystems might be concerned with supplying information tailored for use in the marketing department, for research and product development, or for personnel administration. A variety of information relevant to long-range planning, inventory planning, production scheduling, and many other managerial functions is not a direct output of an AIS. AIS are largely concerned with data of a transactional or financial nature. An MIS processes these as well as other types of data.

Davis (1974, p. 5) provides the following definition of an MIS: "an integrated man/machine system for providing information to support operations, management, and decision-making. The system utilizes computer hardware, software, manual procedures, decision models, and a data base." There are several points to note in Davis's definition of an MIS. The first is "computer-based." Although it is debatable, at least at a philosophical level, whether or not computer technology is essential to an MIS, as a practical matter the question is not whether but how much. The MIS concept requires information; increasingly, computer technology is the most economical method of information processing. A second point is the data base concept. The data base concept refers to information storage, and is a computer technology concept. The data base concept refers to an integration of data (to avoid inefficient storage) and a software system that *manages* this integrated data, performing tasks such as storing and retrieving data items for individual users. A third point is decision models. In Figure 1.1, decision models provide the rationale by which information is filtered as it moves up the hierarchical (pyramidal) organizational structure. For example, an inventory reorder quantity model (that is, one that decides when and what quantity of an inventory stock item to reorder) may become the rationale for determining what information passes from the transaction processing subsystem to the operational planning and control subsystem.

Among various definitions of MIS, there appears to be a consensus that the purpose of an MIS is to provide information that supports management, and, in particular, aids decision making. A thread common to various MIS concepts is the assumption that an information system adds value to an organization. Information is a resource with a price. Information offers a competitive advantage. Decision theory, a subject matter common to management accounting, management science, and other fields of study, provides a framework for this assumption. Information is the raw material of decision making. Information derives value by its impact on some users' productivity or decision making.

Impact on Accounting Activities

From an accounting perspective, the concept of an MIS embraces managerial accounting and management science concepts and techniques. Management accounting is loosely associated with the internal accounting function, but conceptually management accounting theory represents a shift toward decision-oriented accounting data: that is, data that is tailored for use in a specific purpose. Management science models, such as linear programming, inventory models, and statistical decision models are increasingly utilized by business organizations. The data required by such models is frequently different from that routinely accumulated for financial reporting. The American Accounting Association's 1968–1969 Committee on Managerial Decisions Models (AAA, 1969) examined the interaction of decision models and accounting in detail. Their report noted that the information requirements of such models increase both the quantity and types of information required of an organization's information system. Another committee report (AAA, 1971) has observed two trends that relate to an increasing use of formal decision models: first, the increasingly technical capabilities and professionalization of people occupying managerial jobs, and second, the increased range of problems and factors with which this group perceives they must deal in effectively performing their jobs. Both of these factors would seem to be related to increasing educational levels of management personnel. Formal decision models and their information and computational requirements are feasible only in a computer environment; thus several trends seem to reinforce and interact with each other.

This discussion has touched upon several trends related to the MIS concept that are broadening the scope of the accounting function within organizations. Discussion of the MIS concept has emphasized the computer-based and decision-oriented features of the concept in the belief that these features have the most bearing upon the study of AIS. One frequently finds a collection of large computerized transaction processing applications termed an MIS. The concept of an MIS connotes more than reasonably efficient data processing. However, computerized data processing is implied by most MIS definitions, and it is the computerization of transactional information that provides a direct link between the MIS concept and the AIS. The increased volume of data and the variety of alternatives available with current technology are increasing the necessity for accountants to consider explicitly that value of information provided to users of an AIS.

THE ACCOUNTANT AND SYSTEMS WORK

System studies or projects that an accountant might expect to encounter professionally would likely involve him with the topics introduced in this chapter. The design or audit of an AIS must consider the data processing technology employed by the system. The data processing configuration of an AIS is an important factor in the role an AIS occupies in an organization's internal control system. Contemporary data processing technology complicates professional internal control considerations and at the same time introduces powerful capabilities to provide useful information relevant to a wide range of organizational decision-making needs and requirements. Expertise in systems techniques such as flowcharting and scheduling and a familiarity with contemporary data processing technology are essential to an accountant's performance of traditional duties relating to the design and audit of AIS. Systems techniques such as flowcharting and scheduling, principles of internal control, and contemporary data processing principles are discussed and integrated in the following chapters to assist the reader in acquiring the skills and expertise that are increasingly expected and required of an accounting systems analyst or auditor.

The Nature of Systems Work

A *systems analyst* is a person who is qualified to undertake or participate in system studies. A *system study* or project ordinarily consists of three phases: systems analysis, systems design, and systems implementation. These phases are directed at systems problems pertaining to AIS design and audit.

Systems analysis involves formulating and evaluating solutions to systems problems. The overriding principle of systems analysis is an emphasis on the objectives of the entire system under consideration. Basic to this principle is an analysis of trade-offs between system objectives. The general objectives of systems analysis may be summarized as follows:

1. to improve the quality of information;
2. to improve internal control; and
3. to minimize cost, where appropriate.

These objectives are interrelated and often conflicting. Often trade-offs must be made between such qualities as economy versus usefulness, or simplicity versus a realistic, complex system. Often the only method of evaluating such trade-offs is subjective, as the factors involved deny quantification.

Systems design is the process of specifying the details of the solution approach selected by the systems analysis process. System design includes the evaluation of the relative effectiveness and efficiency of alternative system designs in light of the overall system requirements. Systems implementation is the process of placing the revised or newly designed procedures and methods into operation. Systems implementation includes testing the solution prior to implementation, documentation of the solution, and a review of the system when it actually begins operation to verify that the system functions according to the design specifications.

The *systems approach* is a general procedure for the administration of a systems project. The systems approach can be viewed as a process that consists of several steps. Its purpose is to assist in the orderly development of effective systems. These steps can be described as:

Statement of system objective(s)
Creation of alternatives
Systems analysis
Systems design

Systems implementation
Systems evaluation

The systems approach, like a system itself, is composed of subsystems. Thus each step in the above process can itself be subjected to the systems approach. For example, the first step requires that the system objective(s) be stated. Solving this problem by the systems approach involves all six steps. A defined system objective is the purpose being pursued. To achieve this purpose, alternatives can be created. The system might, for example, seek objectives A, B, or C, or some combination of them. One can then analyze these alternative objectives and design, implement, and evaluate the one that seems most suitable.

FIGURE 1.6.   The Systems Approach to Design

Defining objectives of design—develop simple, clear, and precise specifications for effective and efficient systems implementation.

Planning alternate possible designs—develop alternative design plans that meet design objectives.

Analyzing alternative possible designs—includes:
1. separating plans into logical parts;
2. evaluation of the relative effectiveness and efficiency of alternatives against system output requirements;
3. a team approach in many cases;
4. selection of the best alternative to form a design strategy.

Developing detailed design specifications—they should include:
1. enough detail to serve as the basis for implementation process;
2. identification of system inputs;
3. identification of system outputs;
4. strategies for producing system outputs.

Documenting design specifications—should include specifications for every input and output data element and all circumstances for their uses.

Evaluating design specifications—involves testing for the desired output of the design process (specification of an effective and efficient design). The evaluation of the design should consider whether it is:
1. developed according to the systems approach model;
2. based on effective systems strategy produced by a careful and detailed systems analysis;
3. effective, efficient, simple, clear, easy to build, easy to change, and easy to test or evaluate.

Executing each subsequent step in the systems approach can also be viewed as a process that involves all six steps. Figure 1.6 illustrates this with respect to the system design step.

Behavioral Considerations in Systems Work

One cannot overemphasize the importance of dealing effectively and openly with the personnel who are involved in a system. People will run the system. The analyst must meet and talk with personnel in the system, attempt to find out their needs and requirements, and include these considerations in the design of the system. Not to do so may seem efficient at first, but this would be a false economy.

Accountants do not develop AIS in isolation. Multiple parties (management, users, and systems personnel) are necessarily involved in the design and subsequent operation of an information system. Typically a design group or project team, consisting of users, analysts, and management representatives, is formed to identify needs, develop technical specifications, and implement a new system.

Technical, organizational, and project management problems are encountered in the implementation of an information system. A new information system typically creates new work relationships among existing personnel, changes in job content, and perhaps a change in the formal organizational structure to add a new "information systems" department. The related technical, behavioral, situational, and personnel factors should all be considered. Failure to do so may lead to the output of the system not being used, even if the system itself is technically sound. Furthermore, cooperation is continually required from users to operate the system (provide inputs, verify outputs) after its implementation.

The user cooperation needed to operate the system successfully should be insured during the design of a system, not afterward. Most accounting applications are routine in nature: to insure adherence to production schedules, ongoing relationships between users and information system personnel are important. Schedules for inputs, reports, and other items are usually the responsibility of the systems group, but, to implement and maintain these schedules, cooperation is required from users.

A philosophy of *user-oriented* design and operation fosters a set of attitudes and an approach to system design that consciously considers the organizational context. Users should be involved in the design of applications. Careful attention to output, both in quantity and format, in the design phase will prevent users' having to rework data or request new reports once the system is in operation. Outputs should be directed toward decisions; users must understand the nature and purpose of outputs to be able to utilize this product effectively in their activities. Personnel training should be included in the design phase, not initiated after the system is installed. Finally, the system must be prepared to accept and make changes after operation begins. Users will typically request changes; anticipation of this possibility and the other factors mentioned is essential to a user-oriented philosophy of system design. Systems exist to pursue a purpose; the purpose of an information system is to aid users in furthering the goals of an organization. Users cannot profitably be ignored in the design of an information system.

REVIEW QUESTIONS

1. What characteristics are common to accounting systems?

2. Define the term *transaction*.

3. Define the term *transaction cycle*. What are the benefits of a transaction cycle approach to AIS?

4. What are the objectives of an internal control system?

5. What differences exist between the financial and accounting functions in a firm?

6. What title and duties are typically assigned to the person who has direct responsibility for the accounting function within an organization?

7. Identify the components of the data processing cycle. What data processing functions occur in each of these components?

8. Identify several common special purpose business machines and the data processing function(s) they perform.

9. Distinguish between mandatory, essential, and discretionary reporting and give an example of each.

10. How does a management information system differ from an accounting information system?

11. What are the general objectives of systems analysis?

12. Identify several attributes of a user-oriented approach to system design.

DISCUSSION QUESTIONS AND PROBLEMS

13. "A credit sale is not a complete transaction." Discuss.

14. What effect would the following factors have on the relationships shown in Figure 1.5?
   a. Rising starting salaries for clerical help.
   b. More efficient computer equipment and software.
   c. A dramatic decrease in the cost of computer equipment.
   d. Increased demands for information reporting by the government and other agencies.

15. Discuss several differences between the information requirements of top, middle, and lower-level managers in an organization.

16. Discuss factors that should be considered in the organizational location of the internal audit function.

17. Apply the systems approach to the following objectives:
   a. Improve the quality of an AIS.
   b. Improve the image of a university.
   c. Better the competition.

18. Identify several accounting-related decisions that you feel might be made by the following personnel:
   a. President of a company.
   b. Controller.
   c. Accounting manager.
   Do the information needs of these positions differ?

19. The XYZ Co. distributes three product lines to seven vendors. Sales are manually recorded on invoices. Separate invoices are always used to record sales of product line number 1; sales of the other two product lines are always recorded together on a single invoice.

The manager would like to know the total daily sales of each product line in dollars and also the daily sales total for each product line sold to each vendor.

To develop this information manually, the manager will collect all of the invoices at the end of each day. A separate worksheet will be used to record the daily sales total for each product line. Each worksheet will have seven columns with separate headings—one for each vendor. The manager will record each day's sales totals on a separate line of each worksheet.

Identify the data processing functions necessary to develop and record the desired information from the daily batch of sales invoices.

REFERENCES

American Accounting Association, "Report of Committee on Managerial Decision Models." *Accounting Review*, Supplement to Vol. XLIV (1969).

——, "Report of the Committee on Accounting and Information Systems". *Accounting Review*, Supplement to Vol. XLVI (1971).

Arthur Andersen and Co., *A Guide for Studying and Evaluating Internal Accounting Controls* (1978).

Burch, J.G., Jr., F. Strater, and G. Grudnitski. *Information Systems: Theory and Practice*, 2nd. Ed. (New York: Wiley, 1979).

Cushing, B.E. *Accounting Information Systems and Business Organizations*, 2nd Ed. (Reading, Ma.: Addison-Wesley, 1978).

Davis, G.B., *Management Information Systems* (New York: McGraw-Hill, 1974).

Touche Ross and Co. *The New Management Imperative* (1978).

SYSTEMS CONCEPTS AND TECHNIQUES

2

Systems concepts and techniques are frequently encountered in contemporary accounting literature and practice. Modern auditing, for example, includes a major element of systems review. Systems concepts and techniques are relevant to the analysis and design of computer-based AIS. The recent development of small-business computers had made computer-based accounting information systems a feasible alternative for all but the very smallest of organizations. Systems concepts and techniques are increasingly relevant to auditing practice. Most consulting engagements conducted by public accounting firms are system studies concerning AIS. Many internal audit functions, such as operational auditing, also are of a systems nature.

This chapter discusses systems concepts and techniques and their relationships to AIS work. The chapter discussion contains an overview of general systems theory and its relevance to the design of AIS.

SYSTEMS CONCEPTS

The term *system* is in common use. In everyday usage a system is a collection of elements or things that bear some relationship to each other. An AIS is a collection of human and capital resources designed to process transactions; an automobile system is a patterned or organized collection of tires, an engine, and a body.

The words *patterned* and *organized* in the above sentence suggest important attributes of the concept of a system, attributes that are often ignored in common usage of the term. A system is composed of interacting parts that operate together to achieve an objective or purpose. Systems are not random collections of objects. Systems consist of coherent, patterned, purposeful sets of elements.

In specifying a system, one must identify the elements that belong to the system. A system is considered to have boundaries that set it apart from its environment. In the sense that elements are either in the system or not, they are either within the boundaries of the system or outside of them. Figure 2.1 illustrates a classification of systems. A closed system is one that has no exchange with its environment. That is, nothing crosses the boundary of a closed system. A closed system is totally isolated from its environment. A relatively closed system is one that has a controlled exchange with its environment. A relatively closed system accepts certain inputs across its boundary, generates selected outputs, and is relatively but not completely isolated from its environment. Manufacturing systems, computer programs, and accounting application systems are examples of relatively closed systems.

An open system is one that is capable of constant exchange with its environment. An open system differs from a relatively closed system in that an open system does not attempt to control completely its exchange with its environment. An open system is one that is subject to environmental disturbances: thus its inputs and outputs are subject to a wider range of variation than those of a relatively closed system. An organization is an example of an open system.

One of the major mechanisms operating in systems is *feedback*. The term is often loosely used, but the intended meaning here is simply that feedback occurs when part of the output of a system is returned as input to the system. Feedback is information on the results of a process that is used to alter the process itself. The terms *feedback* and *control* are closely related, as the usual purpose of feedback is to aid in the control of a system.

A feedback control system (Figure 2.1) contains five basic components:

1. a process that transforms inputs into outputs;
2. a characteristic of the process that is subject to control;
3. a sensor to assess the characteristic of interest;
4. a criterion to evaluate the process; and
5. an effector, which functions to change the inputs to the process.

A common example of a feedback control system is a thermostat. A thermostat measures the temperature of a system, and triggers an effector to change the temperature when it exceeds or falls below a certain preset level. A thermostat is an example of a negative feedback control system. Negative feedback dampens activity around a norm or target. A thermostat acts to bring temperature back to a preset level. A closed feedback loop is one isolated from environmental disturbances. An open feedback loop is subject to random environmental disturbances.

In the sense that a system is defined by its boundaries, the concept of a

FIGURE 2.1. Types of Systems

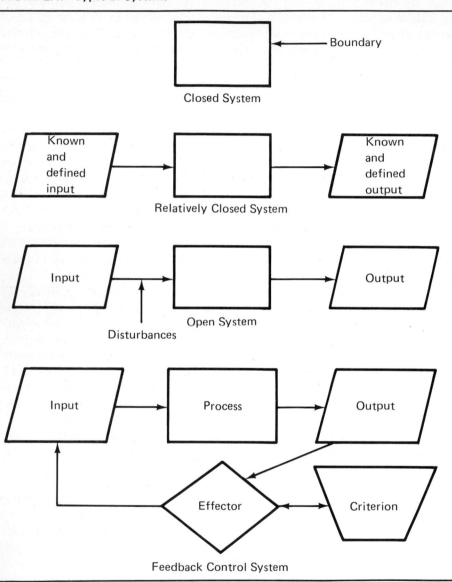

system is relative and depends on the viewpoint of the observer. Consider the number sequence 1, 3, 6, 10, 15, 21, . . . While it is meaningless to many, some may recognize this series of numbers as an abstract system: the number of combinations of n things taken 2 at a time. The numbers

1, 3, 6, and so forth also belong to many other systems. An automobile may be considered within the national transportation system, the local pollution system, or various economic systems when it is bought, sold, or serviced. Systems do not exist in or of themselves; they are coherent, patterned, purposeful sets of elements defined and identified for analytical purposes.

Subsystem Relationships

A system is composed of subsystems, which in turn may themselves be composed of other subsystems. A subsystem is a system whose boundaries are contained within the boundaries of a larger system. Interconnections between subsystems are called *interfaces*. Interfaces occur at the boundary of a system and take the form of inputs or outputs.

Factoring is the analytical process of breaking systems into subsystems. Factoring is often necessary to facilitate the analysis of large, complex systems. Often the intent is to take open systems and, through a careful examination of inputs and outputs, factor an open system into a set of relatively closed systems. Relatively closed systems are sometimes termed *modules* to imply the standardization that usually occurs in factoring. Factoring usually results in a hierarchical relationship between subsystems. For example, an AIS might be factored to include a revenue cycle subsystem, expenditure cycle, production cycle, and finance cycle subsystem. The revenue cycle subsystem might then be further factored to include customer order entry, billing, accounts receivable, and sales reporting. Each of these subsystems would be further factored into specific task-oriented units such as data preparation, processing, and review.

Accounting application systems must communicate, or interface, with each other. Examples of interfaces between accounting application systems would include:

Summaries of sales transactions sent for posting to the general ledger by a billing application system.

Receiving data transferred to an inventory control application from a receiving application.

Interfaces may take several forms depending on the technology and design of the AIS. In manual systems the routing of paper documents from one application area to another serves as an interface. In computer systems the interfaces between accounting applications may take the form of punched cards or other computer-readable media such as magnetic tape. A magnetic tape containing detailed sales transaction data may serve as the interface between a sales reporting application and an inventory control application in that this file of data is separately processed by both applications. In advanced computer systems utilizing on-line processing techniques, interfaces may occur in computer memory and never take a separate physical form. Input of a sales transaction at a point of sale terminal, for example, may simultaneously affect inventory, accounts receivable, and sales reporting applications without a physical transfer that could be observed by a person.

Decoupling is the concept of loosening the interface relationships between systems so that each system can function somewhat independently in the short run. A common example of a decoupling mechanism is a physical inventory of goods kept in a warehouse. A physical inventory allows the production subsystem of an organization to operate somewhat independently of the raw materials acquisition subsystem, and vice versa. An inventory reduces the need immediately to relate short-range changes in production activity to the materials acquisition process. Increases or decreases in production activity are buffered by the supply of goods in inventory.

An important attribute of decoupling mechanisms is the role they play in reducing communication requirements between subsystems. Factoring often results in a hierarchical relation between subsystems. Most system analysts would agree that large systems (or organizations) are associated with large quantities of information. These quantities occur as either the quantity that one would have to receive from the system to study it or the quantity one would have to transmit to the system to control it. In most organizations, the amount of information generated by lower levels of the hierarchical structures is simply too great to be passed along in total to the upper subsystem. This fact creates a need for a *filtering* process, which serves to reduce and/or summarize information transferred on up the hierarchical chain. The AIS filters transactional data to upper levels of management to decouple these personnel from the details of daily operation. The use of minicomputers to distribute overall data processing requirements decouples individual application systems from a central computing facility.

The Proliferation of Variety in Systems

Systems have related parts. This property gives rise to the complexity of systems. Complexity may be discussed by considering variety. *Variety* is the number of elements in a system distinguished or identified by an observer. Variety depends on one's definition of an element. Consider a system with seven basic elements, such as is shown in Figure 2.2. The complexity of a system depends on the attributes the analyst assigns to the elements of the system.

Figure 2.2a shows a collection of elements, the definition of an element being "letter." The variety of this system is seven. The variety of Figure 2.2b is 2. Some of the elements of 2.2b are similar. In Figure 2.2c we show seven letters with a line connecting each pair of letters. We now change our definition of an element from "letter" to a pairwise relation between letters: that is, "A–B," "B–C," and so on. We are now viewing this system not as a collection of parts, but rather as a collection of relationships between parts. The variety is now 21.

Figure 2.2d repeats Figure 2.2c with one difference. Figure 2.2d considers the direction or "pattern" of the pairwise relationship between

---

FIGURE 2.2. Variety in Systems

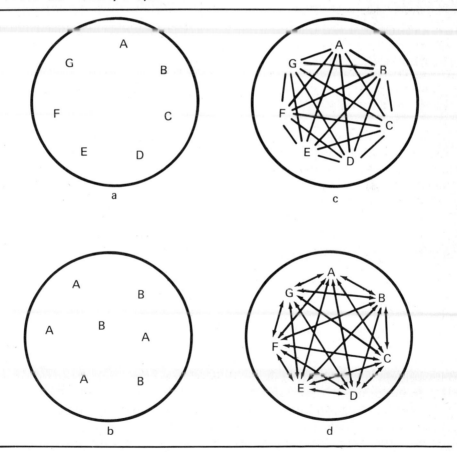

elements. The pattern of a relation is often of significance; for example, B→F may be a sale, while the relation F→B with the same elements would be a sales return. As more information is added, variety increases. In Figure 2.2c, B→F leaves uncertainty; in describing system 2.2d, the element B→F has been clarified. The variety of the system labeled 2.2d is 42.

Finally, we consider a dynamic system. Figures 2.2a–d were static; now we suggest action. It is a *condition* of system operation that relations between parts be capable of change. Consider Figure 2.2d again, except now envision a switch on each relation. For example, B→F may be "off" or "on." In an AIS with seven applications, for example, each application may or may not send a message to (interface with) every other application over a short period of time. We have further enriched our definition of element to include more information concerning the relationships between parts in our system. The variety of this system is now 2^{42}, a number which is greater than 1,000,000,000. This great variety is generated with only seven elements and only pairwise relationships considered in the description of the system as a coherent, patterned, purposeful set of elements.

The Law of Requisite Variety

A systems problem may be seen as a problem in handling variety: being able to adjust and adapt to the number of possible states of a system. AIS are designed to provide management and other users with feedback concerning the operating status of complex organizational systems. The law of requisite variety is a mathematical theorem proposed by Ashby (1954), which states formally that control can be obtained only if the variety of the controller is at least greater than or equal to the variety of the situation to be controlled. Simply stated, "Only variety can destroy variety."

To illustrate the basic idea of the law of requisite variety, consider a manager who is responsible for directing (that is, controlling) the activities of a subordinate. Suppose that the subordinate and manager communicate via a set of standard, preprinted message forms. There are four forms, each requesting the subordinate to undertake different actions. Suppose a situation arises that warrants a response different from those indicated on the four standard forms. If the manager can direct the subordinate only through the issuance of one of the four standard forms, clearly his control over "usual circumstances" is limited. That is, the four-form limited-variety information system allows the manager to react only imperfectly (or not at all) to unusual situations.

The implication for system design is that an information system as a whole must be capable of generating as much control variety (feedback) as the organizational situation is capable of generating uncontrolled variety. The effectiveness of a system may be evaluated in this respect. Requisite variety suggests that to control each possible state of a system's elements there must be feedback that suggests a corresponding control state. As a system increases in complexity, the ability even to identify all possible system states decreases rapidly because of the proliferation of variety.

SYSTEMS THEORY: DESIGN CRITERIA FOR AIS

Systems theory is a field of study concerned with the identification of principles common to viable systems. *Viable* is used in the biological sense; a viable system is capable of existence and development as an independent unit. A viable system survives through time by learning to adapt to its environment. Contemporary accounting theory and practice views accounting as a viable information system that fulfills the needs of its users, those both internal and external to the organization.

Much of the work in systems theory concerns the study of self-regulating systems, systems such as the brain or a living organism, in which no external managerial element is directly identifiable. Yet such systems survive and are viable. They are self-regulating. Systems theory offers insights into the mechanisms of self-regulating systems, mechanisms that would appear to be of increasing value and utility to the management and design of complex information systems.

Ross Ashby, a pioneer in general systems theory, provides a broad overview of the focus of general systems theory (1973, pp. 2–6). According to Ashby, science underwent a major change at about the time of World War II. Prior to this time science had grown rapidly through the application of analytical scientific method. To the ancient Greeks, the world was infinitely complex and not controlled by laws in the scientific sense of the word. Human-like gods were the cause of thunder, spring, and all other natural events. But Newton's law of gravity, Dalton's law of chemical proportions, and other such scientific advances were the fruits of analytical method. Faced with a system, science traditionally reduced the system to its component parts for analysis. Animals were reduced to organs, organs to cells, cells to molecules, and molecules to atoms. Reduction is certainly a valid approach to the study of a large number of systems, but the question of concern is whether system interactions (both internal and external) can be ignored in complex systems.

Some properties of systems, and often those of most concern, involve *relationships* (that is, interactions) that occur between "parts" of systems and are not as such intrinsic to either part. Ashby notes two developments that significantly altered the ability of science to study system inter- actions. Multivariate statistical methods were stimulated by the study of interactions among factors such as rain and soil in agricultural production by R. A. Fischer and other mathematical statisticians. Ashby suggests this was the first major technical step in understanding systems as interactive systems. Another development was the intensive study of the phenomena of feedback in radio systems just prior to World War II. During World War II, previous work on feedback in radio systems was transferred to branches of science that had only a superficial resemblance to radio.

> Then came the automatic pilots, automatic tracking searchlights, self-aiming guns, and a host of other "goal-seeking" devices. System science had begun.
>
> It had now become obvious that systems in one branch of science might be iso- morphic with systems in some other branch that seemed, at first sight, to be wholly different. Banking, say, seems wholly different from the flow of underground water in Arizona, yet when one examines how the deposits in the banks "flow" from place to place in the world's banking network, one may find the dynamics of this system isomorphic with the dynamics of water flow. And today, further examples can be given in almost endless multiplicity. [Ashby, 1973, pp. 4-5.]

The application of systems theory to business systems is relatively recent. System theory suggests we view systems in a biological frame- work, stressing:

1. the "look ahead" or predictive nature of viable systems;
2. the importance of feedback for learning and control; and
3. the necessity of "self-regulation" for viable control in complex systems.

Systems theory also suggests requisite variety: that a device that con- trols a system needs to be as sophisticated as the system it is controlling, and that if it is not, then the system functions inefficiently. Last, systems theory stresses that redundancy within a system is not necessarily a sign of inefficiency. Redundancy and control are related: redundant elements may be significant factors in the ability of a system to adapt to a changing environment.

Control is fundamental to viable systems. An accounting information system itself must be in control if the outputs of the system, such as financial statements and managerial reports, are to possess qualities and characteristics that make them suitable for both internal and external users. In organized systems, control is a function of design. Controls them- selves may be external or internal to a system. Systems theory suggests that feedback controls are essential to the viability of complex systems.

An important responsibility of accountants in the design of information systems is to insure that the system possesses enough feedback controls to remain viable. The following sections illustrate the use of feedback control in the design of information systems.

Feedback Control and the Design of Information Systems

Requisite variety requires that there be as many variations of controls available to a system as there are ways for the system to get out of control. These controls must also be applied within a time period that enables the system to remain viable in its environment. Controls may be external or internal to a system. External controls are often preventive in nature, taking forms such as rules, procedures, policies, and physical devices. Preventive controls attempt to prevent deviations from occurring. In contrast, feedback control systems are expected to deviate out of control occasionally; however, the ability to restore control and the further ability to know or sense when a deviation has occurred are built into feedback control systems themselves.

An information system itself must be in a state of control to remain viable. As information systems increase in complexity, the corresponding increase in the variety of possible system states must be anticipated if the system is to remain viable. Systems theory suggests that complex systems must regulate and control themselves to a large degree if they are to remain viable in an uncertain and changing environment. Control is a property inherent in and internal to viable systems, not something exercised from without.

Information systems can be designed that are inherently capable of responding to unforeseen circumstances. Consider the following illustration drawn from a system study. In an automated steel rolling mill, red-hot steel passed from one operation to another. As in any complex system, the relations were probabilistic; sometimes the hot steel did not behave as it should: it deviated from its intended path, causing serious operational difficulties. The longer the time taken to notice that the hot steel was not passing through the process as it should, the more serious the consequences. The problem was to control this situation. The solution was an information system. Initial efforts placed sensors at various points along the operation where the hot steel might flow if it had deviated from its path to turn off the process quickly if they sensed that an error had occurred. While this system was an improvement, the variety in the steel operation precluded the placement of enough sensors to detect every possible error condition, so that many serious errors still occurred in areas where sensors had not been placed. All of the possible deviations in the process of passing hot steel from one operation to the next could not be foreseen. It was impossible to prevent all serious errors with controls external to the system itself.

A principle of system theory was brought to bear here—the ability of a viable system to look ahead or forecast where something should be and the related ability of being able to detect when it isn't there. With a different set of timing sensors, the steel mill's information system "anticipates." It forecasts where and when the hot steel should be at any moment, and shuts the flow of steel off automatically when this criterion is not satisfied. That is, if the steel is not where it *should* be, control is exercised. Rather than attempting to identify all possible error conditions, the information system considerably reduces variety by considering only where the steel should be at any given moment.

Financial Feedback Control Systems

Several types of financial feedback control systems and related responsibility centers are commonly used for the control of organizational units. A responsibility center is an organization unit headed by a responsible person: that is, a person who is in control of a given function.

Responsibility accounting is the accountant's attempt to classify costs and results of organizational activity according to various decision centers within the organization. These decision centers are dependent on the organizational structure; thus the nature of responsibility centers varies from firm to firm. Responsibility centers may be built around departments, products, territories, individuals, activities, or various combinations of the above.

If an AIS measures only the costs incurred by a unit, that unit is termed a cost center. A cost center is the smallest organizational segment for which costs are traced and accumulated and over which an individual has responsibility. Although every unit classified as a cost center produces some useful outputs, it is neither feasible nor desirable to measure these outputs in monetary terms.

When the performance of a unit can be measured in terms of both the revenue it earns and also the expense it incurs in generating that revenue, it can be controlled as a profit center. Profit centers account for both the inputs and outputs of a responsibility center in monetary values.

The most comprehensive form of financial control system applicable to an organizational unit is an investment center. In an investment center, measures are taken not only of profit but also of the capital employed to generate this profit. The productivity of capital is used as the basis of performance expectation and evaluation. For these organizational units, return on investment is the figure most commonly employed to assess performance.

Responsibility accounting systems can be used in both profit and nonprofit organizations. Profit centers are often called financial performance centers in a nonprofit organization.

Consider responsibility accounting systems as negative feedback control systems. The process is the department, division, or individual that is the "responsibility center"; these centers transform inputs to outputs, and some outputs or input-output relationships are more desirable than others. The performance criterion of major interest is typically cost or profit, the standard utilized in the feedback control system is accordingly budgeted cost, budgeted profit, or the like. The measure of the criterion is typically an accounting report on cost or profit (a responsibility report) provided by the AIS. The effector is the responsible person, the manager who is expected to control his responsibility center. As the manager receives a report (feedback), he is expected to modify the process, if necessary, to direct the system toward its desired or planned state of operations.

The credit control function will serve as another illustration. The process is the credit sales and collection function. The criterion is to minimize financial loss from selling on credit. A standard or budgeted amount of allowable or expected financial loss may exist as policy: regardless, every organization has a limit to the amount of such financial losses it can absorb. Once again, measurement is typically provided by an accounting report showing bad-debt losses or aged accounts-receivables schedules. The effector is the credit manager or other person responsible for this function.

The above two illustrations show the generality of the feedback control analogy. Numerous other examples could be given. The essence of the analogy is to emphasize the important role that accounting information and reports occupy in the control of business systems. Managers are expected to and frequently do base their decisions and hence actions on accounting information. If these reports are not timely, or if they contain irrelevant information, the feedback control system cannot function properly. Consider again the credit collection illustration. There are several ways to measure financial loss: bad-debts expense may be estimated and booked by several alternative methods. Is the selected measure the best? Would other measurement alternatives lead the manager to different decisions? The intent of the analogy is to focus the attention of the systems analyst on the importance of feedback control mechanisms utilized in AIS.

SYSTEMS TECHNIQUES

Systems techniques encompass a range of analytical tools and practices commonly utilized in systems work. The complexity inherent in contemporary AIS necessitates the use of formal techniques in the analysis and design of system and subsystem relationships. Systems techniques serve several important functions in a systems study:

1. organize data for effective analysis;
2. document work performed;
3. provide the basis for a formal presentation; and
4. provide a permanent file for future use.

Systems techniques are largely matters of graphic presentation. Graphic presentation is to the systems analyst what numbers are to a mathematician—a language of abbreviation enabling the understanding of complex phenomena in a relatively short time period. Graphic presentation is an integral part of most professional techniques. Graphics are important in the analysis, design, and documentation of systems. The adage "a picture is worth a thousand words" is especially relevant to systems work.

Flowcharting Techniques

In both the literature and practice, one finds a confusingly large number of flowcharting techniques that have been used in systems work. There is little standardization in this area; perhaps there should not be. Standards reduce communication requirements (that is, symbols may not need to be explained), but in most instances it is the flexibility inherent in flowcharting techniques that is most useful to the systems analyst.

A flowchart is a symbolic or pictorial representation of a system. Flowcharting techniques are conventions that are used to organize and present problems in a form suitable for analysis. Flowcharts are probably the most common graphic presentation method; accordingly, there are many varieties of flowcharting techniques. There are several sets of standard (that is, officially promulgated) flowcharting symbols, most notably in the data processing field. However, even with the use of standard symbols, flowcharting is not a science. This is to say that different people using the same set of symbols to represent the same system will usually prepare slightly different flowcharts. Flowcharting is more art than science; the only important consideration is that a flowchart effectively convey the message intended by its preparer. Of the numerous types of flowcharting techniques available, those particularly relevant to

FIGURE 2.3. System Flowchart Symbols

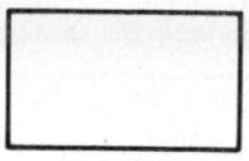 **PROCESSING** — A major processing function	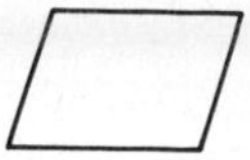 **INPUT/OUTPUT** — Any type of medium or data
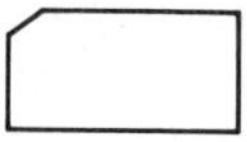 **PUNCHED CARD** — All varieties of punched cards, including stubs	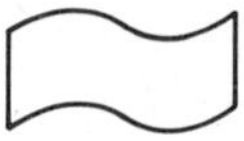 **PUNCHED TAPE** — Paper or plastic, chad or chadless
 **DOCUMENT** — Paper documents and reports of all kinds	 **TRANSMITTAL TAPE** — A proof or adding machine tape or similar batch-control information
 **MAGNETIC TAPE**	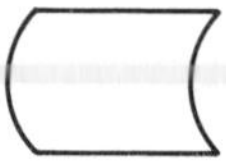 **ON-LINE STORAGE** — Input/output using any kind of on-line storage — magnetic tape, drum, or disk
 **OFF-LINE STORAGE** — Off-line storage of paper or cards or magnetic or perforated tape	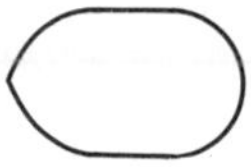 **DISPLAY** — Information displayed by plotters or video devices
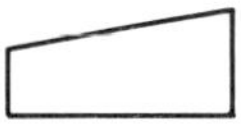 **MANUAL INPUT** — Information input by on-line keyboards, switch settings, pushbuttons	 **SORT** — An operation to arrange a set of items into sequence
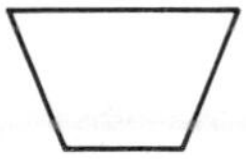 **MANUAL OPERATION** — A manual off-line operation not requiring mechanical aid	**AUXILIARY OPERATION** — A machine operation supplementing the main processing function
 **KEYING** — An operation utilizing a key-driven device	 **COMMUNICATION LINK** — The automatic transmission of information from one location to another via communication lines

◁ ▷ ▽ △   **FLOW** — The direction of processing or data flow

Source: IBM Flowcharting Template, Form X20–8020–1; u/m 010. Courtesy International Business Machines Corporation.

FIGURE 2.4. Sample Systems Flowchart

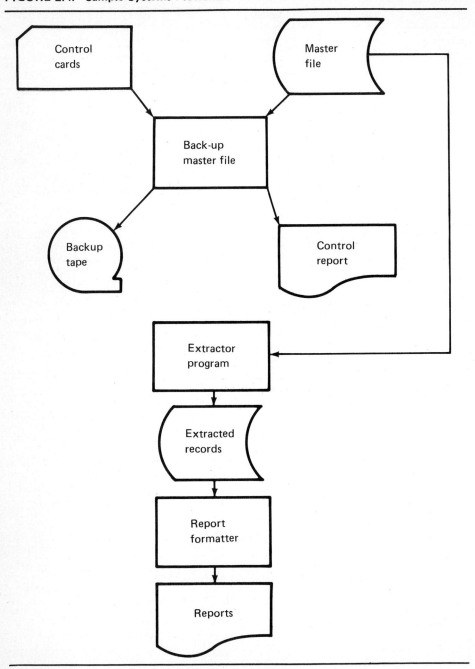

FIGURE 2.5. Program Flowchart Symbols

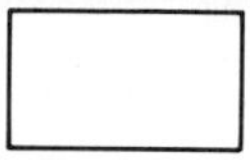

PROCESSING

A group of program instructions that performs a processing function of the program

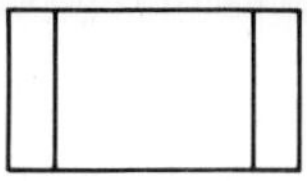

PREDEFINED PROCESS

A group of operations not detailed in the particular set of flowcharts

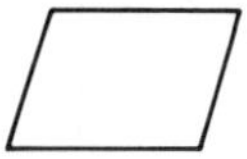

INPUT/OUTPUT

Any function of an input/output device (making information available for processing, recording processing information, tape positioning, etc.)

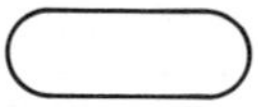

TERMINAL, INTERRUPT

The beginning, end, or a point of interruption in a program

DECISION

The decision function used to document points in the program where a branch to alternate paths is possible based upon variable conditions

CONNECTOR

An entry from, or an exit to, another part of the program flowchart

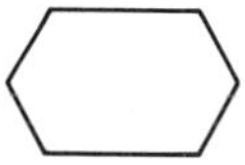

PREPARATION

An instruction or group of instructions that changes the program

OFFPAGE CONNECTOR

A connector used instead of the connector symbol to designate entry to or exit from a page

FLOW DIRECTION

◁ ▷ ▽ △

The direction of processing or data flow

SUPPLEMENTARY SYMBOL FOR SYSTEM AND PROGRAM FLOWCHARTS

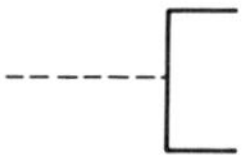

ANNOTATION or COMMENT

The addition of descriptive comments or explanatory notes as clarification

Source: IBM Flowcharting Template, Form X20-8020-1; u/m 010. Courtesy International Business Machines Corporation.

accounting systems work fall into two broad categories: procedural (or operation) flowcharts, and distribution flowcharts.

Procedural Flowcharts

Procedural flowcharts depict data processing procedures. A procedure is a sequence of operations necessary to accomplish a specific task; a set of one or more procedures constitutes a system. A distinction may be made among the levels of the problem being analyzed. A *system flowchart* identifies the overall or broad flow of operations in a system or procedure. A systems flowchart shows where data originates, the sequence and mode (manual or machine) of processing, and the disposition of results. Figure 2.3 presents a set of system flowchart symbols common in data processing environments. Several symbols represents devices, but in general the symbols do not imply a particular method of processing. In systems flowcharting the emphasis is on media and work stations, and not on detail of processing. Figure 2.4 presents a systems flowchart.

A *program* or *block flowchart* is more detailed than a system flowchart. Program flowcharts serve as a source of problem analysis and documentation for computer-related problems. A program flowchart is a step between problem solution and coding for computer processing. Several special symbols are used in program flowcharts (see Figure 2.5). Figure 2.6 illustrates a program flowchart.

There are no formal rules governing the amount of detail to include in a program flowchart. This will depend on the purpose for which the diagram will be used. Programmers will frequently draw a systems flowchart to describe the logic for a particular application. The systems flowchart will then be supported by one or more detailed program flowcharts. Flowcharts provide important documentation; ideally, flowcharts enable other personnel to understand an application to the point where they would be able to make changes in the procedure, if necessary, even though they themselves had not designed the original procedure.

The discussion to this point has been oriented toward a computer processing environment. Several flowcharting techniques are oriented toward manual systems and accordingly utilize different symbols. Figure 2.7 illustrates a *process chart*. The process chart is a special case of the flowchart, utilizing a preprinted form with all symbols repeated on each horizontal line. Selected symbols are blacked in with pencil or ink to depict the flow of operations. The process chart is simpler to draw than a regular flowchart, because no templates or other drawing materials are used. It may be cumbersome for use with procedures that involve many forms or subsidiary activities branching off the main flow lines.

FIGURE 2.6. Sample Program Flowchart

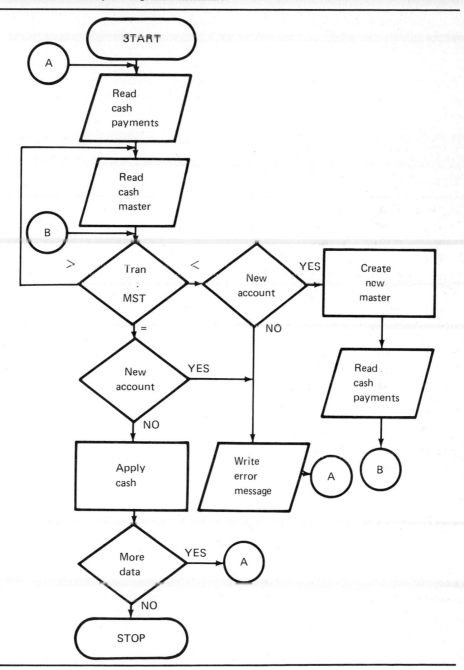

FIGURE 2.7. Flow Process Chart

FLOW PROCESS CHART ☐ ANALYSIS ☐ PROPOSAL PAGE ____ OF ______

DEPT. ____________________ DATE ____________ 19 ____ PROCESS CHARTED ____________________

JOB TITLE & DEPT. NO. OF EMPLOYEE PERFORMING THE WORK		SUMMARY	PRESENT	PROPOSED	SAVINGS
1	7	NO OPERATIONS			
2	8	NO TRANSPORTS			
3	9	NO STORAGES			
4	10	NO INSPECTIONS			
5	11	TOTAL MINUTES			
6	12	DISTANCE TRAVELED			

JOB TITLE CODE NO.	DISTANCE IN FEET	TIME IN MINUTES	OPERATION / TRANS. / STORAGE / INSPECT	STEP NO.	BRIEF DESCRIPTION OF EACH STEP • IMPROVEMENT NOTES
			○ o ▽ □	1	
			○ o ▽ □	2	
			○ o ▽ □	3	
			○ o ▽ □	4	
			○ o ▽ □	5	
			○ o ▽ □	6	
			○ o ▽ □	7	
			○ o ▽ □	8	
			○ o ▽ □	9	
			○ o ▽ □	10	
			○ o ▽ □	11	
			○ o ▽ □	12	
			○ o ▽ □	13	
			○ o ▽ □	14	
			○ o ▽ □	15	
			○ o ▽ □	16	
			○ o ▽ □	17	
			○ o ▽ □	18	
			○ o ▽ □	19	
			○ o ▽ □	20	
			○ o ▽ □	21	
			○ o ▽ □	22	
			○ o ▽ □	23	
			○ o ▽ □	24	
			○ o ▽ □	25	
			○ o ▽ □	26	
			○ o ▽ □	27	
			○ o ▽ □	28	
			○ o ▽ □	29	
			○ o ▽ □	30	
╳				TOTAL	

☐ CONTINUED ON PAGE ______ ANALYZED BY ____________________

FIGURE 2.8. Document Flowchart of a Voucher Procedure

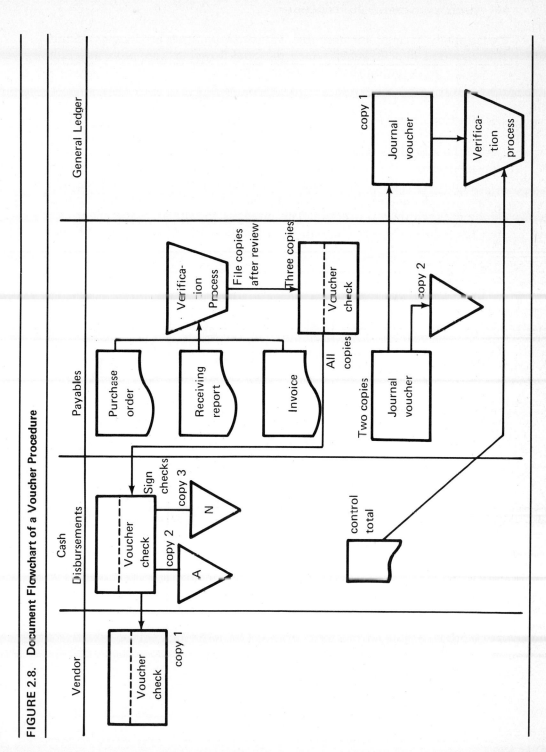

Occasionally it may be desirable to utilize pictures or drawings rather than symbols in a flowchart. Such pictorial flowcharts are more generally useful for presentation than for documentation.

Distribution Charts

Often the systems analyst is concerned more with the flow and distribution of documents in a system than with the mode of processing. Several techniques may be used to analyze the distribution of documents in a system. A *document flowchart* may be used to illustrate the flow of documents within a procedure. The intent is to take each document used in a procedure, identify its point of origination, distribution, and ultimate

FIGURE 2.9. Forms Distribution Chart for a Purchase Order

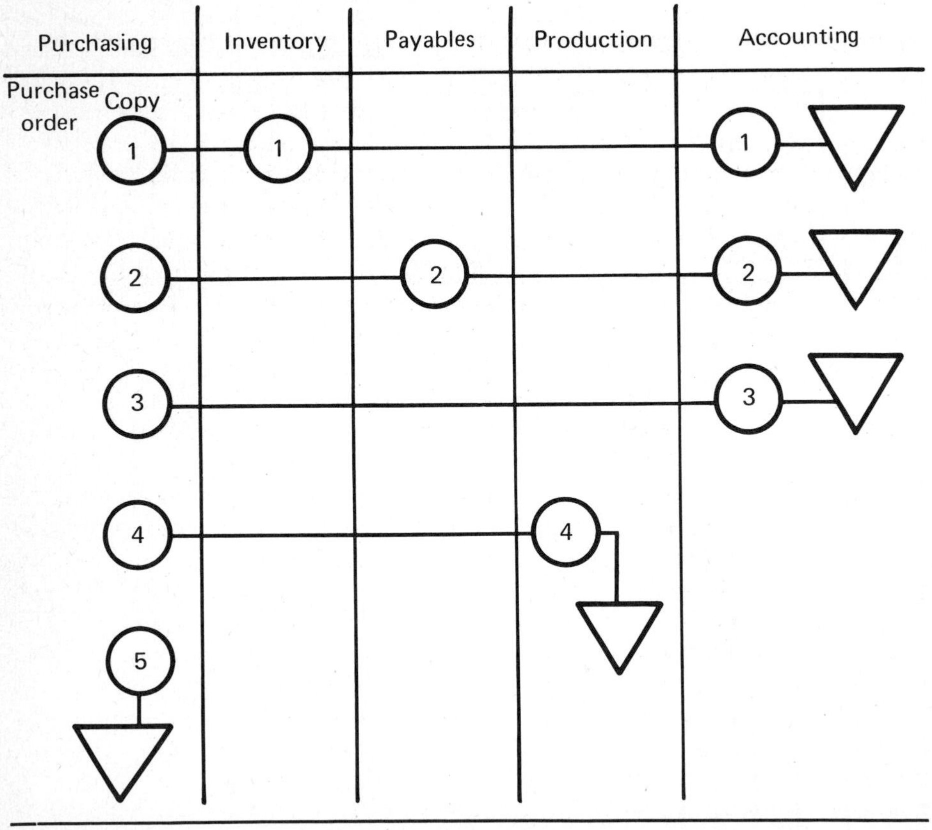

disposition with respect to the various organizational entities (departments or persons) that are affected by the procedure. Document flowcharts are particularly useful in the analysis of internal control systems. System flowcharting symbols are commonly utilized to prepare a document flowchart. To prepare such a chart, one divides a page of paper into several columns, one for each entity in the procedure. Then, after collecting the necessary information, chart the flow of documents, utilizing the symbols. Comments should be added as necessary to clarify the illustration. Figure 2.8 illustrates a document flowchart. A document flowchart usually implies a batch mode of processing; thus each symbol represents a batch of documents.

Closely related to the document flowchart is the *forms distribution chart* (Figure 2.9). A forms distribution chart illustrates the distribution of multiple-copy forms within an organization. The emphasis is on who gets what forms, rather than on how these forms are prepared. Forms may be represented by symbols, reduced photos of the form itself, or simply word descriptions. The form is pictured or designated on the left side of the chart and usually progresses horizontally through the various columns allotted to organizational units. Analysis may be directed toward the elimination of unnecessary copies, unnecessary filing of copies, unauthorized distribution, and so on.

To summarize, flowcharts are basically of two types: those concerned with the flow of procedures and those concerned with the flow or distribution of documents. Procedural flowcharts may be broadly classified as either system flowcharts or program flowcharts, depending on the amount of detail involved. All of these classifications are arbitrary. Although numerous sets of standardized symbols exist, flowcharting is a tool that is heavily dependent on the analyst himself.

Analysis of Resource Requirements

This section discusses several techniques useful in the design and implementation of accounting information systems. The intent here is to present and illustrate certain concepts rather than to provide detailed examples. In all systems work, the level of detail required is a function of the specific problem.

Flowcharts are useful to portray and analyze operations in a given system; however, flowcharting itself assumes an existing or proposed flow of operations. Several techniques are useful in determining the feasibility of a proposed procedure, or, alternatively, in identifying the resources required to implement a procedure. For example, assume that you had prepared flowcharts of a particular procedure, identified the changes that are necessary to accomplish the task at hand, and had obtained approval to prepare (design) the detailed plan of operation and/or implement the newly designed procedure. Clearly, further analysis is required to match the resources at hand with the task at hand. For example, how many clerks or machines will be required to process the data? what type or size of machine is required? and, concerning people, who gets what task?

Questions of this type fall under the broad topic of *work measurement* techniques. Work measurement is a concept or philosophy based on a simple premise: quantitative measurement is essential to the design of efficient procedures. Work measurement includes the variety of techniques used to model, measure, or estimate clerical or other activities in a production framework. In an accounting framework, work measurement is similar to the concept employed in standard cost systems. The essential ingredient is the development of a standard, a yardstick, which may be used to gauge the efficiency of actual operation.

Work measurement involves several basic steps:

1. identify the tasks;
2. obtain time estimates for performing the tasks, utilizing time and motion studies, test runs, historical data, or some other source;
3. adjust these time estimates for idle time and similar considerations; and
4. analyze requirements based on this data.

The following are general examples of step 4:

(average time/unit + idle time/unit)
X average volume   = total task time

$$\frac{\text{total time available}}{\text{total task time}} = \text{capacity utilization}$$

To illustrate the general idea, consider the following excerpt from an actual system analysis:

Our desire to evaluate the relative costs associated with various operating configurations for the CVU Unit led to the programming of a computational model of the CVU operation. The model is essentially a personnel cost model. A constant volume is passed through the CVU operation under certain assumptions as to operating configuration. Costs are accumulated and reported. Costs are calculated in terms of the man hours needed to perform a given operation. A standard computation would appear as follows:

X = volume to be processed
R = processing rate (volume/hour)

$$C = \text{average hourly personnel cost for}$$
$$\text{this processing rate}$$
$$Y = \text{resulting cost}$$

Then,

$$Y = C \cdot (X/R)$$

The standard above is inclusive of such operations as counting, bundle and strap counts, verification, and destruction. In most cases, certain fixed costs are added, such as the cost of observers. As several days are lapsed in processing a given lot, the assumption of a constant volume allows us to calculate the cost/lot. The constant volume used is the average daily volume for the preceding year.

Work measurement techniques may be historically associated with Frederick Taylor's philosophy of scientific management (Taylor, 1947) and the field of study known as industrial engineering. The use of work measurement in manufacturing production situations is widespread and generally considered to be appropriate. Numerous illustrations may be found in Maynard (1971) or similar texts. However, the use of these techniques in office or white-collar situations is a point of disagreement between several management theories. Work measurement may be viewed as a classical approach to management; thus, *detailed* work measurement is not common in an era of relaxed working conditions that exist to promote morale and employee satisfaction. Such conditions are consistent with a contemporary approach to management, which stresses the creation of opportunities and the role of individual choice in organizational activity. McGregor (1966, pp. 14–15), the originator of the "Theory X-Theory Y" dichotomy, provides the following criticism of Theory X management in today's society: "It fails because direction and control are useless methods of motivating people whose physiological and safety needs are reasonably satisfied and whose social, egotistic, and self-fulfillment needs are predominant."

Is work measurement a tool of another, less prosperous, era; a tool that can be used only in dealing with people who have low economic status (most factory workers still receive lower wages than office or white-collar workers)? On the one hand, this question is a matter of philosophy; on the practical side, it is a question of managerial technique: that is, human relations. The success of work measurement in a clerical or white-collar situation is likely to be situation-specific; what is successful or possible in one organization will not necessarily work in another.

With respect to accounting systems, we should note that the trend toward automation of clerical functions increasingly raises work measurement questions with respect to hardware or equipment analysis. Increasingly machines are posting, typing, filing, and so on, and an analysis of machine capabilities is "work measurement." Increasingly, there is less human clerical work to measure, but clerical work more and more often involves some sort of measurable interface with equipment, such as typing or other forms of keyboard entry.

After the operational characteristics of a system have been identified and selected through some form of work measurement, a *work distribution analysis* must be undertaken to assign specific tasks to employees. This analysis may take several forms, but, conceptually we may represent the problem as a matrix (grid or table). Figure 2.10 illustrates a work distribution table.

A work distribution analysis requires detailed information about the functions and responsibilities of all employees involved in the analysis. A task list is used to record each separate item of work performed by an individual and the average number of hours spent on each task per week. The detail of tasks considered would be dependent on the level of work measurement analysis. Figure 2.10 portrays the assignment of several tasks (left-hand column) to employees. Each employee (or department, and so on) is represented by a column; the work assignments are spread across the table to employees. The method of assignment should be rational: that is, one should consider employee qualifications, pay attention to internal control, consider scheduling, timing of events, and so forth. The method of assignment is the choice of the analyst. Formal techniques, utilizing mathematical programming or similar algorithms, may be found in the management science or industrial engineering literature.

FIGURE 2.10.   Sample Work Distribution Table

Task	Estimated Hours per Day	Assignment to Employees		
		Lola	Dale	Neil
Open mail	2	1	1	0
Sort advices	6	2	2	2
Batch control	2	0	0	2
File advices	8	4	4	0

REVIEW QUESTIONS

1. Define the following terms:
   a. system
   b. subsystem
   c. interface

    d. boundary
    e. factoring
    f. decoupling
    g. variety
    h. feedback

2. Identify the basic components of a feedback control system.

3. Is "systems thinking" new? Relate your discussion to several scientific discoveries made since World War II.

4. Describe several types of responsibility centers and their related financial control features.

5. What functions are served by system techniques?

6. Distinguish between "procedural" and "distribution" flowcharts.

7. How does a systems flowchart differ from a program flowchart?

8. Define the following terms:
    a. Process chart
    b. Document flowchart
    c. Forms distribution chart

9. Is flowcharting useful in analyzing the resources required to implement a system?

10. Relate the concept of "work measurement" to the system implementation process.

11. Outline the steps involved in a work distribution analysis.

12. Why are flowcharting techniques important in system analysis and design?

DISCUSSION QUESTIONS AND PROBLEMS

13. Illustrate how the definition of a system affects variety with the following examples:
    a. a course taken at a university;
    b. an order-entry system in a business;
    c. a university.

14. Flowchart the following procedures:
Credit slips and sales slips are keypunched. The cards are sorted by account number. The sorted deck serves as input to the computer together with the accounts receivable master tape. The computer run

produces an updated accounts receivable tape and a sales journal listing. The transaction cards are filed by date.

15.   Analyze the following data incident to machine posting of checks drawn by bank depositors:

Number of checks posted	570
Total elapsed minutes	480
Rest period minutes	20
Interruption and delay minutes	20

Develop a standard time per check. In terms of percentage, what is the rest and delay allowance?

16.   The HRZ Co. maintains a perpetual inventory system. Clerks in the accounting department post the data manually from receiving reports, materials requisition forms, copies of purchase orders, and other transactions such as returns and adjustments to the inventory records. The source documents are filed by posting date. The inventory records are analyzed after each posting to determine if the item should be reordered. If an item needs to be reordered, a purchase requisition is prepared and sent to the purchasing department. There clerks select a vendor from a master vendor file, prepare a purchase order (four copies), and update the vendor file to reflect the order. The purchase order is approved and distributed as follows: original copy to the vendor; copy 2 is filed with the corresponding purchase requisition; copy 3 is forwarded to the receiving department; copy 4 is sent to the purchasing department.

REQUIRED: Flowchart the above procedures.

17.   The XYZ Co. has recently purchased a computer system and is going to automate part of its inventory control systems. An inventory decision rule under consideration by the company for one of its products is as follows:

Sales per Month	Quantity to Order
1–25	20
26–50	50
51–75	80
76–100	100

Does this control have requisite variety?

18.* The independent auditor must evaluate a client's system of internal control to determine the extent to which various auditing procedures must be employed. A client who uses a computer should provide the CPA with a flowchart of the information processing system so the CPA can evaluate the control features in the system. The figure below is a simplified flowchart, such as a client might provide. Unfortunately the client had only partially completed the flowchart when it was requested by you.

   a. Complete the flowchart.
   b. Describe what each item in the flowchart indicates. When complete, your description should provide an explanation of the processing of the data involved. Your description should be in the following order:
       1. "Orders from Salesmen" to "Run No. 5."
       2. "From Mailroom" to "Run No. 5."
       3. "Run No. 5" through the remainder of the chart.
   c. Name each of the flowchart symbols below and describe what each represents.

FLOWCHART SYMBOLS

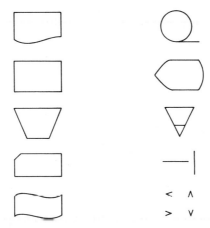

*Material from the Uniform CPA Examinations and Unofficial Answers, copyright © 1967, by the American Institute of Certified Public Accountants, Inc. is reprinted (or adapted) with permission.

FLOWCHART

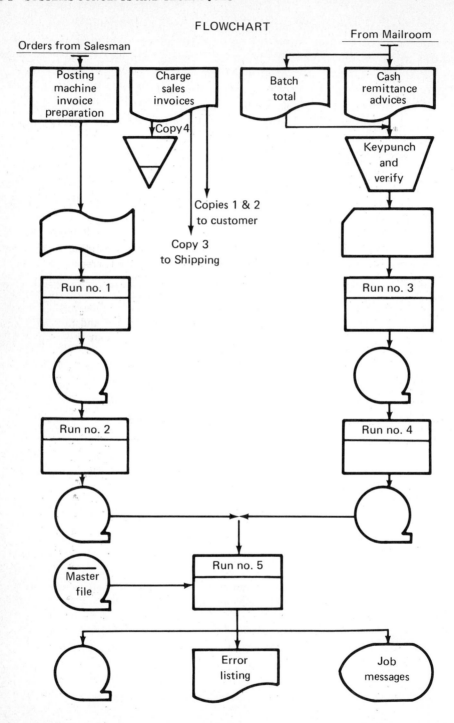

19.*   The Argon County Hospital is located in the county seat. Argon County is a well-known summer resort area. The county population doubles during the vacation months (May–August) and hospital activity more than doubles during these months. The hospital is organized into several departments. Although it is a relatively small hospital, its pleasant surroundings have attracted a well-trained and competent medical staff.

An administrator was hired a year ago to improve the business activities of the hospital. Among the new ideas he has introduced is responsibility accounting. This program was announced along with quarterly cost reports supplied to department heads. Previously, cost data were presented to department heads infrequently. Excerpts from the announcement and the report received by the laundry supervisor are presented below.

> The hospital has adopted a "responsibility-accounting system." From now on you will receive quarterly reports comparing the costs of operating your department with budgeted costs. The reports will highlight the differences (variations) so you can zero in on the departure from budgeted costs (this is called "management by exception"). Responsibility accounting means you are accountable for keeping the costs in your department within the budget. The variations from the budget will help you identify what costs are out of line and the size of the variation will indicate which ones are the most important. Your first such report accompanies this announcement.

Argon County Hospital
Performance Report—Laundry Department
July–September 19X3

	Budget	Actual	(Over) under budget	Percentage (over) under budget
Patient days	9,500	11,900	(2,400)	(25)
Pounds processed (laundry)	125,000	156,000	(31,000)	(25)
Costs:				
Laundry labor	$ 9,000	$ 12,500	$ (3,500)	(39)
Supplies	1,100	1,875	(775)	(70)
Water, Water Heating and Softening	1,700	2,500	(800)	(47)
Maintenance	1,400	2,200	(800)	(57)
Supervisor's salary	3,150	3,750	(600)	(19)
Allocated administrative costs	4,000	5,000	(1,000)	(25)
Equipment depreciation	1,200	1,250	(50)	(4)
	$ 21,550	$ 29,075	$ (7,525)	(35)

*Adapted from CMA Examination

Administrator's comments: Costs are significantly above budget for the quarter. Particular attention needs to be paid to labor, supplies, and maintenance.

The annual budget for 19X3 was constructed by the new administrator. Quarterly budgets were computed as one fourth of the annual budget. The administrator compiled the budget from analysis of the prior three years' costs. The analysis showed that all costs increased each year, with more rapid increases between the second and third year. He considered establishing the budget at an average of the prior three years' costs hoping that the installation of the system would reduce costs to this level. However, in view of the rapidly increasing prices he finally chose 19X2 costs less 3 percent for the 19X3 budget. The activity level measured by patient days and pounds of laundry processed was set at the 19X3 volume, which was approximately equal to the volume of the past three years.

a. Comment on the method used to construct the budget.
b. What information should be communicated by variations from budgets?
c. Does the report effectively communicate the level of efficiency of this department? Give reasons for your answer.

20.* An important concept in management accounting is that of "responsibility accounting."
Required:
a. Define the term *responsibility accounting.*
b. What are the conditions that must exist for there to be effective "responsibility accounting"?
c. What benefits are said to result from "responsibility accounting"?
d. Listed below are three charges found on the monthly report of a division that manufactures and sells products primarily to outside companies. Division performance is evaluated by the use of return on investment. You are to state which, if any, of the following charges are consistent with the "responsibility accounting" concept. Support each answer with a brief explanation.
   1. A charge for general corporation administration at 10 percent of division sales.
   2. A charge for the use of the corporate computer facility. The charge is determined by taking actual annual computer department costs and allocating an amount to each user on the ratio of its use to total corporation use.
   3. A charge for goods purchased from another division. The charge is based upon the competitive market price for the goods.

*Adapted from CMA Examination

REFERENCES

Ashby, Ross, *Design for a Brain* (New York: Wiley, 1954).

—— Editorial, *Behavioral Science*, vol. 18, no. 1 (January 1973).

Beer, S. *Decision and Control: The Meaning of Operations Research and Management Cybernetics* (New York: Wiley, 1966).

Maynard, G.B., ed. *Industrial Engineering Handbook*, 3rd ed. (New York: McGraw-Hill, 1971).

McGregor, D. *Essays in Leadership*. In W. Bennis, ed., (New York: McGraw-Hill, 1966).

Pomeroy, R. "Systems Charting." Chapter 4 in W. Lazzaro, ed., *Systems and Procedures*, 2nd ed. (Englewood Cliffs, N.J.: Prentice-Hall, 1968).

Taylor, F. *Scientific Management* (New York: Harper & Row, 1947).

INTERNAL CONTROL CONSIDERATIONS IN ACCOUNTING INFORMATION SYSTEMS

3

A system of internal control encompasses those policies, practices, and procedures employed by an organization to:

1. safeguard its assets against waste, fraud, and other inefficiency;
2. provide for accurate accounting and other operating information;
3. measure compliance with company policy; and
4. judge the efficiency of operations.

The development of an internal control system is largely a function of the growth of an organization. As an organization evolves from an entity characterized by personal involvement of the owners in daily activities to one marked by specialization and departmentalized operations, the need for internal control increases. The owners become increasingly removed from planning and controlling the firm's activities and become dependent upon a host of operating reports to evaluate financial and operational efficiency. If corrective action is required, this information is communicated through a series of subordinates. The owners, thus, must have certain assurances that the reports generated for planning and control are accurate and that the subordinates carry out the directives in the manner desired. Internal control provides a higher level of confidence in these matters than otherwise might be the case.

ELEMENTS OF INTERNAL CONTROL SYSTEMS

The design of an internal control system is a situationally specific and demanding task of matching a particular set of controls to the organizational situation. A wide range of controls may be utilized in the design of an AIS. This section highlights common control techniques that are utilized to safeguard assets and to check the accuracy of accounting data. These controls provide a set of complementary and supplementary choices to be selected or relied upon as required.

Personnel Practices

Personnel should be competent and have capabilities and/or training commensurate with their duties. In the final analysis, personnel are the key components in any control system. The qualifications established for each job position in a company should reflect the degree of responsibility associated with the position. Qualifications may include experience, intelligence, character, dedication, and leadership ability. Fidelity bonding is common for employees who are directly responsible for the custody of assets. A fidelity bond is a contract with an insurance company, which provides a financial guarantee of the honesty of the individual who is named in the bond contract.

Segregation of Duties

Responsibility for specific tasks should be clearly designated by manuals, job descriptions, or other documentation. This is necessary to implement organizational independence.

Effective segregation of duties depends to a considerable extent on the precise and detailed planning of all procedures and the careful assignment of functions to various persons in the organization. The details of the procedures should be set forth in memoranda that should also show explicit assignment of duties to individual departments or employees. Written procedures, instructions, and assignments of duties will prevent duplication of work, overlapping of functions, omission of important functions, misunderstandings and other situations that might result in weakening the internal accounting controls. Such notes typically form the basis for a formal manual on accounting procedures and policy.

Supervision

In addition to properly selecting and adequately training employees, proper supervision is necessary to insure that duties are being carried out as assigned. Supervision becomes very important in a small firm or other situation in which segregation of duties is not possible.

Job Rotation, "Forced" Vacations

If it is possible to use them, these techniques allow employees to check or verify the operations of other employees by performing their duties for a period of time.

There are several advantages that may be gained:

1. Irregularities which may have been committed by an employee may be disclosed while the employee is on vacation and his duties are assumed by another employee;
2. more than one employee becomes familiar with certain duties and procedures, so that the replacement of employees in cases of emergency is less difficult;
3. rotation frequently serves as a general check on the efficiency of the employee on vacation; and
4. it broadens the training of the personnel in general.

Written Manuals

The accounting and operational procedures should be set forth in accounting and procedure manuals so that company policies and instructions may be explicitly known and uniformly applied.

Chart of Accounts

A chart of accounts will aid in the consistent application of accounting policies, insure proper recording, and facilitate the preparation of financial statements. Control accounts should be used as extensively as possible because they serve as a proof of accuracy between balances and duty-segregated employees.

Double-Entry Systems of Bookkeeping

These systems should not be underestimated as a device that will produce a balanced set of records and statements. To conceal an irregularity under a double-entry system, it is necessary to omit from the accounts both sides of the transaction or to record entries offsetting the amount of the irregularity. Errors are made under a double-entry system, however; the system alone will not prove omission, incorrect entry, or dishonesty.

Dual Control

Closely related to supervision is the concept of dual control. As used here, *dual control* means the assignment of two individuals to perform the same task. The intent of dual control is not work reduction but work redundancy. Each individual is assumed to check the work of the other constantly. Counting cash, for example, is frequently delegated to two or more people working in unison. Multiple control involves three or more people in unison. Dual or multiple control differs from supervision in that a supervisor is expected to supervise several people or operations simultaneously, and therefore may effectively supervise a particular operation less than 100 percent of the time. Dual control is essentially "dedicated" supervision: that is, one employee constantly checks the work of another, and vice versa.

Forms and Documentation

Internal control may be enhanced by the design and effective use of forms that require adherence to prescribed procedures. For example, the use of voucher forms that provide specific space for indication that the required supporting documents have been properly checked and assembled and for the approval of designated employees will immediately call attention to any failure to follow company procedures. The use of prenumbered forms allows verification of the use of each item in proper sequence. This creates clear accountability and helps prevent the use of any form for other than the intended legitimate purpose. Transactions should be supported by sufficient substantiating documentation.

Authorizations

Procedures should provide for a system of authorizations at various levels to prevent unauthorized actions. The fact that an authorization was lacking in a given instance would call for immediate investigation. Proper authorization implements segregation of duties.

Approval

In order to insure that company personnel are acting within the realm of their authority, there should be a system of approval.

Completed transactions should be properly approved by authorized personnel. Several examples where written approval should be required in a good accounting system are:

Approval of bad debt write-offs by an appropriate official.
Approval of payroll by an appropriate employee or officer.
Approval of journal entries by an appropriate official.

Accounting Controls

The accounting system should contain control features that readily confirm or question the reliability of recorded data.

In addition to the points previously discussed, the use of batch totals, control accounts, and the proper voiding or cancellation of invoices and supporting documents after payment are further examples of basic accounting controls. The machine proofs discussed in Chapter 6 are an essential element of accounting control in an automated system.

Budgets

A budget is a plan for action; it summarizes the financial objectives of an organization. In a business organized for profit, the master budget for the entire organization is a good approximation of a formal model of the total organization. The master budget summarizes the organization's inputs, outputs, and financial objectives in monetary units. It captures most of the relevant dimensions associated with the profit motive, the raison d'être of the organization.

This may be contrasted with the master budget of a not-for-profit organization, where outputs are rarely accounted for and often defy definition as well as monetary valuation. Conventional budgeting in the not-for-profit area serves primarily as a device to authorize appropriations and set ceilings for management actions.

Budgets are financial controls in that they set either a target or an amount to which a particular subunit is accountable or by which it is restrained. In the case of a target such as budgeted sales or budgeted travel costs, the subunit has a criterion that may be matched to actual performance. In theory, this is negative feedback control. In the case of a budgeted amount, expenditures may not exceed this amount without specific approval. For example, a subunit may be authorized a budget of $500 to spend as it sees fit; however, in no case may checks be drawn totaling more than $500. In either case, the essential feature of budgets is that they are determined in advance; the system may anticipate what expenditures will be under normal circumstances.

Internal Audit

An internal audit function or staff is common in large organizations to monitor and evaluate internal control on a continuous basis. By measuring and evaluating the effectiveness of organizational controls, internal auditing is itself an important internal control. The extended span of control and the growth in the volume of transactions associated with large organizations were factors in the relatively recent emergence of the internal audit function. The increased reliance on accounting data that is necessary in the management of a large organization, coupled with the increased possibilities of defalcations and improperly maintained accounting records in a large organization have created a need for auditing service on a continuous basis within the organization. In theory this function is independent of other organizational functions and accordingly should report directly to top management. Internal auditing is gradually but continuously moving toward "operational" or "management" auditing. That is, less emphasis is being placed on accounting controls and more emphasis placed on management controls—those concerned with the effectiveness and efficiency of operations. It should be noted that the terms *management audit* and *operational audit* are used without distinction in the literature.

Audit Committees

A recent development relating to financial reporting is the use of audit committees to control an organization's interface with its public accountants. There is a growing belief among investors, analysts, and regulatory agencies that such committees can improve the quality as well as the general acceptance of financial reporting. The Securities and Exchange Commission and the American Institute of Certified Public Accountants have both recommended that publicly owned companies establish audit committees.

The audit committee as envisioned by these institutions is independent of a firm's management, as it is composed directly of members of a corporation's board of directors. The audit committee functions to nominate public accountants, discuss the scope and nature of audits with public accountants, and to review and evaluate reports prepared by a firm's public accountants. Audit committees should be charged with reviewing management's reaction to independent accountants' reviews of internal control.

Physical Controls and Safeguards

Physical controls and safeguards are not accounting functions per se, but as they are concerned with the protection of assets, a brief mention is warranted. It is well documented that physical theft and embezzlement are substantial threats to the solvency of business organizations. Physical controls are directed at reducing the opportunities for thefts and embezzlements.

Safeguarding of assets such as cash, securities, and inventory is accomplished by close supervision, physical protection devices, and segregation of duties. Common examples of physical controls are:

1. cash registers and lock boxes;
2. locks, vaults, and limited-access areas;
3. security forces;
4. closed-circuit TV monitors; and
5. alarm systems

No physical control in and of itself can protect assets; it is the procedures surrounding the use of physical controls that dictate whether or not the controls are effective. For example, every lock has a key; therefore a lock is only as effective as is access to the key.

TV monitors are effective only if watched, or alternatively if personnel believe they are being watched. Limited-access areas are effective only if access is truly limited. The effectiveness of physical controls depends largely on the measures surrounding their use, and not the existence of the devices per se.

HUMAN FACTORS IN INTERNAL CONTROL SYSTEMS

Ethical Considerations

Consider the following hypothetical job description:

> The person who accepts the treasurer's position shall be entirely responsible for the company's securities transactions. The position entails keeping the supporting records, exclusive control over the safe deposit box, and complete discretion over buying and selling of securities.

Would you accept this job?

Many readers will recognize several violations of conventional internal control principles in the above job description. Is this job offering an invitation to fraud? That is, does the lack of conventional controls over the treasurer's duties constitute the equivalent of an invitation to steal? What is an organization's responsibility for the integrity of its employees?

These questions raise issues that should be considered in the design of business systems. The need for an adequate system of internal control can be viewed ethically as well as from the view of efficient management.

The following quotation is representative of this often expressed view:

> I can recall a sizable industrial concern which was headed by a president who was perhaps more interested in his avocation of preaching than in running his business. Attempts to improve internal control in his corporation were constantly rebuffed because he believed that people were fundamentally honest, that his employees could be trusted and, therefore, there was no need for any system of checks and balances. The accountant became increasingly concerned with the company's exposure of its assets to possible defalcation. Finally, he went to the company president and said, "As a good Christian, you have a moral obligation to remove temptation from your employees!" This ethical appeal succeeded where an appeal to good business judgment alone failed, and the company's system of internal control was improved after all. (*Price Waterhouse and Co.*, 1977, p. 16.)

Organizations should have sufficient controls to deter fraudulent actions, if only through reducing temptation by the resultant threat of being caught. On the other hand, overly rigid controls hamper the actions and decisions of individuals, artificially limiting an employee's response to the variety of his task. Accountability and pressures for performance may boomerang; rigid control systems may create or stimulate the types of action that the controls were designed to prevent.

Communicating the Objectives of Internal Control

Internal control must be seen not as a system unto itself but as part of a larger system. It must fit in or it may be totally ineffective or perhaps even harmful. One must not lose sight of what the purpose of internal control is.

People are an essential element in every internal control system. People are not perfect; they commit errors of omission and commission. If people were perfect, internal control would be an unnecessary waste of resources. Internal control is people: an internal control system consists of people checking the work of other people. The principal function of internal control is to influence the behavior of people in a business system.

There is a paradox inherent in developing a system of internal control: controls such as rules and procedures are imposed on people who ideally, from a more humanistic view, should be responsible for their own self-control and self-direction. This inconsistency must be dealt with in every organizational control system.

Management's job is to insure the efficiency of operations: thus behaviors and activities need to be organized and controlled to insure that the organization's goals are attained. A system of internal control does interfere to some extent with an individual's self-control. But by promoting the interests and safeguarding the assets of the overall organization, a system of internal control is really protecting the interest and integrity of each individual employee who is a part of that organization.

The objectives of internal control must be seen as relevant to the individuals who will comprise the control system. The system must be designed such that each employee is convinced that controls are meant to prevent difficulties or crises in the operation of the organization that could otherwise affect him or her very personally.

Goals and Behavior Patterns[1]

An information system has several goals; chief among them is productivity. Reliability of information and the safeguarding of assets are also important goals. These goals are at times contradictory in nature. Productivity in an information system is often constrained by the consideration of reliability. Controls are redundant; they constrain productivity but increase the reliability of resulting outputs. This inherent conflict between internal controls and productivity must be acknowledged and carefully considered by the analyst, since these factors may influence the behavior of people in a control system.

A common behavior caused by this goal conflict is the omission of an internal control duty (such as counting documents) in the interest of increasing production. Consider a clerk manually posting invoices; if the clerk double-checks each posting, the number of postings is approximately 50 percent of what would have been performed without double-checking. If the clerk's performance is evaluated by postings per time period, there is likely to be a temptation to omit the double-checking of at least some items if the clerk falls behind schedule. Internal control duties typically require a trade-off with production. The basic motiva-

[1] This section draws from material published by D. Carmichael, "Behavioral Hypotheses of Internal Control," *The Accounting Review* (April, 1970).

tional problem is that productivity is usually measurable and forms the basis for performance evaluation, whereas reliability or degree of internal control is not as easily measured or incorporated into performance reviews. The systems analyst should keep this in mind in designing and evaluating internal controls.

The goals of an internal control system are achieved through the actions of the people in the system. The reliance upon a formal plan of organization and related methods and measures to attain these goals entails important assumptions concerning collusion, reporting of irregularities, power relationships, and other behavior patterns within the organization. Organizational independence and segregation of duties are consistent with good internal control only if the probability of collusion between two or more duly segregated employees is low.

Collusion is agreement or conspiracy among two or more people to commit fraud. In a purchase procedure, control over acquisitions is obtained when duly segregated personnel from both receiving and stores acknowledge that the materials have been received by stores. Both must sign for the material, and neither could deceive the other without collusion or fraud. Of course errors of omission are possible, such as both parties miscounting quantities. In fact the same error (a shortage) could occur unintentionally as well as intentionally. However, if unintentional, the error would not be covered up and other controls would probably uncover the discrepancy.

Justification for the assumption that the probability of collusion between two or more people will be low is found in the formal plan of organization. For one individual to suggest an irregularity to another person and be rejected would entail prohibitive costs to the first individual. He will be turned in by the second individual and hence lose his job or incur another punishment. This entails a related assumption: that employees will always report irregularities to those higher up in the organization. This assumption in turn requires several others: one is that the formal plan of organization as denoted in procedures manuals and the like solely determines power relations in a system. A related assumption is that actions not specified by a system are dysfunctional or "wrong": that is, deviations suggest irregularities that should be reported to those higher up.

Numerous factors influence an individual's behavior in a control system. One important influence is the formal plan of organization and the related methods and measures employed by an organization. Other factors do exist, however. Groups and other sources of informal pressure bear upon an individual's behavior and may at times mitigate the desired, formally planned relationships between persons in the system. For example, an individual with lengthy service may convince a young coworker that the omission of a control step is OK and need not be reported, since "it's been done that way in the past."

A receiving clerk transferring goods to inventory may convince the inventory clerk just to sign and not waste his time counting the items he is receiving. A clerk performing a bank reconciliation may not examine several checks in detail as it is near quitting time.

What might be called people failure is the source of all theft and fraud in a system and is a prime contributor to serious errors of the production type and other ineffectiveness and inefficiency. One has heard many times that in cases of defalcations "the procedures did not fail, the people did." The variety and complexity of human behavior, the current state of behavioral science, and the value constraints (principles of just, humane, compassionate conduct) we work within, all combine to make the production of "people-proof" procedures infeasible. As long as there are people with access to valuables there will be the possibility of theft, sabotage, and serious error. These possibilities are minimized when employees fully understand, accept, and internalize the objectives of the internal control system of which they are the essential element.

INTERNAL CONTROL AS A PROFESSIONAL TOPIC

As a professional topic, internal control is most closely associated with the public accounting profession. The importance and social relevance of this topic has increased significantly with the passage of the Foreign Corrupt Practices Act of 1977.

Separate and apart from its antibribery provisions, this law amends the Securities Exchange Act of 1934 to require registrants to maintain reasonably complete and accurate books and records and to devise "sufficient" systems of internal accounting controls.

Failure to comply with this law could result in fines and imprisonment. The legal requirement to maintain a "sufficient" system of internal control is a major development. Less than three months after the signing of the Foreign Corrupt Practices Act of 1977, the Securities and Exchange Commission brought its first court action under the accounting standards provisions of the act. It seems clear that the SEC intends to use the recently enacted accounting standards provisions as a tool in future enforcement actions. In April 1979 the SEC proposed rules which would require public reporting on internal control systems.

The specific requirements and definitions included in the act's internal control provisions are very closely related to professional pronouncements of the public accounting profession. These pronouncements are examined in detail in the following sections.

Historical Background and Development

Accountants often use the term *internal control* as a synonym for control within an organization. The term internal control has largely replaced the term *internal check*. Internal check referred to those methods and procedures followed by the accounting and finance divisions of a business for the purpose of minimizing clerical errors and protecting assets, especially cash, from theft or loss. This change in terminology was accompanied by an increasingly expanded conception of both the objectives and activities implied by internal control. In a 1936 AICPA bulletin entitled "Examination of Financial Statements by Independent Public Accountants," internal control was defined as follows:

> . . . those measures and methods adopted within the organization itself to safeguard the cash or other assets of the company as well as to check the clerical accuracy of bookkeeping.

In 1949, the AICPA Committee on Auditing Procedure published a special report entitled "Internal Control—Elements of a Coordinated System and Its Importance to Management and the Independent Public Accountant."* In that report, internal control was defined as follows:

> Internal control comprises the plan of organization and all of the coordinate methods and measures adopted within a business to safeguard its assets, check the accuracy and reliability of its accounting data, promote operational efficiency, and encourage adherence to prescribed managerial policies.

This definition has been reaffirmed by Statement on Auditing Practice (SAP) No. 33 (1963), entitled "Auditing Standards and Procedures," and by SAP No. 54 (1972), entitled "The Auditor's Study and Evaluation of Internal Control." Both of these SAP's were subsequently incorporated into Statement on Auditing Standards (SAS) No. 1 (1973), entitled "Codification of Auditing Standards and Procedures." The broad sweep of this definition indicates that internal control is much more than a device for the detection of fraud and accidental errors in the accounting processes.

Many important elements of internal control systems in organizations are not directly related to the accounting function of processing transactional data. The term *administrative controls* has been given to controls that are necessary to the effective management of an organization but

*Copyright 1949 by the American Institute of Accountants.

that are not directly related to the accounting or financial aspects of a business. One example of an administrative control is a written directive to a personnel department establishing specific standards for hiring new personnel. Training programs, product quality control procedures, and statistical analyses such as employee absence reports or production scheduling reports that are prepared for management are further examples of administrative controls.

Because a review of a firm's existing system of internal control is fundamental to the auditing process, the auditing profession has issued several pronouncements in order to clarify the scope of the independent auditor's review as it pertains to his examination, leading to an expression of an opinion on financial statements. The AICPA Committee on Auditing Procedure issued SAP No. 29, entitled "Scope of the Independent Auditor's Review of Internal Control," in October, 1958, which subdivided the institute's definition of control to include accounting controls and administrative controls. This distinction was reaffirmed by SAP Nos. 33 and 49 and was revised somewhat by SAP No. 54. The revised definitions as incorporated into SAS No. 1 are as follows:

> *Administrative control* includes, but is not limited to, the plan of organization and the procedures and records that are concerned with the decision processes leading to management's authorization of transactions. Such authorization is a management function directly associated with the responsibility for achieving the objectives of the organization and is the starting point for establishing accounting control of transactions.
>
> *Accounting control* comprises the plan of organization and the procedures and records that are concerned with the safeguarding of assets and reliability of financial records and consequently are designed to provide reasonable assurance that:
>
> a. Transactions are executed in accordance with management's general or specific authorization.
> b. Transactions are recorded as necessary (1) to permit preparation of financial statements in conformity with generally accepted accounting principles or any other criteria applicable to such statements and (2) to maintain accountability for assets.
> c. Access to assets is permitted only in accordance with management's authorization.
> d. The recorded accountability for assets is compared with the existing assets at reasonable intervals and appropriate action is taken with respect to any difference.

Internal control in organizations can be viewed as two complementary systems of organization, procedures, and records. Accounting control is a subsystem of administrative control. Accounting controls bear directly on the dependability of the accounting records and the financial statements as opposed to administrative controls, which pertain to operational efficiency and adherence to prescribed policies in all departments of an organization. These control systems are not mutually exclusive, but complementary. Many accounting controls, such as standard costs in a manufacturing firm or budgets, also function as administrative controls in that they are designed to promote operational efficiency.

The Foreign Corrupt Practices Act (FCPA)

Internal control is largely directed at activity which has become to be known as white-collar crime,

> an illegal act or series of illegal acts committed by nonphysical means and by concealment or guile, to obtain money or property, to avoid the payment or loss of money or property, or to obtain business or personal advantage. [Edelhertz, p. 3, 1970.]

The term *white-collar crime* encompasses a wider variety of activity than has traditionally been considered in discussions of internal control, but this limitation is rapidly changing. The SEC and numerous other agencies are increasingly concerned with organizational plans to detect and defer white-collar crime.

By any definition, the cost of white-collar crime is staggering. In 1974 the Chamber of Commerce of the United States, after surveying various sources, came up with a figure of approximately $41 billion annually, not taking into account the cost to the public of price-fixing illegalities and industrial espionage. Quite clearly, figures of this magnitude dwarf into insignificance the total dollar costs of common crimes. White-collar crimes such as embezzlement, tax fraud, unemployment insurance fraud, and the like require some form of procedural analysis (a physical examination and analysis of financial transaction records, and documentation, inventories, etcetera) as a *prerequisite even to finding out and proving that a crime has been committed.*

Thus the social role and responsibilities of the auditing profession have become blurred and debated as the economic necessity for auditors to sample transactions rather than test them 100 percent (which was not uncommon long ago and is sometimes done today) has obvious implications. The importance of systems design and the increasing importance of internal control to businesses is evident as computers continue to take over the processes and environment of white-collar crime. For example, a study completed in 1973 showed that the average losses resulting from bank embezzlement by computer were ten times higher than general bank embezzlement losses (Parker, 1973). Congress has considered legislation that is directed at the subject of computer crime.

An increasing concern for white-collar crime, coupled with increasing government interest in the social role of public accounting firms, stimulated the passage of the Foreign Concept Practices Act of 1977. During the Watergate investigations, the Securities and Exchange Commission (SEC) detected some firms utilizing company funds for illegal domestic political contributions. Later investigations disclosed that these firms had also engaged in questionable payments to foreign officials. It was found that these payments had been made through secret bank accounts and other methods that circumvented internal accounting control systems.

On May 12, 1976, the SEC presented its "Report on Questionable and Illegal Corporate Payments and Practices" to the Banking, Housing and Urban Affairs Committee of the Senate. The SEC's report proposed that Congress enact legislation to improve the accuracy of corporate books and records. In response to the SEC's recommendation, the Foreign Corrupt Practices Act (FCPA) contained standards with respect to company books and internal accounting controls.

Source and Nature of the Act's Accounting Provisions

Section 102 of the FCPA requires all companies who are subject to the Securities Exchange Act of 1934 to:

A. make and keep books, records, and accounts, which, in reasonable detail, accurately and fairly reflect the transactions and dispositions of the assets of the issuer; and
B. devise and maintain a system of internal accounting controls sufficient to provide reasonable assurances that
  i. transactions are executed in accordance with management's general or specific authorization;
  ii. transactions are recorded as necessary (i) to permit preparation of financial statements in conformity with generally accepted accounting principles or any other criteria applicable to such statements, and (ii) to maintain accountability for assets;
  iii. access to assets is permitted only in accordance with management's general or specific authorization; and
  iv. the recorded accountability for assets is compared with the existing assets at reasonable intervals and appropriate action is taken with respect to any differences.

Noncompliance with these provisions could result in $10,000 fines for both the corporation and its officials along with five years' imprisonment for those executives involved. Apprehension has arisen from the fact that there are no objective criteria in either the statute or SEC rules and regulations to enable the evaluation of an internal accounting control system.

The act's accounting requirements and internal control definition are based on auditing concepts and are taken almost verbatim from the AICPA's Statement on Auditing Standards No. 1. Although it may seem reasonable to select an AICPA pronouncement as a source for accounting-related legislation, this selection raises significant problems in meaning and interpretation.

An independent auditing firm performs a review of a client's internal control system only to determine how much that system can be relied on in auditing the books and records and the financial statements generated from it. A comprehensive study is not always made, for it may be cheaper and quicker to check sample transactions and other accounting records to ascertain that financial statements follow generally accepted accounting principles (GAAP). When an internal control review is performed, weaknesses in the system are at times discovered. However, only when a weakness is "material"—that is, significant enough to allow a potential misstatement of the overall financial report on which an opinion is being expressed—will an auditor issue his comments concerning that weakness to management. The comments become part of a confidential management letter issued by the CPA firm to management, and the particular weaknesses are corrected and/or legitimately disposed of by them.

Demonstrating Compliance with the FCPA

Since the passage of the act in 1977, the issue of demonstrating legal compliance with the act's accounting provisions has been surrounded with uncertainty. An organization may take the view that compliance with the accounting standards provisions of the FCPA is encompassed within the external audit of the firm. Assessing the adequacy of internal controls is not the responsibility of the external auditors. Their main responsibility is to provide an opinion on the financial statements. The external auditor tests the internal controls only in the areas where he or she relies on existing controls in formulating an opinion of the financial statement. For example, the auditor may decide to perform direct tests of documentation underlying financial statements, rather than relying on the existing control system. As a consequence, weaknesses in an internal accounting control system may not be detected during an external audit because the auditor has chosen not to rely on existing internal control systems.

Since the external auditors are not responsible for compliance with the act, it is necessary for management to assess and demonstrate compliance. Management should consider the broad guidelines laid down by the AICPA in its publication "Report of the Special Advisory Committee on Internal Accounting Control" (AICPA, 1979). This report differs from other AICPA publications on internal accounting controls in that its primary audience is management rather than the public accounting profession. The committee's procedures for the evaluation of an accounting system are classified into three broad areas. These procedures are an analysis of the factors that encompass the internal accounting control environment, development of a "cycle approach" in the evaluation of accounting controls, and a cost-benefit analysis of an accounting control. While embracing a cycle approach in its illustrations, the report recognizes that some companies may choose to approach their evaluation in another way, for example, by function or operating unit.

The committee's guidelines emphasize that controls start with a corporate environment that has clearly drawn lines of responsibility and authority, as well as divisions of responsibility to provide checks and balances. The guidelines also provide for an evaluation of controls as a coherent, integrated system and state that there should be clear policies for handling and recording transactions.

Specifically, the committee recommended that management take these steps: (1) assess the environment in which internal controls operate, (2) devise a plan to evaluate the adequacy of system procedures, and (3) monitor compliance. By "control environment" the committee means general business practices such as organization and personnel practices, budgetary controls, and internal audit activities. It is unlikely that management can be reasonably assured that internal control objectives are met in the absence of such practices.

Public Reporting on Internal Control

Although effective upon enactment, the FCPA itself did not directly address the issue of how an organization could demonstrate compliance with the act's accounting provisions. Concerning this issue, the SEC in Accounting Series Release No. 242 (February, 1978) stated:

> Because the Act became effective upon signing, it is important that issuers subject to the new requirements review their accounting procedures, systems of internal accounting controls and business practices in order that they may take any actions necessary to comply with the requirements contained in the Act.

Passage of the FCPA stimulated discussion of a management report in which management would publicly address the issue of compliance with the FCPA as well as other matters pertaining to management's responsibilities for financial reporting. The final report of the Commission on Auditors' Responsibilities (AICPA, 1978) suggested a need for a management report that would include, among other items, an assessment of the organization's accounting system and of controls over it. The Financial Executives Institute (FEI) has issued suggested guidelines for preparation of such a management report. These guidelines are generally consistent with those of the Commission on Auditors' Responsibilities.

Although the "Report of the Special Advisory Committee on Internal Accounting Control" (AICPA, 1979) does not deal with the issue of public reporting on internal control, it notes that "companies may be called upon to make public representations about their internal accounting control." (AICPA, 1979, p. 27). This possibility appears to be imminent. In April 1979, just after the final report of the advisory committee on internal accounting control was released, the SEC proposed rules that would require public reporting on internal control. The proposed rules are designed to implement the accounting provisions of the FCPA.

The proposed rules were not a surprise. The SEC had stated publicly many times that firms must demonstrate compliance with the FCPA; the proposed rules would formalize and implement this requirement.

The SEC proposal for a management report does not involve matters other than internal accounting control that might otherwise be included in a management report. As proposed in the Federal Register of May 4, 1979, the SEC's rules would require management to express an opinion as to whether the control system gave reasonable assurances of having met each of the specified control objectives (authorizing and recording transactions, limiting access to assets, and comparing assets and accountability) which are contained in the FCPA. The independent, external auditor would have certain responsibilities under the proposed rules, including examination of and reporting on management's statement on internal control. The proposed rules would require an expansion of the independent public accountant's present responsibilities with respect to internal accounting control. (*Federal Register*, p. 26707, 1979).

The SEC's discussion of the proposed rules stresses the Commission's refusal to prescribe detailed procedures to insure compliance with the FCPA; such procedures are managements' responsibility. The FCPA makes record keeping and internal accounting control requirements a matter of law for organizations subject to SEC regulations. The law has major implications as the legal interpretation of "sufficient internal accounting control" and "reasonable assurance" evolve through court case rulings and SEC regulations.

Reasonable assurance is the concept that the cost of a control should not exceed the benefits likely to be derived from the use of the control. Reasonable assurance is explicitly endorsed by the AICPA in SAS No. 1, and the SEC in Release No. 34-13185 (January, 1977), which pertains to the FCPA. The proposed rules for public reporting on internal control also incorporate the concept of reasonable assurance.

In discussing the proposed rules for public reporting on internal control, the Commission suggests that the determination of whether a system of internal accounting control provides reasonable assurances that the broad objectives of internal accounting control are achieved will generally involve the following:

> First, evaluation of the overall control environment;
> Second, translation of the broad objectives of internal accounting control into specific control objectives applicable to the particular business, organizational and other characteristics of the individual company;
> Third, consideration of the specific control procedures and individual environmental factors which should contribute to achievement of the specific control objectives;
> Fourth, monitoring of control procedures and consideration of whether they are functioning as intended; and
> Finally, consideration of the benefits (consisting of reductions in the risk of failing to achieve the objectives) and costs of additional or alternative controls. (*Federal Register*, p. 26705, 1979).

These guidelines are consistent with those contained in "Report of the Special Advisory Committee on Internal Accounting Control" (AICPA, 1979).

Evaluating both the adequacy of an internal control system and the related cost/benefit relationships is a highly subjective process in which knowledgeable individuals can arrive at different conclusions. Demonstrating compliance with the FCPA is likely to require explicit documentation of an organization's accounting control provisions, the establishment of an independent audit committee, the use of independent management directors, the strengthening of the internal auditing function, and the establishment of a written code of corporate conduct.

The need for the establishment of audit committees and an independent board of directors is evidenced in SEC proceedings against public companies. The proceedings have led to court orders requiring the establishment of these channels. Another encouragement for the establishment of audit committees has come from a New York Stock Exchange rule mandating their existence for its members.

ANALYSIS OF INTERNAL CONTROL SYSTEMS

The analysis of an internal control system requires both an understanding of the system as it is designed and evidenced by formal documentation, such as organization charts and procedures manuals, and also an understanding of the system as it actually operates. The actual system may or may not conform to expectations. Documentation may be outdated, and the system may be operating under new procedures. Procedures may have changed informally to adapt to circumstances not foreseen at the time when the original system was designed and documented.

Internal control systems routinely collect and process information concerning fulfillment of duties, transfer of authority, approval, and verification. This documentation of internal control duties is examined to evaluate the reliability of the system's operation.

The reliability of an internal control system is dependent on the people who administer internal control procedures. To put it succinctly, internal control is people. Designing an internal control system is only the first part of the problem; it is essential that internal control duties are actually performed as prescribed.

There are several reasons why internal control duties may not be administered. New employees, or perhaps even experienced employees, may not understand their duties. More common is the omission, in order to increase production, of an internal control duty (such as counting documents). Other factors were discussed earlier and are mentioned here again to emphasize the role human behavior has in internal control.

Despite the importance of internal control, formal review techniques are largely nonexistent, with one significant exception—the internal control questionnaire. The internal control questionnaire is a guide for the systems analyst or auditor to follow in evaluating internal control. Questionnaires are usually designed so that an affirmative answer to a question indicates an adequate degree of internal control, while a negative answer indicates the need for further information or a potential weakness in the system. Questionnaires are essentially checklists to insure that a review does not omit a major area of traditional importance. Figure 3.1 illustrates a portion of a checklist for sales and shipping procedures that is similar to that which would be found in use by public accounting firms.

Questionnaires are only tools; the manner in which they are used is extremely important. The questionnaire should be filled in on the basis of actual observations and inquiries, but filling in the questionnaire is not the essence of the review. The essence of a review is the analyst's analysis of his or her findings. Questionnaires do serve as documentation that a review was undertaken; however, questionnaires are necessarily "standardized" and therefore are not equally applicable in all circumstances. Their use must often be supplemented with other forms of analysis, such as write-ups, flowcharts, or other charting techniques.

Evaluation of internal control requires that the analyst compare his or her understanding of the existing system to the system that is evidenced

---

FIGURE 3.1. Portion of an Internal Control Questionnaire

Sales and Shipping

1. Are sales orders adequately controlled?
2. Are all orders approved by the credit manager or department before shipment?
3. Is the credit department entirely independent of the sales department?
4. Are sales prices and credit terms based on approved standard price lists?
5. If so, are any deviations from standard approved:
   a. By an officer?
   b. By another? Explain.
6. If not, are all sales prices and credit terms approved by the sales manager or in the sales department?
7. Are prenumbered shipping advices prepared for all goods shipped?
8. Are the quantities shown on the shipping advices double-checked in the shipping department?
9. Does the billing clerk or some other designated employee receive the shipping advices directly from the shipping department? (If so, identify this employee.)
10. Does this employee check the numerical sequence of shipping advices to assure that all are accounted for?
11. Are sales invoices checked:
    a. As to prices?
    b. As to quantities?
    c. As to credit terms?
    d. As to extensions and footings?
    e. Against customers' orders?
    f. Against shipping advices?
    (Identify the department or individual responsible for the above.)
12. Are sales invoices prenumbered?

by formal documentation. Exercising judgment, analysts must determine if any weaknesses or deficiencies exist, and if so, they must find the means to correct them. A cost/benefit criterion is implicit to systems analysis. Cost/benefit trade-offs require an assessment of system reliability.

The use of probability models to measure statistically the concept of system reliability began with the space programs of the 1960s. Since space equipment was expensive to develop and required extensive testing, economies were expected from an integrated statistical program that would model hardware systems reliability. Reliability theory has matured into a well-founded discipline. The discipline has been largely concerned

---

FIGURE 3.1. continued

---

13. Is there a check on the arithmetical accuracy of total sales by means of a statistical or product analysis?
14. Are total sales for the respective accounting periods (e.g., monthly) reported directly to the general ledger bookkeeper independently of the work of the accounts receivable bookkeepers?
15. Are there adequate safeguards against understatement of sales through the suppression of sales invoices or shipping advices?
16. Are returned sales cleared through the receiving department (i.e., the department receiving incoming purchased materials and supplies)?
17. Are credit memos for returned sales supported by adequate data from the receiving department as to quantity, description, and condition?
18. Are the following classes of sales accounted for in substantially the same manner as regular credit sales of merchandise:
    a. Sales to employees?
    b. C.O.D. sales?
    c. Sales of property and equipment?
    d. Cash sales of merchandise?
    e. Scrap and waste?
    (If the answers are in any case in the negative, amplify by a concise description of the procedures.)
19. Is there an adequate check on freight allowances:
    a. By reference to terms of sale?
    b. By checking against freight bills or established and up-to-date schedule of freight rates?
    c. Other? (If any, explain.)
    Comment on adequacy of internal control:

Source: Bower et al, *Financial Information Systems* (1969), pp. 609–611.

with assigning numerical reliability figures to configurations of hardware systems such as switching circuits and power networks.

Reliability theory provides a framework for the measurement of the reliability of an internal control system. This measurement might then be used in a cost/benefit analysis of internal controls (Cushing, 1974). The practicality of reliability measurement in internal control systems analysis has not yet been demonstrated. However, the successful implementation of reliability theory techniques in other disciplines suggests that principles of reliability theory are relevant to the analysis of organizational control systems.

Basic Elements of Reliability Theory[2]

The basic principle of reliability theory is that any operating configuration of components is predictable, once the individual component reliabilities are known. The use of simple multiplicative probability models creates a small paradox:

> Mathematically, it can be shown through the operation of the product rule that the introduction of a component into a system reduces overall reliability. . . . (Meister, 1964, p. 621).

As any individual component is assigned a reliability measure r, $0 \leqslant r \leqslant 1$, its serial introduction into a system necessarily reduces overall reliability. This is a direct consequence of multiplicative probability models. Reliability theory's mathematical counter to this basic feature of probability models is the concept of redundancy. Redundancy refers to the existence of alternative components within a system, to help the system operate in case of failure of one or more components. Common examples of redundancy are standby or backup generators, computers, and, in internal control systems, dual control of procedures. A component may serve to increase system reliability with respect to a particular type of error if it functions in a redundant (that is, parallel) mode. Several parallel models are possible. Figure 3.2 shows a system with parallel channels. A channel contains all the serial components necessary to complete the step from A to B. The step from A to B is completed if either channel functions without an individual component failure. Figure 3.3 shows the same system with parallel components. In this case, the step from A to B is successful if at least one component in each parallel configuration functions. The result (which may be proven mathematically) is intuitive: in Figure 3.2 the system fails if only one component in each channel fails, whereas in Figure 3.3 n components in all may fail without causing system failure.

The primary effects of adding a component depend on whether it functions in series or parallel. However, in either case it may be that the overall reliability of the system decreases. This is so because the overall reliability of any individual component cannot be greater than one. Each component conceptually adds new sources of error: the seriousness of this new source of error depends on the overall system configuration. Enrick (1972, pp. 256-260) gives an example involving electrical switches where redundancy reduces the probability of one type of error, but increases the probability of another type of error. Enrick concludes that redun-

---

[2] Adapted from G. Bodnar, "Reliability Modeling of Internal Control Systems," *The Accounting Review* (October, 1975).

FIGURE 3.2. Redundant Channels

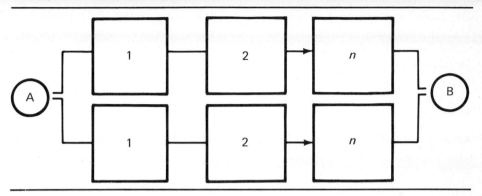

dancy "is not an unmixed blessing." Although conceptually the probability of a stage's (a necessary step in a process) functioning correctly can be made as large as one pleases by adding enough of each type of component in parallel, one must carefully consider the costs of this increase in reliability and also assess the potential increase in other sources of error that redundancy creates. In hardware reliability analysis, these potential increases are usually in the probability that the system will function in an unexpected manner. Such errors, once defined, may be included in the analysis and overall system design may then be optimized. Gordon (1957, pp. 229–243) presents a general formula for determining overall reliability in such cases. It should be emphasized here that the solution depends heavily on the magnitude of the error estimates. In control systems analyses, the addition of more controls is unlikely to increase the proba-

FIGURE 3.3. Redundant Components

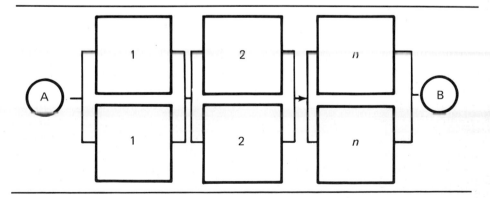

bility that the system functions inadvertently, due to the nature of such systems. However, when the addition involves a human element, there is necessarily an increase in the probability of individual theft, etcetera (that is, the control must be controlled), and possibly an increase in the probability of collusion. Furthermore, unlike hardware systems, one is not a priori guaranteed that the control will function in the manner desired. Although reliability modeling indicates that a parallel configuration is desirable, components arranged in parallel may function as though in series.

Analysis of "Human Reliability" in Systems

The straightforward extension of reliability techniques to human performance dates from the late 1950s. The term *human reliability* has been defined by Meister (1964, p. 621) as "the probability that a task involving a human operator will be successfully performed at any required stage in system operation within a criterion time period." This definition closely parallels the definition of equipment reliability, to indicate what is being measured and predicted is an attribute of a system which is entirely parallel with that of equipment reliability. To ignore human performance in system reliability estimates is to assume that operator performance is invariably perfect. Studies in this area have shown that this assumption is rarely justified.

The simplest means of quantitatively measuring human reliability is to determine the frequency and percentage of errors made in performing a task. Data bases being developed for use by human reliability analysts would appear to indicate the feasibility of a similar approach for use in control system analysis. Theoretical objections against frequency as a concept of probability stress the problem of induction. The question that immediately arises is, how much error implies human *un*reliability? Simple error frequency and percentage are not very meaningful because frequency and percentage cannot be related to a theoretical potential error to which human performance in a given system is susceptible, nor do they say anything about the probability of a given error being repeated in subsequent exercises and particularly in the operational situation (Meister and Rabideau, 1965, p. 243).

The statistical nature of reliability theory precludes an attempt to predict individual operator errors, although the latter are measured individually. Statistical methods extend only to the development of probability predictions for a mean of population responses, and, therefore, any prediction will, to a certain extent, be in error with respect to an individual operator.

This should not pose any serious problems for the analysis of normal errors of the production type.[3] However, for an analysis of the probability of fraudulent behavior this situation is somewhat less satisfying. Assuming a frequency approach, measurement becomes the issue. Conceptually, there are two approaches. First, one may assume that, with respect to fraud, theft, etcetera, all persons are identical. While simplifying in that it is similar to the data bank approach, such an approach may prove unacceptable because it goes against common beliefs, as evidenced primarily by personnel hiring policies. It is unlikely that persons in charge of personnel operations will agree that all persons are equally acceptable for a given task. Security guards, for example, are screened in several attributes. The existence of such practices and common beliefs among management mitigates against the use of a single estimate for all personnel. On the other hand, following this approach to its logical conclusion infers the assignment of unique probabilities to each individual. This approach is well beyond the state of the art in assessing human behavior. Furthermore, for an individual who has not previously committed a defalcation, a frequency approach must yield an estimate of perfect reliability. But obviously this implies little about the future. Furthermore, collecting data on individuals who have committed errors of a criminal nature is very difficult, as often such records are not kept for fear of libel suits. Even if such records were kept, their use might prove very difficult because of questions of fairness and legality. One would be hard pressed to defend decisions based on background (such as race, training, or army records) in today's sociopolitical environment.

This discussion suggests that statistical modeling of production aspects of internal control systems is currently feasible, although in any situation a great many difficulties would be encountered. The experience of the human reliability field demonstrates that, once suitable data bases have been developed, reasonable predictions concerning a population of operator responses are possible. With respect to the perhaps more important concern for "people failure," it seems that numerical analysis is not likely to be directly meaningful. However, generalizations and concepts drawn from reliability theory may serve as useful guides in designing and evaluating control procedures.

---

[3] The terms *production aspects* and *errors of the production type* refer to actions such as counting cash and recording data (as in posting to a ledger). In counting cash one would expect some errors to occur even if employees were perfectly honest. On the other hand, a deliberate error in counting is an example of what has been termed "people failure." The terminology is used to imply the difference between normal errors of omission and errors of commission.

REVIEW QUESTIONS

1. Is supervision in a small business more important than in a large business?

2. How does prenumbering of documents and forms enhance internal control?

3. Discuss the role of the following controls within an internal control system:
    Personnel practices
    Segregation of duties
    Supervision
    Job rotation
    Written manuals
    Chart of accounts
    Double-entry accounting
    Forms and documentation
    Authorizations
    Approval

4. Is an organization responsible for the behavior of its employees in their work environment?

5. What paradox exists in the design of internal control systems? Is this problem different in a manufacturing firm than it is in a professional firm, such as a public accounting firm?

6. Do you feel that people are basically dishonest?

7. Why is it important that the purpose and nature of internal control be communicated to employees within an organization?

8. What is meant by "collusion"? Why is collusion a problem in the design of internal control systems?

9. Discuss the statement "The procedures did not fail; the people did."

10. Give several examples of administrative controls that are not accounting controls. Give several examples of accounting controls that are also administrative controls.

11. What role do physical security devices have in a system of internal control?

12. Why has the internal audit function continued to grow in importance?

13.   What are the functions of an audit committee?

14.   Define organizational independence.

15.   Discuss the advantages and disadvantages of using a questionnaire or checklist in evaluating an internal control system.

16.   Does filling out a questionnaire constitute an evaluation of internal control?

17.   What is the significance of the Federal Foreign Corrupt Practices Act of 1977?

DISCUSSION QUESTIONS AND PROBLEMS

18.   A certain business receives all payments of account by check. Since checks are always received, an analyst wants to use the checks themselves as posting media to the accounts receivable ledger rather than have to prepare and process remittance advices. Discuss the conflict between productivity and reliability that is inherent here.

19.   What potential and problems do you foresee with a formal statistical approach to the evaluation of internal control systems?

20.   What duties should not normally be performed by the same individual in each of the following procedures.
   a.   Bad-debt write-off?
   b.   Payroll preparation?
   c.   Sales returns?
   d.   Inventory purchases?

21.   The president of an organization delegates part of his authority to a controller. Does this make the president any less responsible for the organization's internal control system? Does the size of the organization (large *vs.* small) influence your answer?

22.*   The Internal Auditing Department was told that two employees were terminated for falsifying their time records. The two employees had altered overtime hours on their time cards after their supervisors had approved the hours actually worked.
   Several years ago, the company discontinued the use of time clocks. Since then, the plant supervisors have been responsible for manually posting the time cards and approving the hours for which their employees

*Reprinted by permission of The Institute of Internal Auditors, Inc., from the Certified Internal Auditor Examination (May, 1977).

should be paid. The postings are usually entered in pencil by the supervisors or their secretaries. After the postings for the week are complete, the time cards are approved and placed in the mail racks outside the supervisors' offices for pickup by the timekeepers. Sometimes the timekeepers do not pick up the time cards promptly.

Required:

Assuming the company does not wish to return to using time clocks, give *three* recommendations to prevent recurrence of the situation described above. For each recommendation, indicate how it will deter fraudulent reporting of hours worked.

23. Discuss the purpose of the following questions, which appear on an internal control questionnaire:

a. Does the company have an organization chart?
b. Are the duties of the principal accounting officer segregated from those of the treasurer?
c. Are employees in position of trust bonded?
d. Are bank accounts reconciled regularly by the company?
e. Does the company maintain a ledger of its fixed assets?
f. Are journal entries approved by a responsible official?
g. Are aging schedules of accounts receivable prepared periodically and reviewed by a responsible person?
h. Does the company compare budgeted amounts with actual expenditures?
i. Are trial balances of the accounts receivable ledgers prepared and reconciled regularly?
j. Do the employees who maintain inventory records have physical access to the inventory?
k. Are the inventory records adjusted to physical counts at least once a year?
l. Are remittance advices that accompany receipts separated and given to the accounting department?
m. Are costs and expenses under budgetary control?
n. Is a postage meter used?
o. Are monthly statements of account mailed to all customers?
p. In reconciling bank accounts do employees examine endorsements?
q. Has the bank (or banks) been instructed not to cash checks payable to the company?

24.* B.J. Machine Company is considering developing an internal audit department. A few years ago the company began an expansion program, which included the acquisition of new businesses, some of

*Adapted from CMA Examination

which are located quite distant from the home office. B.J. Machine has used the acquired managements in most past acquisitions and expects to continue to do so. The corporate organization is decentralized, with the parent company (B.J. Machine) setting the general policy. Divisions and subsidiary managements are quite autonomous; their performance is measured against budgets and return on investment targets established at the beginning of each year. The units of B.J. Machine manufacture and market their products. The present companywide volume is $150,000,000.

B.J. Machine has been audited by the CPA firm in which you are a manager. You have supervised the audit of B.J. Machine for the past three years. You have been asked by B.J. Machine Company to prepare a report on the activities that could be undertaken by an internal audit department.

Required:

1. Prepare a report which describes:
   a.   the different objectives of the external vs. internal auditor;
   b.   the types of audits that an internal audit department might be expected to perform;
   c.   the relationship of the internal auditor to the external auditor.
2. The company has indicated that you will be asked to head the internal audit department if it is established. Describe the change(s) in your audit philosophy and in your relationship to the firm management, if any, you believe should occur if you were to take this job.

25.*   The cashier of the Easy Company intercepted Customer A's check payable to the company in the amount of $500 and deposited it in a bank account which was part of the company petty cash fund, of which he was custodian. He then drew a $500 check on the petty cash fund bank account payable to himself, signed it, and cashed it. At the end of the month while processing the monthly statements to customers, he was able to change the statement to Customer A so as to show that A had received credit for the $500 check that had been intercepted. Ten days later he made an entry in the cash received book which purported to record receipt of a remittance of $500 from Customer A, thus restoring A's account to its proper balance, but overstating the cash in bank. He covered the overstatement by omitting from the list of outstanding checks in the bank reconcilement two checks, the aggregate amount of which was $500.

List what you regard as five important deficiencies in the system of internal control in the above situation, and state the proper remedy for each deficiency.

26.*   The Frances Foxx Company, a client of your firm, has come to you with the following problem: It has three clerical employees who must perform the following functions:
1.   maintain general ledger;
2.   maintain accounts payable ledger;
3.   maintain accounts receivable ledger;
4.   prepare checks for signature;
5.   maintain disbursements journal;
6.   issue credits on returns and allowances;
7.   reconcile the bank account;
8.   handle and deposit cash receipts.

Assuming that there is no problem as to the ability of any of the employees, the company requests that you assign the above functions to the three employees in such a manner as to achieve the highest degree of internal control. It may be assumed that these employees will perform no other accounting functions than the ones listed and that any accounting functions not listed will be performed by persons other than these three employees.

a.   State how you would distribute the above functions among the three employees. Assume that, with the exception of the nominal jobs of the bank reconciliation and the issuance of credits on returns and allowances, all functions require an equal amount of time.
b.   List four possible unsatisfactory pairings of the above listed functions.

27.† You were recently appointed the internal auditor for a private college. Your first assignment is to appraise the adequacy and effectiveness of the student registration procedures. You have completed your preliminary survey. Based on your interviews and a walk-through of the student registration operation, you prepared an informal flowchart.
Required:
Examine the following informal flowchart and list *five* internal control weaknesses (such as omissions of certain steps or measures) in the student registration procedures.

Admission—Processing of Registrations

1. *Mail Room*
   Opens all mail, prepares remittance advices, and remittance listings
   Sends copies of advices and listings to:
   A. Cashier (with cash and cheques)
   B. Accounts receivable clerk
   C. General bookkeeper
   Destroys other copies of advices and listings
2. *Registration Clerk*
   Receives three copies of completed registration forms from students
   Checks for counselor's or similar approval
   Records appropriate fee from official class catalog
   If completed properly, approves forms and sends students with registration forms to cashier
   If not completed properly, returns forms to student for follow-up and reapplication
3. *Cashier*
   Collects funds or forwards two copies of registration forms to billing clerk
   Records cash receipts in daily receipts record
   Prepares and makes daily deposits
   Forwards duplicate receipted deposit slips and daily receipts records to general bookkeeper
   Destroys copies of daily receipts records
4. *Billing Clerk*
   Receives two copies of registration form, prepares bill, and makes entries in registration (sales) journal
   Forwards copies of billings and registration forms to accounts receivable clerk and forwards copies of bill to general bookkeeper
5. *Accounts Receivable Clerk*
   Posts accounts receivable subsidiary ledger detailed accounts from remittance listings
   Matches billings and registration forms and posts accounts receivable subsidiary ledger detailed accounts
6. *General Bookkeeper*
   Journalizes and posts cash receipts and applicable registrations to general ledger
   Enters registration (sales) journal data in general ledger

28.* Dragano Inc., a regional distributor of building products with

*Adapted from CMA Examination

headquarters in New York, had been operating on the East Coast for a number of years. By the end of 1971, there were 15 local sales branches and annual sales totaled $15 million.

In an effort to expand its area of sales coverage, Dragano acquired Gruendo, Inc., in 1972 and operated the company as a wholly-owned subsidiary. Gruendo, also a distributor of building products, with 10 branches and annual sales of $10 million, is located in the Midwest with headquarters in Chicago.

Both companies sell to individuals as well as to contractors. Terms of sale to individuals are cash; sales to contractors are made on 30-day open account, provided the contractor's credit is cleared by the head-quarters office. The bulk of the dollar volume of sales is to contractors on account.

Dragano customers are billed from the New York office and Gruendo customers are billed from the Chicago office, on a cycle basis. The billings are completed on the basis of daily sales listings, along with prenumbered charge slips, rendered by the branches to headquarters. The listings identify cash and charge sales separately. All cash receipts are deposited daily and intact by the branches in local depositories. Charge accounts are paid directly to the office from which the account was billed.

Early in 1974, Dragano management became concerned about the apparent excess of accounts receivable on the books of Gruendo relative to Dragano. Both companies utilized the same credit policy and had approximately the same mix of cash and account sales. Gruendo's accounts, however, represented 50 days' sales, while Dragano's represented 30 days' sales.

This concern prompted the management of Dragano to call upon the corporate accounting staff to investigate the situation. In confirming the accounts of Gruendo and clearing exceptions, the accountants conducting the audit discovered that

1. 10 percent of account balances represented invoices already paid by customers, and
2. an additional 20 percent of the account balances represented underpayments by customers on specific invoices.

The audit disclosed that the cashier opened the mail and deposited some checks to a company-named account for which his signature was the only authorized one. He was responsible for preparation of monthly statements and thus was able to remove from the statement invoices already paid by customers.

The underpayment of accounts was the result of arrangements made by the branch salesmen with the knowledge of the credit manager, a long-time employee of Gruendo, whereby favored customers were quoted lower prices than list prices. This granting of discounts in this fashion has been a practice of long standing. The Chicago office billed at list prices, but the customers paid at the quoted rates.

The amount of the overstatements totaled $600,000.

Required:

Assume that you are the Dragano accountant in charge of this job.

1. Comment critically on the accounting and other procedures described above.

2. Recommend any changes that you think should be made in the company's procedures. Explain your answer.

REFERENCES

AICPA Publications

Statements on Auditing Procedure

Scope of the Independent Auditor's Review of Internal Control, No. 29 (1958).
Auditing Standards and Procedures (a codification), No. 33 (1963).
Reports on Internal Control, No. 49 (1971).
The Auditor's Study and Evaluation of Internal Control, No. 54 (1972).

Statements on Auditing Standards

Codification of Auditing Standards and Procedures, No. 1 (1973).
The Effects of EDP on the Auditor's Study and Evaluation of Internal Control, No. 3 (1974).

Other Publications

Examination of Financial Statements by Independent Public Accountants (1936).
Internal Control—Elements of a Coordinated System and its Importance to Management and the Independent Public Accountant (1949).
Report, Conclusions, and Recommendations of the Commission on Auditors' Responsibilities (1978).
Report of the Special Advisory Committee on Internal Accounting Control (1979).

Arthur Anderson & Co., *An Analysis of the Foreign Corrupt Practices Act of 1977* (Chicago: Arthur Anderson & Co., 1978).
Beresford, Dennis R., and Robert D. Neary, "SEC Charges Internal Control Violations," *Financial Executive* (July 1978).
Bodnar, G., "Reliability Modeling of Internal Control Systems," *The Accounting Review* (October 1975), pp. 747-757.
Bower, J., R. Schlosser, and C.T. Zlatkovich, *Financial Information Systems: Theory and Practice* (Boston: Allyn & Bacon, 1969).

Brown, Marilyn V., "Auditors and Internal Controls: An Analyst's View," *The CPA Journal*, 48, no. 9 (September 1977):27-31.

Carmichael, D.R., "Behavioral Hypotheses of Internal Control," *The Accounting Review* (April 1970), pp. 235-245.

Coopers & Lybrand, *Sharpening Controls: Corporate Approaches to Comply with the Foreign Corrupt Practices Act.* (U.S.A.: Coopers & Lybrand, 1978).

Cushing, Barry, "A Mathematical Approach to the Analysis and Design of Internal Control Systems," *The Accounting Review* (January 1974), pp. 24-41.

Deloitte Haskins & Sells, *Internal Accounting Control: Current Developments and Implications of the Foreign Corrupt Practices Act.* (U.S.A.: Deloitte Haskins & Sells, 1973).

Edelhertz, H., *The Nature, Impact, and Prosecution of White Collar Crime.* U.S. Department of Justice, L.E.A.A. (Washington, D.C.: U.S. Government Printing Office, 1970).

Enrick, Norbert, *Quality Control and Reliability*, 6th ed. (Industrial Press, 1972).

Federal Register 44, (May 4, 1979), 26705, 26707.

Gordon, Robert, "Optimum Component Redundancy for Maximum System Reliability," *Operations Research* (May 1957).

Mace, Myles L., "Strengthening the Functions of Internal Auditors," *Harvard Business Review*, 55 (July-August 1977):46-47.

Meister, David, "Methods of Predicting Human Reliability in Man-Machine Systems," *Human Factors* (December 1964), pp. 621-646.

——, and G. Rabideau, *Human Factors Evaluation in System Development* (New York: Wiley, 1965).

Parker, D., "Computer Abuse." Report prepared by Stanford Research Institute, Menlo Park, California (1973).

Price, Waterhouse & Co., *Monitoring Compliance With Control Systems Under the Foreign Corrupt Practices Act* (New York: Price Waterhouse & Co., 1978).

——, "Business Ethics," *Review.* (New York: Price Waterhouse and Co., 1977), 16.

SEC. v. Aminex Resources Corporation. CCH Fed. Sec. L., Rep. Sec. 96,352, D.D.C., March 9, 1978.

Title I of Public Law 95-213, 91 Stat. 1494, December 19, 1977.

Touche Ross & Co., *The New Management Imperative: Compliance With the Foreign Corrupt Practices Act* (U.S.A.: Touche Ross & Co., 1978).

Walker, Michael A. and Thomas Moser, "The Foreign Corrupt Practices Act of 1977: An Auditor's Perspective," *The CPA Journal*, 48 (May 1978):71-75.

Williams, Harold M., "Audit Committees: The Public Sector's View," *Journal of Accountancy*, 144 (September 1977):71-73.

REVENUE AND EXPENDITURE CYCLE APPLICATIONS

4

Revenue, expenditure, production, and finance activities are common to most business organizations. Chapters 4 and 5 provide an overview of common transaction processing applications in each of these major cycles of business activity. Chapter 4 discusses common revenue and expenditure cycle application systems. These systems include sales order processing, accounts receivable, purchasing, and payroll. Chapter 5 discusses common production and finance application systems. These applications include production and inventory control, property accounting, cash receipts, and cash disbursements.

Figure 4.1 provides an overview of the basic transaction flow in a manufacturing company. The application systems to be discussed are oriented toward manufacturing firms: however, with slight modifications these typical application systems are usable in all organizations. A retailing firm differs from a manufacturing firm only in that a retail firm purchases the goods it sells, whereas a manufacturing firm produces the goods it sells. Thus a typical retail firm does not have production application systems, but it does have revenue, expenditure, and finance applications. Service-oriented firms generally maintain fewer inventories than retail or manufacturing firms do, but service-oriented firms have sales, payroll, purchasing, and other applications. Nonprofit organizations, often service-oriented, differ slightly from profit-oriented firms.

INTERNAL CONTROL CONSIDERATIONS

Systems exist to perform specific functions. These functions (such as sales order entry or billing) can generally be accomplished in a variety of manners. Cost, efficiency, and reliability are the relevant considerations in any application system. Cost and reliability usually go hand in hand: the least costly system to operate is usually inadequate when one considers the reliability of the resultant outputs. As an organization grows in size, system reliability—that is, internal control—increases in importance.

Control is a fundamental consideration in any application system. This is the design philosophy of the procedures presented in Chapters 4 and 5. In 1948, an AICPA Committee on Auditing Procedure made a comprehensive study on internal control and published its results in 1949 as a special report entitled "Internal Control—Elements of a Coordinated System and Its Importance to Management and the Independent Public Accountant" (AICPA, 1949). This report attributed an expanding recognition of the significance of internal control to the following factors:

1. The size and scope of the business entity had increased to the point where its structural organization had become complex and geographically widespread.
2. The primary responsibility for safeguarding company assets and for preventing and detecting errors and fraud was management's.
3. A properly functioning system of internal control affords protection against human weaknesses such as fraud, theft, and inefficiency.
4. It had become impracticable for public accountants to make detailed audits of most companies within economic fee limitations.

These factors, of course, are more in force today than they were in the 1940s. Organizations are larger and process large volumes of transactional data with sophisticated data processing technology. Widely publicized cases of computer-related fraud and increasing concern with white-collar crime stimulated the passage of the Foreign Corrupt Practices Act of 1977. The accounting provisions of this act require companies registered with the Securities and Exchange Commission (SEC) to (1) make and keep books, records, and accounts that, in reasonable detail, accurately and fairly reflect the transactions of the registrant and the disposition of its assets and (2) devise and maintain a system of internal accounting controls sufficient to provide reasonable assurances that certain specified objectives are met.

The principle that the management of an organization is responsible for establishing and maintaining adequate internal controls has long appeared in the authoritative literature of independent public accountants. This principle has been embraced by the SEC:

> The establishment and maintenance of a system of internal controls is an important management obligation. A fundamental aspect of management's stewardship

FIGURE 4.1. Transaction Flow in a Manufacturing Firm

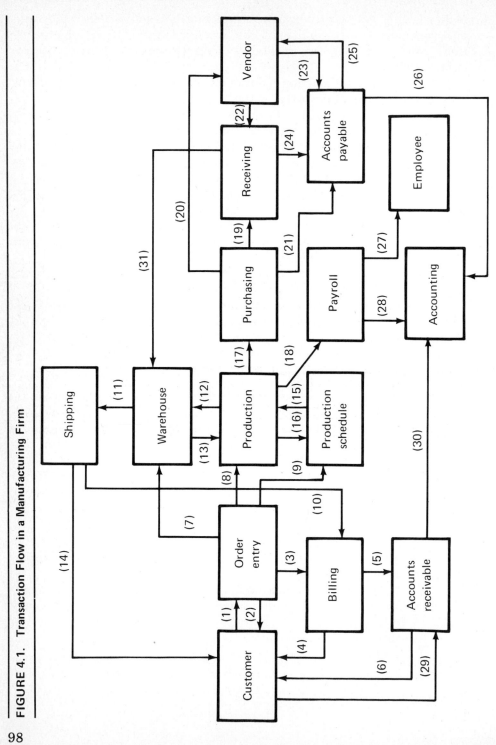

Key

1. Order
2. Acknowledgement
3. Billing memo
4. Invoice
5. Invoice advice
6. Statement
7. Shipping order
8. Production order
9. Production order (if required)
10. Shipping order
11. Goods for shipment
12. Finished goods
13. Production order (if required)
14. Goods to customer
15. Production schedule
16. Production status

17. Purchase requisitions
18. Labor report
19. Receiving advice
20. Purchase order
21. Purchase advice
22. Merchandise
23. Invoice
24. Receiving voucher
25. Payment
26. Payment record
27. Paycheck, etc.
28. Employee payment records
29. Remittance (customer)
30. Cash receipts
31. Purchased goods

responsibility is to provide shareholders with reasonable assurance that the business is adequately controlled. Additionally, management has a responsibility to furnish shareholders and potential investors with reliable financial information on a timely basis. An adequate system of internal accounting controls is necessary to management's discharge of these obligations. [Securities Release 34-13185 (January 19, 1977)]

Internal control is an important professional consideration in the design or review of an application system. It is important to realize that financial recordkeeping and the usefulness of the related reports to management and outside interests are not a separate consideration from the accounting application systems that process transactional data. Acceptable record keeping is rarely attainable without acceptable internal control.

The application systems discussed in this chapter and the next illustrate and emphasize the concept of organization independence (separation of functions) in the design of application systems. As a design criterion organizational independence requires that the custody of an asset be under a separate authority from record keeping functions related to that asset, and that both custody and record keeping functions be under separate authority from any operating functions that utilize the asset. The applications presented are not intended to serve as blueprints that may be duplicated without regard to the specific situation at hand. They do, however, serve a checklist function; they provide a frame of reference against which an analyst may contrast a proposed or existing system to make informed judgments of systems design.

Technological considerations (equipment and devices) are not specifically addressed in the following discussion of common application systems. Although technology may alter the operating configuration of an application system, the same ends should be accomplished regardless of technology. An internal control system includes people with varying authorities and capacities of supervision and with varying abilities to assume or delegate authority:

In a corporation, internal control commences with the . . . enforcement of top policies established by boards of directors and continues down through the organizational structure, taking form in the development and operation of management policies, administrative regulations, manuals, directives, and decisions; internal auditing; internal check; reporting; employee training and participation. [Kohler, 1975, p. 267]

Application systems must implement and maintain the pattern of authority and authorization necessary to give top management assurance that the organization's transactional activities are adequately controlled.

REVENUE CYCLE APPLICATIONS

An organization's revenue cycle includes the functions required to exchange its products or services with customers. Common functions in a revenue cycle include credit granting, order taking and processing, shipment of goods, billing, and accounts receivable. This section discusses two common revenue cycle application systems: sales order processing and accounts receivable. Cash receipts are discussed in Chapter 5 as a finance cycle application.

Sales Order Processing

The sales order system comprises the procedures involved in accepting and shipping customer orders, and the preparation of invoices which describe products, services, and assessments. Figure 4.2 illustrates the transaction flow in a typical sales order application system. The chart illustrates a partial billing (incomplete pre-billing) system in which customer orders are filled from an inventory of finished goods. The invoice (Figure 4.3) is the interface between the various functions necessary to process a customer order. As Figure 4.1 illustrates, a customer order may require a production order prior to a shipping order; this may be necessitated by a special nonstock order which requires a separate production run; it may be standard company practice due to a relatively short production cycle; or it may result from an out-of-stock or back order condition. In any of these circumstances, once the customer's order is ready for shipment, the flow of documents would parallel that presented in Figure 4.2. If the time between receiving a customer's order and the actual shipment of goods is significant, an acknowledgment copy of the invoice is generally appropriate to inform the customer that his order is received and in process.

The receipt of a customer order should normally require a verification of the customer's creditworthiness prior to the actual shipment of goods. For regular customers the credit check involves determining that the total amount of credit granted does not exceed management's general or specific authorization. For new customers a credit check is necessary to establish the terms of sale to the customer. As Figure 4.2 illustrates, the sales order-entry procedure should be subject to the control of an independent credit review function to maintain organizational independence.

Three major functions apparent in Figure 4.2 are the order, billing, and shipping functions. A distinction is usually maintained between billing and accounts receivable: billing relates to invoicing individual

FIGURE 4.2. Sales Order Application System

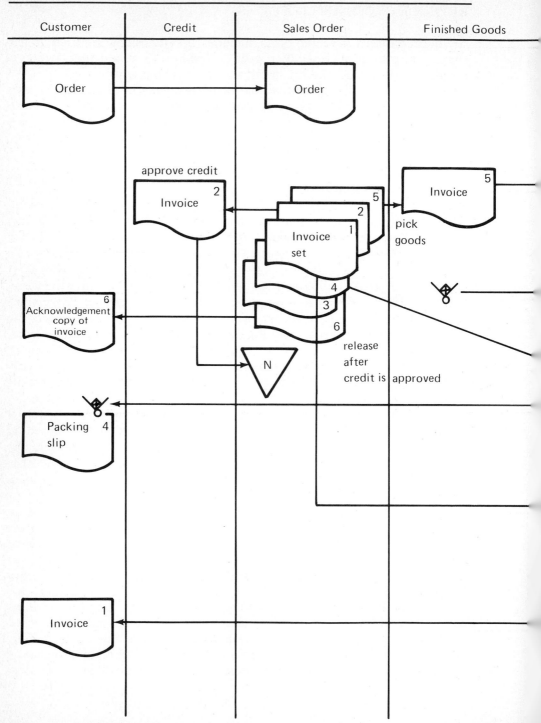

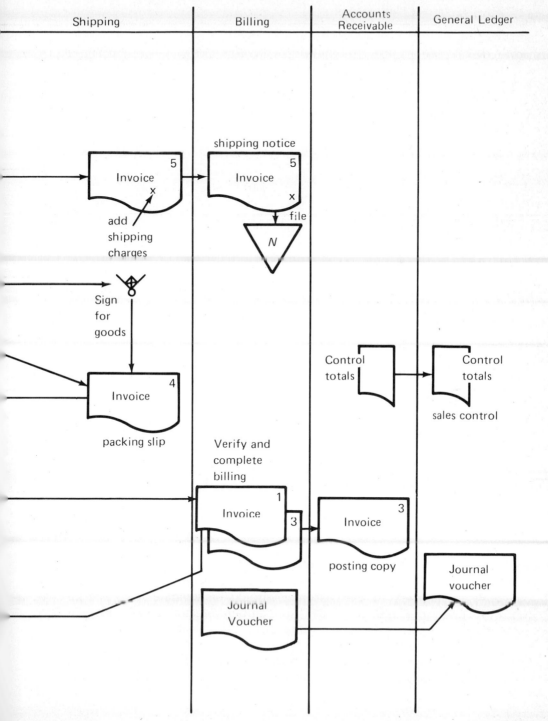

Shipping	Billing	Accounts Receivable	General Ledger

Shipping — Invoice 5 — add shipping charges — x

shipping notice — Invoice 5 — x — file — N

Sign for goods

Invoice 4 — packing slip

Verify and complete billing — Invoice 1 — 3

Invoice 3 — posting copy

Control totals — Control totals — sales control

Journal Voucher

Journal voucher

FIGURE 4.3.   Invoice Illustration

```
SOLD   CITRUS SUPPLY CO                                    INVOICE
TO:    1467 CLAY STREET
       PETERSBURG, WISCONSIN          Burroughs  Ⓑ
       44444


SHIP   CITRUS SUPPLY CO
TO:    1467 CLAY STREET
       PETERSBURG, WISCONSIN
       44444
```

TERMS	ORDER NO.	CUSTOMER NO.	SOLD BY	SHIP VIA	DATE	INVOICE NO.
2-10 NET 30	P87654	102,912	7	OUR TRUCK	NOV 15 76	12,347

CODE	QUANTITY	DESCRIPTION	PRICE	UNIT	GROSS	DISCOUNT	NET
13414522	10	CUTTING TIP TT-3	2.80	EA	28.00	.00	28.00
12415710	10	SCREWDRIVER 6″	1.90	EA	19.00	.38	18.62
15611410	5	WELDING GLOVE #10	1.50	PR	7.50	.15	7.35
12488806	10	DSK	1.00	EA	10.00	.00	10.00
							63.97
					TAX	5.0%	3.20
					HANDLING		25.00
							92.17

YOU MAY DEDUCT $ 1.84 IF THIS INVOICE IS PAID BY DEC 30 76

Courtesy Burroughs Corporation.

sales transactions, while the accounts receivable function maintains customer-accounts information in a subsidiary ledger and is also responsible for sending periodic statements to customers.

This maintains separation of functions: the invoicing operation (billing) does not have direct access to the books of record. Invoices should provide complete descriptions of the products, services, and charges. The descriptive data should include: customer sold-to and customer shipped-to address information, salesman identification, product description, quantities, unit prices, price extension amounts, terms of the sale, applicable discounts, sales taxes, special terms, and total amount due.

The shipping function, the operation responsible for the preparation of goods for delivery to the customer, should be separate from the inventory function (finished goods) to maintain organizational independence. This establishes accountability over the release of goods from inventory.

Several relationships between the order, billing, and shipping functions are feasible under different circumstances. The major consideration is the preparation of the invoice. In a *complete prebilling system*, the complete invoice is prepared at the same time as the shipping order. In this case the shipping order is usually a copy of the invoice. This system minimizes the necessary paperwork. The invoice is released after the shipment of goods. A complete prebilling system requires that all invoicing information must be known prior to the preparation of the invoice-shipping order set. This requires few back order or other inventory problems, and requires that freight and other charges either be absorbed by the seller or be standardized (for example, "add 50¢ for postage"). Any change between the customer order as prewritten and as actually shipped requires the generation of a new invoice and the destruction of the original invoice. If such situations are common, complete prebilling will be very inefficient.

As indicated previously, Figure 4.2 illustrates an *incomplete prebilling system.* The invoice is not completed until the goods are ready for shipment. Freight charges, extensions of actual goods to be shipped, back orders and the like are prepared by billing after goods are prepared for shipment. This system is probably the most common in practice. At the other extreme from complete prebilling is a *separate order and billing* system. The shipping order in this case is prepared in a separate writing from the preparation of the invoice. The invoice is separately prepared after goods are ready for shipment. Separate order and billing are necessitated when there is a significant difference between the information on the shipping order (internal to the seller) and the invoice. For example, technical specifications in the shipping order may not be required or desired on the invoice. Excessive back order and out-of-stock conditions would warrant this approach, since the final content of the invoice cannot be determined until the goods are ready for shipment. In many industries (retailing, for example), alterations or substitution of goods ordered are allowed by customary trade practices (different styles or colors in an order for clothing) or several shipments are made under a single "blanket" order covering several shipments of goods over a specific time period. In the former case (substitution), the changed specifications from the customer's order must be shown on the invoice; in the latter case (blanket order), a one-to-one correspondence between customer order and invoice does not exist. Typically, one blanket order would require several separate invoices, one for each shipment made under the blanket order.

Accounts Receivable

Accounts receivable represent the money owed by customers for merchandise sold or services rendered. Since approximately 90 percent of

FIGURE 4.4. **Accounts Receivable Application System**

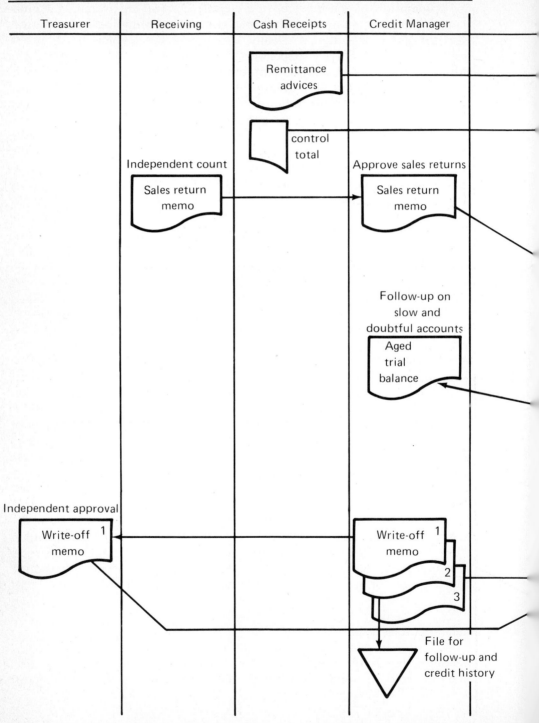

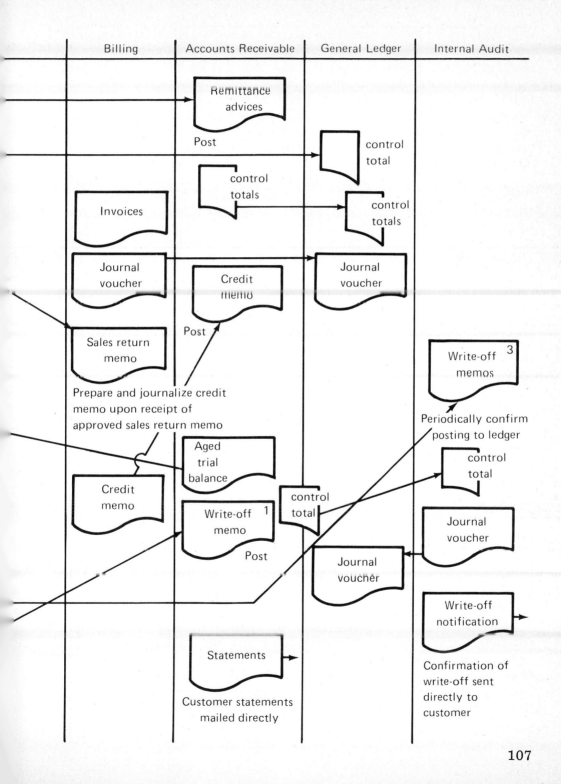

| Billing | Accounts Receivable | General Ledger | Internal Audit |

Remittance advices

Post

control total

control totals

Invoices

control totals

Journal voucher

Credit memo

Journal voucher

Sales return memo

Post

Write-off memos 3

Prepare and journalize credit memo upon receipt of approved sales return memo

Periodically confirm posting to ledger

Aged trial balance

control total

Credit memo

Write-off memo 1

control total

Post

Journal voucher

Journal voucher

Write-off notification

Statements

Customer statements mailed directly

Confirmation of write-off sent directly to customer

U.S. business is done on credit, the accounts receivable application system often represents an accounting for the majority of an organization's working capital. Accounts receivable also provides the facility for maintaining customer credit and payment history information, which is useful in the overall administration of company credit policies.

Figure 4.4 illustrates an accounts receivable application system. Included in Figure 4.4 are provisions for sales returns and allowances and provisions for writing off bad accounts (bad debts). Each of these procedures is discussed in turn.

Conceptually, the accounts receivable procedure is straightforward. Generally a subsidiary ledger of individual accounts will be maintained, with a control account in the general ledger. Remittance advices are routed from the cash receipts function; credit memos and other invoice adjustments are routed to the accounts receivable department from the billing department. Debits and credits are posted to the individual accounts; periodically, statements are prepared and sent to customers. Aging schedules are generally prepared as a by-product of sending statements. Special credit reports may also be prepared.

There are two basic approaches to performing an accounts receivable application: open-item and balance-forward processing. In open-item processing, a separate record is maintained in the accounts receivable system for each of the customer's unpaid invoices. As customer remittances are received, they are matched to the unpaid invoices. In balance-forward processing, the customer's remittances are applied against a customer's total outstanding invoice balance rather than against individual invoices.

Data processing of accounts receivable can be tedious, because of the volume of transactions and number of accounts that may exist. A large insurance company or bank may have close to a million separate accounts. Even with computer processing, mailing all statements at month's end may be impossible. Many businesses use a *cycle billing plan*, in which the accounts receivable file is subdivided by alphabet or account number. The idea is to distribute the preparation of statements over the working days of the month; for example, accounts A to H may be billed on the tenth, H to P on the twentieth, etcetera. These plans often have a beneficial effect on a company's cash flow, as consumers generally pay bills shortly after they are received.

Ledgerless bookkeeping (discussed in Chapter 6) may be used to streamline accounts receivable procedures in certain situations. A procedural question of import is whether copies of sales slips are to be included with the monthly statement. This practice is increasingly uncommon. Usually individual transactions are itemized on the statement, with supporting documents referenced by either code or invoice number. A company is obligated to produce supporting documents at the customer's request; this demands careful attention to the details of filing source documents. Owing to the above procedural aspects, some companies sell their accounts receivable at a discount to collection agencies. This process, called factoring, avoids record keeping costs. This alternative should be considered by the analyst, but one must also carefully consider the potential negative effects of factoring on customer relations.

Sales returns and allowances typically require careful control. Allowances occur when, because of damaged merchandise, shortages, clerical errors, or the like, the customer and the seller agree to reduce the amount owed by the customer. Generally the merchandise is retained or destroyed by the customer. The amount of an allowance is generally negotiated between the customer and the sales order department (or salesman). The allowance should be reviewed and approved by an independent party (usually the credit department); when authorized, billing would issue a form (credit memorandum) to document the reduction to the customer's account. As Figure 4.4 illustrates, sales return procedures (that is, for goods actually returned, usually for full credit) are typically initiated by the receiving department. Once goods are received and returned to inventory for proper control (this would be evidenced by documentation), the credit manager authorizes billing to issue a credit memorandum.

Note that for both returns and allowances, two independent persons are required to approve the transaction, while a third party maintains the records. This is another example of organizational independence. This same principle holds in the write-off of accounts receivable procedure. The central feature in a write-off procedure is an analysis of past due accounts. Typically this is done with an aged trial balance. Numerous techniques are available to collect past due accounts (for example, follow-up letters, collection agencies), but some accounts are ultimately worthless. In this case (as Figure 4.4 shows) the credit manager initiates a write-off, which is approved by another person (treasurer). On approval, accounts receivable is authorized to write off the account; a copy of the authorization is also sent to a third party for purposes of record keeping (auditor). This is necessary because after the write-off, accounts receivable no longer has an active record of the account. Figure 4.4 details the role of the independent third party (the auditor). Note that the auditor confirms write-offs directly with the customer to insure that no collections have been made on written-off accounts. An employee might intercept a customer's payment on account and then arrange for the account to be written off so that the customer does not continue to be billed for the amount.

EXPENDITURE CYCLE APPLICATIONS

An organization's expenditure cycle includes the functions required to acquire goods and services that are utilized by the organization in conducting its operations. The expenditure cycle includes the acquisition of goods for resale or use in production, the acquisition of personnel services, and the acquisition of property and equipment. Common functions include vendor selection, requisitioning, purchasing, receiving, accounts payable, and payroll accounting.

This section discusses two important expenditure cycle applications: purchasing and payroll. Cash disbursements and account payable are discussed in Chapter 5.

Purchasing

In some companies, substantially all purchases of goods and services are channeled through and controlled by a centralized purchasing department. In others, the authority to place orders with vendors is dispersed throughout the company, a decentralized approach. A centralized purchasing function may yield increased quantity discounts, a stronger market position, better inventory control, buyer specialization, and the like. A decentralized purchase function may yield similar benefits because of the increased responsibilities placed on the ultimate user. For example, decentralized buyers may have greater knowledge of the use and specifications of the desired goods, and thereby maintain "optimal" inventory levels. This may be reinforced by shorter lead times between order and receipt of goods, resultant from decentralized (that is, local) buying. As in any organizational decision, the choice is largely one of management style and philosophy.

There are two major aspects of the purchasing function. The first aspect is deciding what to buy, from whom, and for how much. The second aspect concerns the mechanics of ordering, receiving, and approving payment to vendors.

A purchase application system includes several basic functions:

1. Someone outside the purchasing department determines that materials are needed; a requisition is prepared and approved.
2. Bids are requested, a vendor selected, and a purchase order issued by the purchasing department.
3. When the materials are received, a receiving report is prepared by the receiving department. In many cases only a person with technical ability can adequately inspect the materials and give assurance

to the requisitioning or using department. In unusual cases, it may be desirable to have the quality of materials received tested before payment is made. An inspection function may be established for this purpose, either as a part of the receiving department or as a separate department.

4. Details of the invoice submitted by the vendor are compared to the purchase order and to the receiving report. The invoice is checked for mathematical accuracy. If everything is in order, the invoice is approved for payment.

5. A check is prepared and sent to the vendor and all the above documents are canceled to avoid the possibility of duplicate payments for goods purchased.

Figure 4.5 illustrates the flow of transactions in a purchase application system. Note the separation of functions. The receiving operation is separate from stores (inventory): acknowledgment of both functions is required before payment may be authorized. As Figure 4.5 indicates, this is usually accomplished by routing a receiving report through stores; stores indicate that material has been received by approving or stamping the receiving report, and then forwards the report to payables. The purchasing office does not control the actual goods nor does it have complete control over the documentation required for payment. Payables handles only documents, and is not able to obtain merchandise or cash independently. Requests for purchases (requisitions) originate either in the user departments or the stores function; however, it is usually the function of the purchasing office to select a vendor, and to arrange deliveries and terms. How this is done depends, of course, on the relative degree of centralization of the purchasing function. At times requisitions will be altered or overridden by the purchasing department.

Four forms—requisition, purchase order, invoice, and receiving report—are typically used to document a purchasing transaction. A major control over purchasing is obtained through a voucher system (see Figure 4.5). A voucher system is essentially a review technique to insure that all documentation is assembled, verified, and reviewed prior to actual payment. This is called the matching process. This review of documentation assumes that documentation evidences the execution of procedural steps. Voucher systems are discussed further in the cash disbursements application contained in Chapter 5.

The above documentation simply insures that individual orders are received as expected. Purchase orders, receiving reports and the like control individual purchases, but *not* the purchasing application itself. Control of the purchasing application (as opposed to individual purchases) centers largely on the integrity of the buyer-vendor relationship. Bribery, kick-

FIGURE 4.5. Purchase Application System

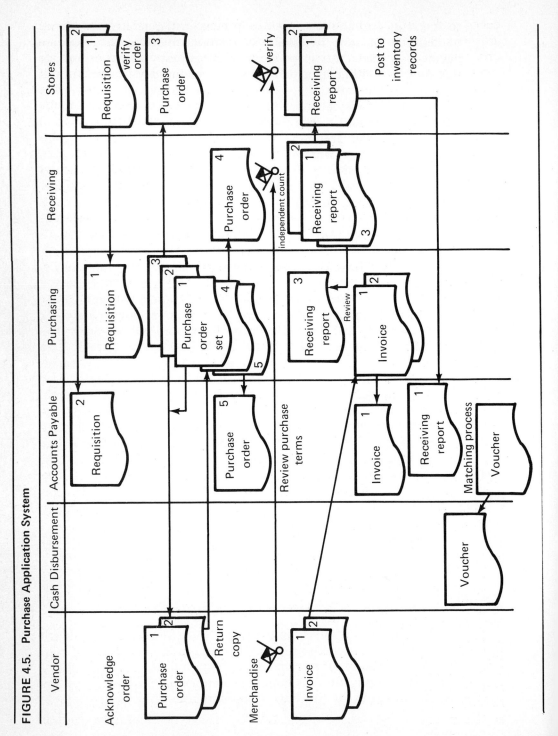

112

backs, and conflicts of interest (such as buying from a relative or friend) are examples of improper buyer-vendor relationships that the purchase order application system must address. Buyer-vendor relationships are more a matter of policy than procedure. Most companies have found it desirable and often necessary to have formal written policy and procedure manuals covering the purchasing function. Purchasing policies may require competitive bidding, usually implemented through a request-for-quotation form.

Buyers must request competitive bids through request-for-quotation forms. Copies of these forms are filed and reviewed by purchasing management. Lowest-cost bid is not always an acceptable basis for selecting a vendor. Methods of evaluating and selecting bids on the basis of several vendor attributes (vendor rating plans) may be formalized, with decisions subject to review by a higher authority. A policy of rotating buyer's responsibilities weakens buyer-vendor relationships, but reduces possibilities for buyer specialization. Approved vendor lists, prepared by an independent function, may be used to restrict a buyer's option to those vendors who have been found to be reliable, financially sound, and free of conflicts of interest. These examples are not exhaustive, but they indicate the types of controls that may be used to insure the integrity of purchasing personnel.

Payroll

A payroll/personnel system involves all phases of payroll processing and personnel reporting. The system provides a means of promptly and accurately paying employees, generating the necessary payroll reports, and supplying management with the required employee skills information. The processing should include a deduction for withholding taxes, specialized deductions, government reporting and internal personnel requirements. An efficient system is necessary in establishing and maintaining good employer-employee relationships.

The subject of payroll processing is extremely complex. In a large organization, payroll processing is often the most complex procedure in operation. This is because of the social significance payrolls have assumed over the last few decades. All levels of government impose payroll taxes of one sort or another; regulations and rates are constantly changed, with the result that a payroll system usually has a relatively short life cycle. The strategy here is to provide an overview of a typical payroll procedure and to provide a discussion of factors influencing the actual calculation of payroll. No attempt is made to provide current rates: tax laws are arbitrary and subject to change, and do change quite rapidly. Payroll processing is one area in which the law imposes not only a fine but a jail sentence for willful negligence in maintaining adequate records. As with any law, ignorance is no excuse. The onus is on the systems analyst to keep current in this area.

Figure 4.6 illustrates the flow of transactions in a payroll application for a manufacturing firm. The main feature is a separation of functions. The employment (personnel) office is responsible for placing persons on the payroll, specifying the basic pay rate, and authorizing all deductions. All changes such as adding or deleting employees, or changing pay rates or deduction levels, must be authorized by the employment office. This function is distinct from payroll processing and also from the timekeeping function. In a manufacturing firm, an hourly employee typically clocks on and off a job. The timekeeping function reconciles employee time cards or reports, and forwards this report to payroll. Note in Figure 4.6 that this time report is typically reconciled to the cost of production (job time tickets). Salaried employees typically are not required to account for their time in the same way that hourly workers do. If no accounting is required, a supervisor's approval often is required to initiate payroll processing. If time reports are required, the analogy to Figure 4.6 is straightforward.

Numerous files must be maintained in a payroll system. Basic employee information, such as name, address, rate of pay, and deductions, is necessary to prepare a payroll. A payroll register or journal must be maintained to document actual payments. Files pertaining to government reports, tax tables used in processing, pension plans, hospitalization and similar plans are examples of information required to support a payroll procedure.

The ability of an organization to maintain and utilize payroll information is dependent on the technology of payroll processing. Manual systems typically utilize some form of one-writing technique. In a typical one-write system (discussed in Chapter 6) the payroll journal is put on a board with a carbon over it. On top of this goes the employee's earnings records, and on top of that goes the stub of the paycheck. All of the columns of the three documents correspond to each other. The person who prepares the payroll actually writes on the employee's check stub, the employee's record of the payroll that he receives with the paycheck. At the same time, what is written on the stub is transferred to the employee master pay record and the payroll journal by the carbon paper. After the pay of each employee has been calculated and processed, all that remains to be done is the footings and extensions on the journal. Systems of this type usually furnish the minimum amount of information required by law. More complete processing of personnel data (as opposed to payroll data) is generally feasible only in a computer environment. Numerous vendors offer economic payroll processing on a contract basis. Payroll, due to its

FIGURE 4.6. Payroll Application System

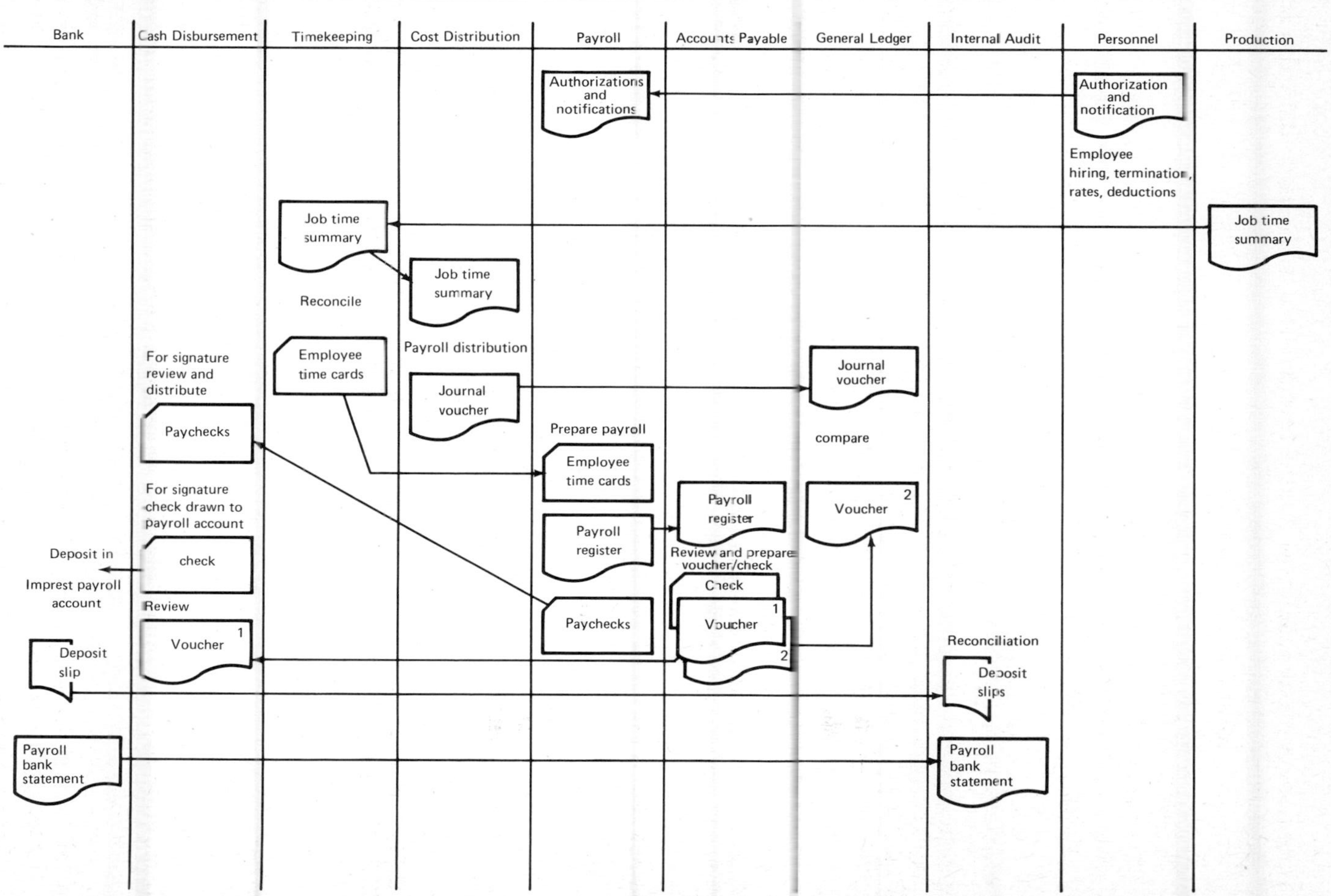

complexity, is typically the first procedure that a company delegates to some form of automated processing.

Payroll Processing Requirements

Social Security and income tax legislation impose four taxes based on payrolls. These taxes are:

1. federal old-age, survivors', disability, and hospital insurance (F.I.C.A.);
2. federal unemployment insurance;
3. state unemployment insurance; and
4. income taxes withheld.

The Federal Insurance Contributions Act (F.I.C.A.) provides that employees contribute equally to funds for old age, survivors', disability, and hospital insurance benefits for certain individuals and members of their families. The contribution is based on a tax rate applied to gross wages. The tax rate has increased gradually over the years and will continue to increase in the future.

The employer is required to deduct the amount of F.I.C.A. tax from each employee's pay each pay period. The employer is then required to match these deductions and deposit the entire amount in a government depository. A 5 percent penalty is levied for failure, without reasonable cause, to make required deposits when due. Taxpayers who willfully claim credit on the record of federal tax deposits for deposits not made are subject to fine and/or other criminal penalties. The employer is responsible for the full amount of the tax even when he fails to withhold from employees amounts representing their contributions.

The Federal Social Security Act and the Federal Unemployment Tax Act (FUTA) provide for the establishment of unemployment insurance plans. Employers with covered workers employed in each of twenty weeks during a calendar year are affected. Payment to the federal government is required quarterly. Unemployment benefits are provided by the systems created by the individual states. Revenues of the federal government under the acts are used to meet the cost of administering state and federal unemployment plans as well as to provide supplemental unemployment benefits.

State unemployment compensation laws are not the same in all states, but all states participate in the federal-state unemployment insurance program. In most states, laws provide for taxes only on employers. The federal legislation applies to all employers of one or more employees.

Tax payment is generally required on or before the last day of the month following each calendar quarter. Most states have a merit-rating plan that permits a reduction in the tax rate for employers who establish a record of stable employment.

Federal income taxes on wages of an individual are collected in the period in which the wages are paid. Our "pay-as-you-go" system of federal income tax requires employers to withhold a portion of the earnings of their employees. The amount withheld depends on the amount of the earnings and upon the number of exemptions allowed the employee. The employee is entitled to one exemption for himself and an additional exemption for each person qualifying as a dependent. Persons over sixty-five or blind are entitled to additional exemptions. A withholding exemption certificate must be prepared by each employee. The certificate states the number of exemptions to which the employee is entitled. This certificate is given to the employer so that he will be able to compute the proper amount of tax to be withheld.

Present regulations provide a graduated system of withholding, designed to make the amount of tax withheld closely approximate the rates used in computing the individual's tax liability at the end of the year.

Employers engaged in interstate commerce are required by the Federal Fair Labor Standards Act (also known as the Wages and Hours Law) to pay overtime at a minimum rate of one and one-half times the regular rate for hours worked in excess of forty per week. Many companies also pay overtime premium rates for night shifts and for work on Sundays and holidays.

Employers must take care to deduct payroll taxes from all employees. A distinction is drawn between employees and independent contractors. Public accountants, architects, attorneys, and other persons who render services to a business for a fee but are not controlled or directed by the client are not employees but independent contractors, and the amounts paid to them are not subject to payroll taxes.

At the close of each quarter an employer is required to file a quarterly return on Form 941 or 941E and pay the balance of undeposited taxes. If the taxes were deposited in full, ten additional days are allowed. This return covers income tax withheld and F.I.C.A. tax for all employees.

On or before January 31 each employer is required to give each employee a completed Form W-2, Wage and Tax Statement. The employer is required to forward a copy of these W-2 forms with a Form W-3 on or before February 28.

Also on or before January 31 employers must file Form 940, Employer's Annual Federal Unemployment Tax Return.

The basic information about what the U.S. government requires with respect to payroll is outlined in the Department of Treasury Internal

FIGURE 4.7.   Sample Payroll Events Timetable

Date	Event
January 31	Form W-2 (Wage and Tax Statement) to be furnished to employees.
January 31	Form 941 (Employer's Quarterly Federal Tax Return) due for 4th quarter of preceding calendar year.
January 31	Form 1099-Misc. (U.S. Information Return for Recipients of Miscellaneous Income) to be furnished to consultants paid directly.
February 28	Form W-3 (Transmittal of Wage and Tax Statements) due with Copy A of each Form W-2; Form 1096 (Transmittal) with each 1099-Misc.
February 28	Duplicate of Form 1096 due with State Copy of Form 1099-Misc.
March 15	File Form 1120 or 1120-S (Federal Corporate Income Tax Return for calendar year.)
April 30	Form 941 due for 1st quarter.
July 31	Form 941 due for 2nd quarter.
October 31	Form 941 due for 3rd quarter.

Revenue Service publication *Circular E Employers Tax Guide.* This publication contains all the latest information on new laws, and detailed information for employers. It tells how to fill out all the forms and reports required, how to compute employment taxes, how and when to make deposits and payments, and the invaluable tax tables are listed. If an employer does not have this publication or access to the information contained in it, it is almost certain that he will sooner or later make an error in his payroll procedure that will cost him a penalty.

Figure 4.7 contains a schedule of payroll-related deadlines that illustrates some of the processing and information that a typical payroll system must provide.

REVIEW QUESTIONS

1. What are several factors that make internal control an important consideration in the design of business procedures?

2. In what circumstances might a customer order require the use of a production order prior to a shipping order?

3. Distinguish between the "billing" and "accounts receivable" functions in a sales order procedure.

4. Briefly describe and contrast the following types of sales order procedures:
   a. Separate order and billing
   b. Incomplete prebilling
   c. Complete prebilling.

5. What accounting journal entry or entries summarize the activities of a sales order procedure?

6. What is "cycle" billing? State two advantages that may be obtained through the use of cycle billing.

7. When is the use of an "acknowledgment copy" of a sales order desirable?

8. Outline the major features of internal control in a sales return and allowance procedure.

9. What functions are served by periodic statements of account?

10. Identify the two major aspects of a purchasing application system.

11. What accounting entry, if any, is necessitated by the issuance of a purchase order?

12. Define and indicate the purpose of the following forms:
   a. requisition
   b. purchase order
   c. invoice
   d. receiving report.

13. What is the "matching process"?

14. Identify several controls that are directed at insuring the integrity of the procurement function.

15. How might budgetary control be exercised over the purchasing function? Give specific examples.

16. What factors or qualifications might be considered in the implementation of an approved vendors list?

17. What are the objectives of a payroll system?

18. What is the basic source of information concerning federal requirements with respect to payroll processing?

19. Identify the major controls in a payroll procedure.

20. Identify each of the following forms:
    a. Form 941
    b. Form W-2
    c. Form W-3
    d. Form 1099-Misc.
    e. Earnings statement

DISCUSSION QUESTIONS AND PROBLEMS

21. Discuss the objectives of the following control procedures:
    a. purchasing policy manual
    b. approved vendors' list
    c. request-for-quotations form
    d. vendor rating plans
    e. rotation of buyers

22. Identify the objective of distributing copies of a purchase order to the following functions:
    a. requisitioning department
    b. receiving department
    c. accounting department

23. What differences exist in approving vendor invoices covering services rendered rather than physical goods sent to an organization? Illustrate with several examples.

24.* You have completed an audit of activities within the purchasing department of your company. The department employs 30 buyers, 7 supervisors, a manager, and clerical personnel. Purchases total about $500 million a year. Your audit disclosed the following conditions:
    1. The company has no formal rules on conflicts of interest. Your analysis produced evidence that one of the 30 buyers in the department owns a substantial interest in a major supplier and that she procures supplies averaging $50,000 a year from that supplier. The prices charged by the supplier are competitive.
    2. Buyers select proposed sources without submitting the lists of bidders for review. Your tests disclosed no evidence that higher costs were incurred as a result of that practice.
    3. Buyers who originate written requests for quotations from suppliers receive the suppliers' bids directly from the mail room. In your test of 100 purchases based on competitive bids, you found

*Reprinted by permission of The Institute of Internal Auditors, Inc., from the Certified Internal Auditor Examination (May, 1977).

that, in 75 of the 100 cases, the low bidders were awarded the purchase orders.

4. Requests to purchase (requisitions) received in the purchasing department from other departments in the company must be signed by persons authorized to do so. Your examination of 200 such requests disclosed that three, all for small amounts, were not properly signed. The buyer who had issued all three orders honored the requests because he misunderstood the applicable procedure. The clerical personnel charged with reviewing such requests had given them to the buyer in error.

Required:

For each of the *four* conditions, state:

a. The risk, if any, which is incurred if each condition described above is permitted to continue.

b. The control, if any, you would recommend to prevent continuation of the condition described.

25.* The customer billing and collection functions of the Robinson Company, a small paint manufacturer, are attended to by a receptionist, an accounts receivable clerk, and a cashier who also serves as a secretary. The company's paint products are sold to wholesalers and retail stores.

The following describes *all* of the procedures performed by the employees of the Robinson Company pertaining to customer billings and collections:

a. The mail is opened by the receptionist, who gives the customers' purchase orders to the accounts receivable clerk. Fifteen to twenty orders are received each day. Under instructions to expedite the shipment of orders, the accounts receivable clerk at once prepares a five-copy sales invoice form, which is distributed as follows:

1. Copy #1 is the customer billing copy and is held by the accounts receivable clerk until notice of shipment is received.

2. Copy #2 is the accounts receivable department copy and is held for ultimate posting of the accounts receivable records.

3. Copies #3 and #4 are sent to the shipping department.

4. Copy #5 is sent to the storeroom as authority for release of the goods to the shipping department.

b. After the paint order has been moved from the storeroom to the shipping department, the shipping department prepares the bills of lading and labels the cartons. Sales invoice copy #4 is inserted in a carton as a packing slip. After the trucker has picked up the

*Material from the Uniform CPA Examinations and Unofficial Answers, copyright © 1965 by the American Institute of Certified Public Accountants, Inc., is reprinted (or adapted) with permission.

shipment, the customer's copy of the bill of lading and copy #3, on which are noted any undershipments, are returned to the accounts receivable clerk. The company does not "back order" in the event of undershipments; customers are expected to reorder the merchandise. The Robinson Company's copy of the bill of lading is filed by the shipping department.

c.   When copy #3 and the customer's copy of the bill of lading are received by the accounts receivable clerk, copies #1 and #2 are completed by numbering them and inserting quantities shipped, unit prices, extensions, discounts, and totals. The accounts receivable clerk then mails copy #1 and the copy of the bill of lading to the customer. Copies #2 and #3 are stapled together.

d.   The individual accounts receivable ledger cards are posted by the accounts receivable clerk by a bookkeeping machine procedure whereby the sales register is prepared as a carbon copy of the postings. Postings are made from copy #2, which is then filed, along with staple-attached copy #3, in numerical order. Monthly the general ledger clerk summarizes the sales register for posting to the general ledger accounts.

e.   Since the Robinson Company is short of cash, the deposit of receipts is also expedited. The receptionist turns over all mail receipts and related correspondence to the accounts receivable clerk, who examines the checks and determines that the accompanying vouchers or correspondence contain enough detail to permit posting of the accounts. The accounts receivable clerk then endorses the checks and gives them to the cashier, who prepares the daily deposit. No currency is received in the mail, and no paint is sold over the counter at the factory.

f.   The accounts receivable clerk uses the vouchers or correspondence that accompanied the checks to post the accounts receivable ledger cards. The bookkeeping machine prepares a cash receipts register as a carbon copy of the postings. Monthly the general ledger clerk summarizes the cash receipts register for posting to the general ledger accounts. The accounts receivable clerk also corresponds with customers about unauthorized deductions for discounts, freight or advertising allowances, returns, etcetera, and prepares the appropriate credit memos. Disputed items of large amount are turned over to the sales manager for settlement. Each month the accounts receivable clerk prepares a trial balance of the open accounts receivable and compares the resultant total with the general ledger control account for accounts receivable.

Required:

Discuss the internal control weaknesses in the Robinson Company's procedures related to customer billings and remittances and the accounting for these transactions. In your discussion, in addition to identifying the weaknesses, explain what could happen as a result of each weakness.

26.* You have been engaged by the management of Alden, Inc., to review its internal control over the purchase, receipt, storage, and issue of raw materials. You have prepared the following comments that describe Alden's procedures.

Raw materials, which consist mainly of high-cost electronic components, are kept in a locked storeroom. Storeroom personnel include a supervisor and four clerks. All are well trained, competent, and adequately bonded. Raw materials are removed from the storeroom only upon written or oral authorization of one of the production foremen.

There are no perpetual inventory records; hence, the storeroom clerks do not keep records of goods received or issued. To compensate for the lack of perpetual records, a physical inventory count is taken monthly by the storeroom clerks, who are well supervised. Appropriate procedures are followed in making the inventory count.

After the physical count, the storeroom supervisor matches quantities counted against a predetermined reorder level. If the count for a given part is below the reorder level, the supervisor enters the part number on a materials requisition list and sends this list to the accounts payable clerk. The accounts payable clerk prepares a purchase order for a predetermined reorder quantity for each part and mails the purchase order to the vendor from whom the part was last purchased.

When ordered materials arrive at Alden, they are received by the storeroom clerks. The clerks count the merchandise and agree the counts to the shipper's bill of lading. All vendors' bills of lading are initialed, dated, and filed in the storeroom to serve as receiving reports.

Describe the weaknesses in internal control and recommend improvements of Alden's procedures for the purchase, receipt, storage, and issue of raw materials.

27.† Antonia, CPA, prepared the following flowchart, which portrays the raw materials purchasing function of one of Antonia's clients, a medium-sized manufacturing company, from the preparation of initial documents through vouching for invoices for payment in accounts pay-

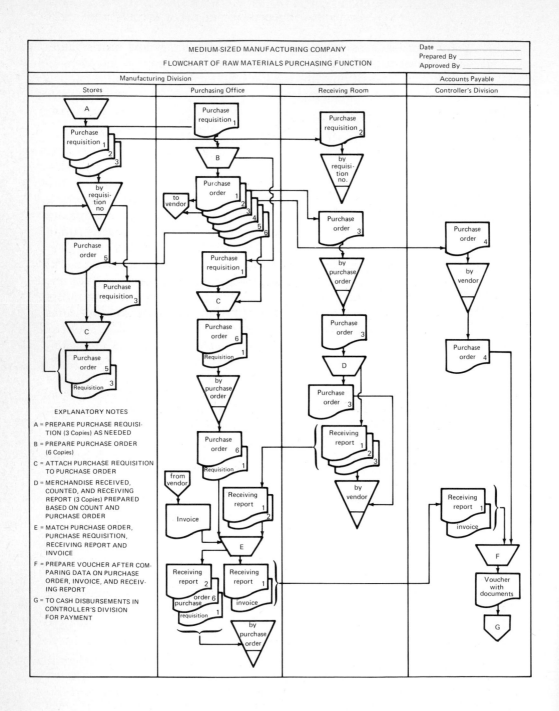

MEDIUM-SIZED MANUFACTURING COMPANY

FLOWCHART OF RAW MATERIALS PURCHASING FUNCTION

Date _____
Prepared By _____
Approved By _____

EXPLANATORY NOTES

A = PREPARE PURCHASE REQUISI-
TION (3 COPIES) AS NEEDED

B = PREPARE PURCHASE ORDER
(6 COPIES)

C = ATTACH PURCHASE REQUISITION
TO PURCHASE ORDER

D = MERCHANDISE RECEIVED,
COUNTED, AND RECEIVING
REPORT (3 COPIES) PREPARED
BASED ON COUNT AND
PURCHASE ORDER

E = MATCH PURCHASE ORDER,
PURCHASE REQUISITION,
RECEIVING REPORT AND
INVOICE

F = PREPARE VOUCHER AFTER COM-
PARING DATA ON PURCHASE
ORDER, INVOICE, AND RECEIV-
ING REPORT

G = TO CASH DISBURSEMENTS IN
CONTROLLER'S DIVISION
FOR PAYMENT

able. The flowchart was a portion of the work performed on the audit engagement to evaluate internal control.

Required:

Identify and explain the systems and control weaknesses evident from the flowchart. Include the internal control weaknesses resulting from activities performed or not performed. All documents are prenumbered.

28.* After a shipment is prepared, the shipping department prepares a shipping order form in three copies. The first copy is included with the goods sent to the customer as a packing slip. The second copy is forwarded to the billing department. The third copy is sent to the accountant. When the billing department receives the second copy of the shipping order, it uses the information thereon to prepare a two-part sales invoice. The second copy of the shipping order is then filed in the billing department. The first copy of the sales invoice is sent to the customer. The second copy of the sales invoice is forwarded to the accountant. Periodically, the accountant matches the copy of the shipping order with the copy of the sales invoice and files them alphabetically by customer name. Before doing so, however, the accountant uses the copy of the sales invoice to post the sales entry in the subsidiary accounts receivable ledger.

Required:

    a. For use in appraising internal control, prepare a flowchart covering the flow of documents reflected in the above situation.

    b. List those deficiencies and/or omissions revealed by the flowchart which would lead you to question the internal control.

29.† The Kowal Manufacturing Company employs about 50 production workers and has the following payroll procedures.

The factory foreman interviews applicants and on the basis of the interview either hires or rejects the applicants. When the applicant is hired he prepares a W-4 form (Employee's Withholding Exemption Certificate) and gives it to the foreman. The foreman writes the hourly rate of pay for the new employee in the corner of the W-4 form and then gives the form to a payroll clerk as notice that the worker has been employed. The foreman verbally advises the payroll department of rate adjustments.

A supply of blank time cards is kept in a box near the entrance to the factory. Each worker takes a time card on Monday morning, fills in his

---

*Reprinted by permission of The Institute of Internal Auditors, Inc., from the Certified Internal Auditor Examination (August, 1974).

†Material from the Uniform CPA Examinations and Unofficial Answers, copyright © 1964 by the American Institute of Certified Public Accountants, Inc., is reprinted (or adapted) with permission.

name, and notes in pencil on the time card his daily arrival and departure times. At the end of the week the workers drop the time cards in a box near the door to the factory.

The completed time cards are taken from the box on Monday morning by a payroll clerk. Two payroll clerks divide the cards alphabetically between them, one taking the A to L section of the payroll and the other taking the M to Z section. Each clerk is fully responsible for his section of the payroll. He computes the gross pay, deductions and net pay, posts the details to the employee's earnings records, and prepares and numbers the payroll checks. Employees are automatically removed from the payroll when they fail to turn in a time card.

The payroll checks are manually signed by the chief accountant and given to the foreman. The foreman distributes the checks to the workers in the factory and arranges for the delivery of the checks to the workers who are absent. The payroll bank account is reconciled by the chief accountant, who also prepares the various quarterly and annual payroll tax reports.

List your suggestions for improving the Kowal Manufacturing Company's system of internal control for the factory hiring practices *and* payroll procedures.

REFERENCES

American Institute of Certified Public Accountants, "Internal Control—Elements of a Coordinated System and Its Importance to Management and the Independent Public Accountant." (New York: American Institute of Certified Public Accountants, 1949).

Bower, J., R. Schlosser, and C.T. Zlatkovich, *Financial Information Systems: Theory and Practice* (Boston: Allyn and Bacon, 1969).

Kohler, E. *A Dictionary for Accountants*, 5th ed. (Englewood Cliffs: Prentice-Hall, 1975).

Securities and Exchange Commission. *Securities Exchange Act Release 34–13185* (January 19, 1977).

PRODUCTION AND FINANCE CYCLE APPLICATIONS

5

This chapter discusses accounting application systems commonly found in an organization's production and finance cycles. As in Chapter 4, the central feature of the illustrated applications is a segregation of duties to achieve organizational independence.

PRODUCTION CYCLE APPLICATIONS

Production control, inventory control, cost accounting systems, and property accounting are typical functions in the production cycle of manufacturing firms. Few if any production cycle activities may exist as separate functions in a nonmanufacturing firm, but to some extent most organizations hold some inventories and manage some type of productive activity such as retailing goods or selling services. Thus principles of production control, inventory control, and cost and property accounting are relevant to most organizations.

This section provides an overview of the transaction flow necessary to support the functions of production control, inventory control, and cost accounting within a manufacturing firm. The discussion of production cycle applications also includes an overview of the basic factors relevant to property accounting application systems.

Production and Inventory Control

Cost accounting systems focus on the management of manufacturing inventories: materials, work-in-process (WIP), and finished goods. There are two basic types of cost systems: job order and process. Job order costing is a procedure in which costs are distributed to particular jobs or production orders. Job order costing requires a production order control system, because costs are distributed to orders.

Process costing is a procedure whereby costs are compiled in process or department accounts by periods (day, week, or month), and at the end of each period, the cost of each process is divided by the units produced to determine the average cost per unit produced. Process cost systems are used where it is not possible or desirable to identify successive jobs or production lots as they pass over the production floors. A classification of processes or departments may be set up for both cost distribution and production reporting purposes. This classification serves the purposes of process cost accounting and repetitive order production control.

"Costs" in either of the above cases may be actual costs or predetermined (that is, standard) costs. The details of these costing procedures are covered in numerous cost and managerial accounting texts, and accordingly are not discussed here.

Figure 5.1 outlines the transaction flows essential to a manufacturing company. Cost accounting systems encompass both production and inventory control; both of these functions are closely related to order entry, billing, payroll, shipping, and purchasing procedures within a firm. These relationships may be examined by reference to Figure 4.1 in the previous chapter.

Internal control over inventories and production is based on separation of functions and basic records and documentation, such as production orders, material requisition forms, and labor time cards. Protection of inventories from physical theft involves security and access provisions, as well as periodic physical counts and tests against independent records.

Production control involves the functions of planning which products to produce and the scheduling of production to make optimal use of productive resources. Basic production requirements are provided by the bill of materials and master operations list. Detail material specifications for the production of a product are recorded on the bill of materials (Figure 5.2). A bill of materials lists all required parts in subassembly order, with any corresponding description accompanying the subassembly. The bill can be used as a ready reference for replacement parts, as an aid in troubleshooting subassemblies, or as a parts list for the end user. By distributing copies of bills to all affected departments, management can insure uniform access to accurate, up-to-date information at every operational level. A master operations list is similar to a bill of materials: detailed labor operations, their sequencing, and their related machine requirements are specified in the master operations list for a product. The bill of materials and the master operations list are used extensively in the production control function. In a firm that uses a standard cost accounting system, the standard material cost and standard labor cost might be included on the bill of material and master operations list.

Determining what products to manufacture requires an integration of the demand for a product, the production requirements, and the produc-

FIGURE 5.1. Transaction Flow in a Production Control Application

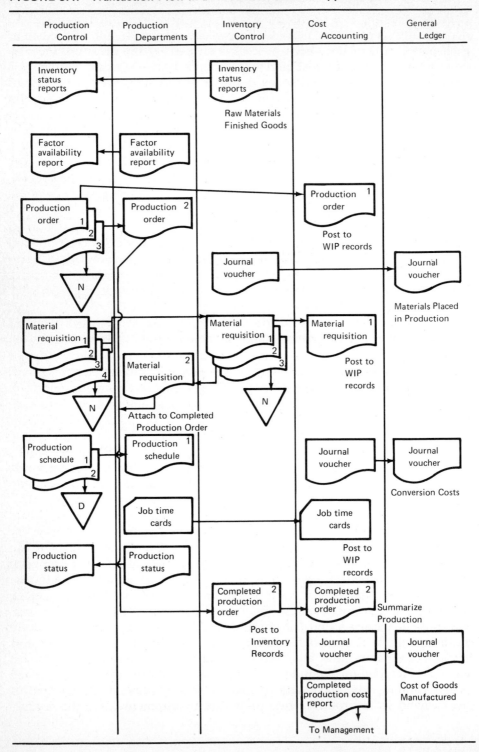

FIGURE 5.2.   A Computerized Bill of Materials Report

XTN SIDE MOUNT CAPSIN
ENG. SPEC 1-456-A-553-1

PART NUMBER	QUANTITY	DESCRIPTION
1001	2	1 INCH TRAY BOLT
1003	1	TINSEL TIN PYLON
1022	2	THREE-QUARTER PLY TINSEL BEAM
1015	2	ALUMINUM SIDE PANEL
1030	12	1 INCH CLAMP
1031	4	2 INCH CLAMP
1040	1	SIDE TABLE−L/R
1041	1	FRONT LOADER TABLE−F ONLY
1050	4	INTERWEAVE FUSE ATTACHMENT
1060	6	SECTIONAL HOSE

ENG. SPEC 1-456-A-553-2

1001	20	1 INCH TRAY BOLT
1003	1	TINSEL TIN PYLON
1009	2	DITMUS CRANE BOLT
1015	2	ALUMINUM SIDE PANEL
1021	2	HALF PLY TINSEL BEAM
1030	12	1 INCH CLAMP
1032	4	SCALED 2 INCH CLAMP
1041	1	TABLE−L/R
1040		

Courtesy NCR Corporation.

tion resources available to the firm. Resources available for production are communicated to the production control function through stock status reports and factor availability reports. A raw material status report details the material resources in inventory that are available for production. A factor availability report communicates the availability of labor and machine resources. Demand requirements for products depend on whether the product is custom-manufactured per customer order or routinely manufactured for inventory. If the product is manufactured for inventory, production requirements depend on a sales forecast, which may be sent to production control from the sales or marketing function. Sales requirements must be related to the amount of a product held in inventory. This information is provided in a finished goods status report, which lists the quantities of products in inventory. The integration of all of the above factors results in a production plan for the organization. The production plan is embodied in a production schedule and production order(s). These documents originate the flow of production data processing.

A production order serves as authorization for the production departments to make certain products. Material requisition forms are issued for each production order. A material requisition form authorizes inventory to release materials to the production departments. The items and quantities shown on a materials requisition are determined according to specifications in the product's bill of materials. Note the flow of the materials requisition form and production order in Figure 5.1. The cost accounting function receives a copy of the production order directly from production control and also from the production departments when the production order is complete. In similar fashion cost accounting receives copies of material requisitions from both the inventory control function and the production departments. This distribution of documents implements segregation of duties and provides accountability for the production departments.

Labor operations are recorded on job time cards. These cards are posted to production orders and forwarded to the cost accounting department. The periodic reconciliation of time cards to production labor reports is an important internal control function. This function was detailed in the discussion of payroll processing in Chapter 4 (Figure 4.6).

Production status reports are periodically sent from the production departments to the production control function. A production status report details the work completed on individual production orders as they move through the production process. This report is used by production control to monitor the status of open production orders and to revise the departmental production schedules as may be necessary.

The central document in the above process is the production order. A copy of the production order is sent to the cost accounting function to establish a work-in-process record for each job.

Cost accounting is responsible for maintaining a file of work-in-process cost records. New records are added to this file upon receipt of new production orders, initiated by production control. Materials costs are posted to this file from copies of materials requisitions. Direct labor costs are posted from job time tickets. Overhead costs are often applied on the basis of direct labor hours or direct labor costs, and therefore are posted at the same time as labor costs. Cost accounting initiates a journal voucher reflecting each batch of job time tickets posted that contains a debit to work-in-process and credits to payroll and manufacturing overhead. This journal voucher is transmitted and posted to the general ledger.

As production orders are completed and goods are transferred to inventory, several documents must be updated. Production control removes the production order from its file of open production orders. Cost accounting closes the related WIP record, summarizes this activity, and communicates a completed production cost summary to various managerial personnel. The finished goods inventory records are updated to reflect the availability of the product.

The information flows just discussed are an important input to the overall production control process. Control of production efficiency requires comparisons of actual production with scheduled production and an analysis of related variances. Production control also requires a comparison and analysis of other factors, including budgeted cost *versus* actual cost for individual production orders and/or departments, and facility usage *versus* facility availability by department. The control of inventory loss and the maintenance of optimal inventory levels is also important to overall production control.

Inventory Control

The control of inventories is accomplished through a series of inventory records and reports that provide such information as inventory use, inventory balances, and minimum and maximum level of stock. Reorder points and procedures are established. A reorder point is the level of inventory at which it is desirable to order or produce additional items to avoid an out-of-stock condition. The development of reorder points requires an analysis of product demand, ordering or production setup costs, vendor or production lead time, inventory holding costs, and the costs associated with an out-of-stock condition such as lost sales or inefficient use of production facilities.

Perpetual inventory records provide the best source of inventory information. The units in the beginning inventory, on order, receipts, issues, and balance on hand should be included in the record. Appropriate control over inventories requires that there be a periodic verification of items that are on hand. This can be done on a rotating basis when perpetual inventory records exist, or it can be done with a periodic physical count. The planning of a physical inventory is essential to control. Only through careful planning is it possible to make certain that all items are properly counted and have been reported.

An important part of inventory control is the evaluation of inventory turnover to determine the age, condition, and status of stock. Special control should be established to write down obsolete and slow-moving inventory items, and to compare the balance to an appropriately established inventory level. A stock status report showing detailed use by period is especially helpful in maintaining the inventory at a proper level, and controlling slow-moving items.

Control over inventory includes methods of storing and handling. Items need to be classified and properly identified so that they can be located appropriately and so that proper verification and reporting is possible. The storage and handling of items must be accomplished to provide security against embezzlement, to protect the material against damage or spoilage, to avoid obsolescence, and to provide assurance of proper control.

Inventory is a substantial investment. An inventory control system should be designed to provide status reports on each active product, so that the company can reasonably meet customer demands. Because of the large number of inventory items and the variety of transactions affecting them, it is difficult to keep inventory and production information up-to-date with manual systems. A computerized inventory control system can result in a substantial reduction in inventory investment: these savings include a reduction in inventory without a corresponding decrease in service, determination of economic order quantities and order points, establishment of adequate safety stocks, and forecasts of future demand based on current and past information. Use records, turnover and obsolescence analyses, reorder points and quantities, and other useful statistics relevant to inventory control are difficult to generate in purely manual systems.

Property Accounting

Property accounting applications concern an organization's fixed assets and investments. An important element of effective internal control is the accurate and timely processing of information relating to a company's fixed assets and investments. Such processing is accomplished through the use of special accounting applications that provide for accounting, operational, and management information needs.

The primary objectives of fixed asset or investment accounting applications are to:

1. maintain adequate records that identify assets in terms of description, cost, and physical location;
2. provide for appropriate depreciation and/or amortization calculations for book and tax purposes;
3. provide for reevaluation for insurance and replacement cost purposes;
4. provide management with reports for planning the use of and controlling the individual asset items.

Fixed assets are tangible properties such as land, buildings, machinery, equipment, and furniture that are used in the normal conduct of a business. These items are of a relatively permanent nature and often represent the largest investment and assets of a company. Transactions that change the amount of investment in fixed assets tend to occur infrequently and to involve relatively large amounts.

A company accumulates many assets over the life of the business, disposes of assets (by retirement, sale, or other means), moves assets from one location to another, and matches the costs (other than land) to revenues by means of periodic depreciation charges over the estimated useful life of the asset. To accomplish these tasks efficiently and to provide adequate control, an automated system is frequently required.

Every organization, including those on a cash basis, should keep a ledger of fixed assets as an aid to effective control. The first step in controlling fixed assets is to know what assets the organization owns. Thus a fixed asset register is basically a listing of those assets in a systematic manner. A separate section of the fixed asset register is usually kept for each major category of asset. This categorization should follow the general ledger account description. For example, an organization may have separate ledger accounts for buildings, furniture and fixtures, and automobiles. There would be a separate section for each of these categories. Assets themselves should be labeled with identifiers linked to the fixed asset register.

When each asset is acquired it should be tagged and entered in the fixed asset register. The total dollar amount shown in the register should agree with the general ledger control accounts. In order to do this, entries must be made in the fixed asset register not only to record additions but also to record asset sales or other dispositions.

Several entries must be made when an asset is disposed of. The first is to record the date of disposal to indicate that the asset has been disposed of. The second entry removes the original cost of the asset in the current period. A third entry is to remove the accumulated depreciation taken to date. A fixed asset register functions as a subsidiary ledger to the corresponding general ledger control accounts.

Investments, like fixed assets, require separate records; typically an investment register is used to provide accounting control over investments. As with all other assets, custody of investments should be separate and distinct from record keeping. The investment register should contain all relevant information such as certificate numbers and par value, to facilitate identification and control. All investment transactions should be duly authorized and documented. A common control practice with respect to the physical handling of investment securities is to require two people to be present when the firm's safe deposit box or other depository is entered.

FINANCE CYCLE APPLICATIONS

Finance cycle applications concern the management of functions relating to the acquisition and use of capital funds. Capital funds include working capital (cash and other liquid resources) as well as long-term funds such as bonds, investments, and capital stock. This section discusses cash receipt and cash disbursement applications as these applications are common to all organizations.

Cash Receipts

Cash, the most liquid of all assets, has historically been subject to rigid controls. "Cash" includes currency and negotiable papers such as checks. In most businesses, checks constitute the bulk of cash volume. In the era of computers, there is a trend toward a "cashless" society. Cash transactions may be totally electronic, involving neither currency nor checks.

The basic objective in any cash receipt application is to minimize exposure to loss. Such procedures as immediate deposit of receipts intact, centralization of cash handling, maintenance of minimal cash balances, and the immediate recording of cash transactions are fundamental control techniques. Physical safeguards such as cash registers, vaults, immediate endorsement of checks, and limited access to cash areas are generally necessary as well.

The most critical phase of cash receipts is the establishment of the initial documentation evidencing a receipt. Once a record has been prepared, cash is subject to accounting control. Prior to this record, misappropriations are not easily determined. Consider a cash sale in a retail store. What guarantees are there that this sale will be recorded? It is possible (and has happened all too frequently) that the attendant merely pockets the cash, releases the goods to the customer, and the transaction is never recorded. Inventory analysis may uncover a cash shortage at some later point; however, this is not direct evidence of misappropriation, and has relatively little legal value. Customer theft may be the reason for the shortages. In any event, the cash is already gone, the system out of control.

Several techniques and devices are useful in controlling the establishment of an initial record. These may be grouped into three major categories: customer audit, supervision, and imprest techniques. *Customer audit* is a general term used to describe procedures in which the customer is expected to function as a control over the initial documentation of a transaction. Pricing items at 99¢ rather than $1.00 is a customer audit technique as well as marketing technique: the idea is to force the recording of a sale, because the customer generally expects change. Techniques relating to sales invoices, such as awarding a customer a free gallon of ice cream if his receipt has a red star or other symbol, are intended to have the customer audit the recording of the sale. Many cash registers sound a bell or buzzer when opened; it is hoped that the customer's attention is drawn to the amount actually being rung on the register. Sending monthly statements of account (to have the customer audit his own account) and providing customers with remittance advices (which they should return with their payments) are common examples of customer audit techniques.

Supervision includes direct supervision over clerical work, as in a mail room where cash receipts are opened. It also includes the use of professional shoppers, people hired to purchase goods in a retail environment with the expressed purpose of observing the recording of the transaction. Supervision also includes the use of test packages. For example, a pre-counted amount of cash may be given to a teller or cash counter (with or without that person's knowledge) to ascertain the validity or error rate of the procedure.

Imprest techniques are used to control cash receipts in the same manner (but usually with less accuracy) that they are used to control petty cash disbursements. A clerk is given a precounted number of tickets, and must account for either their retail value or the tickets themselves. Retail jobbers must account for the retail value of goods in their possession. Inventory control over sales (gross profit or retail sales analysis) is essentially an imprest technique. Such controls cannot be effective enough to remove completely possibilities of manipulation; however, they can serve to limit the size of potential defalcations.

Figure 5.3 illustrates a cash receipts system. The chart includes both cash sales and customer remittances sent on account. The major features of the system are the separation of functions and the generation of initial documentation. Separation of functions insures that no one person has complete control over a cash receipts transaction. Notice that it is not possible for a mailroom clerk, the cashier, the accounts receivable bookkeeper, or the general ledger bookkeeper *individually* to withhold funds or manipulate the records without being detected by the actions of some other party. The generation of initial documentation is controlled by supervision or one of the other methods previously discussed.

Cash Received on Account Procedure

Cash received on account typically comes into a business through the mail or is paid to a clerk or central cashier. In either instance the customer should have the payment acknowledged. He or she should receive a receipt

FIGURE 5.3. Cash Receipts Application System

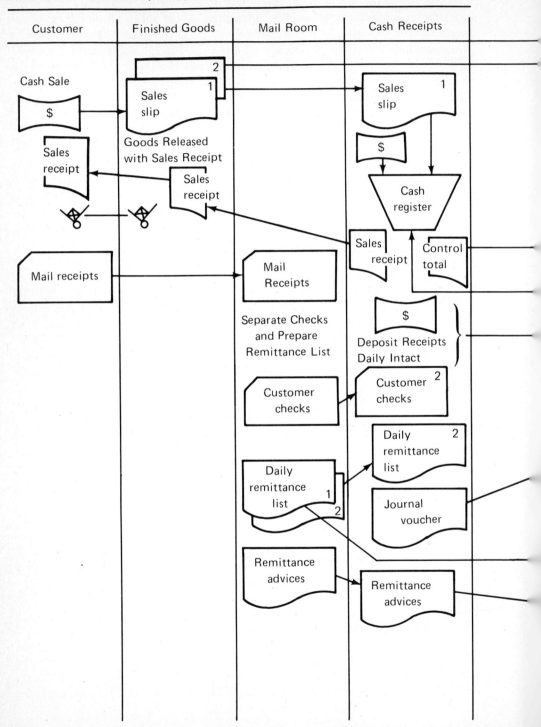

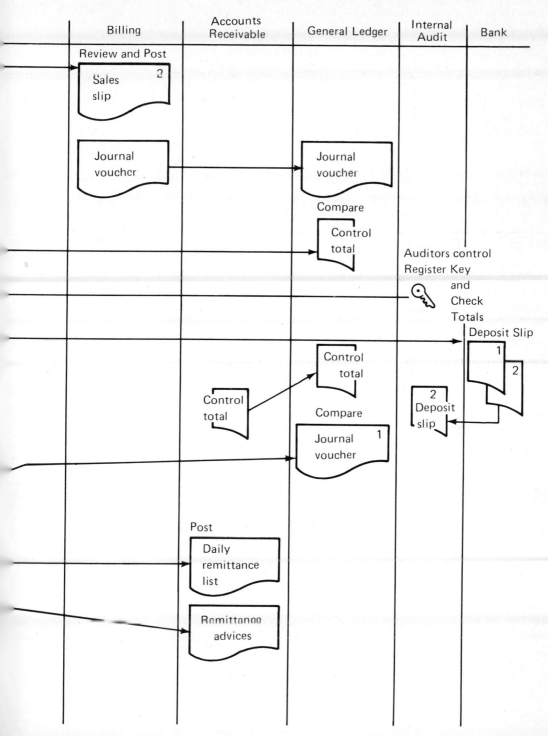

Billing	Accounts Receivable	General Ledger	Internal Audit	Bank

Review and Post

Sales slip 2

Journal voucher → Journal voucher

Compare

Control total

Auditors control
Register Key
and
Check
Totals

Deposit Slip

Control total 1 2

Control total

Compare

Journal voucher 1

2 Deposit slip

Post

Daily remittance list

Remittance advices

or at least a monthly statement with the amount paid shown. In the design of a procedure to control incoming cash received through the mail, it is important that no one in the mailroom, where the correspondence is opened; in the cashier's office, where the money is summarized and a deposit prepared; or in the account receivable section, where the asset reduction is recorded, should have complete control over the transaction. When the mail goes to the mail room, the checks or cash are withdrawn from the correspondence. A remittance advice is prepared and transmitted to accounts receivable. In many procedures the invoice or statement that is sent to a customer is prepared in such a way that the portion with the name and address of the customer is returned with the payment. This is common with telephone, utility, and department store invoices, and provides good documentation for the payment.

In the mail room a prelist of remittance is prepared. One copy of the prelist goes to notify the cashier of the amount of cash being transmitted, and the second copy goes to accounts receivable with the remittance advice. Note that the source of posting the general ledger is the journal voucher notification by the cashier of the amount of the deposit of cash receipts. This amount must agree with the accumulated total of the items posted to the subsidiary receivable file. It should also be noted that validated copies of the deposit slip go to the internal auditor, who will also have responsibility for the reconciliation of the bank account.

The control of actual cash (as opposed to checks) received by mail relies largely on direct supervision. More direct techniques, such as physical examination of employees upon the end of a working shift, are typically not tolerated in our society. Such measures may, however, be warranted in some special cases. More indirect approaches, such as an audit of an employee's lifestyle compared to his income, may be used but are rather costly to implement on a routine basis.

Cash Sales Procedure

The procedure for handling cash received from customers when there is no asset record, such as a recorded receivable, requires a different control procedure from the one in which the accounts receivable are on the books. A cash register often records the first record of such a transaction. A typical "cash received over the counter" procedure when there is no account receivable is illustrated in Figure 5.3.

Note that when cash is received from a customer it is rung up on a cash register at the point where the finished goods are released. Many cash registers validate the sales ticket, returning one copy to the customer. In other situations, a cash register receipt is delivered to the customer to evidence the amount of cash paid in. In situations in which sales tickets are made for cash sales due to inventory control or other needs, copies are sent to the billing department. A summary that must agree with the cash sale figure accumulated is sent to the general ledger. The cashier, who receives the cash from all cash registers, prepares a deposit slip and reports the amount of cash received. In the general ledger section a cash sales clearing account can be maintained to which the amount of cash received is posted from the separate sources. When the cash sales clearing account zeroes out, there has been no error. The amount reported from independent sources are in agreement.

Cash Disbursements

Cash disbursement systems are designed to control check disbursements as well as actual cash disbursement. Typically checks are used for the majority of disbursements, with actual cash disbursements restricted to small amounts drawn from and accountable to a "petty cash" imprest fund. The main concern of this section is with check disbursements; imprest funds will be briefly discussed but not illustrated. A full discussion of petty cash imprest funds may be found in most introductory accounting textbooks.

The imprest fund concept is not restricted to petty cash control; imprest payroll funds and imprest charge or expense funds are common in systems design. An imprest fund is a fund maintained at a specified, predetermined amount. At all times, the amount of cash or funds on hand plus documented expenditures should equal the specified amount of the fund. Periodically an imprest fund is replenished; documented expenditures ("petty cash vouchers") are reviewed and approved, and a check is drawn to the fund or custodian of the fund for the amount necessary to bring the fund back to its specified amount.

Figure 5.4 illustrates a cash disbursements system. The major features of the system are a voucher system to support the drawing of checks, separation of approval from actual payment, and an independent bank reconciliation of cancelled checks. Separate checking accounts may be maintained for payroll and other expense categories, such as dividend payments.

A voucher system is essentially a review technique; the real control over disbursements is a final review of documents evidencing the entire transaction prior to the authorization of payment. Authorization may take the form of physically signing off on a voucher package, or preparing (or signing) a form to authorize an entry in the voucher register. This review process evidences that a procedure or operation has been duly

FIGURE 5.4. Cash Disbursements Application System

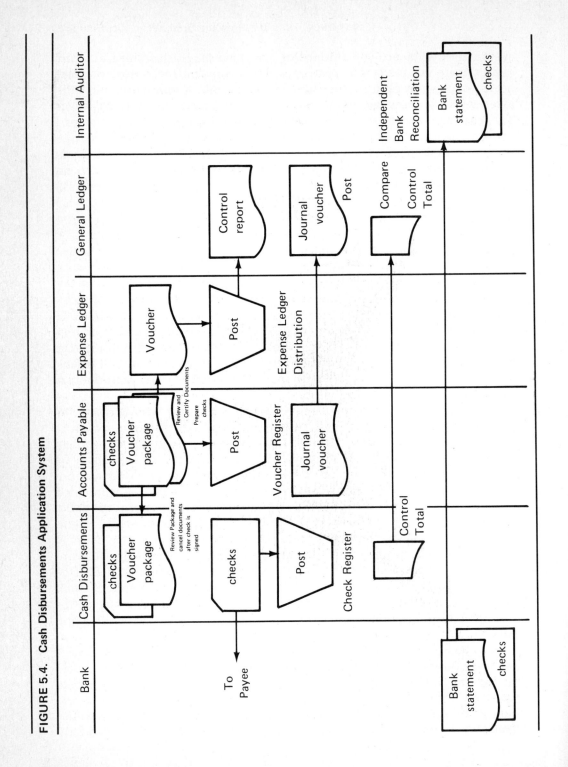

authorized and completed according to system specifications. It is the review process, not the actual signing of checks, that is the control. This is particularly evident in computer applications where checks are "signed" with a signature imprinter at the rate of hundreds of checks per minute.

An accounts payable system typically maintains a subsidiary ledger of creditors' accounts, posting invoices and payments on account to each individual creditor's account. Accounts payable generally refers to trade accounts, whereas a voucher payable system encompasses *all* expenditures, including trade accounts, payroll, capital expenditures, etcetera. In a strict voucher payable system, individual accounts for creditors need not be kept: a voucher system maintains a voucher register or, alternatively, files of voucher packages in numerical or other order. Several vouchers may relate to the same creditor, as opposed to a single account in an accounts payable system. If information on individual creditors is desired, copies of vouchers may be used to generate this information. Numerous voucher/payable files are maintained in most systems as payable information is essential to short-run financial planning.

A voucher system centers around a form called a *voucher*. Vouchers themselves can take several forms, ranging from a simple form or envelope to a voucher-check combination (Figure 5.5). A voucher would show, among other things, the name and address of the vendor, a description of the invoice, total or net amount due, and the accounts to be charged (distribution). In a computer application, most of the items in the matching process would be coded and processed by the computer. At times a voucher system may be implemented by rubber-stamping an invoice or purchase order with a voucher stamp and documenting the matching process on this original document. The form of the voucher itself is not of significance; a voucher system may operate without a human-readable voucher. In this case the "voucher" becomes an approved entry in the voucher register, typically a file on magnetic tape or disk. References to documents rather than the documents themselves are provided in the register, and voucher entries are under strict numerical control.

A basic question in the design of a voucher system is when invoices are to be posted to vouchers payable; that is, when are liabilities "booked" (excluding end of period accruals). After invoices have been approved for payment they may be held until due date and formally posted at that time; alternatively, they may be booked at the time of approval (generally different from the due date). As most firms attempt to pay invoices on due date to maximize working capital, this question relates to whether there is a formal record of amounts owed to creditors. If invoices are booked on due date, there is no formal record of unpaid invoices, as the liability is immediately canceled by payment. If invoices are booked on

FIGURE 5.5. A Computer Processed Voucher–Check

			VOUCHER NUMBER				
			186549				

ALLIED SERVICE INC.
2368 N. MAIN ST.
SOLON, MICHIGAN, 39846

DATE	REF. NO.	AMOUNT	DISCOUNT	BALANCE	VERIFICATION	LINE	MEMO
10-02-75	448963	125.00		125.00			186674.00
10-10-75	589341	75.50		200.50			186874.50
10-25-75	623892	345.50	6.91	539.09			187413.59

THE ABC COMPANY
SOME PLACE, S.C. 29623

1684

62 – 186
—————
132

PAY
TO THE
ORDER OF   ALLIED SERVICE INC.

DATE	CHECK NO.	PAY EXACTLY
10-25-75	1684	$539.09

THE FIRST BANK
SOMEPLACE, S.C.

_____
AUTHORIZED SIGNATURE

NCR Systemedia Division

○ ○

Courtesy NCR Corporation.

date of approval, then a formal record of liabilities exists. This advantage is gained at a cost; the voucher register (or file of vouchers) now must be searched or sorted by due date to facilitate payments. Typically a voucher register is used for numerical control when invoices are booked at time of approval. This is the only feasible alternative in a large organization.

Preparing vouchers for individual invoices in situations where several invoices typically refer to the same vendor in the same time period would result in the drawing of several checks to the same vendor in the same month. This is generally inefficient. Most firms attempt to accumulate several invoices pertaining to the same vendor, and pay these invoices with a single check. Such procedures are called "built-up voucher" procedures.

A built-up voucher system functions essentially as an accounts payable system. After invoices are approved, they are sorted and accumulated by vendor or voucher number. Payments are made at month end or due date. A built-up voucher procedure as just described is a full accrual system; vouchers payable replaces accounts payable in the general ledger.

Note that three files are necessary to maintain useful information: first, a file of approved but unpaid invoices, with access to due date for payment; second, a file of paid invoices, usually in numerical order; third, a vendor file showing both paid and unpaid amounts, ordered by vendor ID. In a manual system, these files are obtained by filing carbon copies of vouchers. In a computer system, separate files may be maintained, or complex processing of a "data base" may yield the same results without having three separate files.

The voucher concept is helpful in the disbursement procedure of any organization in which a basic record is desired and proper authorization and control over disbursements is important. By requiring signatures before disbursement, knowledge and approval of the disbursement are documented. Paid vouchers can be filed in strict numerical sequence to provide documentation for every amount paid. Such a procedure provides orderly records and good documentation and is advantageous in establishing good stewardship of cash.

REVIEW QUESTIONS

1. Distinguish between "job order costing" and "process costing."

2. Identify the accounting journal entries that summarize the activities involved in a manufacturing operation.

3. What is a "bill of material"? A reorder point? A reorder quantity?

4. Identify the main features of control over inventories and production.

5. Define the term *master operations list*.

6. What information might be included on a production order? Identify the source(s) of this information. To whom should copies of production orders be distributed?

7. What are the objectives of a fixed asset or investment accounting system?

8. Identify several controls relevant to fixed assets and investments.

9. What accounting entries are required when fixed assets are disposed?

10. What is the most critical phase of a cash receipts procedure? Identify several techniques that may be used to control this phase.

11. What is a remittance advice? What function do remittance advices play in a cash receipts procedure?

12. Identify the major features of control in a cash receipts procedure.

13. Criticize the following statement: "The major control over cash disbursements is the actual signing of the checks."

14. Identify the major control features in a cash disbursement system.

15. What is a "voucher system"?

16. Identify several files that might be kept in a voucher system to provide useful information.

17. What is the major difference between booking invoices on date of approval and booking them on date of payment?

DISCUSSION QUESTIONS AND PROBLEMS

18. Indicate the objective of each of the following controls:
a. Canceling paid vouchers by perforating them at the time of payment.
b. Simultaneous reconciliation of all bank accounts at an interim date.
c. Using prenumbered checks and carefully accounting for used and unused checks.
d. Maintaining a record of numbers of all stock certificates and bonds.
e. Making surprise counts of imprest funds.
f. Having registers read and cleared by internal auditors rather than cashiers.
g. Comparing totals of mail receipts with duplicate bank deposit records (daily).
h. Periodic comparison of personnel department rosters with payroll registers.
i. Having checks mailed by persons other than those causing them to be drawn.
j. Providing multidrawer cash registers.
k. Offering bonuses to customers for "red stars" or other special symbols on sales tickets.

19. Indicate the objective of the following questions taken from an internal control checklist:

  a. Are all disbursements, except petty cash, made by check?
  b. Are voided checks properly mutilated and held available for subsequent inspection?
  c. Is the sequence of check numbers accounted for when reconciling bank accounts?
  d. Are payroll checks drawn against a separate payroll bank account?
  e. Are the names of employees hired reported in writing by the personnel office to the payroll department?
  f. Are payroll checks distributed to employees by someone other than the foreman?
  g. Are salary payrolls approved by a responsible official prior to payment?
  h. Are bank debit advices (such as NSF checks) delivered directly to a responsible employee (other than the cashier) for investigation?

20. A controller insists that invoices be stamped "paid" prior to his actually signing the checks for payment. Discuss the merits of this policy.

21. Indicate the objective(s) of the following questions on an internal control checklist:

  a. Are all securities registered in the name of the organization?
  b. Are securities periodically inspected and agreed with records kept by internal auditors or other designated employees?
  c. Is the credit department entirely independent of the sales department?
  d. Are detailed plant ledgers maintained for the various units of property?
  e. Is the approval of a designated officer required for the retirement or dismantling of plant items?

22.* You are auditing the Alaska Branch of Far Distributing Co. This branch has substantial annual sales, which are billed and collected locally. As a part of your audit, you find that the procedures for handling cash receipts are as follows:

Cash collections on over-the-counter sales and C.O.D. sales are received from the customer or delivery service by the cashier. Upon receipt of cash, the cashier stamps the sales ticket "paid" and files a copy for future reference. The only record of C.O.D. sales is a copy of the sales ticket, which is given to the cashier to hold until the cash is received from the delivery service.

Mail is opened by the secretary to the credit manager and remittances are given to the credit manager for his review. The credit manager then places the remittances in a tray on the cashier's desk. At the daily deposit cut-off time the cashier delivers the checks and cash on hand to the assistant credit manager, who prepares remittance lists and makes up the bank deposit which she also takes to the bank. The assistant credit manager also posts remittances to the accounts receivable ledger cards and verifies the cash discount allowable.

You also ascertain that the credit manager obtains approval from the executive office at Far Distributing Co., located in Chicago, to write off uncollectable accounts, and that he has retained in his custody as of the end of the fiscal year some remittances that were received on various days during the last month.

Required:

    a. Describe the irregularities that might occur under the procedures now in effect for handling cash collections and remittances.

    b. Give procedures that you would recommend to strengthen internal control over cash collections and remittances.

23. The following is a description of purchasing and accounts payable procedures in effect at the Northwest Manufacturing Co.

Using departments submit purchase requisitions on prenumbered requisition forms. Each requisition is approved by the using department head, who also indicates the accounting distribution on the requisition form. Two copies are forwarded to the purchasing department, and one copy is filed numerically.

Purchasing accounts for the numerical sequence of requisition forms upon receipt. Prenumbered purchase orders are prepared, approved, and distributed: one copy each to the requesting, receiving, and accounts payable departments. A copy of the requisition is also forwarded to accounts payable.

In the receiving department, counters inspect shipments and record their counts on tally sheets. The counters do not have access to purchase orders. The tally sheets are forwarded to the head of the receiving department. She compares the tally sheets to the purchase orders and prepares a prenumbered receiving report. This report indicates the actual quantity received. Items that are returned to the vendor are indicated on the receiving report, and separate prenumbered debit memos are prepared. The department head accounts for the numerical sequence of receiving reports and debit memos. Goods are transferred to the stores department. Copies of receiving reports and debit memos are sent to the requesting, accounts payable, purchasing, and stores departments. Each of these departments files its copy numerically.

Invoices are routed from the mailroom to the accounts payable department. Clerks compare invoice details to those shown on the purchase order, requisition form, and receiving report, and check for mathematical errors. The clerks also account for the numerical sequence of purchase orders and receiving reports.

The clerks withhold invoices until all the above documents are received and the matching process is complete. Upon completion, the clerks assemble the invoice, purchase order, receiving report, and any related debit memos into a voucher package, initial the package to indicate their effort, and forward the package to the accounts payable supervisor. The supervisor reviews the package, initials it to indicate approval for payment, indicates the date payment should be made, and forwards the package to the cash disbursements clerk, who then forwards it to data processing for keypunching. After keypunching is completed, the voucher packages are returned to the accounts payable department.

Checks prepared by data processing are returned to accounts payable, attached to the corresponding voucher package, and submitted to the accounts payable supervisor for a final review before submission to the controller for signature. The controller reviews each voucher package and manually signs the checks. The checks and voucher packages are then sent to the treasurer, who also manually signs the checks. Two signatures are required on all checks. The treasurer's secretary cancels all supporting documents and returns the canceled documents and the checks to the accounts payable supervisor. The voucher packages are filed by a clerk, who also prepared a data processing input sheet showing payee, check number, amount, etcetera. The input sheets are keypunched and processed to produce the cash disbursements records. The accounts payable supervisor forwards the signed checks to the mail room.

Freight invoices, which are substantial in amount, are routed from the mail room to a clerk, who checks their mathematical accuracy. The invoices are then forwarded to the accounts payable supervisor for approval. The supervisor indicates the date payment should be made, and then forwards the invoices for check preparation by data processing. At month's end the cash disbursements book is totaled and a journal entry is prepared by the cash disbursements clerk. It is approved by the accounts payable supervisor and given to the general ledger clerk for posting. The general ledger clerk is independent of all accounts payable and disbursement functions. Monthly bank statements are sent directly to the accounts payable supervisor, who performs the reconciliation.

Required:
  a. Flowchart the present system.
  b. Identify potential internal control weakness in the present procedure. Exclude the data processing department's operations in your review. Suggest modifications to present procedures to support your recommendations concerning potential weaknesses.

24.* The accounting and internal control procedures relating to purchases of materials by the Branden Company, a medium-sized concern manufacturing special machinery to order, have been described by your junior accountant in the following terms:

After approval by manufacturing department foremen, materials purchase requisitions are forwarded to the purchasing department supervisor, who distributes such requisitions to the several employees under his control. These employees prepare prenumbered purchase orders in triplicate, account for all numbers, and send the original purchase order to the vendor. One copy of the purchase order is sent to the receiving department, where it is used as a receiving report. The other copy is filed in the purchasing department.

When the materials are received, they are moved directly to the storeroom and issued to the foremen on informal requests. The receiving department sends a receiving report (with its copy of the purchase order attached) to the purchasing department and forwards copies of the receiving report to the storeroom and to the accounting department.

Vendors' invoices for material purchases, received in duplicate in the mail room, are sent to the purchasing department and directed to the employee who placed the related order. The employee then compares the invoice with the copy of the purchase order on file in the purchasing department for price and terms and compares the invoice quantity received as reported by the shipping and receiving department on its copy of the purchase order. The purchasing department employees also check discounts, footings, and extensions, after doing which they initial the invoice to indicate approval for payment. The invoice is then submitted to the voucher section of the accounting department, where it is coded for account distribution, assigned a voucher number, entered in the voucher register, and filed according to payment due date.

On payment dates prenumbered checks are requisitioned by the voucher section from the cashier and prepared except for signature. After the checks are prepared they are returned to the cashier, who puts them through a check signing machine, accounts for the sequence of numbers, and passes them to cash disbursements bookkeeper for entry in the cash disbursements book. The cash disbursements bookkeeper then returns the checks to the voucher section, which then notes payment dates in the voucher register, places the checks in envelopes, and sends them to the mail room. The vouchers are then filed in numerical sequence. At the end of each month, one of the voucher clerks prepares an adding machine tape of unpaid items in the voucher register and compares the total thereof with the general ledger balance and investigates any difference disclosed by such comparison.

Required:

Discuss the weaknesses, if any, in the internal control of Branden's purchasing and subsequent procedures and suggest supplementary or revised procedures for remedying each weakness with regard to

    a. Requisition of materials.
    b. Receipt and storage of materials.
    c. Functions of the purchasing department.
    d. Functions of the accounting department.

25.* Charting, Inc., a new audit client of yours, processes its sales and cash receipts documents in the following manner:

    a. *Cash receipts.* The mail is opened each morning by a mail clerk in the sales department. The mail clerk prepares a remittance advice (showing customer and amount paid) if one is not received. The checks and remittance advices are then forwarded to the sales department supervisor, who reviews each check and forwards the checks and remittance advices to the accounting department supervisor. The accounting department supervisor, who also functions as the credit manager, reviews all checks for payments of past due accounts and then forwards the checks and remittance advices to the accounts receivable clerk, who arranges the advices in alphabetical order. The remittance advices are posted directly to the accounts receivable ledger cards. The checks are endorsed by stamp and totaled. The total is posted to the cash receipts journal. The remittance advices are filed chronologically.

       After receiving the cash from the preceding day's cash sales, the accounts receivable clerk prepares the daily deposit slip in triplicate. The third copy of the deposit slip is filed by date, and the second copy and the original accompany the bank deposit.

    b. *Sales.* Salesclerks prepare the sales invoices in triplicate. The original and the second copy are presented to the cashier. The third copy is retained by the salesclerk in the sales book. When the sale is for cash, the customer pays the salesclerk, who presents the money to the cashier with the invoice copies.

       A credit sale is approved by the cashier from an approved credit list after the salesclerk prepares the three-part invoice. After receiving the cash or approved invoice, the cashier validates the original

*Material from the Uniform CPA Examinations and Unofficial Answers, copyright © 1969 by the American Institute of Certified Public Accountants, Inc., is reprinted (or adapted) with permission.

copy of the sales invoice and gives it to the customer. At the end of each day the cashier recaps the sales and cash received and forwards the cash and the second copy of all sales invoices to the accounts receivable clerk. The accounts receivable clerk balances the cash received with cash sales invoices and prepares a daily sales summary. The credit sales invoices are posted to the accounts receivable ledger, and then all invoices are sent to the inventory control clerk in the sales department for posting to the inventory control catalog. After posting, the inventory control clerk files all invoices numerically. The accounts receivable clerk posts the daily sales summary to the cash receipts journal and sales journal and files the sales summaries by date.

The cash from cash sales is combined with the cash received on account, and this constitutes the daily bank deposit.

c. *Bank deposits.* The bank validates the deposit slip and returns the second copy to the accounting department, where it is filed by date by the accounts receivable clerk.

Monthly bank statements are reconciled promptly by the accounting department supervisor and filed by date.

Required:

a. Flowchart the sales and cash receipts application of Charting, Inc.
b. Identify potential internal control weaknesses in Charting, Inc., procedures.

ELEMENTS OF
DOUBLE-ENTRY
ACCOUNTING SYSTEMS

6

This chapter examines the basic components and organization of accounting information systems, and explores some basic alternatives in their design and use. The overall tone of discussion is oriented toward manual accounting systems; however, these same basic components (journals, accounts, ledgers, registers) are required in automated systems, and differ more in form than in content. The chapter discusses double-entry, accrual-based accounting systems. There is no attempt to teach basic accounting principles; rather, the discussion in this chapter seeks to explore these basic principles in a data processing environment.

ACCOUNTING AND DATA PROCESSING

Basic bookkeeping is data processing. The repetitive operations of book-keeping consist of sorting, calculating, copying (recording), summarizing, and so on. In a small office, such operations are carried out manually with mechanical aids in the form of a desk adding machine, a typewriter, or the like. Larger offices make increasing use of mechanical devices, and at some point tasks are computerized to the degree that they can be cost-justified. Differences in data processing techniques lead to differences in the speed, versatility, and accuracy of repetitive bookkeeping functions.

Figure 6.1 relates the data processing model to the accounting cycle. The accounting cycle usually begins with papers evidencing business transactions. Such papers are usually called *source documents*. Sales slips, invoices, and purchase orders are examples of source documents. Source documents are recorded in *journals* and/or *registers*. At least one original entry record (a journal/daybook) is fundamental to a complete bookkeeping system, as the steps of double-entry cannot be carried out without at least one journal. The purpose of a journal is to provide a

FIGURE 6.1. Data Processing and Accounting, Diagrammed

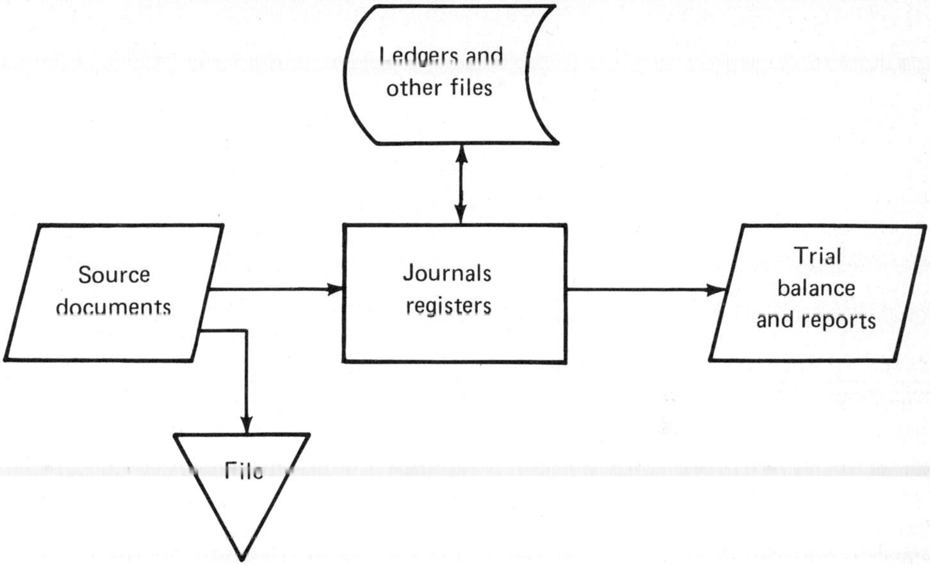

Ledgers and
other files

Source
documents → Journals
registers → Trial
balance
and reports

File

permanent and chronological record of a firm's transactions. In most cases special journals and/or registers may be designed to reduce the clerical effort in bookkeeping. Special journals and registers are used to record and summarize transactions of a similar classification. Journals are associated with monetary amounts whereas registers are typically associated with statistical data (such as receiving reports). Registers are typically auxiliary; they function to record statistical data that is too voluminous to be recorded in a regular journal. However, the terms *registers* and *journal* are sometimes used interchangeably. *Ledgers* and *files* provide permanent, summarized records of a firm's transactions. *Trial balances* and other financial reports are the outputs of the bookkeeping cycle.

Accounting-related forms and papers serve several functions. First, they serve as a physical medium to store and transmit data. This function is necessary both to determine the results of operations and to keep track of (to control) assets. Simply recording transactions and keeping a record of assets (for example, inventory stock cards or a fixed asset register) are basic to the concept of accounting control. Accurate records provide the basis for implementing the concept of organizational independence, and "the books" provide a check or control on the use or misuse of assets. Accounting media also facilitate operations. In an organizational context, forms provide a basis to transmit authority and responsibility. For example, a petty cash slip authorizes the custodian to release cash and transmits responsibility for the use of this asset to the receiver. Literally, the receiver is now accountable for the cash, as evidenced by the petty cash slip. Accounting media also serve to standardize operations. Repetitive processes, such as recording sales, must generally be standardized to insure uniformity and completeness. Forms also assist inexperienced (and often experienced) employees by indicating what data should be recorded in a situation and the format or layout for doing so. Such considerations increase in importance as the level of automation in a system increases.

Source documents provide the initial capture (recording) of transactional data; they are a basic input to an accounting system. In a manual system, data from source documents are usually entered into journals, after which the journalized data is posted to ledgers. In automated systems, source documents are either created in or converted to media forms that are machine-readable. Punched paper cards, tickets, punched paper tape, and magnetic cards and tape are examples of machine-readable media. Clearly the trend in automated systems is toward initial recording of transactions in machine-readable media. In automated systems, journalizing and posting may be simultaneous or carried out in a variety of steps. Frequently, posting precedes journalizing; transactions are often journalized only in summary form. Under either manual or automated systems, the flow of processing must fit the accounting system as a whole. Accounts are the foundation of an accounting system. Each transaction is ultimately interpreted in terms of the organization's chart of accounts. Every transaction, in one way or another, is eventually reflected in an account.

ELEMENTS OF DOUBLE-ENTRY SYSTEMS

The Chart of Accounts

Accounting systems serve to record, classify, and summarize accounting information. Coding is the assignment of symbols (for example, letters) to effect a classification scheme; a coding structure identifies and distinguishes a classification scheme. Regardless of the method of storing data (for example, cards, folders, computer media), data must be coded and stored systematically or later access to stored data is difficult or impossible. Coding and classification are basic to accounting systems.

An account is simply a classification of information; conceptually, an account is simply a place where data relevant to a particular classification or object is recorded and/or summarized. In systems, an account may take physical form on a sheet of paper, a preprinted ledger card, or an allocation of some computer storage medium such as a section of magnetic tape. One can generally classify data in several different ways; the question of what is a relevant classification is best addressed by focusing on the intended or mandatory use of data.

The basic double-entry accounting model contains just three accounts: assets, liabilities, and equity. Each of these accounts is generally subdivided into numerous subclassifications. Assets are classified as current or noncurrent, and further subdivided into cash, inventory, etcetera. Equity is subdivided to contain revenue and expense accounts, among others. Sales revenues are classified as "sales," and increase owners' equity as a result of the closing process. Why not post sales revenues directly to the owner's equity account? The reason is that "sales revenue" is a classification of information that is useful to management and others interested in a particular organization. If sales were posted directly to owners' equity, this information would be combined with other transactions that affect equity, such as additional investments or withdrawals. The process of obtaining sales information would consequently be tedious, as this information would either have to be extracted from the equity accounts or prepared separately. Now consider an organization with several distinct sales outlets. To monitor the operations of individual outlets, management is likely to require sales information by outlet. To post all sales information to one account "sales" might create a situation similar to the one discussed above; accordingly, the organization would likely subdivide its sales account into several subaccounts, one for each outlet. Now consider salesmen: should there be a separate account for each salesman? Perhaps. If this information is relevant, such data will have to be accumulated at some point in the data processing cycle. There are many alternatives, of which a separate general ledger account is only one. Certain accounts may be required by law. Tax laws require an accounting for payroll taxes and related payments; state laws often dictate the accounting for equity components, and many regulated industries must follow a chart of accounts promulgated by the relevant regulatory agency. Public utilities are an example of this later situation; utilities must utilize a chart of accounts promulgated by the Federal Power Commission.

Designing a Chart of Accounts

A chart of accounts must be responsive to both the external reporting requirements and internal information needs of an organization. Figure

---

FIGURE 6.2.   A Chart of Accounts

Assets

Current Assets (100–199)
   101   Cash in Bank
   102   Petty Cash
   110   Inventory
   150   Supplies
   155   Prepaid Rent

Plant And Equipment (200–250)
   201   Land
   230   Office Machines

Intangible Assets (280–299)
   281   Organizational Costs

Liabilities and Equity (300–499)
   310   Accounts Payable
   330   Notes Payable
   400   Bonds Payable
   450   Capital Stock
   460   Retained Earnings

Revenue and Expense (500-999)

Revenue (500–599)
   501   Sales Territory A
   503   Sales Territory B

Expenses (600–799)
   610   Salaries
   620   Power
   630   Supplies
   640   Rent

Summary Accounts (900–999)
   910   Income Summary

6.2 provides a simplified illustration of a complete chart of accounts. The coding system used in Figure 6.2 is discussed in Chapter 7. Although there are similarities among all charts of accounts, specific differences

---

FIGURE 6.3.   Portion of a Chart of Accounts for a Typical Radio Station

---

Direct Expenses (400–499)

40   Agency commissions and other direct expenses
401   Agency commissions—national sales
402   Agency commissions—local sales
403   Other direct expenses

Technical Expense (500–599)

50   Compensation
501   Salaries—supervisory
502   Salaries and wages—nonsupervisory
508   Payroll taxes
51   Other technical expenses
511   Transmitter tubes expense
512   Other tubes expense
513   Transmitter line charges
514   Outside engineering expense
515   Power and light
516   Maintenance and repair of technical equipment
517   Equipment parts and supplies
518   Depreciation
549   Other technical expense

Source: From National Association of Broadcasters, *Accounting Manual for Radio Stations* (1975).

abound in different situations. Accounting for a meat-packing plant is similar to, but also certainly different from, accounting for a radio station. Uniform classifications of accounts have been developed, published, and promoted by trade associations and numerous other groups to encourage good accounting practice. Figure 6.3 illustrates a section of a uniform account classification for radio stations published by the National Association of Broadcasters (1975, p. 22). Many associations that promote a uniform chart of accounts also collect and publish comparative statistics for their industry. Such statistics can be very helpful to an organization; the uniformity among the industry's charts of accounts strengthens the validity of comparing one's own organization to published data. Such comparisons can provide helpful insights into an organization's operations and management policies.

A carefully prepared chart of accounts serves more than the mere provision for slots into which transactions are to be dropped. The accounts selected and their sequence should, at a minimum, meet the following tests (AICPA, p. 11, 1949):

1. facilitate the economical preparation of financial statements and reports;
2. include those accounts that are needed to reflect adequately and accurately the assets and liabilities and the revenues, costs, and expenses sufficiently broken down to be useful to management in its control of operations;
3. describe accurately and concisely what should be contained in each account;
4. delineate as clearly as possible the boundary lines between capital assets, inventories, and expense items; and
5. provide for controlling accounts where necessary.

Documentation

Ordinarily it is desirable to have an account manual with explanations of what should or should not be included in particular accounts. This need increases as an organization grows in size. An account manual is a form of procedural documentation. Ideally, any question raised concerning an accounting system could be resolved by consulting the accounting systems procedures manual(s). Complete documentation of the organization and procedures of an accounting system would include a detailed description of job titles and related duties, the chart of accounts, along with complete specification of standard journal entries and related procedures. If charges and credits to accounts are not carefully defined and controlled, different operating units and/or bookkeepers may record similar transactions in different ways. This is not desirable. Manuals also assist in formalizing internal control procedures. To illustrate these points, consider the following extract from the National Association of Broadcasters *Accounting Manual for Radio Stations* (1975, p. 37) (refer to Figure 6.3):

512   Other Tubes Expense
For those tubes charged directly to expense either because their cost or their life expectancy does not exceed some cutoff level, a sound practice employed in some stations is to require the person requesting a replacement to turn in the old tube before issuing a new tube. See also discussion of account 131.

Journals

"Journalizing" is the process of recording transactions in an appropriate journal. Since the journals contain the initial record of any transaction, they are called the "books of original entry." The data accumulated in each journal are summarized periodically, often monthly, and the journal debit and credit totals are transferred or "posted" to the corresponding general ledger accounts.

Journals are used to provide a chronological record of financial transactions. It is theoretically possible, but not often practicable, to use the two-column general journal as the only book of original entry. However, to effect a division and saving of labor, special journals with special analysis columns are used to record similar and recurring transactions. Some of the more common special journals that may be kept are:

sales journal: used to summarize sales made on account;
purchases journal: used to summarize purchases made on account;
cash receipts journal: used to summarize receipts of cash;
cash disbursements journal: used to summarize disbursements of cash.

The above four types of journal are often used in conjunction with a separate general journal to provide a complete bookkeeping system (see Figure 6.4). Special columns may be used in these books of original entry to facilitate recording transactions or for classification of data.

The design of special-purpose journals is one of the most important steps in the design of an accounting system. Journals must be carefully designed if they are truly to economize clerical effort and at the same time function as true posting mediums in routing debits and credits to the ledger. Properly designed special journals eliminate numerous postings while at the same time enabling one quickly to obtain the totals for all major transactions.

Ledgers

A ledger is a collection of accounts. The terms *ledger* and *account* are sometimes used interchangeably in referring to a single account. The journal-ledger relationship is fundamental to double-entry accounting. The journal supports the ledger and vice-versa. Ledgers and journals should be tailored to a specific organization's needs. While several relevant factors such as the size and shape of the organization, and the detail of posting desired (for example, each sale or total sales) may be identified, there are no hard and fast rules by which one might decide upon a particular configuration. Basic questions in ledger design concern the amount of detail to be posted (that is, detail or totals only) and subdivisions of the ledger to include subsidiary ledgers. If a ledger contains accounts (which may be controlling accounts rather than detailed accounts) for

FIGURE 6.4. A Five-Journal Bookkeeping System

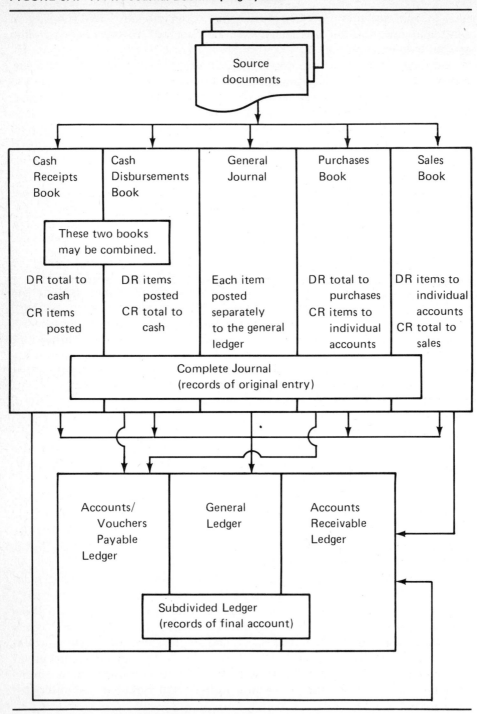

all the assets, liabilities, and equity, including revenues and expenses, it is called a *general ledger*. It summarizes the chart of accounts for the entire organization. Supporting ledgers, called subsidiary ledgers, are used to tabulate and centralize information pertaining to specific accounts such as accounts receivable, fixed assets, and accounts payable. In some cases, where the detail is not voluminous, the general ledger will include the subsidiary detail as well as the control account.

As an organization grows, its general ledger (that is, number of accounts) will tend to expand, creating a need for an organizational structure within the ledger system itself. At one extreme, one may have only a general ledger, which is posted from journals. At some point subsidiary ledgers are required for convenience. Subsidiary ledgers may be kept by the same individual in charge of the general ledger, or by another individual. In a large system, subsidiary ledgers are kept by departments. Ledgers may be further subdivided for groups of related accounts. Accounts receivable, for example, may be further subdivided by sales district or by alphabet or customer number (as in cycle or rotated billing systems). The result is a hierarchical relationship of subsidiary ledgers and control accounts. At the other extreme, the general ledger, though the use of numerous subsidiary ledgers, may consist almost entirely of control accounts.

FUNDAMENTAL DOUBLE-ENTRY PROCESSING ALTERNATIVES

This section illustrates several alternative ways in which double-entry systems may be implemented. This discussion does not directly include computer processing methods, which are discussed in detail in later chapters. A typical system will use a combination of the following alternatives, often in conjunction with some computer processing applications. Systems design is a situation specific task.

There exists a wide variety of data processing alternatives; effective systems design demands an awareness of basic alternatives as well as an understanding of computer processing methods.

There are three basic source document, journal, and ledger processing alternatives:

1. Single Transcription
    Entering source documents directly to journals, and periodically posting from the journal to the ledger. This is the traditional manual system approach. Generally totals only (weekly or monthly) are carried from the journals to the ledger because of the effort involved in this task.

2. Multiple Transcription

    Posting source documents to ledgers first, and obtaining a journal as a by-product of this operation. The principle of multiple transcription is fundamental to both mechanically-aided and computer systems. There are a variety of devices that are used to implement multiple transcriptions.

3. Transcriptionless Systems

    Entering source documents into journals, and then sorting or filing the source documents *themselves* instead of posting these documents to ledgers. The file of source documents substitutes for a separate subsidiary ledger. This approach is called "ledgerless" bookkeeping.

The following sections discuss the second and third alternatives.

Multiple Transcription Techniques

Multiple transcription techniques become essential as the volume of transactions grows. Journalizing and posting both involve copying data from one place to another; often this information is almost identical for both journalizing and posting. Numerous *one-writing techniques* have been designed to reduce the clerical functions of journalizing and posting. Figure 6.5 illustrates a *writing board*, which is often used in manual systems. A writing board is designed to allow simultaneous recording on several documents ingeniously arranged and held on a special board. In preparing a payroll, for example, one must prepare a current earnings statement and check for each employee, a payroll register, and update a cumulative earnings record for each employee. Through the use of a writing board it is possible to prepare all three items, which contain identical data, in one writing. The payroll register is placed over pegs on the writing board first and is covered with carbon paper. Next, a group of paychecks and earnings statements is placed on the pegs over the carbon paper and payroll register. The appropriate earnings record for the first employee is selected and inserted between the first check and the payroll register. When the payroll clerk fills in the earnings statement, the data, because of the appropriate placement of the carbon, are simultaneously recorded on the earnings record and the payroll register. This one-writing technique eliminates the need to transcribe the same data into two additional records. The one-writing technique can be used wherever it is operationally feasible to do so. Other possibilities include invoicing, accounts payable, cash receipts, and cash disbursements. Another advantage of one-write systems is that they insure consistent information; for example, since what appears on the check has been proofread, it isn't necessary to proof the comparable lines on the other media.

Writing boards are an example of multiple transcription capability in a manual system. Multiple transcription is the basic feature of automated systems. A basic example is provided by a class of machinery commonly known as *bookkeeping machines* (often called posting or accounting machines as well). Such machines combine features of adding machines and typewriters, and are generally used to transcribe data to several media in one clerical operation. A basic bookkeeping machine consists of a keyboard, a platen or roller designed to hold two or three related documents at once, and one or more devices (called registers) that accumulate totals during the operation of the machine. These machines were originally mechanical; gradually electronic features, borrowed from computer technology, were added to increase the speed and volume of this machinery. Most companies that originally manufactured mechanical bookkeeping machines have now stopped production entirely, replacing these product lines with a new generation of electronic equipment that in general is more powerful than its predecessors. These new machines may properly be considered as small computer systems, although the terminology in this new area is far from standard. In addition to registers, electronic accounting machines typically have programs and application packages (payroll, receivables, and so on). These programs and packages are internally stored in memory rather than being incorporated in detachable control panels. While most users of electronic accounting machines rely on programs written by manufacturers to perform standard tasks common to all businesses, many of these electronic accounting machines are programmable. The user can work with certain software to write programs to format reports, carry out calculations, and perform other tasks she desires.

Although technologically obsolete, mechanical bookkeeping/posting machines will likely remain in use for several more years. One reason is that optional equipment allows the output of these machines to be captured in a form that is amenable to further computer processing. Bookkeeping machines are often used to process certain applications on site, while other applications are processed at a central computer facility. Contemporary electronic bookkeeping machines often look and operate like mechanical machines, even though they are internally different. The following discusses the basic principles of operation common to both mechanical and electronic bookkeeping machinery.

Bookkeeping machines may be used to process accounts receivable, accounts payable, payroll, and most other accounting applications. In all applications the steps are similar, and these steps depend somewhat

FIGURE 6.5. A Writing Board System

CASH DISBURSEMENT SYSTEM WITH CLIENT LEDGER – GENERAL ACCOUNT

✓	DATE	PAID TO	GROSS PAYROLL	INCOME TAX	SOC. SEC.	STATE		AMOUNT OF CHECK (CR. BANK)		CHECK NO.	BANK DEPOSITS MEMO DATE	AMOUNT	BANK BALANCE
									BAL FWD				9 881 51
	6/1	TELEPHONE CO.	MAY TELEPHONE					346 00	1	2394			
	6/1	PALATIAL REALTY CO.	JUNE RENT					2000 00	2	2395			
	6/1	COPIOX CO.	MACH & SUPP.					427 00	3	2396	6/1	300 00	7 408 51
	6/5	CLERK OF COURT	JONES vs. SMITH					15 00	4	2397	6/2 6/3	2 895 00	12 488 51
	6/8	CLARENCE B SWAIN	EXPENSE ADV.					300 00	5	2398			12 188 51
	6/9	MIDDLETOWN FURN.						87 50	6	2399			
	6/12	MIDDLETOWN INS. AGNCY.	POLICY 825-6321					125 00	7	2400			
	6/12	LEGAL PUBLICATION CO.	BOOKS					37 50	8	2401			
	6/15	POLLY SMITH	180 00	21 30	9 31	3 42		141 97	9	2402			

VINCENT MATHERS CORP.
148 DOGWOOD DRIVE, MIDDLETOWN

PATENT SUIT
PHONE: 521-5215

CASE OR FILE NO. 48302-6-7

BALANCES FORWARDED

DATE	NAME	MEMO	TRUST FUNDS RECEIVED	DISBURSED		DATE BILLED	CK. REC OR CASE NO	FEES RECEIVED	CHARGED	BALANCE	TRUST BALANCE
4/24	VINCENT MATHERS CORP.		500 00		1						500 00
					2						460 00
											400 00
											280 00
											80 00
											70 00
											20 00

REMITTANCE ADVICE   12-345 678

HEALY & MYERS
ATTORNEYS AT LAW
100 STATE STREET
MIDDLETOWN, GEORGIA 31010

2414

PAY   DOLLARS

DATE	TO THE ORDER OF		CHECK AMOUNT
6/30	JOHN LEWIS		25 00

HEALY & MYERS

GENERAL ACCOUNT

NOT NEGOTIABLE

THE FIRST NATIONAL BANK OF MIDDLETOWN
MIDDLETOWN, GEORGIA 31010

CLIENTS LEDGER

From National Association of Broadcasters, *Accounting Manual for Radio Stations.* Courtesy Safeguard Systems.

on the actual machine in use. To illustrate the basic principles of operation, consider a clerk processing a batch of vendor invoices, which we shall assume have been properly authorized and are ready for payment. Certain procedural steps are required to be repeated for each invoice:

1. draw a check;
2. enter related data in the check register or cash disbursements journal; and
3. post the transaction to the accounts payable subsidiary ledger.

MONTH OF_____ 19____ PAGE NO._____

COSTS ADVANCED		5 COSTS ADVANCED	6 REPRODUCTION CHARGE	7 TELEPHONE		8 OFFICE SUPPLIES	9 BOOKS	10 REP & MAINT.	11	12	13
NEW BALANCE	PREVIOUS BALANCE										
					BAL. FWD.						
				346 00	1						
					2						
			427 00		3						
15 00		15 00			4						
					5						
					6						
					7						
					8		37 50				
					9						
					10						
					11						
					12						
					13						
					14						
					15						
					16						
					17		25 00				
					18	31 00					
					19						
					20			15 00			
		25 00			21						
					22						
					23						
					24						
					25						
					26						
					27						
					28						
					29						
					30						

COSTS ADVANCED BALANCE

| |
| 25 00 |

In addition, a summary entry to

DR: accounts payable control
CR: cash

is required after all invoices have been processed.

A bookkeeping machine is essentially a one-writing technique that one operates by depressing a keyboard, as opposed to making hand entries. Figure 6.6 outlines the major features of processing invoices on a

FIGURE 6.6.   Diagram of a Posting Machine

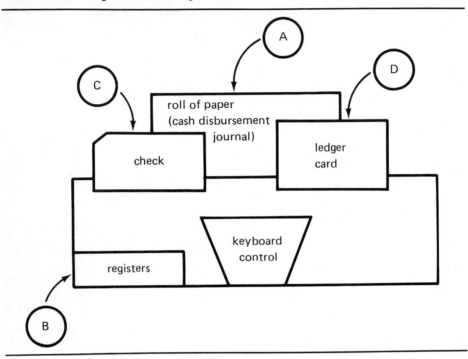

bookkeeping machine. To begin, the machine is loaded with a roll of paper that will ultimately serve as the journal. This roll of paper (keyed "A" in Figure 6.6) is often called the proof sheet, to indicate the role it plays in verifying the posting operation. (This aspect will be discussed further.) In addition to loading the proof sheet, the operator clears any registers that the machine has ("B" in Figure 6.6). Registers are mechanical or electronic devices that store and/or accumulate data during the operation of the machine. Machines differ in the number of registers provided; generally, many registers are useful, but registers are a (relatively) high-priced feature of such machines. Registers that will accumulate totals would be set ("initialized") to zero; other registers may be initialized to such things as the date or the first check number. These later items of data would then be automatically supplied during operation by the machine, reducing the possibility of error and increasing the speed of operation.

Once the machine is loaded, the operator would process each invoice as follows:

1. Place a check (or set of checks, perhaps on a continuous roll) at one printing position/slot (keyed "C" in Figure 6.6).
2. Place the *correct* ledger card in the other print position (keyed "D" in Figure 6.6).
3. Key in the data from the invoice (similar to a typing operation).
4. Depress appropriate keys to
   a. enter machine-controlled data (if any; for example, date or check number); and
   b. enter operator-keyed data onto the media.

Step 4 is the "one-writing" operation; the machine is designed to print simultaneously on two media (the check and the ledger), while the *identical* information is transferred by carbon or similar paper to the proof sheet. The above procedure would be repeated for each invoice. When the batch is completely processed, the proof sheet may be removed. This journal was obtained as a by-product of the posting operation. The information accumulated by the machine's registers may then be used to develop the summary journal entry.

The major feature of electronic machinery, as opposed to mechanical machinery, is that this transcription is also captured and recorded electronically. Thus the keying operation serves both a posting function and a data conversion function: data is automatically converted to machine-readable form. This greatly facilitates further processing of data.

Proofing Techniques

Proofing techniques are a fundamental accounting control. Proofing techniques are used to increase the reliability of the transcription process, whether transcription is done manually or by machine. The following discussion of proof techniques associated with bookkeeping machinery is somewhat detailed, because these same principles are relevant to computer systems as well. Proofing techniques are especially relevant to the input stage of the data processing cycle. The common saying "Garbage In Garbage Out" (GIGO) is particularly relevant to automated systems. Reports and other system outputs cannot be more accurate than the inputs on which they are based.

Figure 6.7 illustrates a simplified proof sheet. The proof sheet remains on a bookkeeping machine through the entire posting operation; it therefore is imprinted with a detailed record of item postings. The postings on this sheet could be directly proofed to the source documents themselves. This would eliminate the need for a detailed, more tedious comparison of the source documents to the postings on the ledger cards themselves.

FIGURE 6.7. Example of Line Proof

| | Items Posted | | | | Line Proof | |
	1	2	3	4	5	6
	Old Balance	DRs	CRs	New Balance	Second Pickup Old Balance	Proof
Jones	115	25		140	115	25
Smith	0	160		160	0	160
Tims	2050	90		2140	2050	90

To facilitate *direct proofing* of posting to source documents, most machine procedures incorporate some type of *line proof*. There are many variations of line proof, but they are all similar in that they each serve to prove in detail each line of posting. In Figure 6.7, columns 1 through 4 are a copy of what was posted to a ledger card; columns 5 and 6, which appear only on the proof sheet, constitute one version of line proof. The old balance is picked up a second time (either automatically or entered by the operator), then subtracted from the new balance. The difference of this operation is printed in column 6, and should equal the amount of the posting. The items in column 6 may be directly compared to the original media. A separate register is typically used to accumulate these line proof amounts and/or posting amounts; these end-of-run totals may be compared to prelisting (batch control) figures.

Distribution proof is used when a distribution is to be effected by the posting operation. In this case, the old balance is again subtracted from the new balance, but this difference is not physically posted, although it is stored in a register. The operator then distributes the total amount by

FIGURE 6.8. Distribution Proof

| | Items Posted | | | | Distribution Proof | | | | |
	1	2	3	4	5	6	7	8	9
	Old Balance	DRs	CRs	New Balance	Second Pickup Old Balance	Sales Outlet A	Sales Outlet B	Sales Outlet C	Line Proof
Jones	115	25		140	115			25	0
Smith	0	160		160	0	100		60	0
Tims	2050	90		2140	2050		90		0

keying in the appropriate subamounts shown in each invoice to the appropriate distribution column. The machine subtracts each subamount as entered from the line proof difference in the register; at the end of the posting, the amount in the register should equal zero (see Figure 6.8) This amount is either printed for visual inspection or subject to machine testing. In this latter case, the machine would lock unless the final balance in the register had "zeroed out."

In electronic machinery, numerous other types of proof techniques are available and commonly used. These techniques are discussed in Chapter 10. More thorough editings are both possible and *necessary* in electronic machinery because of the increased volume of data that is generally processed. This increased volume is subsequently processed automatically, without further need for human intervention (integrated data processing). Although this feature enhances processing speed and economics, it dramatically increases the need for thorough editing of data input to a system.

One should note that the proof methods discussed above help insure the *completeness* of data processing, but do not necessarily insure *accuracy*. Neither of the above proof methods attempts to prove directly that items have been posted to the *correct accounts*. Assuming that account numbers were posted in the machine operation, it would be both possible and desirable to extend batch control and/or line proofing techniques to include the account numbers as well as the amounts posted. This would extend the degree of control over accuracy of data processing.

Ledgerless Bookkeeping

"Ledgerless" bookkeeping systems, a third alternative, attempt a form of integrated data processing in that source documents are filed rather than transcribed ("posted") to other media. The file of source document serves as (and therefore physically replaces) a separate ledger. Accounts receivable and accounts payable systems are typically best suited for ledgerless bookkeeping applications. In a strict sense ledgerless bookkeeping involves no posting. This is possible only under rather restricted conditions. No posting means that statements of account will not be periodically mailed to customers. Thus ledgerless systems are better suited for situations where the industry practice is to pay on receipt of an invoice rather than a monthly statement. A further restriction concerns payments on account: if payments are made in the exact amount of invoices, ledgerless systems may be very cost-effective, since a minimum of clerical effort is required. (See Figure 6.9 for a diagram of this ideal situation.) If partial payments on account are common, or sales returns and allowances and

FIGURE 6.9. Ledgerless Bookkeeping

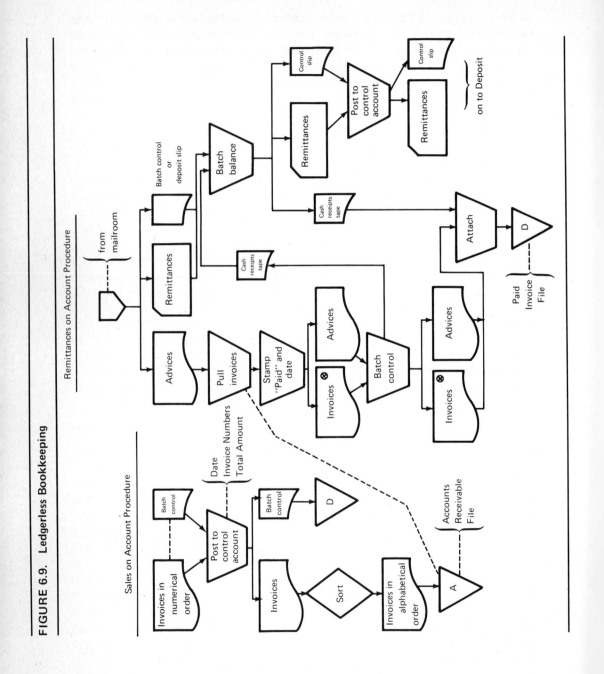

other invoices adjustments are common, "ledgerless" bookkeeping will require significant modifications and postings and will differ very little from a normal system. For example, if partial payments are made, the payment must either be posted to the relevant invoice or a special partial payment slip must be prepared and placed in the invoice file. In addition, some note has to be made in the "paid" file. A situation where ledgerless bookkeeping has traditionally worked very efficiently is one where there are periodic billings for small fixed amounts. This situation is common to monthly magazines and periodicals, which bill small fixed amounts on a regular basis.

Ledgerless bookkeeping systems have less redundancy, and therefore less inherent control, than normal posting systems. Numerical control of documents, prelisting and batch controls, and subdivision of the file to keep batch sizes reasonable are essential steps to compensate for the lack of a second (redundant) record of transactions. If an invoice is lost, misfiled, or posted incorrectly, there exists no second record to assist in locating the error. Careful design of document flow is essential for sound control. To illustrate, note that in Figure 6.9 the cash receipt tape and corresponding advices are filed by date. If a customer complains that a payment was not credited to his account, one may take the customer's alleged payment date and search the file efficiently for evidence of the transaction. If advices were not filed by date, this situation would become much more tedious. Of course filing by both date and customer account is desirable, but this involves some form of transcription, which is precisely what "ledgerless" systems are trying to avoid.

DESIGNING DOUBLE-ENTRY SYSTEMS

This section provides an overview of the steps necessary in the design and implementation of double-entry systems. These steps are essential regardless of whether the resultant system utilizes manual or machine methods to process accounting data. The complexity of these steps will increase as one moves from a manual to a computer-based system.

Basic Considerations

An accounting system must "fit" a particular organization. A variety of factors—the nature and purpose of the organization, its structural and functional characteristics, its physical layout, products, and services, the existing accounting system, and the personnel who operate the system—are all relevant to this consideration. These topics are discussed in subsequent sections. The intent here is to explore double-entry bookkeeping considerations.

Any system has a purpose or objective. The basic objective of an accounting system is to record, process, and report financial information. This objective is best expressed by an organization's financial statements (balance sheet and income statement), the end result and purpose of the accounting system cycle. Accordingly, financial statements are the logical place to begin the overall design of an accounting system. The steps in this process would generally be as follows:

1. Design a rough classification of accounts and related financial statements.
2. Review this with the user or client.
3. Finalize statements and accounts.
4. Prepare a plan of journalizing and design the necessary business papers and procedures to implement and operate the system.

The chart of accounts is used to achieve an organization's objectives concerning financial reporting and control. The accounts in the general ledger provide a separate record for each of the company's assets, liabilities, capital fund balances, revenues, and expenses in which all transactions pertaining to that account are recorded. As previously discussed, there are many sources that provide basic charts of account guidelines and models. Most CPA and other consulting firms have checklists or outlines that are readily adaptable to a particular situation. Other sources have previously been cited.

Once the chart of accounts and related statements have been finalized, a plan of journalizing and posting transactions must be formulated. The basic alternatives by which transcription may be accomplished were previously illustrated. The alternative selected will depend on several factors, most notably the volume of transactions. Regardless of the method of processing selected, a complete set of *standard* or recurring journal entries should be provided to facilitate, document, and complete the system design.

Standard Journal Entries

Standard journal entries are pro forma or hypothetical entries that are expected to occur in the normal operation of the system. Standard journal entries, properly prepared, provide a concise guide through the accounting cycle. They formalize the closing process; in large organizations, standard journal entries allow the closing process to be parceled out (subdivided) to the various responsible organizational subunits, such as divisions or departments. In this case, a file of standard journal entries is accumulated and verified prior to the closing process. A standard journal entry should indicate:

1. the accounts affected by the entry;
2. the source (that is, journal, department, computer run, etcetera) of the entry; and
3. the timing or date the entry is required (weekly, monthly).

In providing a detailed set of standard journal entries, the operation of the accounting system under normal circumstances is described. Not all transactions can be foreseen; accordingly, standard journal entries do not or can not provide for the recording of every transaction. However, an analysis of recurring transactions can indicate ways to streamline the accounting function. Standard journal entries are the source for designing special journals. Figure 6.10 indicates a hypothetical standard journal entry to record sales on account in a retail firm, and a model sales journal designed to facilitate this entry in a manual system. Note the correspondence between the entry and the number of special columnar classi-

---

FIGURE 6.10.   Journal and Journal Entry Relationship

SALES JOURNAL   Page 1

Debits   Credits

		Accounts Receivable		Sales			
Date	Reference number	Customers 120	Other 121	Class 1 511	Class 2 512	Services 520	Tax 550

Standard Journal Entry

No. 15   Monthly

DR. 120	Accounts Receivable — Customers
DR. 121	Accounts Receivable — Others
CR. 511	Sales — Class 1
CR. 512	Sales — Class 2
CR. 520	Sales — Services
CR. 550	Sales — Tax

FIGURE 6.11.   A Standard Journal

STANDARD JOURNAL				Page 1			
Date		Month: January			Month:		
	Particulars	Account Number	DRs.	CRs.	Account Number	DRs.	CRs.
1/31/xx	Commissions	610	1560				
	Wages payable	320		1400			
	Accrued payroll taxes	322		120			
	Withholding tax	325		40			

fications in the journal form. In computer systems, standard journal entries specify the desired outputs from specific applications, such as the payroll system, and indicate how these outputs enter the general ledger.

Recurring adjusting and closing entries should also be included in the set of standard journal entries. Figure 6.11 illustrates an adjusting entry to record commissions earned at month's end, and the use of a *standard journal* to facilitate the recording of this transaction from month to month in a manual system.

Reversing Entries

After the financial statements have been prepared and the books closed, it is often desirable to reverse some of the adjusting entries before entering the regular transactions of the next period. Such entries are called reversing entries.

Adjusting entries are made for prepaid, accrued, and estimated items, whereas reversing entries are usually made only for accrued items and for some prepaid items. The prepaid items that are reversed are those in which the amounts arising from the original transactions were initially entered in expense or income accounts, as opposed to asset or liability accounts.

The question of reversing entries is fundamentally related to the basic plan of operation reflected in standard journal entries. The intent of reversing entries is to facilitate the accounting function with respect to transactions that relate to two or more accounting periods.

For illustration, consider a transaction involving the purchase of fire insurance covering a two-year period. At the time of purchase, there are two alternatives:

1. debit an *asset account* such as prepaid fire insurance; or
2. debit an *expense account* such as fire insurance expense.

This choice is fundamental but also arbitrary; it is a system design choice. The correctness can be evaluated only in light of the total system.

Consider now the adjustment required at the end of the first accounting period. Figure 6.12 contrasts the two alternatives outlined above. If the initial posting is to an asset account, it is necessary to decrease the balance in this account through an appropriate transfer to expense. The determination of this amount (that is, the actual adjustment) depends on the situation at hand. After analysis and posting, alternative 1 begins the new accounting period with the adjusted balance set up in an asset account. Alternative 2, with the initial posting to an expense account, also requires a similar end-of-period adjustment; however, this adjustment reduces the expense account through an appropriate transfer to an asset account. Note now that to begin the new accounting period consistent with the same accounting policy, it is necessary to *reverse* the adjusting entry in

---

FIGURE 6.12.   Comparison of Methods for Adjusting Entries

Reversing Entry Method	*Direct Method*
a. Insurance policy purchased:	
Dr. insurance expense	Dr. prepaid insurance
Cr. voucher payable	Cr. voucher payable
for the total cost of the policy	
b. Adjustment at the end of the first month:	
Dr. prepaid insurance	Dr. insurance expense
Cr. insurance expense	Cr. prepaid insurance
for the unexpired portion	
c. Postclosing entry at the beginning	
of the second month:	
Dr. insurance expense	No
Cr. prepaid insurance	entry
for the unexpired portion	

order to transfer the remaining balance to an expense account. That is, to be consistent with a policy of initially posting new transactions to expense accounts, it is necessary to transfer remaining balances of prior-period transactions to expense accounts as well. This is accomplished through the additional step of reversing entries.

Alternative 2 requires more journal entries than alternative 1; however, these additional entries, which are routine, often serve to reduce the overall workload necessary to close the books. This workload arises from the way in which the procedures necessary to operate the accounting system are organized. Many accounting systems are factored into five basic subsystems (see Figure 6.4):

1.   cash receipts,
2.   cash disbursements,
3.   purchases,
4.   sales, and
5.   general ledger.

The first four subsystems are generally concerned with specific assets (cash, inventory, and accounts receivable); the general ledger subsystem incorporates all remaining assets. In general, each of these subsystems may be considered to a source or book of original entry (for example, the sales journal). The question of reversing entries relates to the choice of method of initially recording transactions that will likely require adjustment. If the cash disbursements subsystem is selected, then one has to provide either extra debit columns for assets (to follow alternative 1), or, as is more common, treat all disbursements as expenses (and fall naturally into alternative 2). To record the transaction initially in the general ledger would circumvent the standard cash disbursements procedure, complicating internal control considerations and probably increasing the paperwork involved. On the other hand, to follow the first alternative, one has to operate a cash disbursements system that involves more complexity (more columns or codes) than would be required under alternative 2. To summarize, the interactions within the procedures that support an accounting system often make alternative 2, the reversing entry method, preferable to alternative 1, even though on the face of it, alternative 1 requires one fewer entry per item. It must be emphasized that under either approach to adjusting entries, someone must always determine the *amount* of the adjustment. This accounting step is necessary to determine income and to reflect assets properly, and is fundamental in either systems design approach.

REVIEW QUESTIONS

1. The text discussed and illustrated an accrual-based five journal bookkeeping system (Figure 6.4).
   a. Which of the five books of entry would not be required under a cash basis system?
   b. What information relevant to a retail firm would *not* appear in the ledger of a cash basis system?
   c. How might the information in part 2 be provided in a cash basis system?
   d. How would each of the following items be reflected on a cash basis income statement?
      i. depreciation
      ii. cash received on account
      iii. inventory merchandise
      iv. cash paid for supplies not yet received
      v. purchase of an asset

2. What functions are served by accounting forms and papers in an organization?

3. How does an organization identify the specific accounts it needs in its chart of accounts?

4. Why are control accounts commonly found in the general ledger of an organization?

5. What is a "writing board"?

6. Outline the major features of posting accounts with a bookkeeping machine.

7. What effect does each of the following have on line or distribution proof?
   a. the incorrect pickup of the old balance
   b. posting to the wrong invoice
   c. posting the incorrect amount
   d. the computation of an incorrect new balance (a machine error)

8. Suggest a proof technique that would control each of the situations listed in question 7.

9. Discuss the advantages and disadvantages of ledgerless bookkeeping.

10. Why do sales returns and other sales adjustments reduce the efficiency of ledgerless bookkeeping for receivables?

11.   How might customer balances and aging schedules be accumulated under a ledgerless bookkeeping system for receivables?

12.   What are the uses of standard journal entries?

13.   What major differences exist between manual and machine posting methods?

14.   Consider the following monthly standard adjusting entry designed by a systems analyst:
DR. Insurance expense—Inventory
DR. Insurance expense—Equipment
  CR. Prepaid insurance
Briefly describe an alternative plan of adjusting insurance expense, illustrating your answer with appropriate entries. Contrast these alternatives.

DISCUSSION QUESTIONS AND PROBLEMS

15.   Discuss the importance of an accounting systems manual to:
    a.   the training of new personnel;
    b.   the uniformity and consistency of reports;
    c.   an external audit;
    d.   the revision of an accounting procedure.

16. Modify Figure 6.12 to illustrate ledgerless bookkeeping when partial payments are made.

17.   The figure below is a schematic diagram of a one-write system. Identify the probable uses of forms A, B, and C if the system is used for the following functions:
    a.   Accounts payable
    b.   Accounts receivable
    c.   Payroll.

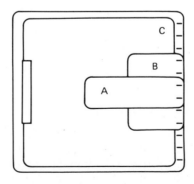

18.   The APP company publishes a monthly newsletter with a mailing circulation of around 100,000 customers. The company accepts subscriptions on a credit basis and maintains a ledgerless accounts receivable system by filing copies of invoices alphabetically. Invoices are typed on a seven-part prenumbered form: copy 1 is the customer original; copy 2 is a file copy, and copies 3 through 7 are follow-up copies. Stencils that contain customer name, address, and invoice number are produced as a by-product of typing the invoice set. The stencils are used to address mailings of the newsletter. The stencils are filed by zip code and name within zip code.

Credit follow-up must be very strict, otherwise customers may receive a number of issues without having made payment. The follow-up days are the first and fifteenth of each month. No follow-up is made on a new customer until the second regular follow-up date following the date of subscription. On each follow-up date, clerks pull each statement set out of the file, examine the date of billing, and if the billing date is more than fifteen days old, tear off a copy of the statement and put it in one or another file, depending upon whether it is a first statement, a second, or a third, and so on. A series of collection letters is sent out with the statements. Each first statement receives a friendly letter, and each fifth statement receives a letter that threatens cancellation.

Most customers pay in full in a single payment, and they send in a statement top, showing name, address, and invoice number, with the remittance. After the cash and checks are separated from statement tops in the mail room the statement tops are sent to the accounts receivable clerk. Here they are sorted alphabetically and used to pull the appropriate sets of statements out of file. Each fully paid statement is then stamped "paid" and put in the paid file. Ninety-five percent of the remittances are accompanied by statement tops.

Review the efficiency of the above procedure, commenting on the filing of invoice sets, pulling follow-up copies, and pulling paid invoices from the accounts receivable file.

19.   The mail is opened by an accounting clerk. Vendor invoices are stamped with a voucher stamp and forwarded to the purchasing agent. The purchasing agent matches the receiving report, purchase order, and vendor invoices. He then forwards the combined voucher set to the controller, who reviews the documents, approves them, and records the account coding within the voucher stamp. He then forwards the voucher set to the accounts payable clerk.

The accounts payable clerk records the approved invoices onto an accounts payable vendor card and a purchases journal, using a one-write system. The clerk then initials the invoice and files it alphabetically by vendor. At month's end, the clerk prepares an accounts payable aging report and totals the columns in the purchases journal, which is used by the controller for preparing a monthly journal voucher.

The controller uses the accounts payable aging report to indicate those vendors to be paid. In addition, the accounts payable clerk files invoices that contain cash discount terms in a calendar according to due date. The accounts payable clerk manually writes the checks, posts the amounts to the vendor cards, and records the amount in the cash disbursements journal, using a one-write system. The clerk then runs the checks through a check protector and forwards them to the check signers.

Two signatures are required. Normally the controller signs the checks first, followed by the office manager. The checks are occasionally signed in advance by the office manager. Normally the supporting invoice vouchers are not given to the check signers. The checks are then returned to the accounts payable clerk, who mails them along with any requested remittance advices to the vendors. The clerk then files the vouchers alphabetically in a paid bills file.

Each month the accounts payable clerk receives the bank statement and canceled checks. Using the cash disbursements journal, the clerk prepares the bank reconciliation and forwards it to the controller for his review and approval.

Required:

   a. Flowchart the above procedure.

   b. Identify potential internal control weaknesses in the above procedure.

20. The campus bookstore has recently come under new ownership. The owner has asked you to design an accounting system to support his new method of operating the store. The store occupies rented space under a lease that covers heat and water, but not electricity or telephone expenses. Assets include miscellaneous office furniture, store fixtures, and machinery such as cash registers, typewriters, and adding machines, in addition to an inventory of books and supplies.

The major changes made by the new owner concern the type of merchandise carried and the terms of sale. In an effort to improve profitability, only cash sales will be made, and several types of merchandise previously carried will be dropped. The store will carry four major classes of merchandise:

   a. textbooks and related materials,

   b. other books,

   c. paper and printing supplies,

   d. miscellaneous desk/office furnishings.

The staff includes the owner/manager, two office employees who handle the accounting/office paperwork, three full-time sales clerks, a part-time janitor, and several part-time sales clerks. The office employees and full-time clerks are paid on the first and fifteenth of each month, and the janitor and part-time clerks are paid weekly. Deductions are made for withholding tax and social security tax. The owner has a drawing account; the store is organized as a sole proprietorship. Sales clerks receive commissions on all sales of merchandise in class d above. The commissions are calculated monthly and paid a few days after the end of each month.

The store will purchase all merchandise on account and sell only for cash. There are three cash registers, which will be used to record sales; these registers may be used to analyze sales by class, but not by salesperson, as there are only five sales keys per register. The store will collect state sales tax. Cash payments ("paid-outs") will be made from one of the three registers. This register has a separate "paid-out" key and accumulator for such items. A paid-out slip will be written for each such payment and kept in the drawer of the register until the cash is balanced at the end of the day. Each register will be provided with a $100.00 change fund. The store maintains a checking account at a local bank. Gross cash receipts less paid-outs will be deposited intact daily. Payroll checks as well as checks for merchandise and supplies will be drawn on this account.

Textbooks will be ordered from publishers under certain return privileges. Other merchandise will be bought subject to terms of 2/10, n/30. There will be about 150 merchandise suppliers. Physical inventories will be taken at midyear and at year-end. The store will utilize a periodic inventory system.

The owner asks you to design a system that will give him proper and timely financial and operating information, and a set of books in which to collect the necessary information.

Your assignment should include:

a. a complete chart of accounts,
b. a draft set of financial statements in outline form,
c. a set of standard journal entries, and
d. a set of journals in draft outline to record the store's transactions.

The store will operate a manual system. Statements will be prepared twice yearly. Be sure to indicate the timing of each of your journal entries. You need not discuss or provide formal closing entries.

REFERENCES

American Institute of Certified Public Accountants, *Internal Control—Elements of a Coordinated System and Its Importance to Management and the Independent Accountant* (New York: AICPA, 1949).

Gillespie, Cecil, *Accounting Systems: Procedures and Methods*, 3rd ed. (Englewood Cliffs: Prentice-Hall, 1971).

National Association of Broadcasters, *Accounting Manual for Radio Stations* (Washington, D.C., 1975).

Thompson, W.R., *Accounting Systems: Their Design and Installation* (Chicago: LaSalle Extension University Press, 1926).

DATA PROCESSING CONSIDERATIONS IN ACCOUNTING SYSTEMS

7

This chapter serves as a bridge between manual and computer systems. Topics relevant to both types of systems—coding, distribution, and forms design and retention—are covered in a discussion that compares and contrasts manual and machine methods. An overview of electromechanical data processing is provided as a general introduction to computer data processing procedures.

CODING SYSTEMS FOR DATA PROCESSING

Coding, the means by which classification schemes are implemented, is fundamental to all but the simplest accounting systems. A code serves two purposes:

1. providing a brief identification; and
2. giving meaning to data in subsequent processing.

The first purpose, brief identification, is a practical consideration. It is more convenient to enter "M" or "F" on a document than "male" or "female"; moreover, data has been compressed. The use of "M" rather than "male" saves three characters; doing so facilitates both processing and storage, especially in automated systems. This example fails to highlight the basic dilemma in coding systems (and classification schemes in general); the more detailed (that is, longer) the code, the better the accuracy of the description; on the other hand, the more detailed the code, the more cumbersome is the processing of that code. Lengthy codes provide more accurate descriptions of data, but lengthy codes require more storage (at a cost) and are more subject to transcription or other conversion errors in usage. To illustrate the second purpose, once an employee has been coded by sex, age, or education, this datum can be combined with similar data, sorted, summarized, and processed to yield information such as a personnel report.

Types of Codes

A coding system consists of a character set: that is, a set of admissible, predefined symbols that are used to identify the object of interest. Numerical codes utilize numbers exclusively. The character set for a typical numerical coding system contains the digits 0, 1, 2, . . . 9. Numerical codes are used extensively in automated data processing. Alpha-numerical codes utilize numbers, letters of the alphabet, and other special symbols such as *, (, and +. Alpha-numerical codes are usually easier for humans to use, but are generally more difficult than pure numerical codes to implement on machinery. This difficulty is due to the manner in which the code itself is coded for machine operation. The subject of machine coding (data representation) is discussed in Chapter 8. Finally, numerous special codes exist; such codes utilize symbols (character sets) that are easily interpreted by machines but not by humans. Special codes are usually designed for machines and are becoming more visible in human activity because of increased usage of computers. The now familiar Universal Product Code (Figure 7.1) is an example of a special code designed for machine usage. This code contains two five-digit fields; the first field is for the manufacturer, the second is for product number.

The fundamental aspect of a code is its character set; the basic building block in a coding system is the individual character. Rules specify the manner in which characters are manipulated: that is, rules specify the meaning given to the value and position of characters. Probably the most

---

FIGURE 7.1. Machine-Readable Universal Product Code

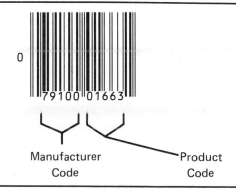

Manufacturer Code

Product Code

common and simplest rule is to assign documents consecutive numbers. For example, checks are usually numbered in sequence. Numbers may be consecutively assigned in either ascending or descending order, with ascending order most common. This scheme is called *sequential coding.* Sequential codes are simple to administer and organize data on the basis of position. A strict sequential code, however, contains no information about a document other than its position in a list. Frequently more descriptive codes are desired. To attain this end, more complex rules are needed.

A *block code* is used to classify objects into certain groups. Characters are assigned sequentially (that is, without any particular meaning other than sequence) within each block. In a block code, the position of a character or group of characters has a special meaning; by contrast, a character in a pure sequential code has no meaning other than relative position (for example, 9 is greater than 8). In Figure 7.1, the first five digits specify, or "block out," a particular manufacturer; the next five digits identify or block out a specific product for a particular manufacturer. In a strict block code there is no classification scheme inherent in each block. Manufacturers in Figure 7.1 are identified only by sequential coding. It is not possible with this code to identify directly the type of manufacturer.

It is common to give meaning to the value as well as the position of a character. Such schemes are interchangeably called *group* or *hierarchical* codes. Group or hierarchical codes implement several subclassifications within each major block of data. Certain characters are reserved for each classification desired. Such codes generally consist of several blocks, called fields; usually the leftmost field is of greatest significance, as is the case in the zip code (Figure 7.2).

FIGURE 7.2.   ZIP Code Example

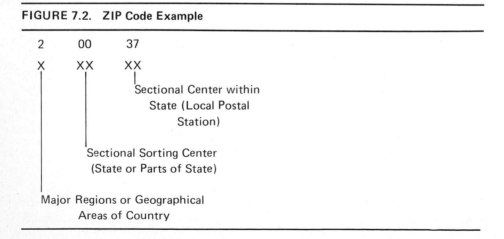

The zip code system is a hierarchical coding scheme in which both the value and position of a character (restricted to decimal digits) have meaning. Characters assigned within each zip code field designate a particular classification within that field. The value 2 in the first zip code field indicates a particular major region of the country. All addresses within this major mailing region begin with a 2 to indicate a commonality of geographical location.

A special variation of hierarchical codes is the *decimal code*. A decimal code differs from a typical block code in that a decimal code allows for unlimited expansion to the right of a decimal point. The decimal point itself is included in the character set. Major classifications are represented by fields to the left of the decimal point, while digits to the right of the point are not standardized and are used to provide subclassifications. Many libraries use the Dewey Decimal Classification. This system divides all knowledge into ten major classifications, and provides subclassification by utilizing extra digits. For example, 610.736 is "special nursing," subcategorized in the major classification "applied science" (600-699). The major advantage of decimal codes is the ability for unlimited, easy expansion; this ability is also the major disadvantage of decimal codes. The lack of complete standardization allows and promotes uneven code lengths; these are a disadvantage in machine processing, and perhaps dangerous even in a manual system. Consider the code 610.73; is this the complete code? Sometimes yes, sometimes no. Questions of this type complicate the usage of coding systems that are not completely specified as to length. Their use should be carefully considered by the analyst.

Considerations in Designing Codes

Several observations can be made concerning the use of codes. Clearly a code must yield the desired classification. A code should also be flexible. In this context it is important to realize that systems are not static. A decimal code is flexible, but the lack of standardization that yields this quality also complicates machine processing. Block codes are usually organized as follows:

1. character position has significance;
2. it has a predetermined number of characters; and
3. all codes are the same length.

Flexibility is built into a typical block coding system by leaving gaps or spaces in the original classification. This allows room for future additions to the scheme without extensive system modification.

Another consideration concerns integration of data files. A sales order, for example, ultimately affects sales, accounts receivable, and inventory. Cross-linking these files in a single code is usually desirable but difficult to achieve. Cross-linking also poses system maintenance and system security considerations. An individual's social security number is a unique identifier that might be used to cross-link several related data files. The security and privacy implications are immense to the individual; this has become a sociopolitical issue that is itself of great import in influencing the future of information processing. There are analogies to the use of company (as opposed to individual) bank account numbers, accounts receivable files, credit files, and the like, not to consider the immense data files collected and maintained by numerous governmental agencies.

Numerous standardization procedures can facilitate data processing. Most of these relate to converting alpha-numerical data to numerical data through use of appropriate codes. Days and weeks may be numbered 1 to 7 and 1 to 52 respectively, and dates put into a condensed "Year-Month-Day" numerical format. For example, September 18, 1976, may be coded as 760918. A twenty-four hour clock avoids A.M.–P.M. confusion. Calendar dating in a machine environment frequently utilizes a Julian calendar system, as opposed to the common Gregorian calendar system that the code 760918 conforms to.

Many accounting applications require the use and manipulation of calendar dates, such as the determination of due dates for vouchers payable. Calendar dating procedures may be standardized through the sequential assignment of dates. This is called Julian calendar dating. In Julian calendar dating, all days are numbered sequentially from an arbitrary date and months and years are not directly identified as such. December 31, 1979 might be Julian coded 286050.; January 1, 1980 would then be the Julian date 286051. The condensed Gregorian calendar code for these same two dates would be 791231 and 800101. Julian calendar dating is more convenient for arithmetic manipulation than the Gregorian system. In Julian calendar dating, the number of days difference between two dates may be determined by simple subtraction. In the Gregorian system one may have to convert a month to days, or a year to months to complete the same subtraction. (Consider the Dec. 31, 1979 example above). While this computation is not too difficult for humans or machines, the potential savings in processing time should be evident. For this reason, machine coding considerations (data representation) favor the use of the Julian system, which is widely used in data processing operations.

One type of code not yet mentioned is the *mnemonic code*. A mnemonic code utilizes an alpha-numerical character set; letters (and numbers) are combined to form shortened or abbreviated codes that are similar to the pronunciation or spelling of the object of interest. SJ for "sales journal," PA for "Pennsylvania," and HQ for "headquarters" are examples of mnemonic codes. Such codes are amenable to human processing, and often facilitate human processing of codes to the extent that one may more readily recall "PA" as Pennsylvania, as compared to a more arbitrary two-digit numerical code for the same state.

A final point concerns the length of codes. Empirical studies have unveiled a bell-shaped curve phenomenon related to human use of codes. Most people can readily work with codes containing 7 ± 2 digits. While larger codes are increasingly in use, the analyst should be cognizant of human limitations in devising such coding schemes. Blocks or fields may be subdivided, if necessary, to make them more amenable to human processing.

Coding Examples

Codes are widely used in accounting systems. This section provides two common examples. The first relates to customer coding, which serves as an example of activity coding, which is closely related to the accounting function of distribution. Distribution is discussed in the following section. The second example relates to the Chart of Accounts.

Many organizations have implemented large coding systems to enable them to analyze activity relating to their customers. A typical customer coding scheme is presented by example. Consider the code 123400193-33103. The first 5 digits (12340) (the first field) might represent an account number. The next 2 digits (01) a geographical code. The next 2 digits (93) a trade classification. The next five digits (33103) indicate sales territory (331) and salesman (03). And so on. Such codes might appear to be cumbersome, but computers manipulate lengthy codes quite readily. The longer the code the better the description. Although such codes are expensive to maintain, their continued and increasing usage implies that organizations have found them to be of value.

The chart of accounts, previously discussed in Chapter 6, may now be described as a hierarchical coding system. Once the accounts have been selected, they must be organized into a manageable framework. This is done by assigning each account a multi-digit code in which each digit denotes a particular classification. A typical account coding structure is illustrated below:

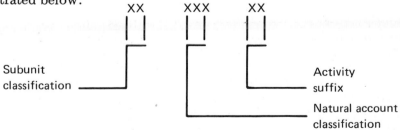

The first two digits of the seven-digit code are used to identify a division, department, profit, or cost center accounted for separately. These subunits may be numbered 01 through 99. Examples include:

01 Electronics Division
02 Research Division
07 Production Department
08 Marketing Department

Note that several digits are skipped in order to provide for future expansion. The next three digits represent specific categories:

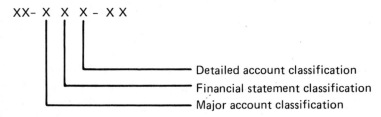

Major account classification can be numbered 100 through 900 (in hundreds), such as:

100 Assets
300 Liabilities
400 Stockholders' Equity
500 Sales
600 Cost of Sales
700 Expenses
800 Other income

Financial statement classifications are the account titles used on a company's financial statements. These accounts can be numbered 10 through 90 (in tens); an example is account 110:

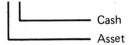

Detailed account classifications are the transaction-level accounts into which information is posted. These accounts can be numbered 1 through 9; an example is account 111:

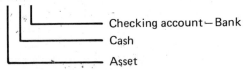

The rightmost two digits (the activity suffix) may be used to denote a company's products or activities within subunits. Examples might be:

01 Product one
02 Product two

Recognize that total expense recorded in the natural expense accounts must equal the total expense recorded in the activity (for example, product line) accounts. The purpose of the activity suffix accounts is simply to view the organization's expenses in a different context. Natural expense classifications delineate expenses by type (for example, office supplies and telephone), while activity classifications delineate the same expenses by the purpose for which they were expended.

The example just presented is just one of numerous ways in which accounts may be coded. The point to keep in mind is that a code should facilitate the desired presentation of information. The desired outputs (reports) must be identified before one constructs a chart of accounts; otherwise, the coding scheme may prevent economical presentation of information desired by management.

Coding and the Distribution Function

Accountants use the term *distribution* to denote the process of extracting and accumulating detail information from data of a transactional nature. Posting invoices to a subsidiary ledger or posting payroll data to an expense ledger are examples of distribution functions in an accounting system.

In manual systems, the cost of distribution often precludes the generation of many useful management reports. "Simply" spreading sales invoices to 5 subunits may involve a tremendous amount of effort. In effect, the basic workload is multiplied by 5; that is, details must be carried or accumulated by each desired object of distribution. Numerous devices and techniques exist to aid the distribution function in a manual system. The basic principle of these methods is to accumulate subtotals prior to actual posting; generally only totals are posted to accounts themselves.

A cash register with multiple sales keys performs a distribution function by allowing the accumulation of several sales subtotals. The cash register's tape may function as a sales journal; posting the subtotals to accounts completes the basic recording function. In the absence of a cash register or similar device, totals of invoices and the like must periodically be developed, usually with the assistance of an adding machine or similar device. Now, unfortunately, one has a fundamentally different problem.

Consider yourself in the situation of having, say 500 invoices (a week's sales activity), and there are 4 subtotals desired (sales by salesmen, for example). With a single adding machine, one has either to first sort the invoices by salesman and then take 4 totals; or alternatively, go through the 500 invoices 4 times, taking 4 separate totals. In the precomputer era, numerous machines to facilitate the taking of multiple subtotals in one pass of the media were in existence. The machines (called analysis, distribution, or tabulating machines) were essentially adding machines with multiple registers (as many as 27). Bookkeeping machines often performed a distribution as well as posting function, if the specific machine was equipped with multiple accumulators. However, extra accumulators were a relatively high-cost option. In a computer system, distribution is handled through the use of codes. In the coding example presented in the previous section, sales may be distributed (spread) to subunits or activities by appropriately coding each invoice, and then accumulating invoices by either prefix (subunit classification) or suffix (activity), or by both.

The important point to note is that there need not be a 1-to-1 correspondence between actual ledger accounts and the objects of distribution. Indeed, in most cases there is not this 1-to-1 correspondence. In the account coding example of the previous section, the 7-digit code allows for 10^7 (10,000,000) classifications; however, the actual ledger accounts would be restricted to at most 1,000 (the innermost 3 digits, 10^3). Distribution may occur prior to or after posting to ledger accounts; posting to the ledger accounts (a distribution itself) may include detail or totals only. In general, the more elaborate (that is, mechanized) the data processing system, the less demanding is the specific function of distribution. The reduction in effort is accomplished through the design of coding systems and subsequent machine manipulation of data.

AN OVERVIEW OF AUTOMATED DATA
PROCESSING PROCEDURES

This section provides an overview of data processing procedures in a machine environment. The specific machinery discussed is electromechanical, card-oriented data processing equipment. Such machinery (excluding one or two input devices) has been supplanted in use by totally electronic equipment (computers). The discussion is accordingly brief, and is organized around a typical accounting file maintenance application rather than the machinery itself. While the machines themselves are now technologically obsolete, the *functions* these individual machines were designed to perform are still relevant in computer pro-

FIGURE 7.3.   A Punch Card

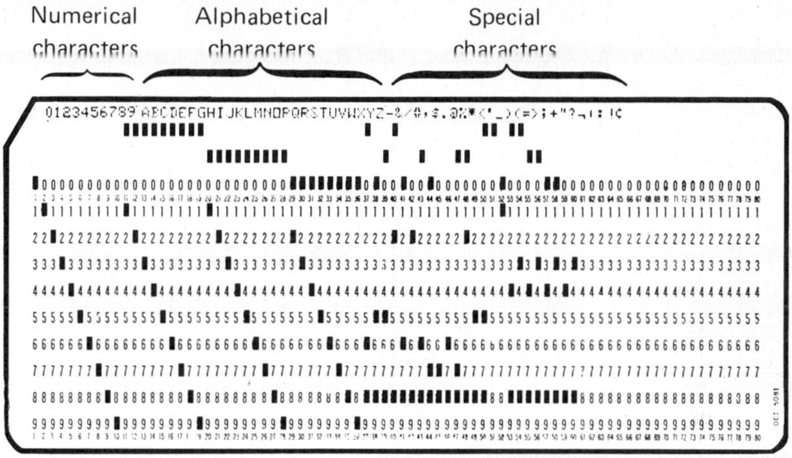

cessing applications. The functions themselves are the basic data processing operations. These functions must be performed in any system. Essentially, a single computer can perform the tasks performed by these various machines at a vastly increased speed. The illustration is provided to introduce both the detailed sequencing of procedures that is required in automated data processing applications and the transformation of ledgers from paper files to machine-readable files.

Electromechanical data processing systems utilize a group of related machines, which accept the standard eighty-column punch card (Figure 7.3) as the basic system input. The punched card is the basic storage medium and serves as input/output (I/O) in all processing steps. The use of punched cards as the exclusive I/O medium (excluding printed reports) is known as the *unit record concept*.

The fundamental operation in electromechanical systems is keypunching. Keypunching is a machine-assisted operation that codes data onto a card or other medium in a form that itself is machine-readable. The traditional method of keypunching codes data by punching holes in a card. (Figure 7.3 illustrates a standard keypunching code.) All relevant data is coded onto cards. In an accounting application, this would include general and subsidiary ledger information, as well as transactional information. The remainder of this discussion will utilize a simplified accounts receivable example.

In a card-oriented system, the accounts receivable subsidiary ledger will be coded onto cards. There will be one or more cards for each indi-

FIGURE 7.4. Flowchart of Electromechanical Data Processing

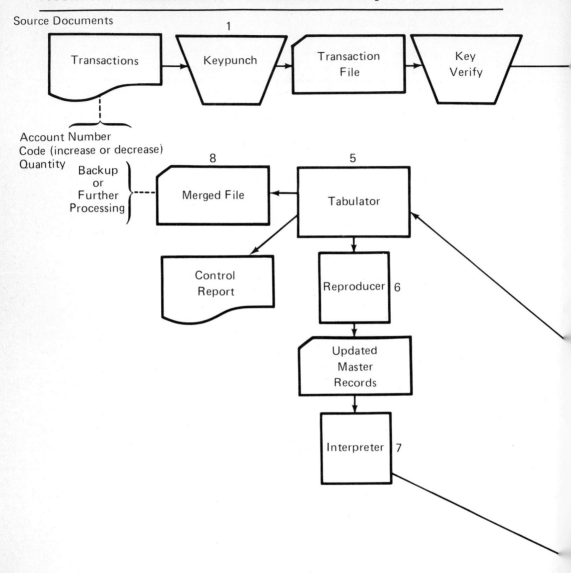

Source Documents

Transactions

1

Keypunch

Transaction File

Key Verify

Account Number
Code (increase or decrease)
Quantity

Backup or Further Processing

8

Merged File

5

Tabulator

Control Report

Reproducer 6

Updated Master Records

Interpreter 7

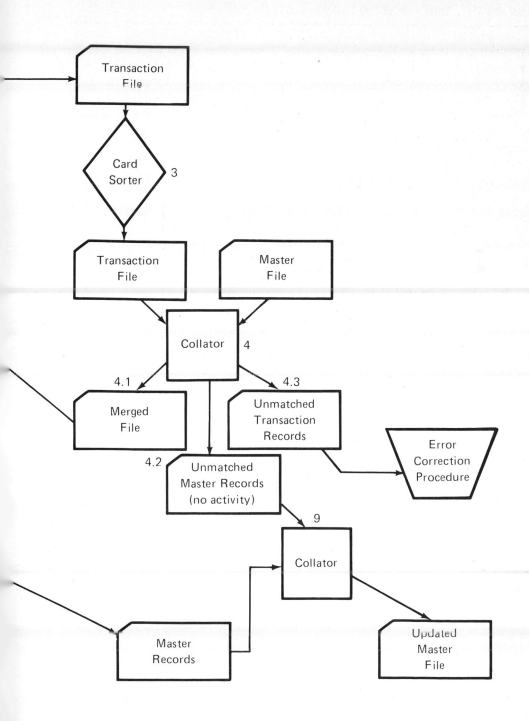

Transaction File

Card Sorter 3

Transaction File

Master File

Collator 4

4.1 Merged File

4.3 Unmatched Transaction Records

4.2 Unmatched Master Records (no activity)

Error Correction Procedure

9 Collator

Master Records

Updated Master File

197

vidual receivable, containing account number and account balance, among other items. The entire set of cards replaces the subsidiary accounts receivable ledger and is called a master file—the accounts receivable master file. To facilitate processing, master files are usually organized in some manner. The most basic method of file organization and, generally speaking, the only practical option in a card system is sequential file organization. The cards are arranged in ascending order by account number. This system facilitates the location of any specific account.

Transactions relating to accounts receivable are normally batched; that is, a reasonable number of transactions are accumulated prior to actual processing. Batching, too, facilitates processing and is discussed in more depth in Chapter 9. At some point the transactional data is keypunched; for example, the account number, a code to indicate a decrease or increase in the account balance (that is, a payment or purchase on account), and the amount of the transaction would be fundamental items in an accounts receivable application.

The basic problem is to post each transaction to the correct account. Figure 7.4 illustrates how this task is accomplished in a typical electro-mechanical system. The following discussion is keyed to the numbers that appear above the symbols in Figure 7.4. (1) Transactions are keypunched; this process transcribes data from a source document to a machine-readable punched card. (2) Verification of keypunched data is a control procedure intended to insure the accuracy of the keypunching operation. Verification can take several forms; the basic idea is to pass the keypunched data through another keying operation. This second keying does not repunch the card. The verifier senses the code already punched in the card, and compares this to the second "keypunching" on the verifier. If a discrepancy exists, the operator is notified and may initiate a correction procedure. This step helps insure that only valid data enters the system. After keypunching, one has a new file of cards—the transaction file. This file is not in any particular order, as transactions occur somewhat randomly. The transaction file is passed through a card sorter (3), a mechanical device that sorts (places) the cards into the same sequence as the master file. Without this step, posting the individual transactions to the correct account would be extremely inefficient. (4) The transaction file and master file are merged by the collator, a machine designed to compare and collate two card decks on a field value such as account number. The collator operation yields three files: (4.1) a merged activity file, which consists of individual master file records followed immediately by transaction cards that pertain to the individual account; (4.2) master file cards that have no activity in this processing (that is, there are not any current transactions pertaining to this set of accounts); (4.3) a set of unmatched transaction file records. This is an error condition; these cards would undergo an error correction procedure. (5) The merged cards are processed by a tabulator. A tabulator (sometimes called an accounting machine) is a device that can add, subtract, and accumulate, as well as prepare printed reports, line by line, as individual accounts are updated. Specific operations are controlled by a wired-control panel. These panels are interchangeable, allowing different applications to be processed on the same machinery. Prewired control panels were a fore-runner of today's computer programs. (6) Concurrent with the tabulator operation, the reproducer, electrically connected to the tabulator, punches a new master file card when the tabulator finishes processing transactions against the old master file card. This new card contains the updated balance as well as the unchanged information such as the account number.

After the tabulator processes the entire deck of cards, several post-processing operations are necessary. (7) The interpreter prints the charac-ters represented by holes along the top of the new master file cards. This step is done to make the cards human-readable. A typical keypunch machine provides this service. The reproducer typically doesn't, neces-sitating another machine, the interpreter. (8) The old merged deck of master and transaction cards goes on to storage (for back-up) or perhaps on to further processing. Reports concerning this file update (for example, a current accounts receivable list) are distributed to users. (9) A final step is to merge the newly updated cards with those that require no updating, again using the collator. After the complete file is assembled, it goes to storage and awaits the next batch of transactions.

The above discussion has been simplified. Error correction and batch control procedures, fundamental to such systems, have not been fully discussed. These topics will be fully discussed in the context of computer systems. At the time of widespread use, the speed of such systems was impressive and yielded significant clerical-cost savings compared to manual systems. A tabulator, for example, could print at speeds of around 100–150 lines per minute. A card sorter had speeds of 650–2000 cards per minute. By contrast, a modern high-speed printer operates at 1200 or so lines per minute. Sorting is typically electronic: 2000 card images could be sorted in a matter of seconds.

Although electromechanical data processing systems are no longer manufactured, the punched card itself is still widely used in data pro-cessing systems. Punched cards can be read and manipulated by people as well as machines. Punched cards are often used as customer remittance advices. A customer returns a punched card remittance advice with his payment: data that has been prepunched on the card, such as customer account number, need not be re-keypunched as input to the data pro-cessing system. Documents utilized as both output and input to a data processing system are referred to as *turnaround documents*. Punched cards are commonly used as turnaround documents in computer processing systems to reduce overall processing costs.

FORM DESIGN AND RECORDS RETENTION CONSIDERATIONS

Many accounting systems are built around a single form; the production and handling of the form is the major function of the system. The func-

FIGURE 7.5. Form Displayed on a Video Terminal

Courtesy International Business Machines Corporation.

tion of a billing system is to process invoices; a sales system processes a customer order. Forms are used to collect information and also to provide evidence that an operation (a specific stage in a system) has been performed. A receiving report provides evidence that goods have been received and verified prior to actual payment. Procedures and forms must be designed as a single integrated system. Forms are used to standardize the inputs and outputs of a data processing application. Forms themselves may be paper documents or formats displayed on computer input/output devices such as video display terminals (Figure 7.5). A completed form is called a record in data processing systems.

Form Design Considerations

The fundamental consideration in form design is the user. If the user does not understand a form, or can't use it, the result is evident. Clear instructions as to how the forms should be filled out, adequate spacing for entries, and shaded or blocked areas to indicate sections that are not to be utilized are examples of details that should be considered in the design of a form. A coordination of data items on a form or set of related forms is usually desirable. For example, a form that will eventually be keypunched (that is, coded for computer processing) should have its data items arranged in the same order in which they will be keypunched. If multiple-color paper forms are used, the same color should be used for the same department in all multiple forms used in the organization. Color itself should not, however, be relied upon exclusively, as color blindness is more common than most people realize.

Concerning paper forms, optional design features such as multiple colors, prenumbering, and rigid specifications for size and quality of the paper stock are often desirable, but they adversely affect the cost of printing the form itself. These extra-cost features should be related to the intended use of the form. There are several basic considerations: (1) the number of times the form will be handled; (2) storage time or active use; (3) the type of handling—machine or manual; (4) the quantity that is used; and (5) whether all copies in a multiple-copy form will be identical with respect to preprinted information and quality of paper stock. From a systems design viewpoint, the most fundamental choices are the number of copies of a form, its destinations, and whether the first copy is the same as all other copies. In all of these decisions, the analyst must be cognizant of one point: forms preparation and handling costs are usually far in excess of the cost of printing the form itself. If an extra-cost feature such as prenumbering or having another copy can save a procedural step at another point in the system, the extra cost in printing the form will be recovered many times over.

Form design and control is essential to systems work. The printed form on a clerk's desk, in a typewriter, or displayed via a video terminal is often a more eloquent device for directing the flow of work than the written procedure that is filed away in the supervisor's bookcase. Large organizations have found it expedient to create media or form control units, perhaps as large as a department, to standardize and thereby reduce the cost of using forms. A typical form control unit has authority and responsibility to review and approve all requests for forms. Most units also have responsibility for technical aspects of form design; in this respect they function much like a purchasing department, offering design assistance to users and interfacing between the user and the printer. Along the same lines, form control units are usually responsible for inventory control, dealing with supplies (running out versus overstocked) and organization (form numbering systems).

Records Retention Considerations

Records retention requirements must be considered in the design of an AIS. Various governmental and tax regulations set specific guidelines and legal requirements over records retention. Records retention must also be considered from the internal viewpoint of information storage and usage. Nonessential outdated forms occupy space and may hinder efficient access to more current information.

Keeping current with federal and, in particular, Internal Revenue Service requirements is the responsibility of the systems analyst. There are several basic reference sources. A *Guide to Record Retention Requirements* is published periodically in the *Federal Register;* the latest guide is available through the office of the Superintendent of Documents, U.S. Government Printing Office, Washington, D.C. The *Guide* is a digest to the provisions of federal laws and regulations relating to the keeping of records by the public. It indicates what records must be kept, by whom, and for how long.

Basic tax-related records-retention requirements may be found in the current volumes of specialized tax-reporting services, the Commerce Clearing House (CCH) and Prentice-Hall tax guides being the largest services. Revenue Ruling 71-20, "Expanded Record Retention Requirements," set guidelines, but not specific rules, pertaining to the retention of EDP and microfilm records. An adequate audit trail must be maintained in any system utilized by a taxpaper. When EDP and other machine-readable media are used, the IRS may require that such media be kept in order to permit the IRS to employ electronic auditing methods. Since specific rules are not available, a taxpayer must request the IRS to make a "record evaluation" of his records and sign a records-retention agreement with the IRS if he is to make sure of IRS satisfaction with his practices.

REVIEW QUESTIONS

1. What are the basic objectives of coding systems?

2. Define and give an example of the following types of codes:
   a. sequential
   b. block
   c. group
   d. decimal

3. What is the major disadvantage of a decimal code?

4. Identify several standardization procedures pertinent to the coding of calendar data.

5. Distinguish between Julian and Gregorian calendar dating. Which is more advantageous in data processing environments?

6. What is a mnemonic code?

7. Define the term *distribution*? How do coding systems facilitate the distribution function?

8. Define the term *unit record concept*.

9. Briefly define the functions of the following electromechanical data processing equipment:
   a. keypunch unit
   b. key verification unit
   c. card sorter
   d. tabulator unit
   e. collator unit
   f. interpreting unit

10. Has data that has been keypunched onto a card been coded? Explain.

11. Identify the major differences between manual and electromechanical processing of accounting data.

12. What is a "turnaround document"? Give several examples.

13. Are forms always paper documents? Explain.

14. Identify several basic considerations in form design.

15. Identify a fundamental principle of form design that pertains to the features contained on the form itself.

16. What are the functions of a "form control unit"? Why is forms control important in large organizations?

17. Why are records retention requirements an important consideration in system design?

18. Identify several sources that list federal records-retention requirements.

DISCUSSION QUESTIONS AND PROBLEMS

19. What is meant by "payroll distribution"? Contrast this function in a manufacturing firm to that in a CPA firm.

20. The items listed below should normally be obtained and reviewed prior to the design of an accounting system. What relevant information might the analyst extract from each of the following items? What problems might arise from a failure to review these items?
- a. chart of accounts
- b. organization chart
- c. product listings
- d. detail on facilities and operations
- e. financial statements
- f. account forms and journals
- g. original documents

21. A form should permit the right thing to be done at the right time. What form would you want as proper authorization to perform the tasks named below?
- a. To assemble the items ordered by a customer and prepare them for delivery.
- b. To arrange for the purchase of goods for your company at the best price.
- c. To write a check, except for signature, in payment of a company bill.
- d. To assign work to factory operators in your department.
- e. To issue materials and supplies to employees for use in their work.
- f. To post charges (debits) to customers' accounts.
- g. To make out the payroll summary each week.
- h. To disburse petty cash.
- i. To repair equipment that is not functioning properly.
- j. To release operators of cash registers at the end of their shift.

22.* Olivia Mace has recently been appointed controller of a family-owned manufacturing enterprise. The firm, S. Dilley & Co., was founded by Mr. Dilley about twenty years ago, is 78 percent owned by Mr. Dilley, and has served the major automotive companies as a parts supplier. The firm's major operating divisions are heat treating, extruding, small parts stamping, and specialized machining. Sales last year from the several divisions ranged from $150,000 to over $3,000,000. The divisions are physically and managerially independent except for Mr. Dilley's constant surveillance. The accounting system for each division has evolved according to the division's own needs and to the abilities of individual accountants or bookkeepers. Ms. Mace is the first controller in the firm's history to have responsibility for overall financial management. Mr. Dilley expects to retire within six years and has hired Ms. Mace to improve the firm's financial system.

Ms. Mace soon decides that she will need to design a new financial reporting system that will:

a. Give managers uniform, timely, and accurate reports on business activity. Monthly divisional reports should be uniform and available by the tenth of the following month. Companywide financial reports also should be prepared by the tenth.

b. Provide a basis for measuring return on investment by division. Divisional reports should show assets assigned each division and revenue and expense measurement in each division.

c. Generate meaningful budget data for planning and decision-making purposes. The accounting system should provide for the preparation of budgets which recognize managerial responsibility, controllability of costs, and major product groups.

d. Allow for a uniform basis of evaluating performance and quick access to underlying data. Cost center variances should be measured and reported for operating and nonoperating units, including headquarters. Also questions about levels of specific cost factors or product costs should be answerable quickly.

A new chart of accounts, as it appears to Ms. Mace, is essential to getting started on other critical financial problems. The present account codes used by divisions are not standard.

Ms. Mace sees a need to divide asset accounts into 6 major categories: that is, current assets, plant and equipment, etcetera. Within each of these categories, she sees a need for no more than 10 control accounts. On the basis of her observations to date, 100 subsidiary accounts are more than adequate for each control account.

No division now has more than 5 major product groups. The maximum number of cost centers Ms. Mace foresees within any product group is 6,

*Adapted from CMA Examination

including operating and nonoperating groups. She views general divisional costs as a nonrevenue-producing product group. Altogether, Ms. Mace estimates that about 44 natural expense accounts plus about 12 specific variance accounts would be adequate.

Ms. Mace is planning to implement the new chart of accounts in an environment that at present includes manual records systems and one division which is using an EDP system. She expects that in the near future most accounting and reporting for all units will be automated. Therefore, the chart of accounts should facilitate the processing of transactions manually or by machine. Efforts should be made, she believes, to restrict the length of the code for economy in processing and convenience in use.

Required:

A. Design a chart of accounts coding system that will meet Ms. Mace's requirements. Your answer should begin with a digital layout of the coding system. You should explain the coding method you have chosen and the reason for the size of your code elements. Explain your code as it would apply to *asset* and *expense* accounts.

B. Use your chart of accounts coding system to illustrate the code needed for the following data:

1. In the small parts stamping division, $100 was spent by foreman Bill Shaw in the polishing department of the Door Lever Group on cleaning supplies. Code the expense item, using the code you developed above.

2. A new motorized sweeper has been purchased for the maintenance department of the extruding division for $3,450. Code this asset item using the code you developed above.

23. The purchasing agent of the Hirz Co. has approved the design of the purchase requisition below. Criticize the design of the purchase requisition, limiting your comments to the original copy which is illustrated.

HIRZ COMPANY Washington, D.C.		
TO: Purchasing Agent		No._____
Quantity required	Description	Amount

24. The following procedures relating to accounts receivable are in effect at the Pepper Co. The Pepper Co. uses an electromechanical data processing system.

Approved applications for new charge accounts are keypunched and key verified. Copy 1 of the application is filed; copy 2 is sent out to have a credit card made. The credit card is forwarded to the customer by the manufacturer of the cards. The transaction cards are sorted by account number and then merged with the old master file. The updated master file is processed on a tabulator to generate a customer name and address report, and then filed.

Sales slips, credit slips, and payment memos are processed daily. These documents are assembled in batches, then keypunched, verified, and sorted into account number sequence. The sorted transaction cards are processed on a tabulator to generate a daily accounts receivable register, then merged to build a week-to-date customer transaction file.

At the end of each week the weekly customer transaction file is processed on a tabulator to generate a weekly accounts receivable summary report. The cards are then sorted into account sequence and merged with the month-to-date customer transaction file.

Monthly processing includes the maintenance of the customer name and address file and the generation of customer statements. Clerks utilize correction memos to manually extract customer name and address cards for customers who have name or address changes, as shown on the correction memos. New cards are keypunched and verified, and then physically inserted in the customer name and address file. The old cards and correction memos are destroyed. The updated name and address file is processed on a tabulator to generate a customer name and address report.

Customer statement processing begins with the merging of the updated customer name and address file and the month-to-date customer transaction file. This operation yields three files: (1) transaction cards for which there is no matching customer name and address record; (2) name and address cards with no matching transactions; and (3) a file of matched cards.

The file of matched cards is processed on a tabulator to generate monthly customer statements; the tabulator is connected to a reproducer to generate updated customer master records. The merged file is filed by date. The updated master records are merged with the name and address cards for which there were no transactions; the newly updated file is processed on a tabulator to generate a delinquent account report, and then filed. Transaction cards for which there were no matching customer name and address cards are investigated, corrected, and inserted into the file of matching records prior to its processing by the tabulator.

Required:

Flowchart the above procedures.

25. The order-billing procedure employed by the SALT Co. has been revised several times over the last few years as the company has grown in size. The current procedure is presented below.

Customer orders are sorted from the incoming mail and forwarded to the office manager, who edits the order, approves the order for credit, and passes it to a pricing clerk.

The pricing clerk prices all items on the order and completes all extensions and additions in pencil on the customer's order. The order is then passed to the order typist.

The order typist types the complete invoice-order set, including extensions and additions. The invoice-order set is composed of five copies. Two of the copies are for the customer and one copy each for the salesman, accounting department, and billing department. The typist records the numbers of the invoices typed and sends all five copies to the shipping department.

The shipping department pulls from stock all the items listed on the order-invoice. A packing slip and label is prepared after all the available items have been assembled. If the quantity shipped does not agree with the quantity on the order, the shipping clerk pencils in the quantity shipped on the first copy of the invoice-order. The items are then packed and shipped with the packing slip enclosed. The first copy of the invoice-order is stamped and dated as shipped, and all copies are returned to the order-billing department.

The order typist checks off on his control list all invoice-orders returned by shipping. The typist retypes all invoice-orders on which changes in the quantity shipped have been made. He also types back orders on the special back-order form for all items ordered but not shipped. The original copy of the back order is sent to the customer. The duplicate is sent to shipping, and the triplicate is filed in the billing department by customer name. The retyped invoice-orders are extended and footed, and a control is taken of all shipments for the day.

The customer's copies are then mailed; the salesman's copy is sent to the sales department, the accounting copy to the accounting department, and the billing copy is filed numerically.

The company's growth has made it increasingly difficult to maintain an adequate inventory. In addition, certain merchandise has been in short supply, causing frequent out-of-stock conditions that cannot be avoided. Both of these factors have contributed to a situation in which approximately 25 percent of orders received have items to be back ordered.

In the past, all orders have been shipped prepaid, freight or postage allowed. A change in policy to bill all shipping charges for orders of less than $75 is to go into effect. Shipping charges will be calculated by the shipping department after the order is processed.

Forms currently used in the above procedure appear below as exhibits 1 to 4.

Exhibit 1.   Backorder Form

SALT Co.

Invoice #   Backorder #
Date order received

Sold   ⌐   ⌐   Ship   ⌐   ⌐
to: to:

                              Terms:

Description	Units backordered	Unit price	Salesman number	Product number	Date available

Customer Copy

Shipping Copy

Billing Copy

Exhibit 2.   Packing Slip

SALT Co.

Sold   ⌐   ⌐   Ship   ⌐   ⌐
to: to:

Carrier: Date shipped:

Description	Units	Unit price	Total	Product Number

Exhibit 3.   Invoice Set

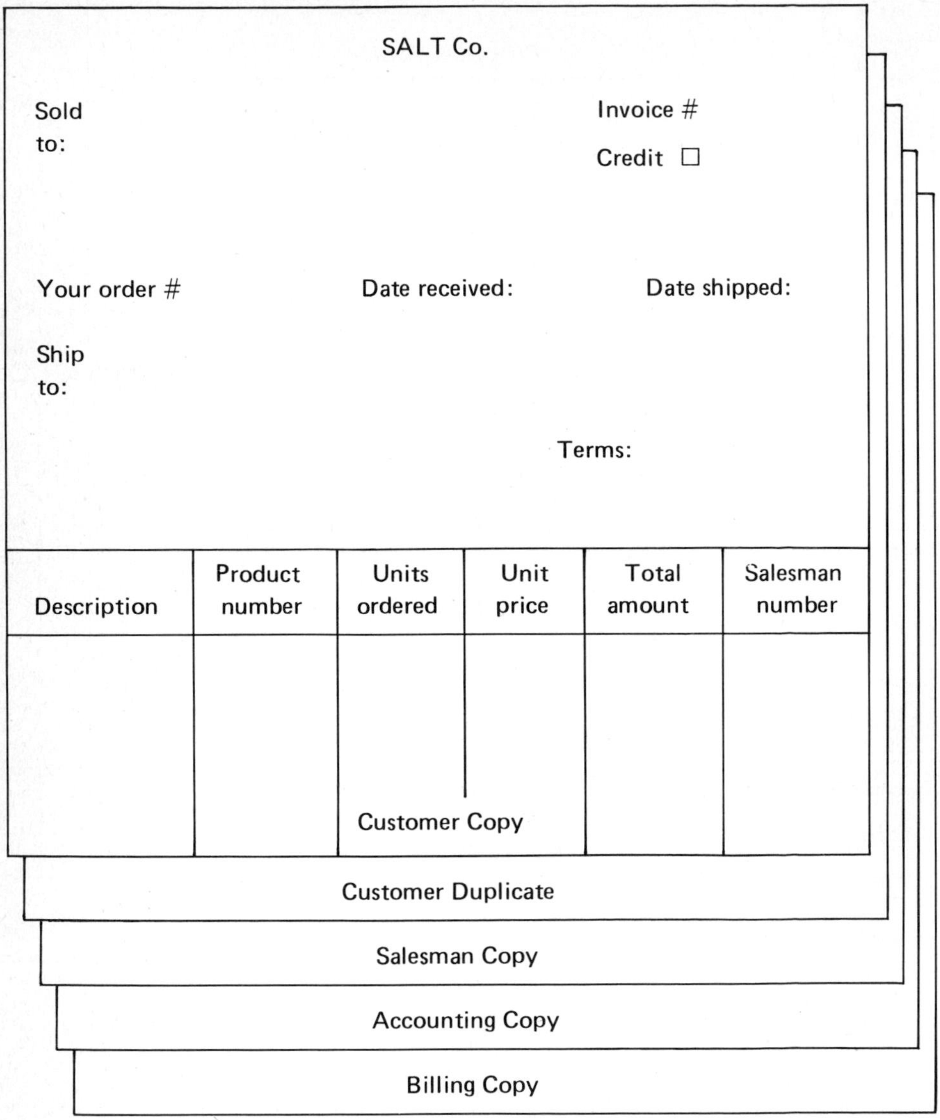

SALT Co.

Sold
to:

Invoice #

Credit ☐

Your order #   Date received: Date shipped:

Ship
to:

Terms:

Description	Product number	Units ordered	Unit price	Total amount	Salesman number
		Customer Copy			

Customer Duplicate

Salesman Copy

Accounting Copy

Billing Copy

Exhibit 4.   Label

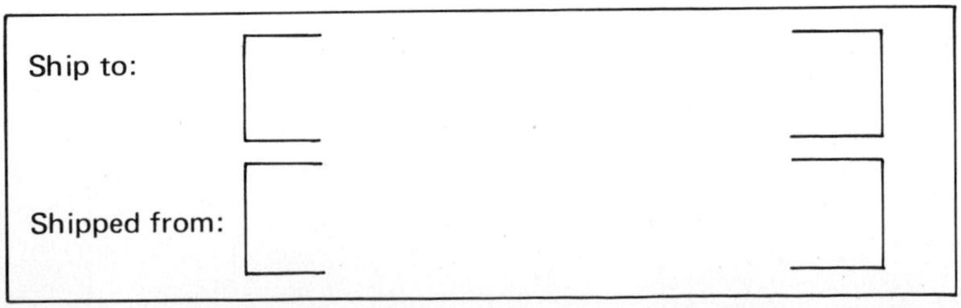

Ship to:

Shipped from:

Required:

Prepare a proposal, including form design, to revise the procedure as necessary in the circumstances.

REFERENCES

Bower, James, R. Schlosser, and C.T. Zlatkovich. *Financial Information Systems* (Boston: Allyn and Bacon, 1969).

Mitchell, William E. "Records Retention Schedule," *Journal of Systems Management* (August 1977).

Myers, Gibbs, "Forms Management, Part 1: Why Forms Management?" *Journal of Systems Management* (September 1976).

—— "Forms Management, Part 2: How to Design Business Forms," *Journal of Systems Management* (October 1976).

ELEMENTS OF COMPUTER DATA PROCESSING SYSTEMS

8

This chapter provides an overview of data processing concepts and technology in a medium-to-large-size computer environment. Smaller ("mini") computers and their unique features are discussed in Chapter 14. A large variety of computing machinery exists; accordingly, the discussion concentrates on logical rather than physical components of computer data processing. Physical devices are discussed only as necessary to provide an understanding of data processing alternatives and design considerations. A more detailed discussion of computer hardware features is contained in Chapter 14.

AN OVERVIEW OF COMPUTER DATA PROCESSING SYSTEMS

The physical components of a computer system are:

1. hardware: the name applied to computer equipment;
2. software: programs (that is, sets of symbols) that operate on computer hardware;
3. procedures: operating instructions and schedules;
4. personnel: operators, programmers, and analysts; and
5. files: data used and processed by the system.

Traditionally, a definition of the term *computer* included the following characteristics:

1. electronic device;
2. internal storage capabilities (memory);
3. internally stored program logic (instructions); and
4. program modification (ability to change instructions as well as data during processing).

Rapid advances in computer technology have made this definition obsolete: numerous hand-held calculators and other devices today would qualify as "computers" under the above characteristics. Contemporary computer technology encompasses a wide spectrum of symbol processing equipment, all of which performs what may be considered as "data processing," but only a subset of which is directed at typical business applications.

Historically (prior to the mid-1960s), one spoke of computers as being scientific- or business-oriented. Scientific processing applications require relatively little input and output, but large amounts of computation. Business data processing applications are typically the opposite: relatively large input/output requirements, but relatively little calculation. Prior to the mid-1960s this distinction was important as second-generation computers (produced roughly between 1958 and 1966) were generally designed to be efficient for one type of application or the other, but not both. With the advent of the third generation of computers (circa 1965), this distinction has largely lost importance with respect to hardware. This is because the third generation of computers and later models are truly general purpose machines, equally efficient for either type of processing.

Computer generations are counted in terms of processing speed. A generation represents an order-of-magnitude improvement over preceding hardware. For example, if the second generation was capable of doing 1,000 additions per second (10^3), the third generation did 1,000,000 (10^6). The third generation of computer hardware was substantially different from (noncompatible with), the second, representing a major advance in computer technology. Although there have been increases in both speed and performance, more recent computer models do not possess this same order-of-magnitude difference in performance capabilities. Whether we are in the third-and-a-half or fourth generation, the important point about newer machines is that they are largely compatible with third-generation machinery, making transition of files and procedures much easier than was the shift from second- to third-generation equipment.

We are concerned solely with the digital computer, a two-state (or binary) device used to store and process information. Regardless of the two physical states used by computers, logically the states are represented as either 0 or 1. From an intellectual as well as practical point of view, the significant feature of modern computers is their generality as symbol processors. A book or accounting form is essentially a collection of characters or symbols, and hence of a form susceptible to computer processing. Most number representations and the procedures for doing arithmetic and higher mathematics are also capable of being described by symbol strings (equations or even words), and are thus subject to computer processing.

Hardware and Software

From the viewpoint of its logical structure, a computer system is best described as a collection of two kinds of resources: hardware and software. The general organization of the hardware of a typical computer system is shown in Figure 8.1. It consists of the following kinds of devices:

1. a central processing unit (CPU), responsible for all arithmetic and other data processing and control functions;
2. a fast, expensive main storage of relatively small size that holds the information (data and instructions) currently needed by the CPU;
3. slow, cheap, but large auxiliary storage (typically rotating magnetic disks or magnetic tape) for holding information, most of which is not in main storage at any one time;
4. a punched-card reader and punch for entering and delivering information in punched-card form;
5. a high-speed printer;
6. terminals with typewriter-like keyboards for direct human communication. Terminals typically connect to telephone lines.

A major feature of Figure 8.1 is the isolation of the fast CPU (the arithmetic-logical unit) from direct contact with the other devices. The CPU is in contact only with main storage, which communicates, through devices called input-output channels, with all other devices. The solid lines show only flow paths for data; the central processing unit has control lines (not shown) to initiate and stop flow along all such paths. Figure 8.1 illustrates the data processing pattern employed by most medium-to-large computer systems. Another feature is the different storage devices, such as main storage, disk, and tape. This is purely for economic reasons: fast storage is much more expensive (per unit) than slow storage; to keep costs down, most storage is slow storage. It should be noted that all of the data required in a typical application could not be stored at the same time in main storage. Although sizable, main storage is dwarfed by a typical accounts receivable or payroll file's storage requirements.

Software, the other major computer resource, consists of the sets of instructions (called programs) used to operate computers. Software may

FIGURE 8.1. Typical Computer System Hardware Organization

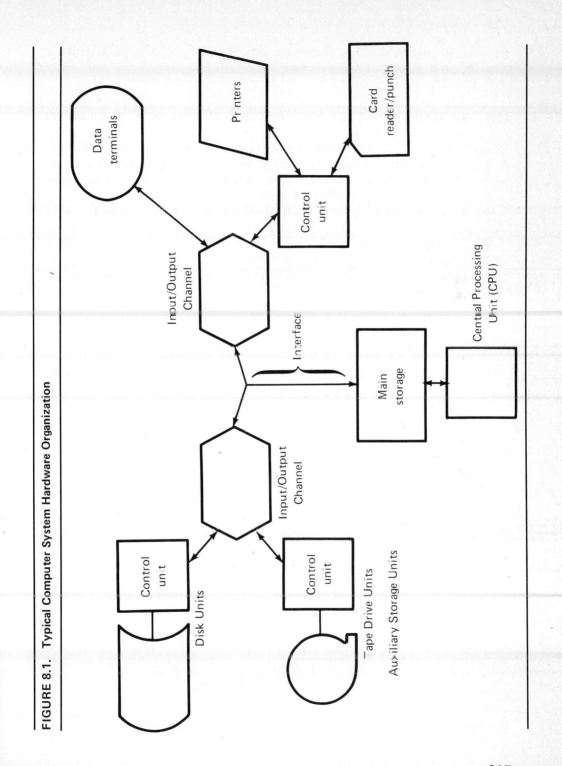

be classified as systems software, which is generally purchased from a vendor, and applications software, generally developed by the user. Systems software includes:

1. operating systems: programs that facilitate and monitor the use of hardware;
2. compilers: programs that translate user-oriented symbolic instructions into machine-oriented instructions (that is, machine language)
3. utility programs: programs designed to standardize and facilitate common functions such as sorting; and
4. canned programs: mathematical and statistical programs available to all users.

Applications software is that developed and retained for use by a specific organization or subunit within an organization, such as payroll or accounts receivable application software.

Batch Processing and Time-Sharing

The traditional and still widely used mode of giving work to a computer is called batch processing. Typically, a user writes a program, which he transcribes onto punched cards, using a keypunch machine. A program and its data comprise a job, physically consisting of a deck of punched cards, which is taken to the computer room. There, several jobs accumulate into a batch until human operators decide to pick up the decks and feed them to the system's card reader, which sends their electrical image to main storage. When the job processing is done, a system program electronically moves the job-output information to the high-speed printer. Every so often, the human machine operators collect the printouts, which are on continuous-form perforated paper. They then separate the jobs and place these and the decks in output baskets for retrieval by users. Because of the necessary human operations and many other factors, typical job "turn-around time" (that is, the time from job submission to return of results) is on the order of tens of minutes to hours, even for short jobs.

The time-sharing mode of computer use contrasts sharply with batching. The former system is designed for direct communication between individual users and the computer system. Time-sharing systems are said to be interactive or conversational. Each user has his own typewriter-like terminal. When he types a line, he always ends it by striking the carriage-return key. This sends an end-of-line signal to the computer. A system program in the computer analyzes the line just entered, does what is requested, and then responds by either typing a result or a message, or simply unlocking the keyboard so the user can make the next request. For most such interactions, the user waits about one second for the computer response.

Because both the batch and time-sharing modes have advantages and disadvantages, both continue as means of using a computer. Generally, time-sharing is most appropriate for fairly small problems; batch processing is most appropriate in the production running of programs or large projects. Both forms of processing are common in accounting systems.

CODING DATA FOR COMPUTER PROCESSING

There are many levels of coding in computer systems. For example, letters, words, and sentences are successive levels of coding in natural language. There is no obvious base level. We cannot say, for example, that the word is always the most meaningful code level in written natural language. Words are made up of letters. Letters, in computers, are made of bits. Bits, in turn, are made up of electrical voltages induced by magnetic fields. The point of view of the observer determines what level is relevant.

Data Coding Structures

There are three basic terms used to describe the data coding structure of third- and later-generation computers:

1. *bit*—a contraction of the words *bi*nary dig*it*; a bit is the smallest possible element of information;
2. *byte*—a group of bits treated as a group, usually 6 or 8 bits;
3. *word*—a group of bytes, typically 3 or 4 bytes.

Both bytes and words may be addressable in computers, whereas the content of a bit is generally not directly addressable. "Addressable" means that the content or value of a byte or word is accessible to a program.

A byte is used to code a character; that is, a digit from 0 to 9, a letter from A to Z, or a special symbol such as + or –. Thus the terms *byte* and *character* are used interchangeably.

A bit has two possible states, represented symbolically by either 0 or 1. When bits are grouped, permutations—that is, different patterns of 0's and 1's—may be used as codes. With 1 bit, there are 2 possible codes;

with 5 bits, 32 permutations are possible; thus 32 different codes are possible. The general formula for bit permutations is

$$2^N,$$

where N is the number of bits in a group. Thus with 6 bits, $2^6 = 64$ codes are possible.

There are 26 alphabetical letters, 10 digits, and 12 or so basic special symbols. Thus, a minimum of 48 codes is necessary to establish a basic character set. A 5-bit "byte" is too small (32 codes); thus a 6-bit code is sufficient and is commonly used to encode a character set. Most computers utilize an 8-bit byte; this allows use of an expanded character set with up to 256 unique codes.

Storing alpha-numerical data requires a minimum of 6 bits per character; numerical information, on the other hand, requires only 4 bits, as there are 10 digits and $2^4 = 16$. In solely numerical applications, this fact is often used to reduce data storage requirements.

The formal terminology for the coding schemes just discussed is as follows:

1. BCD: binary coded decimal, a 6-bit coding scheme;
2. EBCDIC: extended binary coded decimal interchange code, an 8-bit coding scheme utilized by IBM 360/370 computers, among others;
3. packed decimal: a 4-bit scheme for numbers. Two numbers may be "packed" into an 8-bit byte that could otherwise hold only 1 alpha-numerical character.

Arithmetic operations are typically *not* done in BCD or EBCDIC, although this is possible if the computer is so designed. For computation, most systems *convert* (as opposed to *code*) numbers into the binary number system. There follows a brief discussion of number systems.

Number Systems

We are most accustomed to working in the decimal, or base 10, number system. Other bases, such as 2, 8, or 16, are possible. All number systems use the convention of *positional expansion*. The decimal number 4921 really means:

$$4 \times 10^3 + 9 \times 10^2 + 2 \times 10^1 + 1 \times 10^0.$$

In general, any number may be represented as

$$a_1 b^{N1} + a_2 b^{N2} + \ldots + a_K b^0,$$

where

$$b = \text{base of the number system}$$

$$N_i = \text{exponent}$$

$$a_i = \text{coefficient.}$$

Thus 4, 9, 2, and 1 in the decimal number 4921 are coefficients. Only coefficients are shown in the usual presentation of numbers in the decimal system. The position of a coefficient indicates the power (value of the exponent) of the base. This is the key to computer arithmetic.

Most computers are capable of performing decimal arithmetic, but this requires the computer to add digits serially—that is, one at a time, much as humans do mathematical calculations. Other number systems, the binary system in particular, allow the computer to perform calculations by "parallel processing," essentially adding all digits simultaneously in a single operation. This is much faster and more efficient, especially in larger computers. Parallel processing requires that decimal numbers be converted to their equivalents in other number systems. In Fortran, for example, all arithmetic is done in binary (base 2), to allow parallel processing.

Some digital computers make use of the octal system:

$$1(8^2) + 3(8^1) + 2(8^0) = 90.$$

Using subscripts to denote the base,

$$132_8 = 90_{10}$$
$$213_8 = 139_{10}.$$

That is, 132_8 and 90_{10} represent the same *quantity*. Quantity is a concept that may be represented (coded) in many different numbers systems. The position of a coefficient indicates the power of the base.

$$13.4_8 = 1(8^1) + 3(8^0) + 4(8^{-1}) = 11.5_{10}$$

One can count and do arithmetic in the octal system just as in the decimal system.

$$0_{10} = 0_8$$
$$1_{10} = 1_8 \qquad\qquad 8_{10} = 10_8$$
$$\cdot \qquad\qquad \text{but} \qquad 9_{10} = 11_8$$
$$\cdot$$
$$\cdot$$
$$7_{10} = 7_8$$

FIGURE 8.2.   Data Coding and Conversion in a Computer System

```
┌──────────────┐         ╱──────────╲
│ Data in      │        ╱            ╲
│ human-readable│ ───→  │     Key     │
│ form         │        ╲            ╱
└──────────────┘         ╲──────────╱
     Input

                      ╱──────────────╲
                     ╱ Coded          ╱   Hollerith (punch card) or other
                    ╱  Input         ╱            code system
                   ╱───────────────╱
────────────────────────────────────────────────────────────
                   ┌──────────────┐      ⎫ Convert to Binary or
                   │              │      ⎬ Recode to EBCDIC or BCD
                   │              │      ⎭ for Computer Processing
                   └──────────────┘

                   ┌──────────────┐
                   │   Process    │
                   │              │
                   └──────────────┘

                   ┌──────────────┐      ⎫ Convert Internal Code to
                   │              │      ⎬ Human-Readable Code
                   │              │      ⎭
                   └──────────────┘
────────────────────────────────────────────────────────────
                ╱──────────────╲      ┌──────────────┐
               ╱                ╲     │ Data in      │
              ╱     Print        ╲ ──→│ human-readable│
             ╱                    ╲   │ form         │
            ╱──────────────────────╲  └──────────────┘
                                              Output
────────────────────────────────────────────────────────────
```

In general, the largest coefficient in any number system is one less than the base. To illustrate:

$$77_8 + 1_8 = 100_8$$

The binary system (base 2) utilizes only two digits, 0 and 1. Digital computers are two-state. This correspondence and the simplicity of binary arithmetic vastly increase computing speed as compared to performing base 10 (decimal) computations. While it will not be detailed here, all arithmetic functions (multiplication, and so on) are essentially converted to addition in binary arithmetic. Doing this vastly simplifies hardware design considerations and contributes to the speed and efficiency of binary arithmetic.

FIGURE 8.3. Representative Input Codes

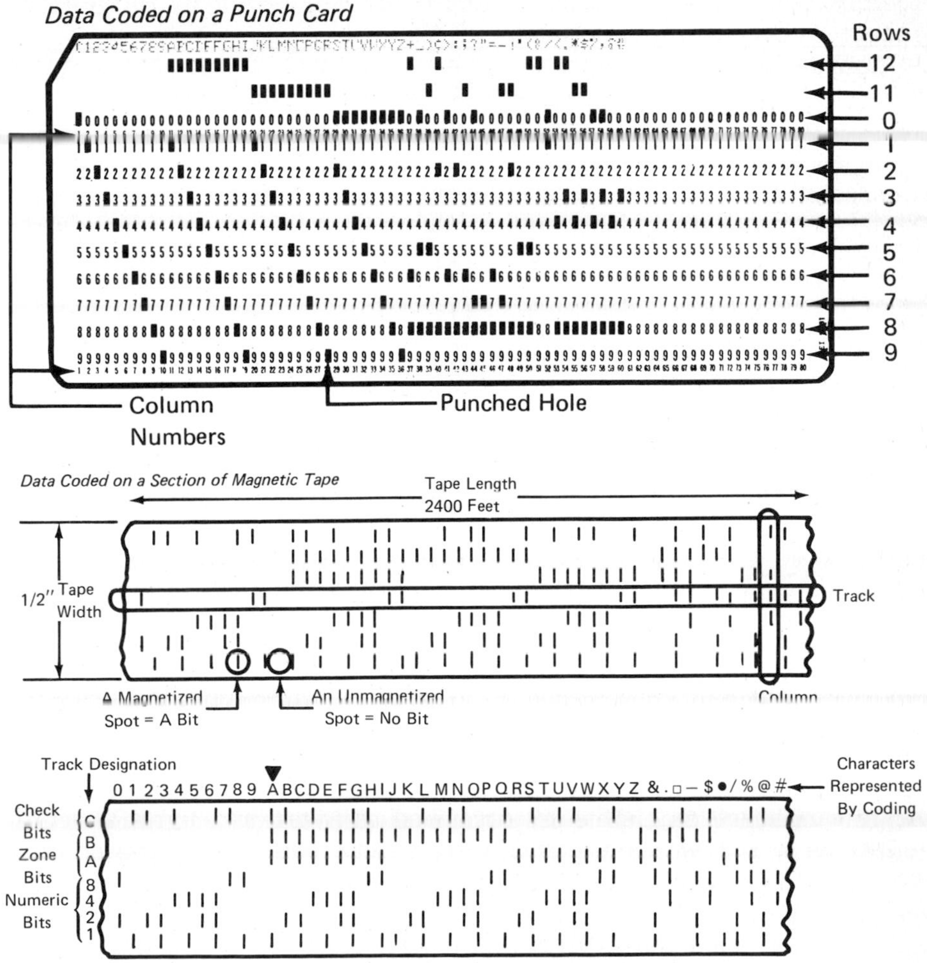

Data Coded on a Punch Card

Data Conversion Sequence

Figure 8.2 is a schema of the data coding and conversion sequence from input to output in a computer system. Input is typically coded (not converted) by a keying operation on some input device such as a card punch or paper or magnetic tape device. Figure 8.3 illustrates two typical input coding schemes, one for cards (the Hollerith code) and one for magnetic tape. For arithmetic, the next step is to convert these coded quantities into their binary equivalents. For alpha-numerical data, these input codes may or may not be converted into other codes; this depends on the input device and the computer system. Translating code to code is straightforward and quite rapid; converting code to binary is more tedious, but this extra effort is more than made up for by the resultant reduction in computational time.

Conversion from one number system to another is essentially a process of repeated division (see figure 8.4). Computers take advantage of the relationships between certain number systems to speed the conversion from decimal to binary numbers. A binary-octal relationship is based on the fact that $2^3 = 8$. This means that each digit in an octal number may be replaced by its 3-digit binary equivalent, viz.:

$$5_8 = 101_2$$
$$7_8 = 111_2$$
$$57_8 = 101\ 111_2$$
$$.1_8 = .001_2$$

The relationship holds equally well for converting binary into octal numbers. This and similar relations are used to speed data conversion: repeated division of a decimal number by 8 is quicker than repeated division by 2. Transforming octal numbers to binary numbers requires no calculation, only direct substitution. Accordingly, conversion time is substantially reduced.

IBM 360/370, as well as other machines, uses hexadecimal (base 16) numbers. The above discussion applies to this system; that is, each hexadecimal digit may be replaced by its 4-digit binary equivalent, as $2^4 = 16$.

Data coding in computers can be summarized by noting that a unit of computer storage consists of some number of bits, each bit representing either 0 or 1. Bits are organized as bytes, and bytes as words; both bytes and words are usually separately addressable. The contents of a hardware byte or word always consists of a number of bits; that is, a string of 0's and 1's. Contents are decoded and interpreted as either instructions, character-coded data, or numerically converted data (binary

FIGURE 8.4.   Conversion of Decimal System to Binary through
Repeated Division

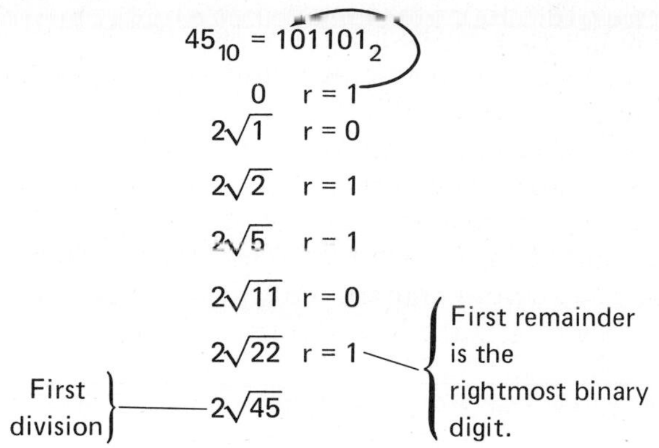

$$45_{10} = 101101_2$$

$$
\begin{array}{ll}
0 & r = 1 \\
2\sqrt{1} & r = 0 \\
2\sqrt{2} & r = 1 \\
2\sqrt{5} & r = 1 \\
2\sqrt{11} & r = 0 \\
2\sqrt{22} & r = 1 \\
\text{First} \\ \text{division} \Big\} \!\!-\!\!-\!\!-\!\! 2\sqrt{45}
\end{array}
$$

First remainder
is the
rightmost binary
digit.

numbers). That is, physical systems are interpreted in terms of numerical and logical systems.

A final point to be noted concerns rounding error. Most business applications demand an equality of debits and credits, and/or penny accuracy in computation. Doing business problems on computers may create problems unless the analyst is aware of the fact that binary-decimal equivalences are not always exact. Rounding errors exist in decimal arithmetic as well as in binary (for example, is 1/3 .333 or .334?), but a decimal calculation involving fractions will often yield a slightly different result from the equivalent binary calculation. Business-oriented programming languages such as Cobol usually accommodate binary-coded decimal arithmetic. While slower than comparable binary arithmetic, the intent is to "mimic" human calculations. Fortran does all arithmetic in binary. Other languages, such as PL/1, give the programmer a choice: BCD or binary calculations. The point is that rounding errors should be expected and hence provided for in any computer-based business application that uses binary arithmetic.

Data Hierarchy and Data Independence

A series of terms is commonly used for specifying the level of codes (hierarchical structure) of computer data representation. From the smallest element of data up to the largest, these terms are bit, character (byte), field, record, file, and data base:

bit—binary digit

character (or byte)—a group of bits treated as a unit; a more meaningful amount of data than contained in a single bit

field—a group of characters treated as a unit, having meaning as a data item beyond the meaning of its component characters

record—a group of fields treated as a unit, aggregating all fields related to some common entity

file—a group of records treated as a unit, all of similar type and aggregating information of common type and purpose

data base—a group of related files. Logically, the term *data base* (or *data bank*) should imply a set of files that are themselves logically compatible in structure and content; however, this is rarely implied when "data base" or "data bank" is used in general publications.

Figure 8.5 illustrates the data hierarchy terminology in a simplified invoice.

In computer-related work, it becomes increasingly important to maintain a distinction between logical and physical data structure. A logical record is the set of information elements descriptive of a single subject, or entity. A physical record is the medium on which information is written or a physically separable portion of a recording medium. Examples are a sheet of paper, a punched card, or the recorded information between gaps of specified size on a magnetic tape. A logical record may require more than one physical record to contain it. Similarly, a physical record might contain more than one logical record. In this case the physical record is called a *block* and the number of logical records it contains is called the blocking factor. Figure 8.6 illustrates both situations. Separating the two concepts of logical and physical structures is called *data independence*. Data independence is an important characteristic of data base systems. Data base concepts are discussed in Chapter 9.

FIGURE 8.5.   Part of a Data Hierarchy

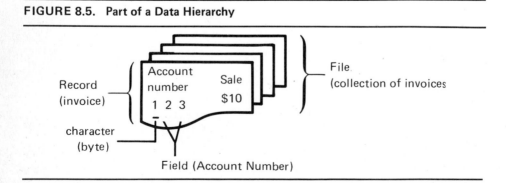

FIGURE 8.6. Logical and Physical Records

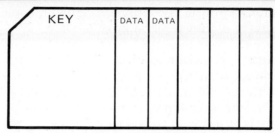

(A) Logical Record Same as Physical Record (One Card)

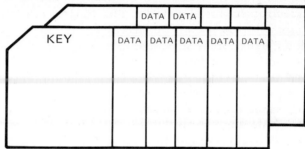

(B) Logical Record More than Physical Record (Two Cards)

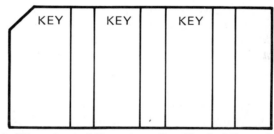

(C) Blocked Records (Three Logical Records on One Physical Record)

ORGANIZATION AND OPERATION OF HARDWARE UNITS

Overlapped Processing and Multiprogramming

To process data on a modern computer system, a specific input unit must be activated, the input read, decoded, and checked, and the data transferred to some form of storage. The circuitry that operates a particular hardware unit is called a control unit. Control units themselves are essentially small computer systems: they accept input, process data, and control output relevant to a particular hardware unit, such as a card reader or tape unit. Control units continue to grow in sophistication and ability as the integrated circuit technology of the late 1970s continues to mature through the 80's.

A "channel" is a hardware unit whose circuitry allows it to control several independent hardware units simultaneously. Channels are used to interface with and decouple the central processing unit from the much slower electromagnetic storage devices and other peripherals (see Figure 8.1). Channels provide independent data paths to and from the main memory. A channel may serve only one high-speed device; in this case it is called a selector channel. Typically channels serve several relatively slow electromechanical devices; this is called multiplexing. These concepts, though perhaps with different terminology, exist in all computers. For example, channels are sometimes called peripheral processors.

Channels and interfaces are associated with third-generation technology. This technology allows *overlapped* or simultaneous processing of independent computer tasks. This distribution of processing tasks between various hardware units greatly increases the overall throughput of a modern computer system.

The goal of overlapped processing (see Figure 8.7) is to keep the fast, expensive central processing unit active on productive tasks. Program requests for input or output are delegated to channels to control rather than having the CPU itself control data transfer between main storage and other devices. This is a decoupling mechanism used to adjust for the vast speed differences between the CPU and other devices.

Several channels and devices may operate simultaneously, moving data to and from buffer areas in main storage. A buffer area is a partition of main storage reserved for a particular program. Several programs are resident (stored) in separate buffer areas in main storage at the same time in most computer systems. However the CPU typically works on (processes) only one program at a time. This procedure is called multiprogramming.

Under multiprogramming, a specific program request to transfer data to or from auxiliary storage causes an interrupt. An interrupt is a control step executed by the multiprogramming operating system; through this software procedure the CPU transfers/delegates this task to a channel for execution, and the CPU moves to work on another program while awaiting execution of the data transfer operation. Without overlapped processing, the CPU would be idle until completion of the relatively slow data transfer operation between main storage and an auxiliary storage device.

There are many input-output (I/O) and secondary storage devices. A

FIGURE 8.7. Overlapped Processing

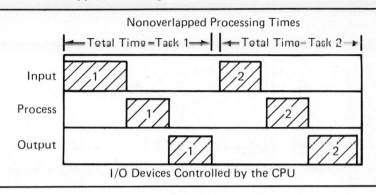

Nonoverlapped Processing Times

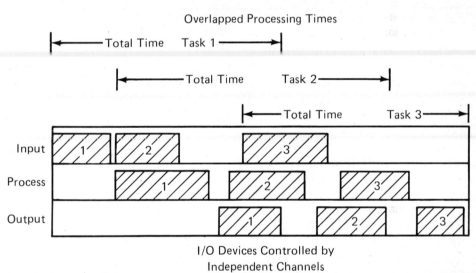

card punch, card reader, and line printer are common to most systems. These devices are not storage devices per se, but their media (cards and paper) are frequently used as secondary storage. Two other devices that are common to file processing are tape and disk drive units. Tapes and disk units are discussed below in turn, as their structure is essential to an understanding of the mechanics of file processing.

Magnetic Tape

Magnetic tape and associated drive units are very common to computer operations. Tape units operate analogously to common reel-to-reel units

FIGURE 8.8.   Magnetic Tape Schematic

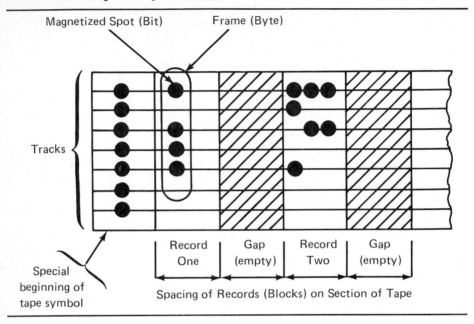

for home use, except that they typically utilize a digital rather than audio recording technique. They are large, of high quality, and of relatively high cost. We are more interested in the tape than the tape drive unit.

Magnetic tape (Figure 8.8) typically allows the coding of one character per "frame" in either a 7-track (6 bits + parity) or a 9-track (8 bits + parity) format. Nine-track tape is typically associated with EBCDIC (IBM 360/370), 7-track with BCD. The tape unit has a separate read/write head for each track. The tape itself is marked with special beginning- and end-of-tape symbols, which are sensed and used by the tape drive control unit. The tape operates like common recording tape—it can be read, erased, and rewritten.

One significant difference that warrants attention is the blocking of data records on magnetic tape. To operate properly, the tape must pass under the read/write heads at a certain speed, otherwise the pickup is distorted. In order for the tape to accelerate and stop without losing (bypassing) data, gaps (blank tape) must be left between records. A typical tape recording density is 1,600 Bpi (bytes per inch). A punched card holds 80 characters, and a 3/4″ gap is required by most tape drive units to start or stop. If card images were placed on tape one by one with separating gaps, the tape would have this format:

FIGURE 8.9. Storage Device Comparison

Storage Device	Average Access Time	Maximum Transfer Rate	Typical Storage Capacity
Semiconductor Memory	.5 microsecond	8000 KB/sec	100 KB
Core Memory	1 microsecond	4000 KB/sec	100 KB
Disk (Large)	30 milliseconds	806 KB/sec	800 MB
Diskette	500 milliseconds	31 KB/sec	250 KB
Magnetic Tape	1 minute	320 KB/sec	10 MB
Cassette Tape	5 minutes	400 Bytes/sec	120 KB
Punch Card	1 minute	1 KB/sec	80 characters per card
Sheet of Paper	1 minute	—	1000 characters per page

micro = 1 millionth   KB = Kilobyte   (1000 bytes)
milli = 1 thousandth   MB = Megabyte (1000 000 bytes)

3/4″ gap   1/20″ data (card image)   3/4″ gap.

Approximately 3 percent of the tape would be used for data; the rest would be blank. Thus, logical records are typically "blocked" on tape to increase storage efficiency. That is, several logical records are physically written as one unit between gaps. Blocking ten cards, for example, would raise storage efficiency to 25 percent. Once in main memory, logical records are unblocked and separately processed by the logic of the related program.

The most significant feature of magnetic tape is that it is inherently a sequential recording medium. Data on tape must be accessed sequentially. Other features are a large data capacity and high speed of operation when compared to standard punch cards (see Figure 8.9). A tape is relatively low in cost (about $20) and is reusable, unlike punched cards. A single reel of tape can hold data equivalent to that which could be placed on thousands of punched cards. For these reasons, keypunched data is typically transferred to magnetic tape prior to processing.

Magnetic Disk

The most common high-speed random-access storage medium is the disk. This consists of a rotating magnetically coated surface and an arm that can position a head over any section of the disk. As the disk rotates, every position on the track under the head becomes available. Any position on the disk can be accessed by a combination of head movement and rotation. There are some disks that have a head per track. These are called fixed-head disks, because the heads do not move to get to a particular track. These fixed-head disks have a higher access rate: that is, it takes less time to get to a particular sector since there is no head movement. They are, typically, more expensive, since there are more heads and more electronics required. The moving-head disk has only a single recording head. It takes longer to get to a specified sector, since the time taken to move the arm may be quite long relative to the disk rotation time. Another distinction is fixed versus removable disks. Some disk units have only a fixed disk: that is, the magnetic disk is part of the disk unit and cannot be simply removed or exchanged for another disk. Other units have only removable disks: that is, the recording disks can be removed from the disk unit. Doing this permits the storage and exchange of data. Many disk units have both a fixed and a removable disk. These permit some of the stored information, such as programs and tables, to be maintained, while the variable data can be taken off-line and stored, or moved to other disk systems. A recent development is the advent of removable disk packs which contain the read/write head as part of the removable package. The full-size disk systems are quite large and expensive and require sophisticated interfaces and power supplies. They have high reliability, large capacity, and a long history of operation.

A disk itself is similar to a phonograph record, except that there are several concentric tracks, as opposed to a single spiraling track. (Figure 8.10) A disk pack is a collection of disks that revolve at high speed on a common drive shaft. A single track holds several thousand bytes, so several records typically reside on a single track. Tracks are addressable by specifying the device (disk drive or pack), the face (surface), and the track number itself. Records within a track itself are not directly addressable. Newer disk systems approach specific record retrieval through software controls that divide a disk face into several sectors. These sector numbers become part of the disk addressing system.

Records on disks (and all other direct access storage devices, abbreviated DASD) may be retrieved directly as opposed to sequentially—as is necessary on common magnetic tape.

Records on a disk may also be retrieved sequentially—if they are organized to facilitate this form of retrieval. When used to store records sequentially, a moving-head disk system utilizes the concept of a cylinder —a vertical collection of tracks (that is, track 1, face 1; track 1, face 2, . . . track 1, face N). (See Figure 8.10.) Records are often grouped by cylinder on disks to minimize the physical movement of read/write heads, which is relatively slow compared to the electronic read/write operation itself.

FIGURE 8.10.   Magnetic Disk Schematic

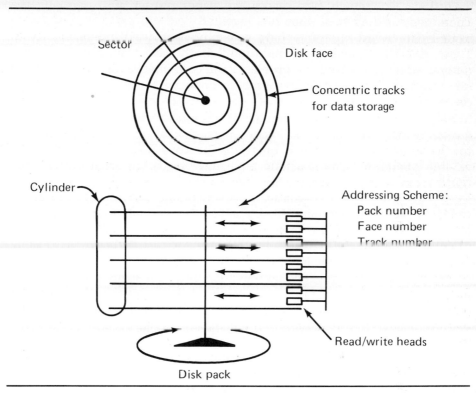

There are other DASD's (drums and data cells, for example), but their differences, mainly cost, volume, and access time, are not significant for discussion here. Disks are by far the most common DASD. Disks allow direct as well as sequential accessing of data. Disk storage is expensive compared to tape for off-line storage, but comparable for on-line storage, as the cost of the respective drive units is about the same. The average access time for disk storage is less than that of tape, and a disk can typically transfer data at a higher rate than magnetic tape (see Figure 8.9).

Computer Output on Microfilm

A final class of devices to be discussed concerns computer output on microfilm (COM). Computer systems are inherently plagued by an imbalance of speeds. Over three generations of computers, processing speeds have advanced from milliseconds to microseconds to nanoseconds (one billionth of a second). However, I/O devices have not shared in this evolution. The punch card reader and paper printer are essentially the same today as they were when first invented.

Computers and microfilm have generally been used independently to cope with the "paperwork explosion." Both have been successful, but neither alone has solved the problem. The combination of computers and microfilm is increasingly being used to cope with the computer output problem.

The COM is a device that records computer data on microfilm in human-readable form. It is a recorder which may be connected directly to the computer for on-line operation or to a magnetic tape unit for off-line operation. The magnetic tape unit "reads" information into the COM from a magnetic tape that previously has been recorded directly from the computer. Alternatively, independent vendors allow outside processing of files into microfilm, a service increasingly available to firms who do not wish to buy or lease the necessary and relatively expensive COM equipment.

There are several similar techniques for generating COM. The most common method produces computer-generated microfilm records with no intervening paper copy. This is achieved by converting the computer digital signals to voltages, which are applied to a cathode ray tube. This process results in the information's being displayed on the cathode ray tube screen in human-understandable form. The microfilm record is produced by photographing the information displayed on the cathode ray tube.

The most obvious advantage of computer output on microfilm is the speed at which data is recorded. A COM may "print" upward of 32,000 lines per minute, as compared to 1,200 lines per minute for an impact printer. This means that one COM device can handle the volume of about 30 impact printers. Important secondary advantages are reduced record sizes and weight, which entail cost reductions for storage, handling, and supplies. Space reductions of 90 to 95 percent are typically realized through the use of COM.

REVIEW QUESTIONS

1. Identify the physical components of a computer data processing system.

2. Identify the major features of the hardware organization of a typical computer system.

3. Define the term *software*. What different types of software are used in computer systems?

4. Distinguish between batch processing and time-sharing in a computer system.

5. Define the following terms:
   a. bit
   b. byte
   c. word
   d. BCD
   e. EBCDIC
   f. packed decimal

6. Why is an arithmetic operation performed by a computer not always exactly equal to the same computation performed manually?

7. Define the term *data hierarchy* as it relates to computer data processing.

8. Are a physical record and a logical record always the same in computer data processing? Explain.

9. Why are multiprogramming and overlapped processing important attributes of computer processing?

10. What role does an input/output (I/O) channel occupy in a computer system?

11. Define the following terms concerning magnetic tape operation:
    a. track
    b. block
    c. interrecord gap
    d. frame

12. Define the following terms concerning magnetic disk operation:
    a. track
    b. face
    c. cylinder
    d. disk pack

13. Contrast the record retrieval capabilities of magnetic tape and magnetic disk.

14. Disks and other DASDs are said to be "updated in place," while magnetic tape is not. Explain. What significance might this hold for backup considerations of an important data file?

15. What is COM? What uses and advantages does COM offer as an alternative to printed output?

16. Indicate the role(s) that each of the following devices plays in the data processing cycle (input, storage, process, output):
    a. CPU
    b. magnetic tape drive unit
    c. card reading unit

    d. magnetic disk unit
    e. COM
    f. video display terminal

DISCUSSION QUESTIONS AND PROBLEMS

17. What is the binary (base 2) representation of the following base 10 values:

a.	7	d.	71
b.	13	e.	93
c.	28	f.	428

18. Compute the decimal (base 10) equivalents of the following numbers:

    a. 111000 (base 2)
    b. 101010 (base 2)
    c. 106 (base 8)
    d. 3001 (base 8)
    e. 121 (base 16)

19. Discuss whether the use of computer output microfilming would be appropriate in the following situations:

    a. filing name and address changes on a customer mailing list
    b. storage of canceled checks and bank statements
    c. storage of charge sale slips

20. A disk has 200 cylinders. There are 10 recording surfaces per disk pack and each track can hold 7,200 bytes.

  a. What is the maximum capacity of each cylinder? Of the entire disk pack?
  b. Assume that a file has 1,200 records, each 600 bytes long. Calculate:
    1. records per track;
    2. number of tracks required; and
    3. number of cylinders required for the file.

21. A recent study has indicated that about 60 percent of all computer-related fraud in the government might be attributed to the input of fraudulent data for computer processing.

What does this suggest concerning the design of computer-based AIS?

22. Batch processing and time-sharing are two general approaches to computer processing. Discuss the relative appropriateness of each of these approaches in the following application areas:

    a. posting customer payments and withdrawals made at a bank
    b. payroll processing in a manufacturing firm
    c. order-entry in a wholesale distributor
    d. depreciation calculations and debt amortization

23. Discuss the effect of computer technology on AIS in terms of:
    a. speed of processing and retrieval of data
    b. volume of data processing
    c. complexity of system design and operation

24. Inventory records will be stored on magnetic tape. The tapes that will be used are 2400 feet long with a density of 1600 bytes per inch. The interblock gap is .6 inch. The inventory records are a fixed length of 400 bytes each.
    a. How many records may be stored on a reel of tape if four records are combined as a block?
    b. How many records may be stored on a single reel if the blocking factor is increased to eight records per block?
    c. By storing the inventory records in "packed decimal" format, 60 percent of the data in each record could be stored at two characters per byte of storage. If the blocking factor is kept at four records per block, how many records could be stored on a reel of tape?

25.* Huron Company manufactures and sells eight major product lines with fifteen to twenty-five items in each product line. All sales are on credit, and orders are received by mail or telephone. Huron Co. has a computer-based system that employs magnetic tape as a file medium.

All sales orders received during regular working hours are typed on Huron's own sales order form immediately. This typed form is the source document for the keypunching of a shipment or backorder card for each item ordered. These cards are employed in the after hours processing at night to complete all necessary record keeping for the current day and to facilitate the shipment of goods the following day. In summary, an order received one day is to be processed that day and night and shipped the next day.

The daily processing which has to be accomplished at night includes the following activities:
    a. Preparing the invoice to be sent to the customer at the time of shipment;
    b. updating accounts receivable file;
    c. updating finished goods inventory;

*Adapted from C.M.A. Examination.

    d. listing of all items backordered and short.

Required:

    a. Identify the master files that Huron Company should maintain in this system to provide for the daily processing. Indicate the data content that should be included in each file and the order in which each file should be maintained.

    b. Employing the symbols shown in the chapter, prepare a systems flowchart of the daily processing required to update the finished goods inventory records and to produce the necessary inventory reports (assume that the necessary magnetic tape devices are available).

26. This problem is a continuation of the Pepper Co. problem at the end of Chapter 7 (page 207). The Pepper Co. has decided to purchase a computer system. Your task is to provide systems flowcharts for the revised accounts receivable application system. Assume that all master files will be stored on magnetic tape.

ORGANIZING DATA FOR COMPUTER PROCESSING

9

This chapter discusses concepts and techniques that are used to organize accounting data for computer processing. Most accounting application systems process and maintain files of data. Examples include processing sales transactions against accounts receivable files, purchase orders against inventory files, and payroll data against employee master files.

Basic file processing alternatives can be illustrated by analogy to a file of documents contained in a single drawer of a file cabinet. Consider a search for a single document in this file. One might begin with the first document, and search the subsequent documents sequentially until the desired document is found. If the file were subdivided by some observable index (such as key letters or numbers displayed in plastic tags), a better starting point for the search could be found by using the index to bypass unwanted documents. And if each *document* were identified by some observable code such as a plastic tab, it would be possible to locate the desired document directly, without having to examine any other documents. These basic alternatives in data manipulation are fundamental in computer data processing as well, and are discussed in the following sections.

ELEMENTS OF FILE ORGANIZATION

In the data hierarchy, a file is a collection of records. File organization concerns the position of records relative to each other. It is necessary in most cases to distinguish between logical and physical file structure. The physical organization of records is concerned with where they are placed in storage and how they are blocked together. Records that are organized sequentially need not be placed contiguous to each other, nor need they be used in the order in which they are stored. That is, a file's logical structure may be different from its physical structure. Alternatively, these may be the same, as in a sequential file on punched cards.

Record Key and File Sequence

An important concept is that of a record identifier or key field. A file is usually sequenced on its most-often-used or its most important field, called the sort or record key. A telephone book is most often searched by name. When we wish to search a file by a field other than the one that determines the sequence, we are not lacking information about the structure of the file, but we are unable to find beforehand where the record we wish is located. This is a condition of *relative random order*. A file that is sequenced, for example, on employee's names will be in random sequence relative to date of birth. A minor (or subordinate) sort key is a field used to determine relative position among a set of records when the primary key, or sequencing field, has the same value in each record of the set. An automobile manufacturer might keep a cumulative sales file sequenced on make (for example, Chevrolet, Buick, or Pontiac), body style (sedan, convertible), color, and region of the country where sold. This file has four sort keys and two other fields (sales registered and orders received) relative to which the file is in random order. Correlation among fields within a record is illustrated by a library catalogue sequenced on document accession number. If access numbers are assigned sequentially as new documents arrive, then a file in this sequence is approximately in sequence by date of publication of the documents being catalogued. Sequentially numbered purchase orders are approximately in sequence relative to the date on which the purchase order was issued.

Record Design Considerations

Records within a file may be either of fixed length or variable length. In a fixed-length record, both the number of fields and the length (character size) of each field are fixed. Fixed-length records are easier to manipulate in computer applications then are variable-length records because the size of fixed-length records is standardized. Most records stored and processed on direct-access storage devices (DASDs) are fixed-length.

The drawback of fixed-length records is that each field in a fixed-length record must be large enough to contain the maximum expected entry in the field. This typically results in wasted space, as in leaving twenty-five or so spaces for a name, where many names have eight characters or fewer. Variable-length records may be of any size. The end of a variable record must be indicated by a special symbol or a record-length field contained within the record itself. Variable-length records efficiently utilize available storage space, but manipulating such records is relatively more difficult.

One approach to variable-length records that does not require programming system support of variable-length records is to use fixed-length trailer records. A trailer record is an extension of a master record. It is separate from the master and written as required. Using an open-item accounts receivable file as an example, the master records contain information common to all accounts, and the number of invoices sufficient for most of the accounts, while the trailer record contains more invoices. A master may have as many trailer records associated with it as are required. The trailer records may be written immediately after the associated master record. As with most computer design, record-length design requires trade-offs between storage efficiency and usage efficiency.

Hardware Considerations

Computer equipment affects the cost and speed of file operations, and these are typically important measures of performance in a data processing system. If a file is seldom used, has modest requirements placed upon it for search completion time, and is searched only on its key field, it can safely be placed on a slow, inexpensive storage medium such as magnetic tape. A file that is frequently searched or requires quick responses, or one for which any of its fields might be used as search parameters calls for faster memory, such as disk storage. Economic and other factors may change the relative merits of the various storage media. For example, it may be cheaper to maintain multiple copies of files on less expensive, sequential-search media, and to search in parallel, than it is to obtain a single, high-access-speed, very expensive memory unit.

File organization is a design problem largely for one reason: there is a finite access time for information stored in any storage device. Access time is the time required to find information stored at a known location; it depends on such factors as disk rotation speed and the rate at which a reading device traverses tracks on a disk. The computer's main memory is quite fast, although it, too, has a finite access time. The kinds of files with which we are concerned are generally so large that they do not fit in main memory and reside instead on larger-capacity, slower, and less expensive auxiliary memories, such as magnetic disks or tape. Except for primary memory, access time is variable and depends on where the particular item of information is stored relative to the location or status of a reading device. Access cost is largely a function of access time.

Since a typical access time to a magnetic disk record is on the order of tens of milliseconds (ten to one hundred milliseconds) and a computer can execute on the order of one to ten million instructions per second, a computer could execute tens of thousands of commands during a single disk seek cycle. If the machine is so programmed as to take maximum advantage of this (multiprogramming), the cost of access delay is little or nothing. If the delay time cannot be used to advantage, the computer may spend most of its time doing nothing but waiting for input or output commands to be carried out. Information can be moved in memory only at a cost. To insert an item between adjacent items requires moving one of them or changing the concept of file organization so that records may be in logical order without being in physical order; that is, the order of retrieval can follow a sequence different from that in which records are stored.

Access Methods

There are three categories of access, of which only two are typically available for file organization.

1. Equal access, often called "random" access, is true only for totally magnetic storage devices. A computer's main (primary) storage is the best common example. In equal access, access time is independent of the previous access. This is not true for electromechanical storage devices (DASDs and tape). This is the most expensive and quickest form of storage, and usually the most limited. Such storage is typically not used for accounting application files.

2. Direct access: this category is best illustrated by magnetic disks. The characteristic of disks is that access to any given record can be gained by moving the read mechanism at high speed directly to the track containing the record, without reading all intervening data. This access is fast compared to magnetic tape access time, even when data-read rates are comparable. Reading from a disk is sequential within a track, usually a fixed-length region within a disk. Access time to a point on a disk includes a starting time for the read mechanism to overcome inertia, stopping time, the time required to move at a constant speed across the face of the disk, and the time to await the beginning of the track rotating under the read head. Direct access, then, applies to storage devices that do not have equal access characteristics, but which do allow a reading device to move directly to a desired area in storage without reading all intervening information.

3. Sequential access: magnetic tape, paper tape, and a deck of punched cards stacked in a card reader are illustrations of a sequential access memory. In these media it is necessary to start at one end of a file and work sequentially down toward the other end to do a search. It is not normally possible to skip or bypass any portion of the storage area.

File organization techniques utilize some combination of the above access methods: typically direct, sequential, or a combination of these two. Common file organization techniques are discussed in the following section.

FILE ORGANIZATION TECHNIQUES

There are many factors to consider in the organization of a file of data for computer processing. First, one should identify the objective—that is, the intended uses—of the file itself. These objectives must then be balanced against available access methods, type of equipment (DASD, tape, card), the size of the file itself, and the user-oriented constraints of cost, security, and privacy considerations. These considerations are truly interacting.

The main objectives for an accounting-related file are processing (keeping records current) and inquiry/search (obtaining selected information on a subset of a file). With respect to objectives, the most important consideration is timeliness. In what time frame should transactions be posted and requests for file data provided? For example, it may be desirable to post withdrawals to a bank's customer files as quickly as possible after the transaction occurs. But this time frame may not be appropriate to posting payments to a retail firm's accounts receivable file. As a general rule, the shorter the time frame, the more expensive the associated processing costs. These increased processing costs, however, must be balanced against the value of having current and timely information available to users.

The three most common file processing techniques are sequential, direct, and indexed-sequential. This section discusses in turn each of these file organization techniques.

Sequential File Organization

In sequential file organization, records are stored physically in order by the record key. (If, for example, the records are for employees and the key is employee payroll number, employee 475 will precede employee 478 on the physical file storage.) Sequential file organization is very common because it makes effective use of the least expensive file medium —magnetic tape—and because sequential processing at periodic intervals using a batch of transactions is very cost-efficient. A disk storage device can be used much like a magnetic tape. The data records are stored sequentially by cylinder to minimize access time. Records may be stored in either ascending or descending order.

With respect to processing sequential files, two points must be noted.

First, transactions are normally batched and must be sorted into key order prior to processing them against the sequential master file. Second, the entire file must typically be passed, regardless of the number of records to be processed against the file.

Sequential file organization is simply a sequential listing of records on a sequential access storage medium, commonly magnetic tape. Computer processing of a sequential file requires that the file be loaded on a reading device and read from beginning to end regardless of the number of specific records that are to be located. The total cost of locating one, ten, or a thousand records is about the same, since the entire file must be read in each case. Accordingly, the average cost per record located decreases as the number of records located increases. Batching groups of transactions to be processed against a sequential file lowers the average cost of each transaction processed.

Figure 9.1 is a program flowchart of sequential file processing. This figure illustrates the necessity of sorting transactions into the same sequence as the master file to the overall efficiency of sequential file processing. Locating a record in the master file for each transaction requires that transactions be in the same sequence as the master file. Once a record in a sequential file has been read and released, and the following record has been located, the previous record cannot economically be retrieved. If transactions are processed out of key field sequence, many transactions will not be processed because their corresponding record in the master file will have already been located and released in this pass of the file. Doing this would severely reduce the efficiency of batch processing. Thus both batching and sorting of transactions are fundamental to the efficiency of sequential file processing.

Direct-Access File Organization

Direct-access file organization techniques utilize on-line equipment (DASDs) to speed record processing. Each record in a direct-access file has a storage location (address) that bears some relationship to the records key field. In direct-access files, a record key connotes the absolute location of the record; in a sequential file, record key connotes only relative location. In a sequential file we know that the record for employee 475 is located before the record for employee 478; however, it may or may not be *immediately* in front of record 478, depending on whether or not there is a 476 and/or 477.

Different DASDs influence direct access organization to some extent, but the principles are basically the same. We shall utilize disk as our example. There are several addressing methods used to store and locate

FIGURE 9.1.   Sequential File Processing Logic

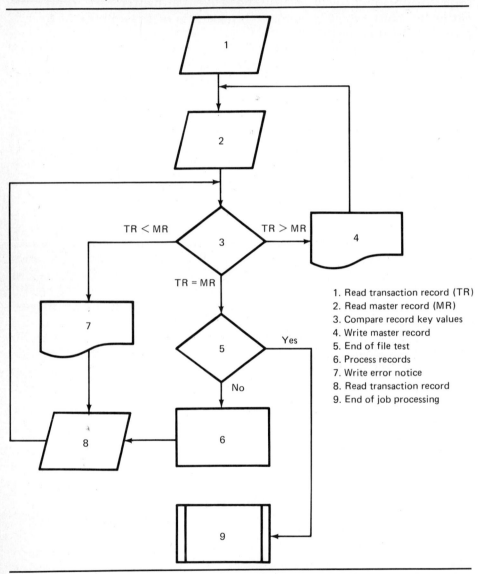

1. Read transaction record (TR)
2. Read master record (MR)
3. Compare record key values
4. Write master record
5. End of file test
6. Process records
7. Write error notice
8. Read transaction record
9. End of job processing

records in a direct access file. One method is to have a record's key field correspond directly to the coding scheme used by the computer itself to identify the physical address on a DASD. A related method is to store physical device addresses as a field within a file's records. Neither of these methods requires any conversion of the key prior to access. Neither of these methods is widely used, as storage location addresses are rarely suitable as record identifiers, and there are security and systems man-

---

FIGURE 9.2.   The Use of a Direct-Access File

Processing Logic Flowchart

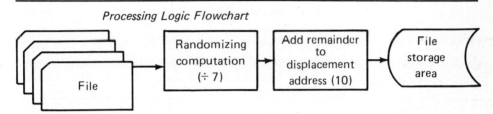

File Loading Illustration

Record	Key	Remainder after division by seven	+	Displacement factor (initial address of file area)	=	Record storage address	
1	15	1		10		11	
2	17	3		10		13	Overflow
3	11	4		10		14	
4	22	1		10		11	

Storage Area Contents after Loading

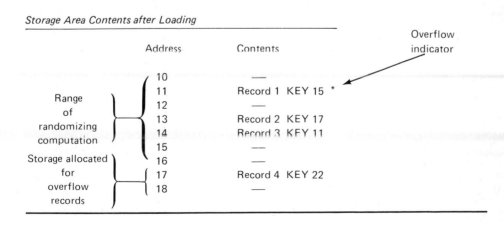

agement problems associated with users' knowing actual physical storage locations.

Most direct-access file systems convert a key to a storage location address through use of either an index (table) or a randomizing transformation. Indexing is relatively straightforward, but indexes are relatively expensive to maintain. The index must be searched for every access to the file. Depending on the file size, this can be a time-consuming operation. Indexes may be factored into subindexes to speed access, but this increases maintenance costs. Indexes are discussed in more detail in the section on indexed sequential files.

A randomizing transformation is a widely used method of storing and locating records in a direct-access file. Figure 9.2 illustrates the use of a randomizing transformation to load a file on a disk. There are four records in the file; in turn each record key is used in a mathematical calculation (divide by seven, note the remainder, and add a displacement factor). Once the file is loaded, any record may be directly accessed by passing the key through the randomizing calculation to determine its address; the device then directly accesses this particular record, bypassing all other records in the file.

Figure 9.2 illustrates several important concepts relating to direct-access file organization. The first is the use of a randomizing transformation to store and access individual records. Note that dividing by 7 yields 7 possible remainders (0 through 6); dividing by a prime number yields remainders that should tend to be uniformly and randomly distributed (thus the term *random access* is often used synonymously with *direct access*). In addition, it is very likely that several different records will randomize ("hash") to the same physical address. Both of these points are significant. The first means that the storage space required for the file is largely determined by the range of the transformation results (0 to 7 in the example), even if the file is expected to be smaller than this. The second point is called overflow, and means that some method of storing and retrieving overflow must be built into the system. In Figure 9.2, two records are hashed to the same address, requiring that one of them be stored in a different location. Overflows occur when two or more records (called synonyms) yield the same address; in such cases, a special pointer field is used to indicate the addresses of the locations used to store overflow records. Note that overflow considerations required storage space in addition to that required by the randomizing transformation. The overall result is that storage efficiency is typically not high in direct-access files.

The drawbacks of vacant storage and overflow considerations are typically more than offset by the advantages of direct-access file organization. Direct access permits nonsequential updating—there is no need to sort and batch transactions. In fact, in a straight direct-access file update, nothing would be gained by batching and sorting transactions. Another major advantage of direct-access files is the speed of access to individual records. Often such speed is essential—as in an airline reservation system or a stock market quotation system. In addition, direct-access organization permits simultaneous updating of several related files. A sale affects both inventory and receivable files. If the inventory and receivable files are direct-access, both may be updated in a single pass of an invoice by noting both inventory number and customer number, using each key to directly access and update the respective records. If both files were sequential, separate passes (and separate sorts) would be needed to accomplish this same task.

Indexed Sequential File Organization

An indexed sequential file is a sequential file stored on a DASD, with an address index based on record key. Such files are commonly referred to as ISAM files, a contraction of the name indexed sequential access method. ISAM is a powerful compromise between sequential and direct-access file organizations, providing the capabilities of both at a reasonable increase in cost over either. ISAM files typically require more software support and maintenance than either sequential or direct files do. Software packages are usually bought from a vendor (as are most file organization software systems). ISAM organization is supported by Cobol and other business-oriented languages and is increasingly being supported by manufacturers of small-business computers.

The concept of ISAM may also be illustrated by an analogy with the location of a name in a telephone book. A search for a particular name is facilitated through the use of the index appearing at the top of each page (first and last name on the page). A user starts his search by selecting the appropriate telephone book (by analogy the correct file), then searches the page index (by analogy, an index where the "pages" are appropriate storage quantities: for example, a cylinder in a disk system); finally, after locating the correct page, the user searches the page sequentially until the desired entry is located. An ISAM file, like a telephone book, is basically a sequential file with an index that is used to provide a good starting point for individual record inquiries. The use of the index allows a search to bypass unwanted entries without having to retrieve them, which is necessary (and time-consuming) in a pure sequential file. However, since an ISAM file is in sequential order, it may be processed sequentially. Doing so does not require the use of the index. Direct-access files cannot be processed sequentially.

Thus, the twin objectives of file usage—processing and inquiry—are both addressed by ISAM organization. The processing of a batch of records may be done sequentially, while individual inquiries to the file may be handled through the use of the index. Inquiries are not as "direct" as they are in a direct-access file, but, as direct-access files themselves may be based on indexes, this difference is a matter of degree.

The more detailed the index, the quicker the access; the trade-off occurs in maintaining the index. Consider first a main file in sequence and an index (list of keys and record locations) to that file. If every record key is represented in the index (not normally necessary), then each time a main file record is added or deleted, the index must be changed. If, as is more likely, only every nth record, or the first or last record in a major memory subdivision, is represented in the index, then the index need not be changed so often, but it is always necessary to check to see whether this is the case. Depending on file volatility (the number of additions or deletions to a file), the cost of maintaining indexes can be high.

Economic Relations between File Organization Techniques

The file organization techniques just discussed (sequential, direct, and ISAM) are appropriate in different circumstances. The basic economics of file processing are largely determined by the size of the files, activity ratios (the number of active records/the number of records in the file), and the desired response time for processing and inquiries.

Figure 9.3 compares the average cost/transaction processed for these three techniques over a range of activity ratios. Sequential organization is essentially a fixed-cost approach to file processing as contrasted to direct-access organization which is essentially a variable-cost approach. In direct-access, each record processed costs about the same, regardless of the number of records processed. For high activity, this is expensive relative to sequential. In sequential, the total costs are largely fixed (loading and passing the entire tape); as these costs are spread over more and more transactions, the cost per transaction decreases rapidly. ISAM offers a middle ground; for low activity, records may be accessed through the index; for high activity, the index is ignored and the file is processed sequentially. For either low or high activity, ISAM is less attractive than either direct or sequential; however, for a file with both low and high activity requirements, ISAM offers economic advantages over either of the other two methods.

A second dimension concerns response time. Figure 9.4 outlines the

FIGURE 9.3.   Unit Costs and File Activity

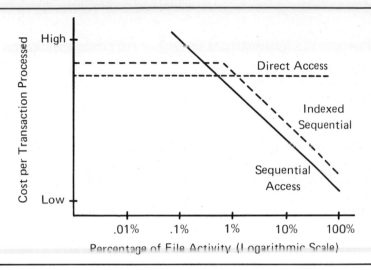

Adapted with permission from *Information Systems—Technology, Economics, Applications, Management* (SRA, 1979) by Chris Mader, p. 191.

FIGURE 9.4.   Unit Costs and Response Time

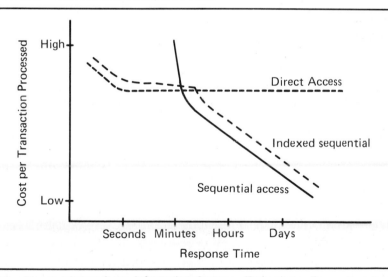

Adapted with permission from *Information Systems—Technology, Economics, Applications, Management* (SRA, 1979) by Chris Mader, p. 192.

basic relationships of cost per transaction to response time for the three file methods. Direct-access files are necessary for very quick response times; longer response times (hours or more) can be economically handled by sequential files. Such inquiries are typically appended to file processing runs. For example, a copy of customers' records can be obtained as a by-product of posting invoices to the accounts receivable file. ISAM again offers a middle ground. Short-response-time requests may be processed through use of the index; longer-response-time requests may be appended to any sequential processing runs against the file.

Although this discussion has been brief, it has made and supported a major point—the economics of file processing require that file organizations be carefully matched to the anticipated use of a particular file. The major considerations are file activity and response times. A careful analysis of these factors, and others, is essential to the design of file processing systems.

DATA MANAGEMENT CONCEPTS

The file organization techniques just discussed—sequential, direct, and indexed-sequential—concern the organization of files by a single key field (the record identifier, such as employee or customer number) selected at the time the file is initially created. The organization of files on the basis of any one single key offers minimal data retrieval abilities to the users of an AIS.

A customer file, for example, is typically organized on the key field "customer number." Consider a user request for a report that lists "all customers in the state of New York whose outstanding balances are greater than $5000." Access to the customer file is based on customer number, but customer number is not the attribute that is the object of this inquiry. The customer file is in relative random order with respect to state and outstanding balance when it is organized on the key field customer number. The production of the requested report would thus entail the examination of every individual record in the customer file to determine whether the state and outstanding balance qualified that record for inclusion in the report. This task would probably necessitate the development of a special application program to be processed against the customer file. The net result would likely be a significant cost and time delay to the user who requested the report. Problems of this type are very common in computerized AIS.

The above example illustrates that just because data is stored and processed by a computer it is not always readily and/or cost-effectively available in a form desired by a user. Since the mid-1960s, the use of large-scale computerized information systems by all types of organizations and the subsequent dependence on the computer-based information system to provide information to a wide variety of users has increased concern for the type of problem just illustrated. The need to integrate scattered files and data into a more cost-effective data base has stimulated a great deal of interest in the concept of data management.

Data management is a term that refers to the overall management of an organization's data base. A *data base* is the collection of all data files stored as part of an information system. Data management refers to the problems of developing and utilizing programming languages (software) to handle various types of data structures. The objective of data management is to increase the utility of an information system.

Organizing Data for Information Retrieval

Data structure concerns both the physical and logical organization of individual data items (records or fields) in a data base. Data structures may be distinguished on the basis of relative levels of complexity. Sequential, direct, and index-sequential file organization techniques each support a data structure based on a single attribute: the key field value. Such techniques offer minimal data retrieval abilities. Several other techniques have emerged since the mid-1960s to alleviate the mismatch between the complex, multiattribute information retrieval demands of users and the single-attribute retrieval capabilities supported by traditional file organization techniques. These techniques concern the physical organization and logical relationships of data on storage devices and typically require the use of DASDs.

There are two basic techniques used to organize data to facilitate multiattribute inquiries. One is to create inverted files; the other is to add pointer fields to records that point to (that is, supply the address of) the next logical record with the same attribute. Inverted files themselves may utilize pointers; upon close analysis, pointers and inverted files are seen to differ mainly in form, not concept. The basic idea is to organize data prior to its use through some sort of coding process.

Inverted Files

Any record attribute can be extracted from the records in a file and used to build a new file whose primary purpose it is to provide an index to the original file. A secondary purpose/advantage of maintaining this redundant information is back-up control over the original file. Such a file is called an inverted file, the name derived from the changing of the sequence of records. For example, if a bibliographical file is sequenced on document serial numbers, the authors' names and the serial numbers can be extracted, resequenced by name, and a new, inverted file produced. Now, in order to search the main file for an author's name, the faster method would be to search the inverted file first, determine the serial numbers of all documents written by that author, then retrieve the bibliographical records containing the known serial numbers by direct lookup in the serial file. The degree of inversion means the extent to which field values and pointers to corresponding records are placed in separate inverted files. The higher the degree of inversion, the larger the number of fields (attributes) inverted. One hundred percent inversion means that every field value has been inverted, thus providing fast access via any attribute to the original file of records. Note that an inverted file must have every record of the main file represented, unlike an index, which is in the same sequence as the main file and which can therefore represent only every nth record as necessary.

If the main file has many additions or deletions, the cost of inverted file maintenance can be high. Because the file is inverted, not ordered on the same key as the main file, a separate search operation is needed to find each inverted file entry (or to find the place where one is to be inserted). Since inverted files are ordered, entries must be inserted in the proper physical position, with consequent reshuffling of records, or chaining techniques used, which slow searching.

Pointer Fields

Chaining requires the use of pointer fields. Direct-access files typically handle overflow through the use of a pointer field. Overflows are chained to their intended storage location (the one that they hash to) through the pointer field. Pointers may be used to structure an entire file. In a *list organization*, each record contains one or more pointers (fields) indicating the address of the next logical record with the same attribute(s). An invoice record may contain a field that contains ("points to") the key of another invoice from the same vendor. A record may be part of several lists. This is called multilist organization. A customer record, for example, may contain pointers for geographic location and customer type (industrial, and so on). By including a pointer in a record to point to the next logical record, the logical and physical organization of a file can be completely different. Figure 9.5 illustrates a simple list structure and a *ring structure*. A ring differs from a list in that the last record in the list points back to the first record. In addition, all records in a ring may point "backward" as well as forward through the use and maintenance of additional pointer fields. In a multiple-ring structure, several rings pass through individual records.

The maintenance and design of such structures is complicated and

FIGURE 9.5.   List and Ring Structures

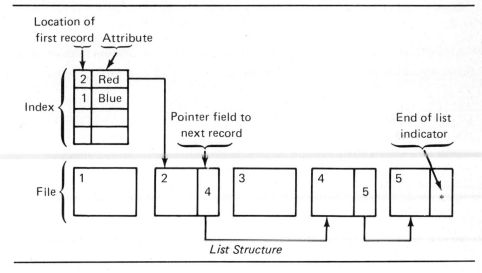

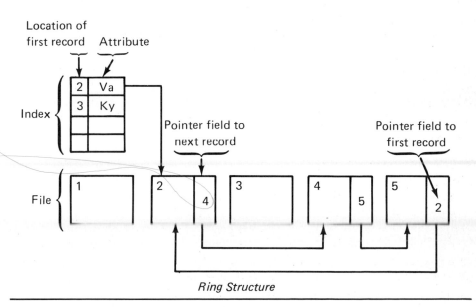

requires extensive software. Updating pointers is necessary every time a record is added or deleted. The relationship between inverted files and pointers indicates the general problem in obtaining nonkey information from files. At one extreme, an inverted file may totally duplicate the information in a main file. The only difference is that this inverted file is organized by a different key: that is, a key different from that of the main file. In this case there is no need for pointers to the original file—the same (redundant) information is contained in both files. At the other extreme is a fully inverted file—records in this file contain only the new key and pointers (no content) to the original file. An inverted file may contain pointers to all records with the desired attribute (as in the bibliographical serial–author name example), or a single pointer that allows entry to a list or ring that is searched sequentially for the desired records. The use of pointer fields minimizes the duplication of information (saving storage). Between these extremes, one may employ any combination of pointers and/or duplicate information to facilitate user requests. Pointers group logical records with a saving in storage; but this saving is gained with relatively complicated software techniques. Note also that pointers themselves require storage; excessive pointing may require more storage than simple file duplication.

Data Management Systems

The above techniques (pointer fields and inverted files) are used in numerous variations and combinations, often with inconsistent terminology, in the wide variety of data management systems that have come into existence since the mid-1960s. Data management systems (DMS) deal with computer programs (software) that enable a user to create and update files, to select and retrieve data, and to generate output reports.

The term *data management system* refers to a particular software package that maintains a data structure which supports the capability of storing and retrieving data on the basis of more than just the primary access key of the underlying physical data structure. The sophistication of the DMS determines the complexity and effectiveness of information retrieval capabilities provided to users.

DMS take many forms and differ widely in their capabilities and design features: "it is unfortunate that the terminology commonly used in the data management world is quite varied, and at times confusing and inconsistent" (Cardenas, 1979, p. 18). The subject matter is further confused by the terms *data base* and *data base management systems* (DBMS). A data base is a group of files that are logically interrelated via some form of cross-reference mechanism. A DBMS has the capability to process the multiple data files that comprise a data base; DBMS is thus an extension of DMS.

There are several attributes common to all data base systems (Cardenas, 1979, pp. 16–17). Common to all data base systems are the ability to:

1. Define the logical structure of every instance of data that comprises the data base. The overall logical structure of a data base is termed a *schema;* the schema is defined via a special data description language by a data base administrator (DBA). Centralization of the responsibility for the schema in the DBA is central to the data base concept. The DBA may define several independent data bases.

2. Define and control access to any logical subset of the data base. The term *subschema* is used to refer to a logical subset of a data base. Any number of subschemas can be defined on a schema; subschemas can overlap and may be shared by several applications. A subschema is a user's view of the data base, while in actuality it is a subset of the overall schema which is shared by multiple users.

3. Provide access to the data base through the use of a special data manipulation language (DML) or a nonprocedural query language designed to facilitate user's inquiry requests.

4. Define the physical structure (organization) of the actual data base on storage devices. This is the task of the DBA. Figure 9.6 illustrates the overall structure of a data base management system as defined above.

The area of "data base software" is plagued with inconsistent and confusing terminology as well as a wide variety of technological approaches to the same problems. There are no industrywide standards although CODASYL's Data Base Task Group (DBTG) 1971 report has the intent of an eventual industry standard for data base systems. The DBTG is a committee comprised of system vendors and users that has been working since 1969 on concepts and specifications for DBMS. The terms *schema* and *subschema* were originally introduced by CODASYL in the 1971 DBTG report. Figure 9.6 is compatible with the data base concepts contained in that report.

As was mentioned earlier in this section, data management systems— both DMS and DBMS—are software systems whose major objective is to reduce overall programming efforts relating to data base processing and inquiry. The value of data management systems can be appreciated only by tracing the history and development of computer programming languages. Chapter 13, "Software Systems," discusses the development of programming languages and provides further discussion of the 1971

FIGURE 9.6. Structure of a Data Base Management System

Application program written in a programming language—typically Cobol, containing data manipulation language (DML) commands

Application program 1 · Application program 2 · Application program 3 · Application program 4 · Application program 5

User work area · User work area · User work area · User work area · User work area

Application programmer's data description via subschema data description language; e.g., in Cobol data division

Subschema A · Subschema B · Subschema C

Global logical data base description via schema data description language

Schema

Physical data description via a device/media control language; in practice done in a variety of ways

Physical data base description

Designed and maintained by a data base administrator (DBA)

External data storage devices

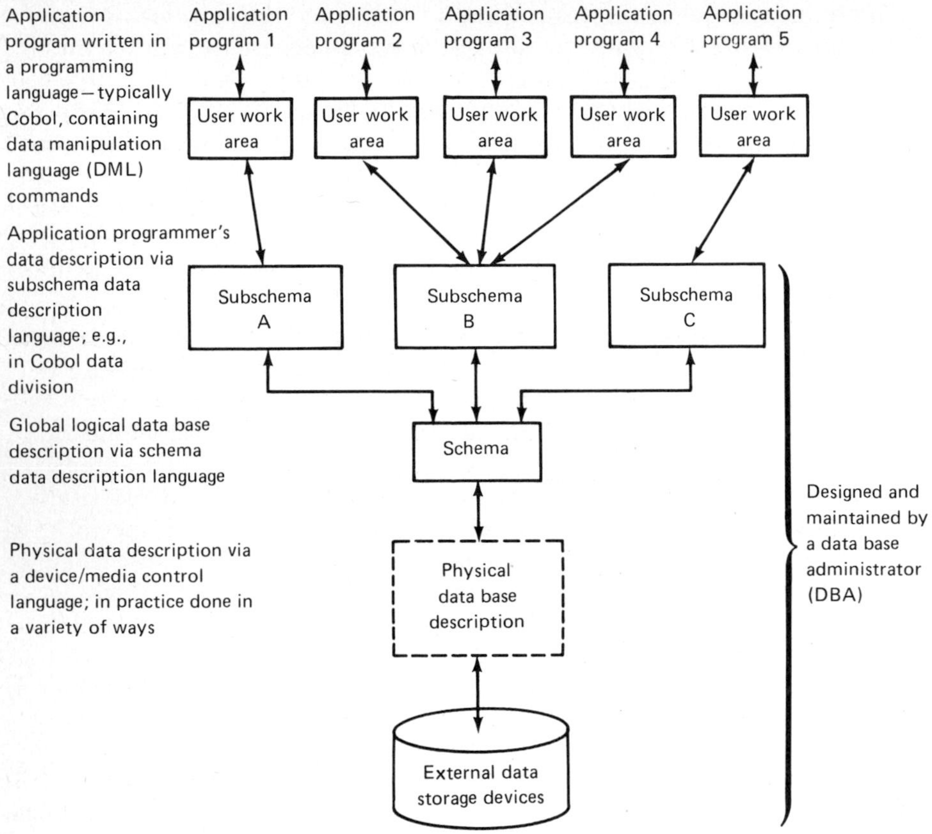

Cardenas, *Data Base Management Systems* (1979), p. 17.

CODASYL DBTG report. The final section of this chapter illustrates the major attributes of data base software systems.

Data Base Software Systems

Data base software systems are intended to simplify and standardize the repetitive aspects of file maintenance and processing from the user's viewpoint. This "file," however, may be part of a broader data structure, which must be called a data base for lack of a better term. We shall consider these aspects in the context of processing sequentially organized files.

The traditional approach to data processing is to have each application area such as payroll or receivables develop and maintain its own independent file(s). This is the cheapest and simplest approach to implement. There are several disadvantages to this approach, however. The first and most obvious is that the same data item may be used in several different application areas—with independent files, this data item has to be fed into each application file. A sale, for example, affects the inventory file, accounts receivable file, and various revenue and expense files. Inputing the same data element numerous times (once for each application it is used in) is time-consuming and potentially expensive; furthermore, there is a greater chance for errors and inconsistencies among the various representations of a piece of data in several independent files.

Second, because files must be rigidly defined early in the system implementation process, procedures may be constrained by the existing file structure rather than the file structure's being determined as the application develops. Finally, independence among files often leads to different structures for the same data, different coding systems, different abbreviations, and different field lengths, to name a few examples. Comparison and reconciliation of supposedly identical data may become a difficult task under these conditions. The result of inconsistent data is that inconsistent reports are produced from the various application programs. Such instances seriously question the integrity of an information system.

In addition to the data management and storage problems just discussed, independent files each require their own processing and maintenance instructions, as neither the content nor the structure of the files is standardized. Inquiry capability concerning nonkey information is restricted, since each individual application program must specify detailed instructions concerning the physical handling of data.

The solution to these disadvantages lies in the separation of the physical handling of data from its logical use. This requires two fundamental changes: first, data storage (that is, files) is integrated into a single data base and second, all access to the integrated set of files (data base) is through a software system designed to manage the physical aspects of data handling and storage. These are the essential characteristics of the data base approach to data processing.

In a sense the word *file* loses meaning in a data base environment. A single master file may be logically subdivided into numerous subsystem files and these files combined and recombined into numerous other files. Data base software separates the physical and logical aspects of file use, and in doing so opens up a broad spectrum of information-processing capabilities simply not feasible without such software.

Figure 9.7 illustrates several data base software concepts. Data base

FIGURE 9.7. Data Base Software Concepts

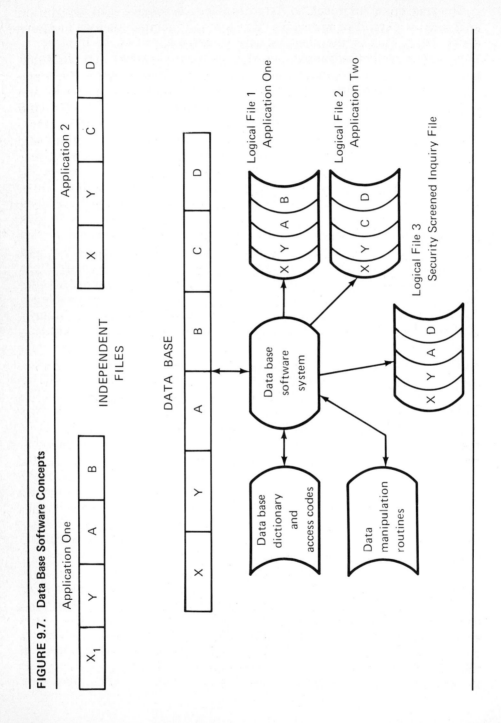

software (DBS) systems possess two essential features: a data description ability and a data manipulation ability. Various DBS systems available differ widely in their capabilities in these two areas.

Data description ability refers to specifying the content and characteristics of the data base itself and its interactions with users. The data-descriptive capabilities of a DBS are used to describe the schema and subschema of the data base. The data manipulation ability of a DBS refers to the data processing capabilities it provides to the user to facilitate data manipulation of user-requested logical files which are structured and processed—from the user's viewpoint—by the DBS. These routines, once they are defined, are stored in a data manipulation routine file by the DBS, which subsequently performs them on request from a user program. Sorting, totaling values, and concatenation are examples of data manipulation routines that might usefully be supplied by a DBS. Figure 9.7 shows two independent application files, each containing four fields per record. Note that two data items, X and Y, are common to both files. Below these files is a data base—a single file that contains all of the nonredundant information previously found in the two physically independent files. This data base file is structured and managed by a DBS system. Upon requests from user programs, the DBS structures logical application files (that is, subschema) through the use of a data base dictionary file. A *data base dictionary* is a collection of all data item names in a data base, along with a description of the standardized data representation form of these data items (for example, its size, type of data—numerical, alphabetical, etcetera.) The data base dictionary is defined and controlled by the data base administrator.

Logical files 1 and 2 (Figure 9.7) are temporary files constructed by the DBS for use by applications one and two. At the completion of processing, the updated values in the logical files may be copied to the actual physical data base. Logical file 3 is a new file created for a specific nonroutine use, such as an inquiry or a special accounting data analysis. The ability to construct such special files quickly and efficiently is a major advantage stemming from DBS systems. This ability is provided through the DBS's maintenance of inverted files, lists, rings, or other data structures designed to facilitate information retrieval by users.

The above attributes are enhanced by the general ability of such software to assign security codes to data items and their processing attributes. Part of the data dictionary file contains a list of authorized system users and their assigned security and access codes. Each of the six unique data elements in Figure 9.7 could be assigned a numerical priority code. These codes would specify which data items may be retrieved by each user of the DBS; furthermore, such codes may also be used to restrict and define the processing a user may do to any data item.

Application one in Figure 9.7 could have authority to request only items X, Y, A, and B and authority to modify/update only fields A and B. Application two could request X, Y, C, and D and modify only C and D. The user of logical file 3 may have authority to access any data items, but not to modify any. And so on through a hierarchy of security or privacy coding applied to data items in the data base.

REVIEW QUESTIONS

1. Define the following terms:
   key field
   minor sort key
   fixed-length record
   trailer record
   randomizing transformation
   overflow record
   activity ratio

2. Distinguish among the following terms:
   equal access
   sequential access
   direct access

3. Discuss the following statement: "Sequential file organization is appropriate when transactions are batched prior to processing. Direct-access file organization is necessary for immediate (that is, 'real-time') posting of transactions."

4. Distinguish between an index and an inverted file.

5. Why are DASDs required when using direct or indexed sequential file organization?

6. Are a file's logical and physical structure always the same? Explain.

7. What is a randomizing transformation?

8. How does a "list" structure differ from an inverted file? From an index?

9. Define the terms *data management*, *data base*, and *data management system*.

10. Identify several attributes of data base systems.

11. Define the terms *schema* and *subschema*.

12.   List and explain four methods of addressing records in a direct-access file.

13.   Contrast the relative advantages and disadvantages of using pointer fields as opposed to inverted files in a data management system.

DISCUSSION QUESTIONS AND PROBLEMS

14.   Discuss some of the differences between the traditional approach to data processing and the data base approach.

15.   Discuss the advantages and disadvantages of having an industry-wide standard to which all data base software systems conform.

16.   For each of the following applications, specify a file organization method (sequential, direct, indexed sequential). Briefly justify your selection in terms of the anticipated activity ratio, processing time frame, file size, and response time to inquiries about file status.
  a.   General Motors stockholder file, updated weekly, and used for mailing dividend checks, quarterly reports, and proxy requests.
  b.   A salesman commission file, updated at the time of sale from a point-of-sale data entry terminal.
  c.   A bank's customer account file, updated daily for deposits and withdrawals, and used for mailing monthly statements of account.
  d.   An inventory file, updated daily, which is also used to ascertain product availability and other related inquiries during daily operations.
  e.   A master payroll file, used biweekly to process payroll and also quarterly to process various tax reports.

17.   The West Co. maintains a master accounts-receivable disk file. Approved applications for new charge accounts are keypunched and verified. The resultant card deck is sorted and processed against the disk file in a computer run. The card deck is filed for backup, in case it becomes necessary to recreate the disk file because of some operator or mechanical failure.

The current master disk file is strictly sequential. What are some advantages and disadvantages that might accrue from changing the file organization method to either a random or index-sequential structure?

18.   For each of the following application files, discuss the relative merits of sequential, direct, and indexed sequential file organization:
  a.   Open-order file in a large manufacturing firm.
  b.   Accounts-receivable file for a magazine publisher.
  c.   Inventory file for a large automobile dealership.

    d. Accounts-payable file for a retailing firm.

    e. Fixed-asset file in a manufacturing firm.

19. Identify an inquiry for (1) a specific record and (2) a group of related records that might be made for each of the following files. Discuss how these inquiries might be satisfied if the file organization method was sequential, direct, or indexed sequential.

    a. An employee master file.

    b. An accounts-receivable file.

    c. A work-in-process file.

20. This problem requires the use of the flowchart presented in Figure 9.1. Assume that the master file and the transaction file are composed of the record numbers shown below in the sequence given:

        Master   11, 15, 31, 84, 87, 99

        Transaction   11, 12, 31, 31, 15, 84, 99

The record number 99 in each file is used to indicate the logical end of the file.

Process this data, using the flowchart in Figure 9.1. Indicate (a) which master records are updated; (b) which master records are not updated; and (c) the disposition of each transaction record (that is, posted to the master or an error condition).

21. Consider an open-purchase order file in a manufacturing company. Identify several other files to which the purchase order file might be linked ("chained") through the use of pointer fields.

22. A personnel file contains a record for each employee in an organization. Each record contains four fields: name, division, specialty, and age. Below are four sample records:

Storage Location	Name	Division	Specialty	Age
22	Ash	New York	Audit	30
28	Fox	New York	Audit	25
64	Luh	Chicago	Marketing	29
106	Smith	Los Angeles	Personnel	40

Each of the four fields is expected to be an important search parameter in the personnel application system. Design an index (directory) to invert the above file fully.

23. Discuss the relative advantages and disadvantages of inverted files and lists or ring structures (pointer field structures) in answering inquiries of the following types:

a. Are there any records that have both attribute 1 and attribute 2 (sales greater than \$5,000 and location equal to the state of New York)?

b. How many records have attribute 1, attribute 2,   attribute n?

REFERENCES

Cardenas, A., *Data Base Management Systems* (Boston: Allyn and Bacon, 1979).

CODASYL (Conference on Data Systems and Languages), "Data Base Task Group (DBTG) Report, 1971" (New York: Association for Computing Machinery, April, 1971).

Mader, C., *Information Systems*, 2nd ed. (Chicago: Science Research Associates, 1979).

ACCOUNTING PROCEDURES AND CONTROLS IN A COMPUTER ENVIRONMENT

10

This chapter discusses basic processing procedures and controls associated with computer-based accounting applications. The discussion of controls in this chapter focuses on user-related data controls in a data processing environment. The first part of this chapter provides a complete overview of the processing of accounting data in a typical batch processing application. This discussion is followed by an elaboration of the techniques utilized to insure control over the processing of accounting data in a computer environment.

The procedures and controls illustrated in this chapter are relevant to all computer-based accounting applications. The following two chapters provide illustrations of specific computer-based accounting application systems. Chapter 11 illustrates revenue and expenditure cycle applications, Chapter 12 discusses production and finance cycle application systems.

COMPUTER BATCH PROCESSING OF ACCOUNTING APPLICATIONS

Figure 10.1 outlines the processing of accounting data as it occurs in a batch processing system. Source documents are accumulated, batched, and periodically posted in detail to subsidiary ledgers. The detail in these ledgers is an important data base for report generation. Standard journal entries (journal vouchers) are prepared to summarize (filter) the voluminous data recorded in the subsidiary ledgers. These journal vouchers are posted to the general ledger, and a trial balance and financial reports are prepared from the updated general ledger. This section illustrates this sequence of processing accounting data in a computer environment. All accounting applications, such as sales orders, accounts receivable, purchases, and payroll, could be and often are implemented in this fashion.

Sequential File Processing Procedures

Sequential or "classical" file processing procedures are a straightforward application of computer technology to the processing sequence illustrated in Figure 10.1. The essential features lie in the machine coding of data (a conversion step), and the media and devices on which the actual data reside. Sequential file processing is a very common method of computerizing accounting applications. Probably 90 percent or more of all accounting application systems utilize sequential file processing techniques. A full understanding of sequential file processing and related control techniques is fundamental to contemporary accounting systems work.

Sequential file processing involves the maintenance of a sequentially organized master file. This file—an accounts-receivable master file for illustration—commonly resides on magnetic tape. Sales transactions affect the information on the accounts-receivable file. These transactions and others—such as new accounts and payments on account—must be reflected on the file. Figure 10.2 outlines the procedural steps in sequential

---

FIGURE 10.1.   Batch Processing Sequence

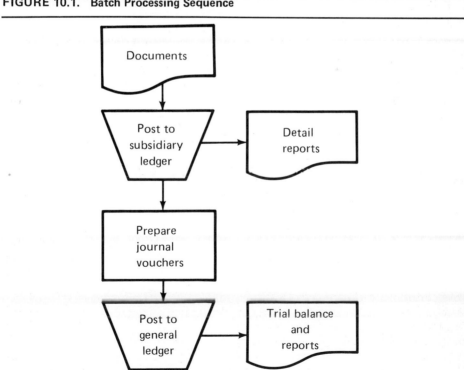

FIGURE 10.2. Systems Flowchart of Sequential File Processing

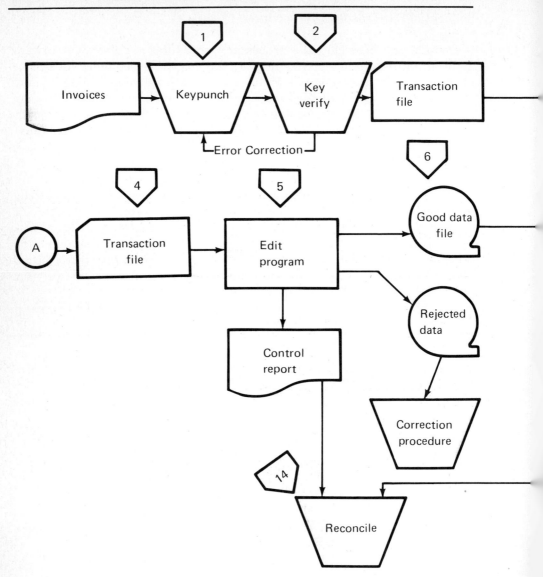

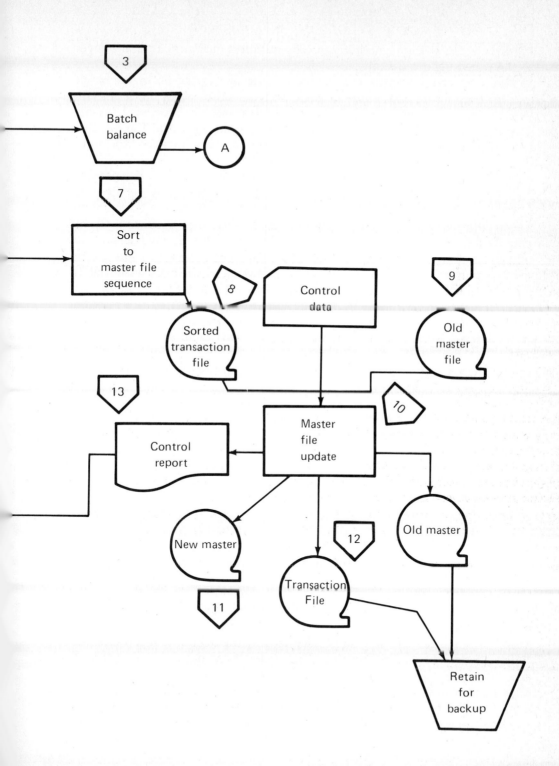

file processing with magnetic tapes. The numbers in Figure 10.2 are keyed to the following discussion.

The economic advantages of sequential file processing lie in the batching of transactions to insure a high activity ratio when updating the master file. This minimizes the cost per transaction processed, as discussed in Chapter 9. As the costs of processing a sequential file on magnetic tape are essentially fixed because of the devices involved, the more transactions processed, the lower the unit cost.

Batches of documents are a fundamental unit in sequential file processing. As Figure 10.2 illustrates, data are keypunched (1), key verified (2), and subject to batch balancing procedures (3) to insure that all documents are accounted for prior to computer processing. The resultant file of transactions is on punched cards (4). This file is processed against an edit program (5) to screen the data before further processing. Data editing of the source documents prior to keypunching is logically essential to insure the reliability of the data processed. The processing system itself can perform certain data editing functions by incorporating the essential features of negative feedback control into the overall processing logic. Data editing techniques are detailed later in this chapter. At this point note that key verification is a control over only the keypunching step itself: that is, key verification is designed to capture errors in keypunching, not to edit data.

In addition to screening data, the edit program (5) is also used to accumulate new batch control totals over the reassembled transaction data as this data is transferred from card to magnetic tape. This transfer from cards to tape typically occurs because tape is capable of higher data transfer speeds, which facilitate further processing. The outputs of the edit program include a control report. This report commonly contains a detailed listing of all transactions (a transaction register) to document inputs to the application. The file of edited transaction data (6) is sorted to master file sequence (7) to facilitate the matching process inherent in the logic of sequential file processing. The sorted, edited transaction file (8) is subsequently processed against the old master file (9) in the accounts receivable application program(s) run (10). This program or set of programs posts the detail of accounts-receivable transactions to the accounts-receivable master file. The new "updated" master file (11) will serve as the basis for generating reports and other detailed information. This master file is a subsidiary ledger, the accounts-receivable subsidiary ledger in this illustration. The transaction data (12) and the old master file are retained for back-up control, as illustrated in Figure 10.2. The control report (13) which is printed at the completion of the processing is reconciled (14) with the batch totals/control report produced by the edit program. This reconciliation of input to output control totals is a fundamental user control. This reconciliation is performed by the user department, a special control unit, or the internal audit function. The control report (13) would normally include a detailed listing of transactions processed against the master file. This transaction register is the equivalent of a journal produced in a manual system.

In terms of Figure 10.1 (a batch processing sequence), the above procedure has accomplished the second step in the diagram, posting transaction detail to subsidiary ledgers. The general ledger has not yet been updated. Part of the output of sequential file processing of accounting applications is the information needed to prepare standard journal entries. This information may be printed and utilized to update a manual general ledger, or subsequently machine coded for processing against a computerized general ledger system. Alternatively, the standard journal entries may be output initially in machine-readable form. The following section continues the discussion of batch processing procedures with an overview of a computerized general ledger system. The discussion illustrates the procedures necessary to complete the processing sequence outlined in Figure 10.1, the processing of journal vouchers against a computer-based general ledger system.

A Computer-based General Ledger Application

Every organization must maintain some type of general ledger accounting system. Data must be collected, recorded, properly classified and entered into the appropriate records for further financial report summations. A general ledger system is the cornerstone of an accounting system. Typical procedures and files used in a computerized general ledger system are discussed in this section.

There are three basic functions that are needed to automate a general ledger system. First, the chart of accounts must be computerized. Typically this is a sequential file organized in account sequence and containing the symbols, titles, and dollar amounts of the general ledger. Second, all revenue and expense data must be regularly collected, summarized, and posted to the general ledger file. In a typical computer-based AIS, most of this summary data is available in machine-readable form as output of individual accounting application systems, as discussed in the previous section. Finally, reports must be generated and printed. Programs to process the general ledger must be coded, tested, and implemented.

There are two major aspects to the operation of a computerized general ledger system. One concerns the direct processing of the general ledger programs, most of which takes place on a monthly basis. The second aspect concerns the processing in other computer application systems in order to prepare the inputs to the general ledger system. One of the tasks to be undertaken in designing a general ledger system is the creation of a pro forma set of journal entries providing for the collection and updating of all data needed for financial reports. The typical approach is to have each relevant application system (such as payroll or accounts payable) generate general ledger transactions (standard journal entry data) to be used as input at the proper time. Doing this implies the use of a separate transactions file in the general ledger system.

Journal Vouchers

Typically all entries into the general ledger are documented via journal vouchers, which represent the transactions expected to have occurred during a given period, identified to the chart of accounts. The preparation of journal vouchers and the related procedures and documentation surrounding their use are equivalent to the standard journal entries discussed in Chapter 6. As in the manual procedure, responsible departments originate the input data to the general ledger system. This may entail the manual preparation of journal vouchers, or in cases where this data is already contained in other application programs, the adjustment (formatting) of this data in journal voucher form.

The journal voucher format (Figure 10.3) is typically the same in context in most organizations and includes the journal voucher number and date, the control and subaccounts (as applicable) and the debit and credit amounts. There may be one or several accounts entered on one journal voucher dependent upon the complexity of the transaction and the system design. Journal voucher numbers are established to code the type of transaction (cash, receivables, sales, etcetera). The column headed by ID designates that the journal is an original entry or the reversal of a prior entry. The account and debit/credit amounts are self-explanatory.

All departments have responsibility for the preparation and submission of journal vouchers as they affect their operations. The time schedule for preparation is dependent upon the availability of the basic or raw data, and management dictates concerning the intervals at which reporting should occur. This basic format may be expanded to include other information relevant to a particular system. Examples of such data are detailed cost ledger information (to support a subsidiary cost file) and details of expenses by organizational unit for responsibility reports. Either of these data items might be used in conjunction with a separate master budget file to produce reports showing "budget vs. year-to-date," and so forth.

Journal vouchers are typically keypunched, edited, transferred to tape,

FIGURE 10.3. A Journal Voucher Form

Journal Voucher			
Number	Month	Year	ID
Accounts		Debit	Credit
			Received from:

sorted to account number sequence, and run against the general ledger master file and general ledger budget file to produce reports. This process is sequential file processing. A fourth file common to most systems is a file of historical data from earlier reporting and accounting periods.

Updating the General Ledger

Figure 10.4 provides an overview of a typical general ledger file update. As they are released by the general ledger department, journal vouchers are used to build a journal voucher file (the transaction file). This file is

FIGURE 10.4. Systems Flowchart Showing a General Ledger Update

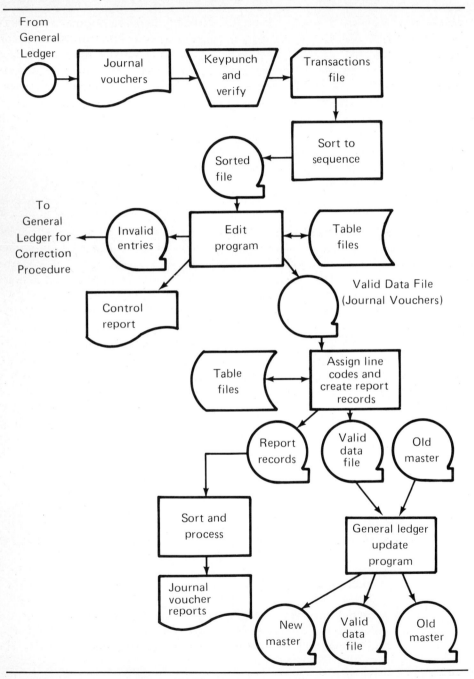

sorted and edited as to validity with respect to the proper journal and account numbers as well as determining if the accounts are correctly associated with their related journals. Invalid data are reported as "exceptions" to established standards and returned to originating sources for correction and reentry. The edited journal voucher file may be sorted and structured to produce a variety of reports. The current journal voucher transactions are processed against the previous month's general ledger master file (the old master) in order to update that file and produce the current period's general ledger register. Note the general similarity between the processing sequence outlined in Figure 10.4 and that previously discussed with respect to Figure 10.2. This similarity exists in all computer batch processing applications.

Computer processing of accounting data is typically a two-step procedure. The first step produces preliminary reports, which are forwarded to the accounting department for review and audit relative to the journal voucher listings and general ledger listing. After the audit and submission of corrections or additional data, the second step is a run that produces the final listings and financial schedules. Numerous reports may be prepared. Doing so requires a link between the general ledger accounts and the report(s) in which they appear. This process is called line coding.

Line coding is a procedural step, typically accomplished by a table look-up (that is, matching) process between the updated general ledger file and a line-coding file. Table files (see Figure 10.4) are items or records that are not a part of data files but are an integral part of the processing function. Tax tables and line-coding assignments are examples of table files typically stored on DASDs in accounting applications. The result of the line-coding procedure is several report files, which are ultimately printed and distributed to users. Figure 10.5 illustrates a line-coding assignment.

A specific general ledger account, let's say marketable securities, is located in the line-coding file. The line code is then used to structure

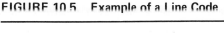

FIGURE 10.5   Example of a Line Code

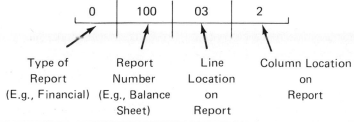

the report. In Figure 10.5, the first field (one digit) indicates the type of schedule—a financial one in this illustration. The second field identifies the specific report—a balance sheet in our example. The third and fourth fields locate the item in the report structure. Marketable securities is the third line item on the balance sheet, and this account value is placed in column 2. In a balance sheet one typically has four columns of data: (1) actual this period, (2) beginning-of-year balance, (3) budget, and (4) variance between (1) and (3). As an alternative to the procedure just described, line codes could be stored within the general ledger file itself.

In addition to financial reports and schedules, common reports from a computerized general ledger system would include the following listings:

1. journal voucher in sequence;
2. journal voucher within general account;
3. general ledger by account;
4. a general ledger summary; and
5. working trial balance.

Item 3 is a summary of this month's activity in the general ledger; item 4 is a year-to-date summary; and item 5 is a sort/summarization of the year-to-date general ledger in trial balance format. Typically, financial statements and trial balances contain details summarized from the general ledger, rather than a listing of all of the individual accounts, because of the large number of detailed general ledger accounts required in a large organization. Detailed reports for lower levels of management may be prepared from the relevant subsidiary ledger files.

CONTROL OF COMPUTER PROCESSING

A major distinction between manual and computerized data processing is the increased speed and processing capabilities gained through common data use, or, as it is more often called, integrated data processing. Each element of transactional data may be used for a variety of reports and purposes. In manual operations, the same data element may be transcribed several times to a number of summary worksheets or ledgers to meet particular reporting needs. Computer processing, however, provides the capability for one-time acquisition of information. The computer uses the data for many reports or necessary calculations. Computer processing eliminates errors involved in human transcription of data from one record to another.

The common data-use concept consists of three major points:

1. original data are recorded at their point of origin in a machine-readable form;
2. once in machine-readable form, data are processed exclusively in a mechanical manner;
3. all processing of data is integrated (designed) so that the original recording of data in machine-readable form serves all subsequent applications.

As an organization moves toward common data usage, numerous manual procedures may be subsumed or eliminated by machine operations. This elimination of human processing yields increased speed; however, controls and checking mechanisms associated with manual procedures are eliminated along with the procedures themselves. Thus, a major consideration is to insure that such controls or their equivalent, are an integral part of a computer processing system.

There are numerous levels of control essential in computer processing. As analysis and design of processing proceeds from subsystem to system, different levels of control appropriate to each system processing level are essential. We are primarily concerned with the controls attendant to implementing accounting applications in computer processing systems. In this framework we shall adopt the controls classification promulgated by the American Institute of Certified Public Accountants (AICPA) in SAS 3.

SAS no. 3, entitled "The Effects of EDP on the Auditor's Study and Evaluation of Internal Control" and issued in 1974, discusses the effects of computer processing on accounting control. SAS no. 3 describes computer electronic data processing (EDP) accounting controls as follows:

> Some EDP accounting control procedures relate to all EDP activities (general controls) and some relate to a specific accounting task, such as preparation of account listings or payrolls (application controls). (p. 3).

General controls comprise:

1. the plan of EDP organization and operation;
2. general operating procedures (documentation, approval, testing);
3. hardware control features; and
4. equipment and data access controls.

General controls affect all EDP applications. Application controls relate to specific applications, such as payroll or accounts receivable. Their function is to provide reasonable assurance that the recording, processing, and reporting of data are properly performed. Application controls are subdivided into input controls, processing controls, and output controls.

There is a considerable variety of alternatives in application controls. General controls apply to all EDP applications and are not a substitute for application controls. It is possible to have relatively strong general controls with relatively weak or nonexistent application controls. General controls may thus be seen as necessary but not sufficient for adequate control over accounting-related applications.

General Controls

Separation of Duties. As defined in SAS no. 3, general controls relate to all EDP applications. General controls are directed at the overall processing system. The most basic general control is to achieve organizational independence at each level in the organizational plan relating to data processing. Effective internal control over data processing is based on effective segregation of duties. Data processing (record keeping) as a system should be independent of the system that has physical control of assets. The data processing system itself should be independent of the system that verifies the validity and accuracy of data processing output. And within the data processing system itself, segregation of duties should be designed with the objective of having no one person responsible for both performing a function and verifying or checking the results of that function. At each system level, segregation of duties is essential to provide some control over the human element in data processing systems. Since EDP systems tend to integrate formally separate and distinct procedures under machine control, incompatible duties may be more likely to be combined in EDP than in manual processing.

Documentation. General controls include the procedures relating to documenting, reviewing, testing and approving the development and subsequent modification of applications software. Segregation of duties in these related procedures is essential to internal control. Initial documentation and the current revision of documentation is essentially a decoupling mechanism: without documentation, an organization is closely coupled to the single person or group who performed and has knowledge of the object in question. Without documentation, failure or loss of this component may cause a larger system to experience difficulties. To illustrate, consider a programmer who modifies a payroll program, fails to document his changes, and subsequently quits his job. Suppose that after he quits the program fails to run. The lack of documentation to back up the programmer will be likely to be a serious problem.

Documentation is redundant in that it does not directly facilitate production. The "extra copy" inherent to documentation is necessary only if its master is lost, destroyed, or incorrectly altered, or fails to satisfy processing requirements in some other manner. Documentation often includes more than a mere copy of information. Typically, documentation is designed to add more information; to explain, provide details, or illustrate the procedure for a potential user. The point is that a degree of reliability is attained with documentation. This reliability is attained through the increased control possible with multiple, redundant sources of information pertaining to an essential component in a system.

Minimum documentation for an EDP application centers around the design and maintenance of a *run manual:* an organized collection of documents pertaining to the procedures surrounding a particular application. The run manual provides documentation pertaining to the description of the application system (its purpose), detailed program description (the parts of the system), and detailed operating instructions. System flowcharts and record layouts are fundamental components of a run manual. A system flowchart indicates the source and nature of all input, machine, computer, and manual operations, and the nature and disposition of all outputs. Record layouts provide detail on field names, field location and size, blocking factors, and other such detail. In addition, any other information necessary to describe the system should be included in the run manual. Detailed program description is provided through flowcharts and a source listing of the program in human-readable form. These two items allow a reader to trace the coding flow and logic; they also serve as back-up.

Operating instructions are a guide to the actual running of the program. Such instructions are essential because a fundamental segregation of duties in EDP is to have the persons who designed the programs independent of the persons who actually run the programs. Accordingly, operating instructions should define the operator's duties in starting, running, and terminating the program. Nothing should be left to the operator's imagination. The operating instructions should provide a basic understanding of the program, detailed instructions as to how to start and stop the program, and details as to labeling, disposition, and retention of program inputs and outputs. As additional documentation, copies of all test input should be preserved. Every time a program is modified or changed, the test input should be processed and the output compared with the original test output.

Hardware Controls. General controls include controls built into EDP equipment itself, commonly referred to as hardware controls, which are designed to guard against machine malfunctions. Machine reliability is in general quite high; accordingly, such controls are only briefly noted herein. Three important hardware control features that are common to most EDP equipment are parity checking, redundant read-write operations, and checkpoint/restart procedures.

Parity checking is a hardware control over data transfer at the level of an individual byte or character. The general idea of parity checking will be illustrated with a six-bit byte. Consider the 0–1 sequence 101 101, which we shall assume is a code for the letter A. Parity involves the addition *to each byte* of an extra bit—the parity bit—and machine determination of the value of the parity bit. In even parity systems, the parity bit is initially set at value 0 or 1 by the machine so that the total number of 1 bits is even. In our example, the parity bit would be set at 0, since the number of 1 bits in the six-bit code for A is even. When the content of the byte is transferred, parity is recomputed for the first six bits transferred; the resultant parity is checked against the value of the seventh bit transferred. If these bits do not agree, a machine error has occurred in the data transfer. The machine will attempt either to retransfer the data or to signal to the operator that an error has occurred. Parity checking is a very effective control over the validity of machine data transfer. Note that the codes discussed in Chapter 8—BCD and EBCDIC—require a seventh and a ninth bit respectively for parity (see Figure 8.3). Odd parity systems function with the parity count being odd rather than even. Parity is checked each time a byte of data is transferred. Parity checking is a fundamental machine-control feature.

Duplicate (redundant) read-write operations may be used to ascertain the validity of data transfer. Most magnetic tape drives utilize two sets of read and/or write heads; data is sensed twice—once by each set of heads—and compared bit by bit to insure a proper pickup. Some card readers incorporate duplicate reading operations, but such operations are not common to DASDs. CPUs typically incorporate duplicate read and/or write operations. The necessity for such features depends on many factors, but, other things being equal, duplicate read-write operations are desirable.

The term *checkpoint-restart procedures* refers to periodic copying of the results of a program prior to its completion. The basic idea is to provide against having to restart a lengthy program from its beginning if the system happens to fail sometime during the running of the program. Periodically (say at fifteen-minute intervals), the program is stopped, its contents are copied to a storage device under control of the system, and the program continues. If the system fails, the program may subsequently be restarted at its most recent checkpoint rather than at its beginning. Checkpoint-restart procedures are essential when lengthy programs are regularly processed.

Access and Data Transfer Controls. General controls also include procedures relating to the access and transfer of data and programs. Segregation of duties is the fundamental criterion in the design of such procedures, and documentation is essential in order to foster adherence to prescribed procedures. Programming and operating personnel should be separate and distinct. Custody of master files and programs should be separate and distinct from both programming and operations. Custodial functions are usually centered under a file librarian. The file librarian is responsible for maintaining a separate storage area, the file library, for control of files and programs. The file librarian should maintain an inventory of all files and programs in the library and should keep a record of files and program copies that are checked out for use by other systems personnel.

File and program control standards should be formalized and enforced. Control over the file storage area should be sufficient to reduce unauthorized access to program and data files. Back-up copies of critical programs and files should be maintained and stored at remote locations. Procedures should require the use and maintenance of human-readable external labels

---

FIGURE 10.6. An Input Control Form

		[Prenumbered]
	Batch Control Form	150

Originating Department _____

Date _____

Preparer's Signature _____

Control Totals

Batch Number └─┴─┴─┴─┴─┘

Number of Documents └─┴─┴─┘

Field Totals (list):

Field Number	Name	Total

FIGURE 10.7. Batch Control

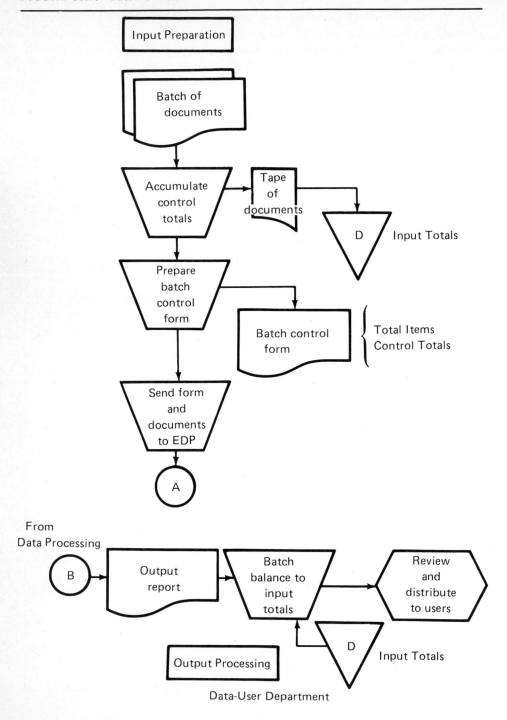

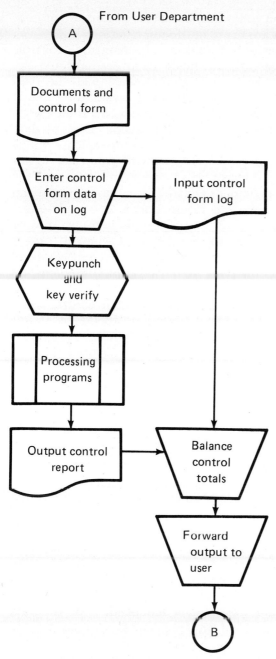

From User Department

A

Documents and control form

Enter control form data on log

Input control form log

Keypunch and key verify

Processing programs

Output control report

Balance control totals

Forward output to user

B

Data Processing Department

on all files. The use of files and programs should be recorded and controlled through registers and accompanying documentation.

Batch control and data transfer registers are fundamental controls over data transfer. The absence or inadequacy of procedures for the control of data transmitted between user departments and the data processing department could represent a significant weakness, since it presents an opportunity for unauthorized and/or fraudulent transactions to be introduced into the processing system. Submission of input data should be accompanied by the completion of an input document control form similar to that shown in Figure 10.6. The control group should not accept data unless some form is present to evidence and reference the transfer of this data. The input document control form may be dated and time-stamped and the batch checked to insure that it is complete and consonant with control procedures; for example: proper accounts, proper authorization, proper timing. Information in the batch control form is typically entered in a data transmission log (register) to provide a control over the disposition and use of this data. Batch control is fundamental to this process. Document counts are a simple form of batch control. Figure 10.7 illustrates the development and use of batch control totals in a computer processing application. In addition to document and/or record counts, batch totals may be taken for all or several numeric fields in the original data file. These totals may be used throughout the data processing cycle to monitor the completeness of processing.

Internal Audit Functions. Typically a separate control group is established to monitor EDP operations; in particular, to control documentation procedures. A separate control group is necessary to segregate EDP operations from the related record-keeping (documentation) function. The EDP control group is normally part of the internal audit function.

As the internal audit function continues to grow and mature within organizations, an EDP auditing specialty has evolved within the internal auditing function. This specialty has evolved as organizations have become increasingly dependent on computer-based information systems and management increasingly concerned about the reliability and security of complex computerized information systems. As computer data processing systems increase in complexity, the need for internal auditors to possess data-processing-related skills and knowledge increases if internal auditing is to remain organizationally and functionally independent of the data processing department. Organizational independence is basic to the concept of internal audit.

There is a trend toward increased internal-audit participation in the system development cycle. Such participation is essential to insure that appropriate audit and control features are designed into computer application systems. Audit considerations cannot be considered independently of control in computer-based systems. This is the overriding conclusion of a recent study, *Systems Auditability and Control*, published by the Institute of Internal Auditors (1977):

> The changes in data processing have caused changes in the traditional role of the internal auditor. To understand this changing role, one must understand the changes occurring in internal control that are being brought about by increasing automation and new data processing technology. In addition, audit and control must be considered together, rather than separately, because they are completely interrelated. Internal controls in the data processing environment govern transaction processing, record keeping, reporting, and environmental security; internal auditing is the evaluation and verification of these controls and the results of data processing. Thus, internal controls and the records and reports produced by data processing are the objects of internal audit. Because of this interrelationship, one cannot consider internal audit without considering internal control [p. 3].

The study also notes that a survey of organizations that utilize computer data processing indicates that approximately 70 percent of the organizations that have EDP audit functions have founded that function since 1970 (*Systems Auditability and Control*, p. 33). The EDP audit specialty, we see, is a relatively recent control practice.

Application Controls

Application controls function to insure that the recording, processing, and reporting of data are properly performed. Application controls may be divided into input, processing, and output controls.

Input Controls. Input controls are designed to detect errors in the conversion of source documents to machine-readable format. It is usually not practical to check input 100 percent. A balance must be achieved between the cost of error detection and the possible consequences of undetected error. Batch control over input established by user departments before source documents are submitted for key transcription is a fundamental user data control. These totals (adjusted for corrections) may be compared to output totals generated by the processing program, once again in the user department, to validate the processing (see Figure 10.7). This use of batch control over the entire data processing input-process-output sequence is fundamental to organizational independence. Proof and control functions should be performed outside the machine room and under the control of people who are not involved with machine operation.

Original source documents should be maintained for a period of time sufficient to facilitate error corrections. Procedures should be designed to insure that source documents are not processed more than once. The control principles discussed in Chapter 3, such as the use of prenumbered forms, supervision, and the like, apply to EDP applications as well.

With respect to input media, several basic software controls are relevant. In general, all input should be subject to key verification or the equivalent. Since key verification does not edit data, it is essential that data be edited at the program level to insure valid content. Program data editing is a software technique used to screen data prior to processing. It should be used in addition to data editing of source documents before key transcription, for several reasons. First, key transcription errors can occur that will pass key verification. Incorrect recognition of a character on a source document is one possibility; another is the simple omission of a necessary input item. As this second example illustrates, data editing at the programming level is a control over the initial data-editing function. Last, the volume of data in EDP operations, coupled with the fact that once data is entered in the system it may be used without reconversion (integrated processing), necessitates a methodological screening of all input data.

Data editing is analogous to negative feedback control. Certain logical, historical, and design requirements serve as standards to which data should conform. Individual items are compared to these standards in a computer program. The data that passes is assumed to be correct; data that fails is presumed to be in error and is sent to error correction procedures.

Data editing routines may take numerous forms, depending on the nature of the input data. This discussion will trace data editing through the basic data hierarchy. The most basic editing is used to insure that all data fields required by the processing system (1) appear in the input records and (2) contain valid characters. Numerical fields should be checked for digits only; letters in a numerical field may be interpreted as numbers by the processing program.

Checking alphabetical fields character by character is possible, as well as alpha-numerical fields. If a data item should be a specified size, this can be tested. If a sign should always be negative (or positive), this can be checked by program statements.

After the presence of all characters has been verified, the contents of fields can be edited as being within proper limits or reasonable. Such relationships are established on logical, historical, or design considerations. The basic approach is to establish a table file that contains valid field entries. The edit program compares the actual value of a field to the acceptable values in the table. A valid customer code list may be used to verify the content of a customer code field. Note that this match insures only reasonableness of the account, not accuracy. Transaction and department and all other codes may be verified by table-lookup procedures. Combinations of field values may be tested as well: for example, only certain transaction codes may be relevant to certain department codes.

Numerical data values, as opposed to numerical codes, should in general fall within certain ranges; thus, checking numerical data as being within certain limits requires a check only against extreme values of the range. For example the field payroll hours may typically not be less than none nor more than, say, one hundred for a two-week pay period. Sales in a certain department should generally be within a range of zero to some upper limit based on historical data.

It is possible to edit numerical data with respect to being outside acceptable ranges; in such cases the data is rejected. At times it may be desirable to discriminate further among acceptable items as well. For example, a payroll field may contain a value that is acceptable but so high or low as to warrant investigation. This data may be accepted for processing and a control report listing this item may subsequently be audited to verify these slightly questionable, but nevertheless acceptable, items. Alternatively, such input items may be held in suspense of processing until the data are reverified. Such controls, referred to as operational audit controls, incorporate the basic features of feedback control at the processing level of a computer system.

As an alternative to table-lookup procedures, codes can be verified through the use of a check digit. A check digit is an extra, redundant digit added to a code number, much as a parity bit is added to a byte. The check digit is computed when a code is initially assigned to a data element. Check digits are computed by applying mathematical calculations to the individual digits in a code number in such a way as to generate a result that is a single digit. This digit becomes the check digit and is added to the original code. In subsequent processing, this same arithmetic operation can be performed to insure that the code has not been incorrectly recorded.

There are numerous check digit procedures. The following illustration is one version of a technique known as Modulus 11:

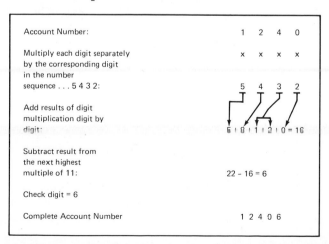

The use of check digits is very common because of the high reliability of this procedure. Commercial check digit packages catch 100 percent of transposition errors and a very high percentage of random errors. No control system is perfect, check digits do not guard against all input errors.

Processing Controls. Processing controls are largely directed at files, which are collections of input records. Processing controls are used to provide reasonable assurance that a file has been processed according to intended specifications and that no records have been omitted or inserted subsequent to the last batch control-total verification point. Fundamental processing controls include label checks, record sequence tests, and control-total verification.

Each file should have as its initial record a special record header identifying relevant information, such as an identification number or title (a minimum), the last processing date, special totals, etcetera. Programs may be coded so as to check the header record of an incoming file to determine if it is the correct file before processing is begun. Each file should be subject to some form of back-up—either a duplicate copy or the ability to reproduce the file from other files not on-line to the system—in the event that a file is incorrectly processed or is destroyed.

Sequence tests should be used to verify any sequentially ordered field in a file. Input to magnetic tape files should always be sequence-checked before conversion to or processing with tape. An out-of-sequence tape can cause processing errors and serious time delays. Accounting for pre-numbered documents demands that sequence be tested.

Control totals should be maintained on all files. Totals should be subject to verification every time a file is processed. Programs should generate totals that can be balanced against input control totals. Control totals can take many forms: card counts, records counts, financial control totals, and hash totals. Hash totals are used to batch balance nonfinancial numbers—such as numerical codes—just as financial totals are used to batch balance-dollar amounts. Hash totals are sums that are nonsensical (for example, the total sum of department codes), but are nevertheless useful for batch balancing.

Control totals are used to insure *completeness* of data processing, but, like the line proofing methods discussed in Chapter 6, control totals do not necessarily insure accuracy of data processing.

Output Controls. Output controls are designed to check that the input processing resulted in valid output and that outputs are properly distributed. Reports should be reviewed critically by supervisory personnel in user departments for general reasonableness and quality in relation to previous reports. Control totals should be balanced to control totals generated independently of the data processing operation, as discussed earlier.

Clerical procedures should be established to provide assurance that errors are reported to the controls group. These procedures must assure that such errors are entered into controls, corrected, and properly reentered into the system for further processing. Corrections should be subject to the same testing as original data. The distribution of output should be controlled in such a manner as to minimize the danger of unauthorized access to confidential data.

Output distribution is controlled through documentation and supervision: typically an output distribution register is maintained to control the disposition of reports. This register and its attendant documentation would be periodically reviewed in the internal audit function.

Control Systems Overview

There are many levels of control essential in the operation of a computer system. Top management has overall responsibility for authorizing and evaluating systems changes. Top management should monitor the overall performance of the EDP function through the use of budgets and other periodic responsibility reports. Top management is also responsible for the overall organizational structure of the EDP function.

The next level of management control involves the overall plan of procedures, management of personnel, and management of the EDP facility itself. People are an essential component of an EDP system; the careful selection, training, and management of EDP personnel is essential in an EDP system, as in any other business system. The internal control principles discussed in Chapter 3—such as bonding or insuring employees—are relevant to EDP systems and need not be redetailed at this point.

The security of EDP facilities is important both in terms of safeguarding the physical data processing assets and in preventing the compromise or destruction of vital computer data, programs, and documentation. Reasonable precautions should be taken against natural hazards, personal inefficiencies, and maliciousness, all of which can affect the operations of the computer room. Security is but one of the many internal control factors that must be considered. There are many effective alternatives available to insure security at an installation. While certain security control features are applicable to all installations, others must be tailored to fit the circumstances of the particular case in recognition of the type of processing being done and of the economic consequences involved. What level of security is to be applied in any given installation is a decision that must be made by management. Physical security devices have too indirect a relation to the processing of accounting data to warrant further discussion here.

Most of the material in this section has been directed at the control of file-processing media and procedures. The nature and extent of such controls will vary according to the type of system in use. A fundamental consideration in the design of such procedures is the resultant *audit trail*. A fundamental system requirement is ability to trace any transaction from a source document through the processing sequence to the totals in which it is aggregated. Likewise, any total should be traceable to the transactions or other elements that were summed to arrive at the total. Basic card-oriented computer systems traditionally produce substantial amounts of printed material that will generally satisfy audit trail requirements. The use of magnetic input, output, and storage media or the use of certain data communication devices may concentrate processing references and results of processing on non-human-readable media. Care must be taken to insure that the controls that are used provide for a complete audit trail through the processing system.

REVIEW QUESTIONS

1. Define the following terms:
    a. activity ratio
    b. master file
    c. table file
    d. data transmission log
    e. line coding

2. Why are transactions typically batched rather than processed separately against a sequentially organized master file that is stored on magnetic tape?

3. What three basic functions are necessary to computerize a general ledger accounting system?

4. Identify four files that are commonly utilized in a computerized general ledger accounting system. Must these four files always be physically separate files? Must these files always be stored on magnetic tape?

5. Identify two fundamental controls attendant to the flow of data in a data processing system.

6. Identify three points that are fundamental to the concept of integrated data processing (often called common data usage).

7. Distinguish between general controls and application controls in a computer data processing environment and give an example of each.

8. Briefly define and explain the purpose of each of the following controls:
   a. run manual
   b. parity checking
   c. checkpoint-restart procedures
   d. external file labels
   e. check digit
   f. internal label check
   g. programmed limit checks

9. For each control listed in question 8 above, indicate whether the control is a general control or an application control.

10. Distinguish between key verification of input data and data editing of the same data. Are key verification and data editing complementary or mutually exclusive control procedures?

11. Criticize the following statement: "Control totals are used to insure accuracy in a data processing system."

12. Distinguish between a table look-up procedure and a check digit procedure such as might be used to verify codes (such as a customer account number) that are input into a data processing system.

DISCUSSION QUESTIONS AND PROBLEMS

13. What is an audit trail? Discuss the following statement: "Computer processing of accounting data has resulted in the loss of a visible audit trail."

14. This question requires the use of the check digit formula presented in this chapter (page 289).
   a. Calculate check digits for the following hypothetical account numbers: 4388; 5100; 9106.
   b. Verify the following codes (which include a check digit): 10307; 50008; 22222.

15. Consider the following numerical input data utilized in an accounts receivable application:

Account Number	Invoice Number	Gross Amount	Discount	Net Amount
Col 1–4	Col 5–8	Col 9–15	Col 16–21	Col 22–28
4012	1003	265000	15000	250000
4810	1007	321550	27130	294420
7188	1008	108010	11500	965100

a. For the above data, calculate an example of each of the following: hash total; financial total; record count.

b. You are to design an edit program that will be used to screen the above data before it is processed against a sequentially organized accounts receivable master file. Assuming that the input data the edit program receives will be sorted in ascending order by account number, what detailed editing procedures would you include in the design of the edit program?

16. Indicate the objective of the following questions, which are abstracted from an EDP internal control questionnaire. What error or weakness might exist if the answer to a specific question is "No"?

a. Do management and user departments review and approve all new systems design work?

b. Have back-up procedures been documented and are the arrangements up-to-date?

c. Is there an organization chart of the electronic data processing function?

d. Are computer operators required to take vacations?

e. Does more than one programmer or a supervisor have a working knowledge of each specific program?

f. Are internal file labels tested by computer programs to validate file setup?

g. Are check digits used where appropriate?

h. Are changes to master files, such as pay rates or price changes, properly authorized and is their posting to the file verified by the originating department?

i. Are output reports reviewed critically by supervisory personnel in user departments for general reasonableness and quality in relation to prior periods?

17. What control or controls would you recommend in a computer processing system to prevent the following situations from occurring?

a. Working through the main control console, the night-shift computer operator made a change in a payroll program to alter his rate of pay in his favor.

b. A customer payment recorded on a remittance advice as $55.05 was entered into the computer from punched cards as $550.50.

c. A new program to process accounts receivable was unreliable and would not handle common exceptions. The programmer who wrote the program recently quit the organization because he was repeatedly asked to document this program (which he never did do).

d. The payroll master file was incorrectly loaded on a tape drive that was supposed to hold the accounts receivable master file. The accounts receivable program was nevertheless run, destroying the payroll master file.

e. A weekly payroll check issued to an hourly employee was based on 96 hours rather than 46.

f. The master inventory file, contained on a removable magnetic disk, was destroyed by a small fire next to the area where it was stored. The company had to take a special complete inventory in order to reestablish the file.

g. The magnetic tape containing accounts receivable transactions could not be located. A data processing supervisor said that it could have been put among the scratch tapes available for use in processing.

h. In preparing payroll checks, the computer omitted 12 of a total of 1,570 checks that should have been processed. The error was not detected until the foremen distributed the checks.

i. A sales transaction document was coded with an invalid customer account code (7 digits rather than 8). The error was not detected until the updating run, when it was found that there was no such account to which the transaction could be posted.

j. During keypunching of customer payments, the digit 0 in a payment of $123.40 was mistakenly punched as the letter O. As a result, the transaction was not correctly processed.

k. A systems analyst keypunched a special routine one evening after work. The next day she obtained the program that calculates interest payments on customer accounts, and processed it to add her routine to the program's logic. Her routine adds the fraction of a cent of each customer's interest, which would otherwise be rounded off, to her own account at the bank.

l. A salesman entering a customer order from a portable data entry terminal entered an incorrect but valid product number. As a result, the customer received a delivery of 100,000 kilograms of industrial salt rather than industrial sugar.

18. Discuss the role of an internal audit function in the control of computer data processing systems. Identify several changes that are occurring in the internal audit function that relate to computer processing systems.

19.* You have been engaged by Central Savings and Loan Association to examine its financial statements for the year ended December 31,

---

*Material from the Uniform CPA Examinations and Unofficial Answers, copyright © 1968 by the American Institute of Certified Public Accountants, Inc., is reprinted (or adapted) with permission.

19X7. The CPA who examined the financial statements at December 31, 19X6, rendered an unqualified opinion.

In January 19X7 the association installed an on-line real-time computer system. Each teller in the association's main office and seven branch offices has an on-line input-output terminal. Customers' mortgage payments and savings account deposits and withdrawals are recorded in the accounts by the computer from data input by the teller at the time of the transaction. The teller keys the proper account by account number and enters the information in the terminal keyboard to record the transaction. The accounting department at the main office has both punched-card and typewriter input-output devices. The computer is housed at the main office.

In addition to servicing its own mortgage loans the association acts as a mortgage servicing agency for three life insurance companies. In this latter activity the association maintains mortgage records and serves as the collection and escrow agent for the mortgagees (the insurance companies), who pay a fee to the association for these services.

Required:

You would expect the association to have certain internal controls in effect because an on-line real-time computer system is employed. List the internal controls that should be in effect solely because this system is employed, classifying them as:

1. Those controls pertaining to input of information.
2. All other types of computer controls.

20.* Simmons Corporation is a multilocation retailing concern with stores and warehouses throughout the United States. The company is in the process of designing a new integrated computer-based information system. In conjunction with the design of the new system, the management of the company is reviewing the data processing security to determine what new control features should be incorporated. Two areas of specific concern are (1) confidentiality of company and customer records and (2) safekeeping of computer equipment, files, and EDP facilities.

The new information system will be employed to process all company records, which include sales, purchase, financial, budget, customer, creditor, and personnel information. The stores and warehouses will be linked to the main computer at corporate headquarters by a system of remote terminals. This arrangement will permit data to be communicated directly to corporate headquarters or to any other location from each location through the terminal network.

At the present time certain reports have restricted distribution because not all levels of management need to receive them or because they contain

*Adapted from C.M.A. Examination.

confidential information. The introduction of remote terminals in the new system may provide access to this restricted data by unauthorized personnel. Simmons's top management is concerned that confidential information may become accessible and may be used improperly.

The company is also concerned with potential physical threats to the system, such as sabotage, fire damage, water damage, power failure, or magnetic radiation. Should any of these events occur in the present system and cause a computer shutdown, adequate back-up records are available so that the company could reconstruct necessary information at a reasonable cost on a timely basis. However, with the new system, a computer shutdown would severely limit company activities until the system could become operational again.

Required:

a. Identify and briefly explain the problems Simmons Corporation could experience with respect to the confidentiality of information and records in the new system.

b. Recommend measures Simmons Corporation could incorporate into the new system which would ensure the confidentiality of information and records in the new system.

c. What safeguards can Simmons Corporation develop to provide physical security for its (1) computer equipment, (2) files, and (3) EDP facilities?

21. The Big Plastic Co. manufactures a variety of plastic utensils, employing approximately 400 factory workers. Foremen are paid a salary for a 40-hour week, but receive overtime for hours worked in excess of 40. Foremen record hours worked on a weekly time card, clocking in and out at the beginning and end of each day.

Factory workers are paid on an hourly basis. Activity rates are assigned to the operation of various machines in the factory; a worker assigned to a machine is paid the higher of either the machines activity rate or the standard hourly pay rate. Workers clock in and out of each assigned activity on a daily basis. Foremen record the activity code and elapsed time for each entry on a machine operator's daily time card. Foremen maintain a record of machine operator overtime. All workers must account for 8 hours a day, and receive time-and-a-half for hours worked in excess of 8 per day.

A timekeeper collects time cards on a daily basis. Foremen time cards are collected at the end of each week. Time cards are compared to an authorized employee list, initialed by the timekeeper, and forwarded to the payroll department.

In the payroll department a clerk verifies timekeeper initials, batches the cards in groups of 40 or fewer cards, and prepares a prenumbered batch control form for each batch. This form contains total regular hours, overtime hours, date, and number of documents in the batch. The payroll clerk transcribes the contents of each batch control form onto an input batch control log to record and maintain control of each batch. The time cards are then submitted to the computer processing department, where they are keypunched, key verified, and processed by a payroll system edit program to produce a detailed listing of the input items. At the end of the listing, control totals are printed for the valid and the rejected items. If any item in a batch is rejected, then all items in the batch are rejected to maintain batch integrity. The payroll clerk corrects rejected items, prepares a new batch control form, using the original batch number plus a suffix to identify the batch as a correction batch, and resubmits the batch to the computer processing department. This procedure is repeated throughout the week until all errors have been corrected.

The payroll is processed weekly to produce an updated payroll master file, employee checks, and payroll register. These reports are distributed to the payroll department, where a reconciliation with the input controls is performed.

Required:

a. Flowchart the above payroll procedure.
b. Briefly criticize the payroll procedure's input and processing controls.

22.* You are assigned to review the documentation of a data processing function.

Required:

a. List *three* advantages of adequate documentation for a data processing function.
b. Below are two columns of information. The left column lists 6 *categories of documentation*, and the right column lists 18 *elements of documentation* related to the categories. Match each of the elements of documentation with the category in which it should be found. List letters A through F on your answer sheet. After each letter, list the numbers of the elements that *best* apply to that category. Use every element but none more than once.

Categories	*Elements*
A. Systems documentation	1. Flowcharts showing the flow of information
B. Program documentation	
C. Operations documentation	2. Procedures needed to balance, reconcile, and maintain overall control
D. User documentation	
E. Library documentation	3. Storage instructions
F. Data entry documentation	

*Reprinted by permission of The Institute of Internal Auditors, Inc., from the Certified Internal Auditor Examination (May, 1978).

Categories	*Elements*

4. Contents and format of data to be captured
5. Constants, codes, and tables
6. Verification procedures
7. Logic diagrams and/or decision tables
8. Report distribution instructions
9. Messages and programmed halts
10. Procedures for back-up files
11. Retention cycle
12. Source statement listings
13. Instructions to show proper use of each transaction
14. A complete history from planning through installation
15. Restart and recovery procedures
16. Rules for handling blank spaces
17. Instructions to insure the proper completion of all input forms
18. List of programs in a system

23. The HOW-TOO Co. has recently purchased a card-oriented computer system and is considering the implementation of the procedure shown below. Credit and sales slips would be accumulated throughout the day and processed as a single batch the following morning. What application controls, if any, would you recommend the company add to the proposed procedure?

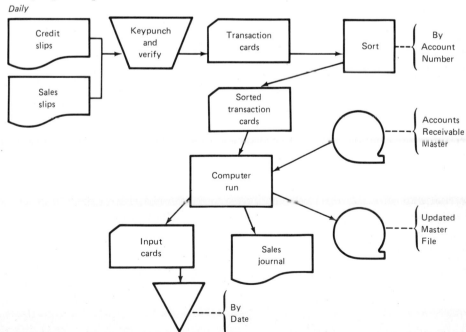

REFERENCES

American Institute of Certified Public Accountants S.A.S. no. 3, "The Effects of EDP on the Auditor's Study and Evaluation of Internal Control" (New York: AICPA, 1974).

Canadian Institute of Chartered Accountants, *Computer Control Guidelines* (Toronto: CICA, 1970).

Institute of Internal Auditor's, Inc., *Systems Auditability and Control Study* Data Processing Control Practices Report (Altamonte Springs, Fla.: IIA, 1977).

REVENUE AND EXPENDITURE CYCLE APPLICATIONS II

11

This chapter contains two illustrations of computer-based accounting application systems. As noted in the previous chapter, computer processing tends to integrate several functions that are separate and distinct in purely manual systems. This integration of functions is apparent in the applications discussed in this chapter.

The first illustration is a revenue cycle application—a batch processing sales-order application system. Order processing, accounts-receivable processing, and inventory-processing functions that are separate and distinct in a manual system are integrated in a computer batch processing system. The discussion of the sales-order application system focuses on the flow of transactional data and the related processing procedures. The overall flow of processing is very similar to that presented in the discussion of computer batch processing in Chapter 10. The illustrated sales order processing application utilizes sequential file processing techniques.

The second illustration contained in this chapter is an expenditure cycle application. This application utilizes direct-access file processing technology to integrate purchases, payables, and inventory management functions. This application system utilizes on-line as opposed to batch processing techniques. The discussion of the expenditure cycle application focuses on the control practices utilized in the system rather than on the attendant file processing techniques.

A BATCH PROCESSING SALES ORDER APPLICATION

This section illustrates the transaction flow in a computer batch processing sales-order application. The system illustrated utilizes punched-card input and maintains the necessary master files on magnetic tape.

Figure 11.1 illustrates the flow of documents in a typical batch-oriented sales-order application. The system illustrated may be contrasted with the sales order application presented in Chapter 4. The major differences between a manual system (Figure 4.2) and a computer batch processing system may be summarized as follows:

1. The computerized application utilizes a separate order and billing procedure, whereas its manual counterpart commonly utilizes an incomplete prebilling procedure. In the computer application, the sales order is a separate internal document; in an incomplete prebilling procedure, the invoice is immediately prepared and serves as the interface among the various departments. This interface function in a computerized batch processing system is fulfilled by a computer file that is shared by several different computer programs.

2. The functions of billing, accounts receivable, and inventory control are *integrated* in the computerized sales-order application. These functions are performed by the computer department from the input data provided on the sales order. Completed sales orders are forwarded to the computer department, keypunched, and the resultant transaction data is used in an integrated series of computer runs that produce invoices, update the accounts receivable file, update the finished goods inventory file, and produce a series of reports relevant to sales, accounts receivable, and inventory. In a manual procedure the above functions are performed by separate departments.

The effect of computer batch processing is minimal on the functions of sales-order preparation, credit checking, inventory, and shipping. These functions are performed in essentially the same fashion in both computer batch processing and manual application systems. Upon receipt of a customer order, a sales order is prepared and processed through credit review, the inventory (finished goods) department, and the shipping department in a manner very similar to that employed in a manual system. The major differences begin after the order has been shipped: the computer assumes the clerical functions of billing, accounts receivable posting, and inventory posting that were formerly performed manually.

Figure 11.2 presents a systems flowchart of the sales order processing application. There are four major subsystems: input preparation, billing and accounts-receivable processing, inventory processing, and reporting. Each of these subsystems is discussed in turn.

Input Preparation

Sales orders are accumulated in batches and forwarded each day to data processing. Sales orders are keypunched onto cards. These input cards are then key verified prior to further processing. The input preparation function should be subject to batch control procedures, as discussed in

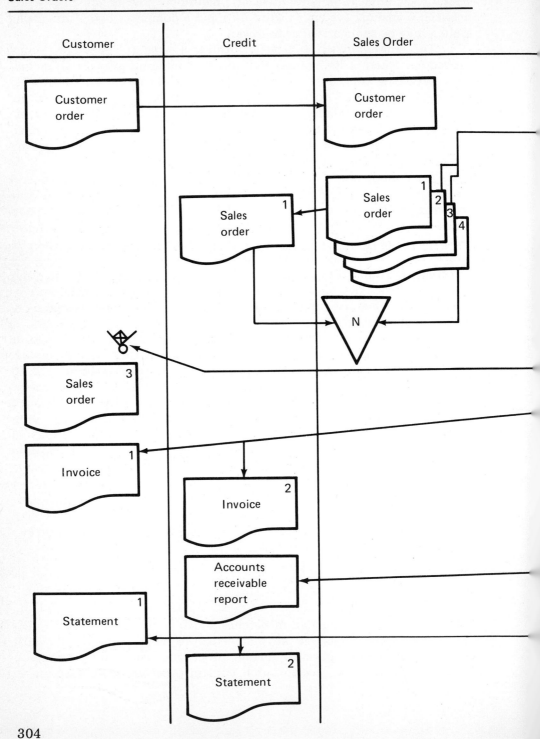

FIGURE 11.1. Document Flowchart for Computer Batch Processing of
Sales Orders

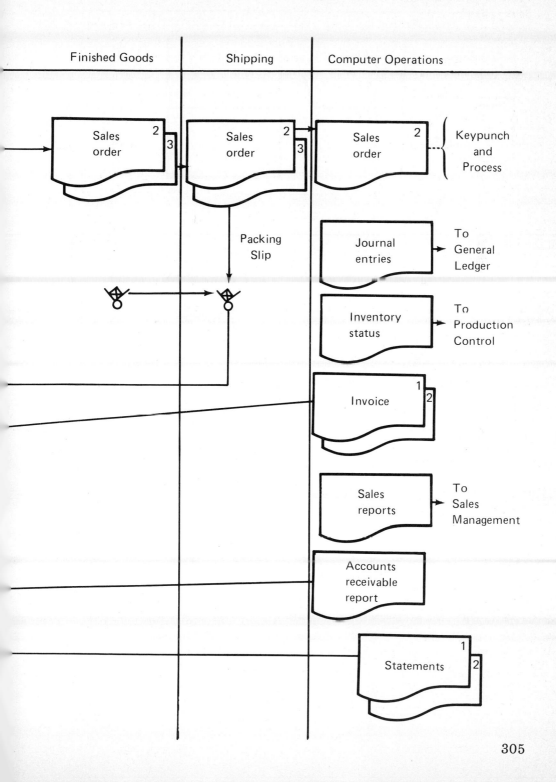

Finished Goods | Shipping | Computer Operations

Sales order 2 3

Sales order 2 3

Sales order 2 — Keypunch and Process

Packing Slip

Journal entries — To General Ledger

Inventory status — To Production Control

Invoice 1 2

Sales reports — To Sales Management

Accounts receivable report

Statements 1 2

305

FIGURE 11.2.   Systems Flowchart of Sales Order Processing

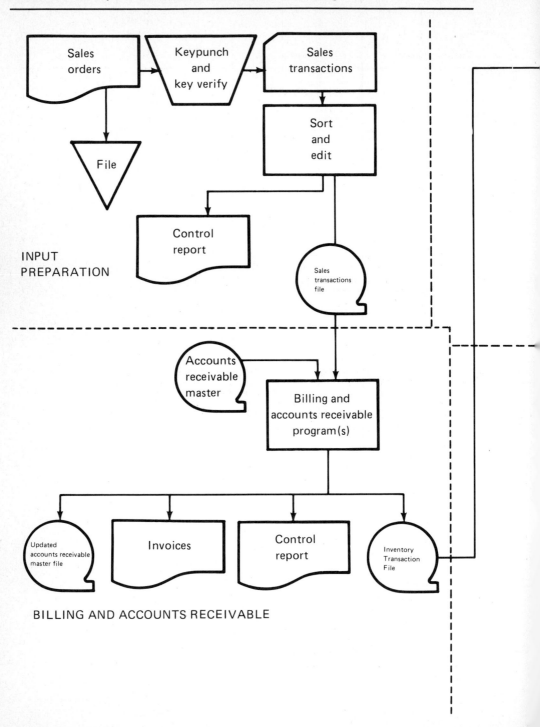

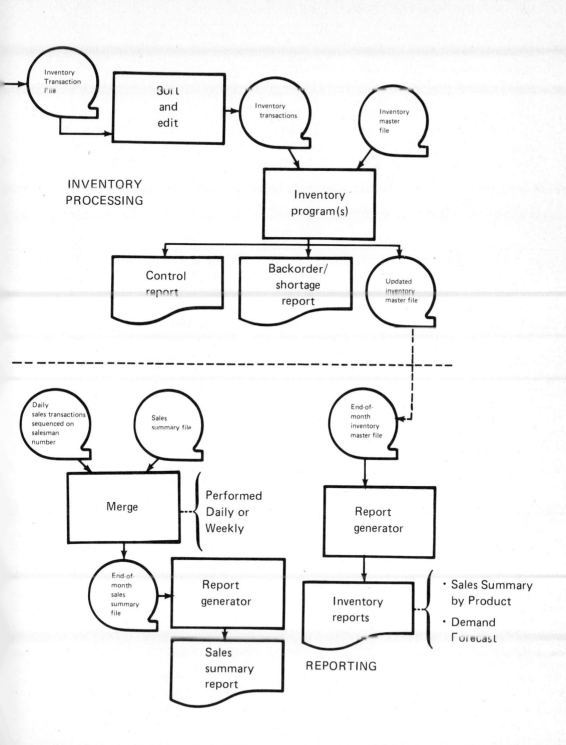

INVENTORY
PROCESSING

Inventory
Transaction
File

Sort
and
edit

Inventory
transactions

Inventory
master
file

Inventory
program(s)

Control
report

Backorder/
shortage
report

Updated
inventory
master file

Daily
sales transactions
sequenced on
salesman
number

Sales
summary file

End-of-
month
inventory
master file

Merge

Performed
Daily or
Weekly

Report
generator

End-of-
month
sales
summary
file

Report
generator

Inventory
reports

• Sales Summary
  by Product

• Demand
  Forecast

Sales
summary
report

REPORTING

Chapter 10. The transaction cards contain information relevant to billing, accounts receivable, inventory, and reporting applications. Such information would normally include customer account number, salesman number, product numbers and quantities of items shipped and of those items back ordered (if any), and unit prices. The transaction file is sorted into customer account number sequence and transferred to magnetic tape to complete the input preparation function. Normal data editing functions and error correction procedures that were detailed in the discussion of Chapter 10 are omitted herein to facilitate discussion of the application.

Billing and Accounts Receivable

The sales transaction file is input each day to the billing and accounts-receivable application program(s) along with the accounts-receivable master file. (See Figure 11.2.) Both the sales transactions file and the customer accounts file are sequenced on customer account number. The billing program generates invoices from the sales order transaction data. The accounts-receivable file is updated to reflect the new customer billings. A control-summary report of the billing–accounts receivable application is output along with an inventory transaction file that will be utilized in the inventory control application. The inventory transaction file contains information pertaining to shipments and back orders. This information is obtained from the sales transaction file. The control-summary report would contain information pertaining to batch and application controls as well as summary journal-entry data debiting accounts receivable and crediting sales for the batch totals.

Inventory Processing

The inventory application program updates the perpetual inventory file for shipments and back orders. Prior to this updating, the inventory transaction file output by the billing program is sorted into sequence by product number. The resultant transaction file is input to the inventory application program(s) along with the inventory master file. The inventory application program posts shipments as reductions to the on-hand quantity shown in the inventory records and records back order information as appropriate. The outputs of the inventory application include the updated inventory master file, a control-summary report containing batch and application control information, which includes the summary journal entry debiting cost of sales and crediting inventory for shipments, and a back order–shortage report, which may be used for purposes of inventory control.

The inventory file in a computer-based system frequently contains much more information pertaining to products than would be found in a manually processed inventory file. Computer files and processing frequently integrate accounting data with operational data. An inventory file would normally include accounting data pertaining to quantity, costs, and price; a computerized inventory file would include this accounting data as well as product-related operational data such as forecasted demand for each product, reorder points, reorder quantities, and vendor-related data such as vendor identification, vendor delivery (lead) time, and other such data. The capability to economically maintain and process operational as well as accounting data pertaining to transactions is a major advantage of computer versus manual processing techniques.

Reporting

The billing–accounts-receivable and inventory applications are run each day. Reporting applications are run at less frequent intervals, such as once a month or perhaps weekly. A wide variety of reports pertaining to sales order processing may be produced. Two common reports are a sales summary by product type and a sales summary by salesman.

Figure 11.2 illustrates the processing sequence necessary to obtain these reports in the application being illustrated. The sales summary report is produced by processing a sales summary file. The sales summary file is a sequential listing of sales transactions ordered by salesman identification number. Daily sales transaction files used by the billing and accounts-receivable application are sorted into sequence on salesman identification number and merged—that is, combined—to produce a sales summary file. This processing might occur at the end of the daily billing and accounts-receivable application or be postponed to the end of each week. The sales summary file is processed by a reporting program which generates the sales summary report.

The sales summary by product type report is obtained by processing the end-of-month inventory master file. The inventory master file is sequenced on product identification number. This file is processed by a report-generating program (Figure 11.2) to produce the sales summary by product-type report. This processing would generally produce several inventory status reports, depending on the detailed operational data maintained by the inventory application. A demand forecast, for example, might be produced by accumulating detailed product-demand information, which is stored on the inventory file.

The general procedure for generating any end-of-month report is similar. The relevant file of data is updated to reflect the month's transactional data, and then sorted into the sequence which is necessary to produce a report. The file is processed by a special report generating program which outputs the desired report. Formatting the desired report requires the use of table files and line coding assignments; these concepts were detailed in Chapter 10.

AN ON-LINE EXPENDITURE CYCLE APPLICATION

This section provides an illustration of an on-line expenditure cycle application. This application integrates purchases, payables, and inventory management functions. This application is representative of contemporary AIS found in business organizations.

The discussion focuses on control practices rather than on the underlying processing techniques. This illustration was originally published in the *Systems Auditability and Control Study* prepared for the Institute of Internal Auditors, Inc. (1977). This study was prepared to examine contemporary data processing control practices. The *Data Processing Control Practices Report*, one of three volumes that constitute the *Systems Auditability and Control Study*, contains four illustrative case studies, which are presented not as ideal models of control but rather as representative applications found in large organizations. The following illustration is one of these case studies, and is reprinted herein with the permission of the Institute of Internal Auditors, Inc.

Application Overview

The basic objective of an inventory management system is to assist corporate management to maintain a level of inventory that achieves the optimum balance between on-order, on-hand, and out-of-stock. The inventory management system reviewed herein is described as follows:

> The engineering department inputs its requirement into an inventory management system. This information, together with other inventory data, is used to calculate reorder points and quantities. Information files are checked regarding inventory part specification, suppliers, open purchase orders, and purchase orders are prepared for material planner review. Material buyers notify suppliers and the material is ordered. Upon receipt of the ordered material, receiving memos are prepared, the purchase order closed, and the material warehoused. The following control illustration describes in more detail the inventory management system.

Background

This control illustration describes an on-line inventory management system that is currently being used by a large manufacturing company. This system, which operates in both an on-line and batch processing mode, has more than 400 terminals in daily operation, and operates on a large-scale computer with a second computer available for backup if necessary. The terminals that are being used are basically typewriter models, although audio response terminals are being used in the material-receiving operation. This inventory management system, in addition to controlling supplier files, purchase order files, and work order files, also controls five inventory data files that consist of four facility inventory files and one surplus inventory file. These inventory files consist of more than 80,000 separate inventory items, and approximately one-fourth of the inventory items are disbursed and received monthly.

The inventory management system and the 25 control points of the system are illustrated in Figure 11.3.

Application Description and Control Practices

All the terminals are activated at the beginning of each business day. Those terminals that connect to the inventory management system through a dial-up system use a password sign-on feature, while those terminals that connect to the system through leased lines have no special password sign-on procedures. There is, however, a terminal/transaction matrix resident in the computer that governs the use of these controls.

Control Point 1—Terminal Transaction Control

A matrix of approved transaction codes is maintained by the inventory management system. This matrix, prepared by data processing and approved by the Materials Management Department, is checked as each terminal request is made. Those transactions not approved are rejected, and the terminal operator is not allowed access to the inventory management data base files. As a further control, special passwords stored in the matrix are used by those terminals that have approved transactions when changes such as payments and credit codes are being made to certain data elements of the Supplier File. All rejected transactions are recorded on the computer log tape (see Control Point 2).

All information that is transmitted to and from the inventory management system is recorded on a computer log tape.

Control Point 2—Transmission Log Control

The data recorded on the computer log tape are used primarily for terminal statistical reporting. A monthly report is produced by terminal identification number that reflects all transmissions to and from the inventory management system. This report is used by data processing, EDP auditors, and material management personnel to monitor terminal activity and to review unauthorized attempts at terminal usage. Special reports may be requested from the computer log tape.

All information that is to be processed by the inventory management system is first edited or validated by a generalized validation system that is used for all on-line application processing.

Control Point 3—Data Validation Control

Edit routines have been developed in a validation application system that is generalized for all the organization's on-line application systems. This valida-

FIGURE 11.3. Inventory Management Flowchart

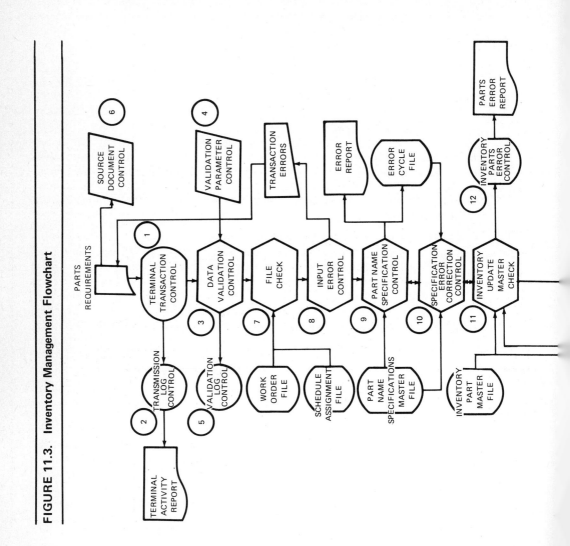

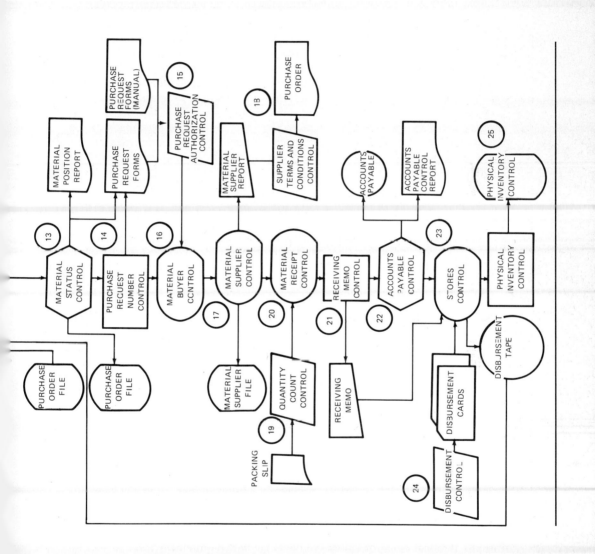

From *Systems Auditability and Control Study.* Copyright © 1977 by The Institute of Internal Auditors, Inc. (Altemonte, Fla.: 1977). Reprinted with permission.

tion system performs checks on all input transactions. Some of the data valida-
tion routines include verification that the number of input characters does not
exceed the number allowed, check digit calculation, mandatory presence of a
data element, and calendar data edit. Once an error is detected in a data ele-
ment, no further checking on that data element is performed. However, editing
on other data elements of the input transaction continues until all data elements
have been checked or until a third data element in error is detected, at which
time the input transaction is immediately rejected. After the data being entered
by the terminal operator have been validated, the transaction is recorded on the
generalized validation system log tape (see Control Point 5) and the transaction
is then passed to the appropriate application system for processing, in this in-
stance the inventory management system. Input transactions that are rejected
are reentered by the terminal operator after corrections have been made by the
department preparing the input. Rejected transactions are not recorded on the
generalized validation system log tape as this log tape may be used for system
recovery purposes.

Control Point 4—Validation Parameter Control
The parameters within the generalized validation system can be changed as nec-
essary to accommodate the validation requirements of an application. Changes
to the parameters are made via a memo signed by the departmental manager
responsible for the application system. A copy of this change memo is filed
in the data processing department and is periodically reviewed by the EDP
auditors.

Control Point 5—Validation Log Control
The data recorded on the computer tape of the generalized validation system
are used primarily for file recovery. Special reports are printed from this log
tape when, as an example, the EDP auditors are reviewing validation parameter
changes. The tape as a rule, however, is printed only when difficulties are being
experienced in file recovery. All transactions that enter the inventory manage-
ment system via batch processing are kept on magnetic tape. These tapes, which
contain only valid transactions, are retained for three inventory management
system update cycles. When it is necessary to restore the data files, these tapes
are merged with the computer log tape of the generalized validation system.
The tapes are not printed routinely but only when difficulties are encountered
in file restoration.

When an engineering change has to be made to a product, an engineering blueprint
is reviewed by a parts requirement analyst who prepares a parts requirements form
for those sections of the engineering blueprint where parts will be required. The
parts requirement form is given to a terminal operator for entry into the system.
After the terminal operator enters the data, the part requirement form is filed by
engineering drawing number.

Control Point 6—Source Document Control
The parts requirement form that contains the engineering drawing number is
filed by that number in a temporary file at the terminal operator's station,
where it is used for correcting any data errors or answering part requirement
questions as they relate to the drawing.

The part requirement transaction, after having been edited by the generalized validation program, is then processed by the inventory management system. The Work Order File, which is maintained and controlled by the Finance Department, is interrogated. The Schedule Assignment File, which is maintained and controlled by the Manufacturing Department, is also interrogated.

Control Point 7—File Check
The Work Order File is checked to obtain the contract number and to validate the account number against which the items required will be charged. If neither the correct record on the file nor the account number can be verified, the input transaction is rejected (see Control Point 8). The Schedule Assignment File is checked to obtain the "need" date for the part. This data element is required as it is basic data input to ordering and stocking calculations of the inventory master update program. If the appropriate master record cannot be located on the Schedule Assignment File, the part requirement transaction will be rejected (see Control Point 8).

Control Point 8—Input Error Control
All on-line input transactions that are rejected by the inventory management system are transmitted immediately to the inputting terminal, where the hardcopy printout of the transaction and the reason for rejection are attached to the source document (part requirement form) and returned to the originating department for correction and resubmission. The managers of the departments inputting data to the inventory management system have the responsibility to ensure that all transactions that are rejected are corrected and resubmitted.

The next step in the inventory management system is the exploding of the part requirements into component or item inventory requirements. These requirements are held on magnetic tape for the next processing of the inventory control segment of the inventory management system. The item inventory requirements that will be processed weekly and in a batch mode will be checked against a Part Name and Specifications File.

Control Point 9—Part Name/Specification Control
Each component or inventory item that resulted from the parts requirement explosion is checked against a Part Name and Specification File. If the item is not a new inventory item, it is only validated against the file. Any item that cannot be found on this file is printed on an error report and recorded on an error cycle file (see Control Point 10). The weekly error report that reflects the input transaction (after the parts explosion) and the reason for rejection is sent to the originating department for correction and resubmission.

Control Point 10—Specification Error Correction Control
Most of the input transactions that are rejected are new inventory items that are input to the system as transactions prior to the updating of the Part Name and Specification File. The Error Cycle File is merged with weekly input transactions for reprocessing. If the transaction is rejected again, it is reported on a weekly error report, which is sent to a material planner and again recorded on the error file a maximum of six times, when it will be dropped. All transactions to be dropped are so noted on the weekly error report. A transaction on

the Error Cycle File may be erased prior to the sixth cycle by the material planner entering a void transaction as part of the regular weekly update.

The data from the parts requirements explosion, as well as inventory adjustment and disbursement transactions, are processed by the Inventory Control Master Update Program. The Master Update Program contains all the formulae that have been developed to control the timing and quantity of stocking levels, replenishments, and stock locations of inventory items. The input transactions to the Inventory Control Master Update Program are checked against the Purchase Order File and the Facility Inventory Part Files. When the Inventory Control Master Update Program determines that inventory items are required, purchase records are created on the Purchase Order File and "to-be-ordered" quantities of the Inventory Parts Records are updated.

Control Point 11—Inventory Update Master Check
The input transactions are checked against the Purchase Order File, to obtain status information regarding any open purchase orders for each inventory item that is required. This status information will later be printed on the Purchase Request to assist the material planner in controlling stocking levels and the buyer in placing the purchase order.

The input transactions are also checked against the Facility Inventory Files to validate the inventory part number and also to ensure that the amount of inventory to be disbursed does not exceed the allowed quantity to disburse. All transactions that are rejected because of invalid part numbers or disbursement quantity problems are printed on an error report, which is sent to the originating department for correction and resubmission. The error is also recorded on an Inventory Parts Error File.

Control Point 12—Inventory Parts Error Control
The Inventory Parts Error File operates in the same manner as the Error Cycle File discussed earlier (see Control Point 10). The exception is that the transactions in error will not be eliminated after six processing cycles. Positive action, namely the inputting by the material planner of a transaction to erase the erroneous transaction, is the only way to eliminate an error transaction from the Error Cycle File.

A material position report together with purchase request forms are prepared by the inventory management system for the material planner's review.

Control Point 13—Material Status Control
The material position report reflects the quantity on hand, quantity on order, and quantity to be disbursed for each item of inventory to be ordered. The material planner, in reviewing the report, may increase or decrease the quantity to be ordered. The material planner may even cancel the purchase request completely. When a purchase request is cancelled, the material planner stamps the request cancelled, initials it, and submits it to a terminal operator for entry to the inventory management system. The purchase request record on the Purchase Order File is erased and the "to-be-ordered" quantity of the Inventory

Parts Record is reduced by the quantity on the erased purchase request record. When the decision is made to increase or decrease the quantity to be ordered, the Inventory Parts Record is changed accordingly and the purchase request record on the Purchase Order File is also changed.

Control Point 14—Purchase Request Number Control
When a purchase request is printed, the computer generates a purchase request number to eliminate the possibility of duplicate purchase request numbers being assigned to potential purchase orders. This request number, which is an eight-digit number, includes coding that identifies the department requesting the materials. This tie-back to the requesting department serves as a means of tracing a purchase request if something delays it in the purchasing order cycle. Manually prepared purchase requests are prenumbered forms, with the area for the requesting department number left blank. The department number is entered by the requesting department when the purchase request is completed. Purchase requests are prepared manually only when the requirement for an inventory item is such that the material planner cannot wait for the weekly processing of the Inventory Control Update program that prints the purchase requests. Manually prepared requests are entered via the terminal operator and the data are validated as discussed in Control Points 7, 8, 9, and 11. All errors detected are transmitted to the input terminal where they are corrected by the material planner and resubmitted.

When the material planner approves a purchase request, the request is stamped "approved" and initialed by the material planner. It is then submitted to a material buyer.

Control Point 15—Purchase Request Authorization Control
The purchase request must be stamped "approved" and initialed before any material buyer action can take place. If the purchase request is not stamped, it is rejected by the buyer. Computer prepared purchase requests are sent to the material planning supervisor, where they are investigated and resubmitted for buyer action if appropriate. Manually prepared purchase requests that are not stamped "approved" are returned to the manager of the requesting department for investigation and resubmitted for buyer action if later approved by a material planner.

The material buyer, when processing a purchase request, prefixes the purchase request number with his two-digit buyer code.

Control Point 16—Material Buyer Control
Each material buyer has a two-digit buyer code that is prefixed to the purchase request number. This code is entered into the computer by the terminal operator and becomes an integral part of the purchase request number. The buyer code serves as a means of tracing purchase orders and also as a means of monitoring and evaluating the performance of a buyer.

Before the buyer contacts the material supplier and obtains the purchase terms and conditions, the supplier information on record is checked in the inventory management system.

Control Point 17—Material Supplier Control
The Material Supplier File is checked via a terminal located in the purchasing department to verify that the supplier is approved. If the supplier is not considered an approved supplier, because of such things as poor material quality or late deliveries, then another supplier's record is reviewed. If no other supplier is on the Supplier File, then the buyer notifies his supervisor and the purchase request is held until an approved supplier can be located.

When an approved material supplier is contacted and the purchasing terms and conditions are obtained, they are entered by the terminal operator into the inventory management system and recorded on the Purchase Order File.

Control Point 18—Supplier Terms and Conditions Control
The final value of the purchase order, if it is more than a predetermined amount (this amount may vary by project), is reviewed by the buyer supervisor, who has the authority to cancel the order if he deems it appropriate. If the order is cancelled, then the terms and conditions recorded on the Purchase Order File are erased through the terminal by the terminal operator and another supplier is located. The purchase request, which is now considered an order, is further checked by representatives from product assurance and packaging. Any disagreements are resolved by the manager of the department requesting the materials.

When the ordered material arrives at the plant receiving dock, it is counted by a representative of the material inspection department.

Control Point 19—Quantity Count Control
The material is counted and compared to quantity count on the attached vendor-supplied packing slip. If the count does not agree with the packing slip, the material inspection department manager is notified and the material is impounded until the quantity difference is resolved. Resolution usually results in the supplier authorizing the material inspection department manager to change the packing slip count to agree with the actual count.

When the actual quantity and packing slip quantity agree, the packing slip is submitted to a terminal operator in the material inspection department for entry into the inventory management system.

Control Point 20—Material Receipt Control
The terminal operator enters the packing slip number, the purchase order number (from the packing slip), and the quantity received. If there is no match against the Purchase Order File, the packing slip and the material are held for a maximum of two days. The terminal operator reenters the information several more times in the two-day period. This mismatch is often caused by material being expedited before computer records can be updated. Failure to match the material data to the Purchase Order File within two days results in the buyer supervisor being notified by the material inspection department manager, and the matter is investigated. If the difference is a mismatch in terms of over or under shipment as compared to the quantity ordered on the purchase order, or if the arrival date is significantly different from that reflected on the purchase order, the following occurs:

If the material received arrives more than 30 days ahead of schedule, the material investigation group must be advised and a decision made as to whether to return the material or to impound it until such time as it is needed. If the material received is overshipped by 5% or $50, the material investigation group must be advised. If the overshipped material is accepted, then the requesting department must increase the purchase order request quantity to agree with the shipped quantity and these data must be recorded on the Purchase Order File. If the material is undershipped, usually by 5% or $50, and the purchase order is not being closed out (finalized), the shipment is accepted. If, however, there is an undershipment and the purchase order is being closed out, a special change order must be prepared by the material planner and recorded on the Purchase Order File. The purpose of this control point is to record the fact that the ordered material has arrived, but because of discrepancies is being held.

When the material is considered acceptable (shipped quantity equals ordered quantity and receiving date is within 30 days of requested date), a computer-generated receiving memo is prepared on the hard-copy terminal at the receiving location.

Control Point 21—Receiving Memo Control
A receiving memo with a computer-generated control number is printed and attached to the material. The control number, which consists of eight digits including a check digit calculated using the modulus 10 weighted formula, is recorded on the purchase order record indicating that the material has been received and is currently located in the material inspection department.

When the receiving memo is printed by the inventory management system, an accounts payable transaction tape is generated for accounts payable application system processing.

Control Point 22—Accounts Payable Control
In addition to supplying a tape for processing, an audit trail report of all transactions is prepared. This audit trail report, which reflects vendor name, purchase order number, and amount due, is reviewed by the personnel of the accounts payable department, as the policy at the organization interviewed is that all procurements under $5,000 are paid automatically. This represents 90% of all procurements. If, however, the value of the purchase order is over $5,000, then an accounts payable check is not issued, and the supplier will not receive payment until such time as an invoice is submitted.

When the material arrives at the stores location, the stores attendant, via an audio response terminal, enters the receiving memo control number from the receiving memo that is attached to the material.

Control Point 23—Stores Control
When the receiving memo control number is entered into the inventory management system, the check digit is calculated and if there is an error, the audio response terminal responds, indicating an incorrect receiving memo control number. After several unsuccessful attempts have been made, stores management advises the data processing department, since a control number reject at this point is indicative of a software problem. When the control number is

successfully entered, the quantity data from the Purchase Order File are entered on the Inventory Parts Record. The purchase order record on the Purchase Order File is retained for historical purposes and after approximately 12 months will be recorded on microfilm.

When inventory items are going to be disbursed from stores, disbursement cards that reflect part number, "need" date, unit of issue, issue quantity, and work order number are reviewed by the material planner.

Control Point 24—Disbursement Control
The material planner must authorize inventory disbursement. The stores keeper is not allowed to disburse any inventory item without a disbursement card signed by the material planner.

When parts are disbursed from stores, the approved disbursement cards are transmitted via the card-reading terminal located in the stores area to the inventory management system. The disbursement information is stored on tape for weekly processing of the Inventory Control Master Update Program (see Control Point 11).

A physical inventory is taken on a cycle basis over at least a year. High-value parts, such as microelectronic parts, are counted more frequently. The inventory management system generates a card containing the part number, part description, and unit of issue when a physical inventory is to be taken.

Control Point 25—Physical Inventory Control
The actual item count is entered on the card and is processed by the inventory management system. The actual count is compared to the "quantity-on-hand" count in the Inventory Parts Master and a report of exceptions is produced for the Material Management and Finance Departments. If the exception value is $200 or less, the "quantity-on-hand" count of the Inventory Parts Master is adjusted and the part dollar value is written off by the Finance Department. If the exception value is more than $200, then a part recount is ordered. If the exception still exists after the recount, the Material Management Department will review every transaction pertaining to that particular part since the last physical count. When the discrepancy has been resolved, the Inventory Parts Master is adjusted.

REVIEW QUESTIONS

1. What manual functions are integrated in a batch processing sales-order application system?

2. Identify the journal entries necessary to summarize the results of sales-order processing and their source in a batch processing application.

3. Identify the major master files that must be maintained in a batch processing sales-order application.

4. What is a data access matrix?

5. What are the advantages of having an application program automatically assign sequential document control numbers to input records entered on-line?

6. What purposes are served by prefixing purchase requisition numbers with a material buyer code?

DISCUSSION QUESTIONS AND PROBLEMS

7. Develop a systems flowchart for an on-line sales-order processing application. Indicate several application controls you would include in the design of the application.

8. Consider the systems flowchart of the batch processing sales-order application system discussed in the chapter (Figure 11.2). Indicate several changes in the processing sequence that might be made if magnetic disks were utilized for file storage rather than magnetic tape.

9. The Morphy Co. operates an accounts-payable system. Purchase orders, receiving reports, and payment records are keypunched. The card deck is read into the computer, where a card-to-tape utility program transfers the information to a tape, in an unsorted arrangement. A sort utility program is then used to sort the tape transaction records by account number. This tape is then used with the accounts-payable master file to create an updated accounts-payable master file and a listing of the day's activity. The current date of the run is read into the computer from the console keyboard.

Describe application controls that you would recommend be included in the above procedure.

10. Would payroll processing be suited for on-line processing? Discuss, considering separately the input, processing, and output requirements of payroll processing applications.

11.* The Vane Corporation is a manufacturing concern that has been in business for the past eighteen years. During this period, the company has grown from a very small family-owned operation to a medium-sized manufacturing concern with several departments. Despite this growth, a substantial number of the procedures employed by the Vane Corporation have been in effect since the business was started. Just recently, Vane has computerized its payroll function.

*Adapted from C.M.A. Examination.

The payroll function operates in the following manner. Each worker picks up a weekly time card on Monday morning and writes in his name and identification number. These blank cards are kept near the factory entrance. The workers write on the time card the time of their daily arrival and departure. On the following Monday the factory foremen collect the completed time cards for the previous week and send them to data processing.

In data processing, the time cards are used to prepare the weekly time file. This file is processed with the master payroll file, which is maintained on magnetic tape according to worker identification number. The checks are written by the computer on the regular checking account and imprinted with the treasurer's signature. After the payroll file is updated and the checks are prepared, the checks are sent to the factory foremen, who distribute them to the workers or hold them for the workers to pick up later if they are absent.

The foremen notify data processing of new employees and terminations. Any changes in hourly pay rate or any other changes affecting payroll are usually communicated to data processing by the foremen.

The workers also complete a job time ticket for each individual job they work on each day. The job time tickets are collected daily and sent to cost accounting, where they are used to prepare a cost-distribution analysis.

Further analysis of the payroll function reveals the following:

a. A worker's gross wages never exceed $300 per week.
b. Raises never exceed $0.55 per hour for the factory workers.
c. No more than 20 hours of overtime is allowed each week.
d. The factory employs 150 workers in ten departments.

The payroll function has not been operating smoothly for some time, but even more problems have surfaced since the payroll was computerized. The foremen have indicated that they would like a weekly report indicating worker tardiness, absenteeism, and idle time, so they can determine the amount of productive time lost and the reason for the lost time. The following errors and inconsistencies have been encountered the past few pay periods:

1. A worker's paycheck was not processed properly, because he had transposed two numbers in his identification number when he filled out his time card.
2. A worker was issued a check for $1,531.80 when it should have been $153.81.
3. One worker's paycheck was not written, and this error was not detected until the paychecks for that department were distributed by the foreman.
4. Part of the master payroll file was destroyed when the tape reel

was inadvertently mounted on the wrong tape drive and used as a scratch tape. Data processing attempted to reestablish the destroyed portion from original source documents and other records.

5. One worker received a paycheck for an amount considerably larger than he should have. Further investigation revealed that 84 had been punched instead of 48 for hours worked.

6. Several records on the master payroll file were skipped and not included on the updated master payroll file. This was not detected for several pay periods.

7. In processing nonroutine changes, a computer operator included a pay rate increase for one of his friends in the factory. This was discovered by chance by another employee.

Required:

Identify the control weaknesses in the payroll procedure and in the computer processing as it is now conducted. Recommend the changes necessary to correct the system. Arrange your answer in the following columnar format:

| *Control Weaknesses* | *Recommendations* |

12.* Peabock Co. is a wholesaler of softgoods. The inventory is composed of approximately 3,500 different items. The company employs a computerized batch processing system to maintain its perpetual inventory records. The system is run each weekend so that the inventory reports are available on Monday morning for management use. The system has been functioning satisfactorily for the past 15 months, providing the company with accurate records and timely reports.

The preparation of purchase orders has been automatic as a part of the inventory system to insure that the company will maintain enough inventory to meet customer demand. When an item of inventory falls below a predetermined level, a record of the inventory item is written. This record is used in conjunction with the vendor file to prepare the purchase orders.

Exception reports are prepared during the updating of the inventory and the preparation of the purchase orders. These reports identify any errors or exceptions identified during the processing. In addition, the system provides for management approval of all purchase orders exceeding a specified amount. Any exceptions or items requiring management approval are handled by supplemental runs on Monday morning and combined with the weekend results.

A system flowchart of Peabock Co.'s inventory and purchase order procedure appears on pages 324 and 325.

*Adapted from C.M.A. Examination.

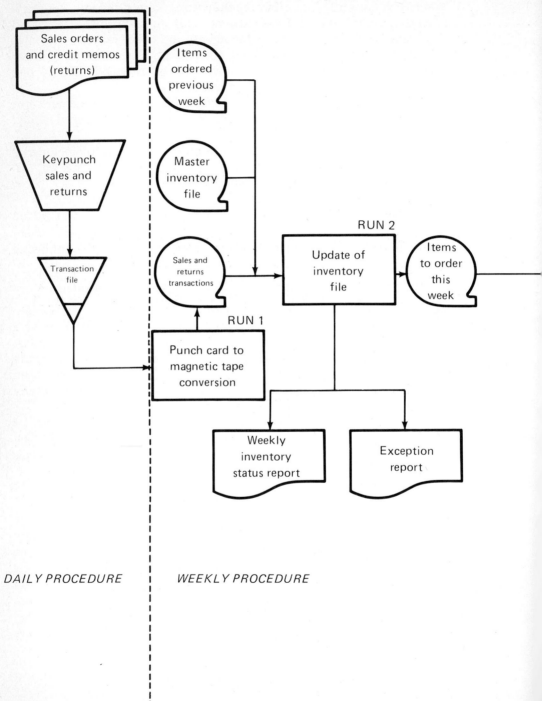

Inventory and Purchase Order System,
Peabock Co.

Sales orders
and credit memos
(returns)

Items
ordered
previous
week

Keypunch
sales and
returns

Master
inventory
file

RUN 2

Update of
inventory
file

Items
to order
this
week

Transaction
file

Sales and
returns
transactions

RUN 1

Punch card to
magnetic tape
conversion

Weekly
inventory
status report

Exception
report

DAILY PROCEDURE

WEEKLY PROCEDURE

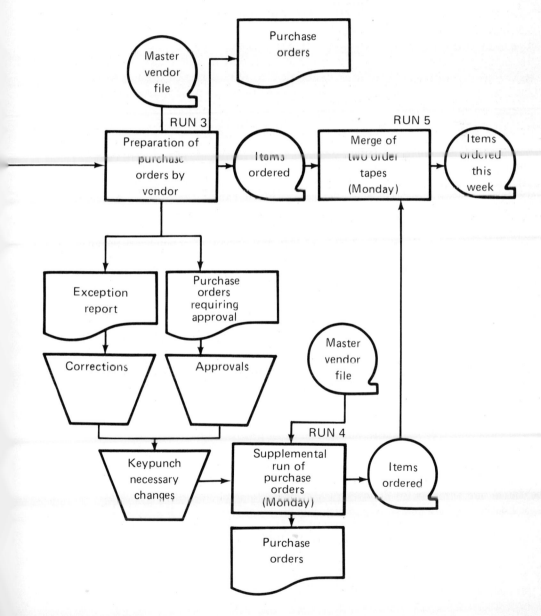

Required:

a. The illustrated system flowchart of Peabock Co.'s inventory and purchase order system was prepared before the system was fully operational. Several steps that are important to the successful operations of the system were inadvertently omitted from the chart. Now that the system is operating effectively, management wants the system documentation complete and would like the flowchart corrected. Describe steps that have been omitted and indicate where the omissions have occurred. The flowchart does not need to be drawn.

b. In order for Peabock's inventory–purchase order system to function properly, control procedures would be included in the system. Describe the type of control procedures Peabock Co. would use in their system to assure proper functioning and indicate where these procedures would be placed in the system.

13.* Georgia Beemster, CPA, is examining the financial statements of the Louisville Sales Corporation, which recently installed an off-line electronic computer. The following comments have been extracted from Ms. Beemster's notes on computer operations and the processing and control of shipping notices and customer invoices:

To minimize inconvenience Louisville converted without change its data-processing system, which utilized tabulating equipment. The computer company supervised the conversion and has provided training to all computer department employees (except keypunch operators) in system design, operations, and programming.

Each computer run is assigned to a specific employee, who is responsible for making program changes, running the program, and answering questions. This procedure has the advantage of eliminating the need for records of computer operations because each employee is responsible for his own computer runs.

At least one computer department employee remains in the computer rooms during office hours, and only computer department employees have keys to the computer room.

System documentation consists of those materials furnished by the computer company—a set of record formats and program listings. These and the tape library are kept in a corner of the computer department.

The company considered the desirability of programmed controls but decided to retain the manual controls from its existing system.

Company products are shipped directly from public warehouses, which forward shipping notices to general accounting. There a billing clerk enters the price of the item and accounts for the numerical sequence of shipping notices from each warehouse. The billing clerk also prepares daily adding machine tapes ("control tapes") of the units shipped and the unit prices.

Shipping notices and control tapes are forwarded to the computer department for keypunching and processing. Extensions are made on the computer. Output consists of invoices (in six copies) and the daily sales register. The daily sales register shows the aggregate totals of units shipped and unit prices, which the computer operator compares with the control tapes.

All copies of the invoice are returned to the billing clerk. The clerk mails three copies to the customer, forwards one copy to the warehouse, maintains one copy in a numerical file, and retains one copy in an open invoice file that serves as a detail accounts receivable record.

Required:

Describe weaknesses in internal control over information and data flows and the procedures for processing shipping notices and customer invoices, and recommend improvements in these controls and processing procedures. Organize your answer as follows:

Weakness	Recommended Improvement

14.*   You are reviewing audit work papers containing a narrative description of the Tenney Corporation's factory payroll system. A portion of that narrative is as follows:

Factory employees punch time clock cards each day when entering or leaving the shop. At the end of each week the timekeeping department collects the time cards and prepares duplicate batch-control slips by department, showing total hours and number of employees. The time cards and original batch-control slips are sent to the payroll accounting section. The second copies of the batch-control slips are filed by date.

In the payroll accounting section, payroll transaction cards are keypunched from the information on the time cards, and a batch total card for each batch is keypunched from the batch-control slip. The time cards and batch-control slips are then filed by batch for possible reference. The payroll transaction cards and batch total card are sent to data processing, where they are sorted by employee number within batch. Each batch is edited by a computer program, which checks the validity of employee number against a master employee tape file and the total hours and number of employees against the batch total card. A detail printout by batch and employee number is produced, which indicates batches that do not balance and invalid employee numbers. This printout is returned to payroll accounting to resolve all differences.

In searching for documentation you found a flowchart (below) of the payroll system, which included all appropriate symbols (American National Standards Institute, Inc.) but was only partially labeled. The portion of this flowchart described by the above narrative appears on the following page.

Required:

a.   Number your answer 1 through 17. Next to the corresponding

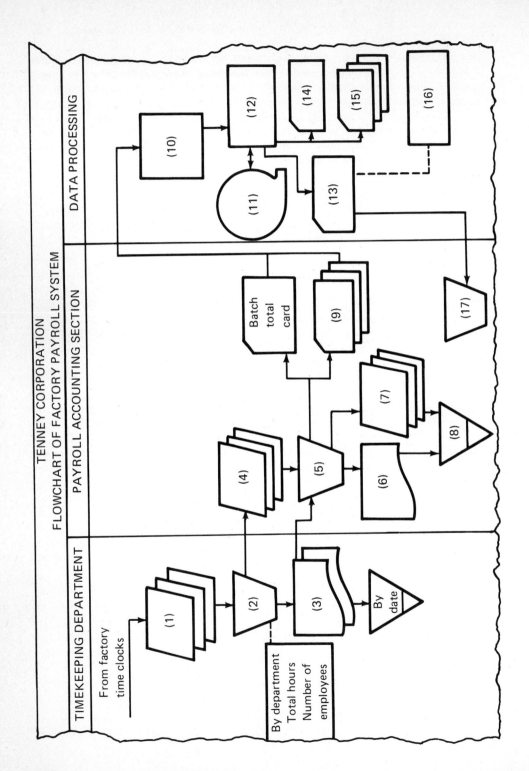

TENNEY CORPORATION
FLOWCHART OF FACTORY PAYROLL SYSTEM

number of your answer, supply the appropriate labeling (document name, process description, or file order) applicable to each numbered symbol on the flowchart.

b. Flowcharts are one of the aids an auditor may use to determine and evaluate a client's internal control system. List advantages of using flowcharts in this context.

REFERENCE

Institute of Internal Auditors, Inc., *Systems Auditability and Control Study* (Altamonte Springs, Fla.: IIA, 1977).

PRODUCTION AND FINANCE CYCLE APPLICATIONS II

12

This chapter illustrates three accounting application systems. The first illustration discusses the application of batch processing techniques to the production control function in a manufacturing concern. The discussion of the production control application focuses on the processing sequence of production control data. The second illustration is an on-line cash remittance application. This application utilizes on-line terminals and direct access files to perform the posting of customer remittances to the accounts-receivable file. The discussion focuses on accounting controls utilized in the system.

The final illustration in this chapter is a point-of-sale application in a retail store. Electronic cash registers serve as the primary input device in a point-of-sale system. Sales transaction data is processed on-line; this capability significantly increases the overall processing capabilities of the store's AIS. The discussion of the point-of-sale application focuses on the overall processing configuration of the system.

PRODUCTION CONTROL APPLICATIONS

The volume of products coupled with their detailed material and labor operation requirements qualifies the production cycle as an ideal area for computer processing techniques. This section illustrates the use of computer batch processing techniques in a manufacturing production cycle. The illustration assumes the use of punched-card inputs and the storage of all necessary master files on magnetic tape.

Figure 12.1 illustrates the document flow accompanying production-cycle batch processing computer applications. Comparison of Figure 12.1 with the transaction flow found in a manual system (Figure 5.1 in Chapter 5) reveals the following differences.

1. The computer is used to prepare and maintain most of the docu-

ments that are prepared manually in a manual system. These documents include production orders, material requisitions, production schedules, production status reports, and all related summary reports.

2. Accordingly, the clerical functions associated with production control, inventory control, and cost accounting are integrated in a series of computer runs.

3. The integration of clerical functions changes the flow of documents to and from the factory departments. Production orders, material requisitions, production schedules, and production reports are forwarded to the production departments from the computer department. Production status data is forwarded from the factory departments to the computer department for processing rather than directly to the production-control or cost-accounting department.

The net result of these changes should be more complete and up-to-date information pertinent to all phases of the production cycle. The following sections present systems flowcharts and a discussion of the flow of processing attendant to production planning, production scheduling, and cost accounting. The discussion assumes the use of a standard cost-accounting system. All files are sequentially organized.

Production Planning

Production planning involves two major phases: determining the products to be produced and, subsequently, converting the planned production into detailed production schedules and production orders. As in a manual system, the determination of which products to make requires an integration of product demand, detailed production requirements, and production resources available to the firm.

The AIS assists the production-planning function by providing product information from several sources. Up-to-date sales summary reports and detailed sales forecasts may be provided by a computerized sales-order processing system, as discussed in the previous chapter. Up-to-date finished-goods stock status reports, including operational statistics related to turnover and relative profitability of product items, may be provided by a computerized inventory control system. Raw-material status reports would also be provided by a computerized inventory-control system.

In addition to these manual system counterparts, a computerized AIS is able to provide a wide range of detailed reports containing relevant production-control information that would normally be impossible to generate in a purely manual system. Figure 12.2 illustrates several production control reports provided by a commercial production-control software package. The overall production plan itself might be generated by

FIGURE 12.1. Document Flowchart for Computer Batch Processing of Production-Cycle Transactions

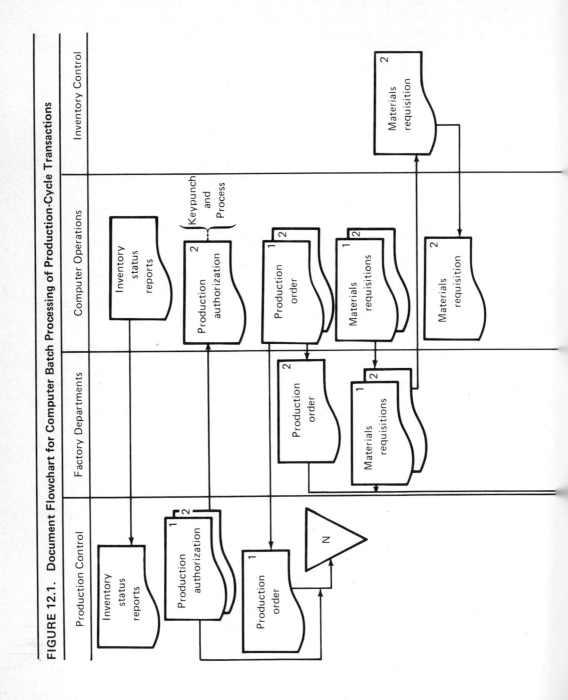

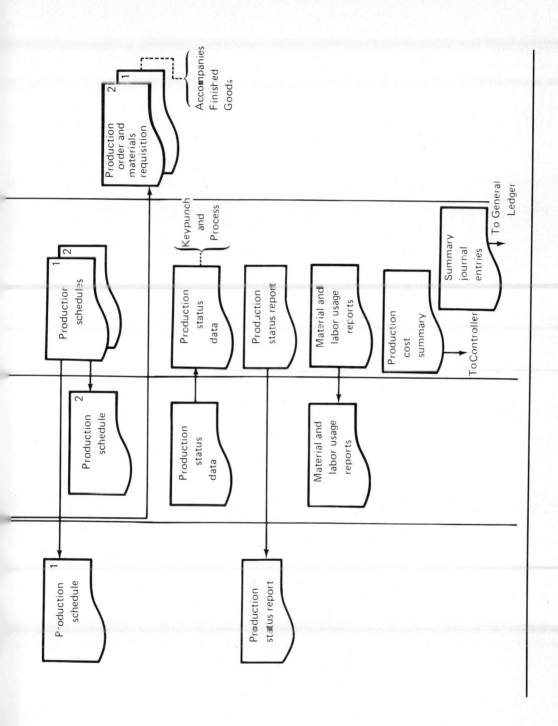

FIGURE 12.2. Production Control Reports

ABC COMPANY

BUYER'S GUIDE

DATE 03 01 7-

C	PRD CAT STOCK NUMBER DESCRIPTION-REFERENCE	VNDR NO	STD ORD QTY / RE-ORDER PT	STOCK BALANCES AVAILABLE ON ORDER	ON HAND	SAFTY STK	UNIT AVG CST / UNIT RPL CST	CURRENT ISS PER TO DTE / YEAR TO DTE	PREVIOUS ISS PER TO DTE / YEAR TO DTE	DATE LAST ISSUE / RECEIPT	LEAD TIME DAYS
A	004 12415710 SCREWDRIVER 6"	2141678	250 / 500	755	755	100	1.185 / 1.193	703 / 1,203	479 / 1,090	02 25 7- / 02 10 7-	015
C	004 12415730 SCREWDRIVER 8"	2141678	250 / 500 **	383	983	500	1.3152 / 1.32	613 / 1,251	534 / 906	02 13 7- / 01 28 7-	015
A	004 12415740 SCREWDRIVER 10"	2141678	250 / 500 **	450	450	200	1.47 / 1.5215	345 / 612	476 / 820	02 27 7- / 02 20 7-	015
B	004 12415750 SCREWDRIVER 12"	2141678	250 / 500 **	315	315	200	1.6554 / 1.6554	282 / 571	321 / 530	02 26 7- / 02 26 7-	021

ABC COMPANY

POTENTIAL EXCESS STOCK ON 03 01 7-

DATE 03 01 7-

CL	PRD STOCK NUMBER CAT DESCRIPTION-REFERENCE	NET ISSUES THIS YEAR CURRENT PER / YEAR TO DATE	NET ISSUES LAST YEAR CURRENT PER / YEAR TO DATE	QUANTITY ON HAND ON ORDER	NO OF PRDS ISS ON HND PER / YR TO DATE	THEORETICAL MAX QTY OH STANDARD ORDER QTY	POTENTIAL EXCESS QUANTITY CURRENT PER / YEAR TO DATE	POTENTIAL EXCESS VALUE CURRENT PER / YEAR TO DATE	LEAD TIME DAYS
A	004 12415710 SCREWDRIVER 6"	703 / 1,203	479 / 1,090	755	1.1 / 1.3	350 / 250	405 / 253	480 / 300	015
A	004 12416101 PLIERS 6"	12 / 31	8 / 41	75	6.3 / 4.8	40 / 20	35 / 49	111 / 156	021
B	004 12447401 PLIERS 8"	423 / 792	520 / 1,025	1,295	3.1 / 3.3	600 / 200	695 / 712	2,853 / 2,923	021
C	004 12447601 PLIERS 10"	363 / 699	203 / 509	801	2.2 / 2.3	200 / 100	601 / 637	2,545 / 2,698	021

TOTAL PRODUCT CATEGORY 004   5,989 / 6,077

GRAND TOTALS   78,436 / 105,295

Courtesy Burroughs Corporation.

a computerized production-planning application that integrates production demand and resource availability information through the use of linear programming or some other management-science technique.

Once the production plan is set, it must be converted or related to the current production schedule and implemented by generating production orders. In a manual system, production orders are generated by the production-control department. In a computerized system, the production-control department authorizes the generation of production orders by issuing production-authorization forms. These forms are sent to the

FIGURE 12.3. Production Control Application

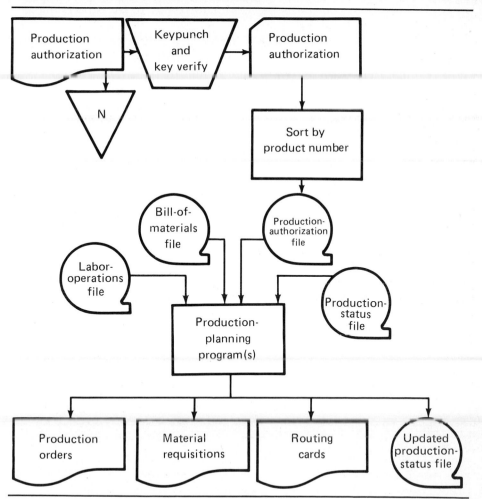

computer department for processing into production orders and related documentation.

Figure 12.3 presents a systems flowchart of the production-control application. Production authorizations are sent in batches from the production-control department. These forms are keypunched and key verified. The resultant card file is sorted into sequence on product number to be processed against the computerized production-status, bill-of-materials, and labor-operations files. This process generates production orders, routing cards, and materials requisitions, and updates the production-status file. The production-status file contains both accounting data and operational data pertaining to the status of production orders. This file integrates production-order data pertinent to state of completion of projects; the production-status file is a major input to the scheduling and cost accounting applications.

The bill-of-materials file contains a record for each product manufactured. Each record contains the detailed material requirements and standard material cost of the product identified by the record's key field value. The labor-operations file contains similar data related to each product's detailed labor operation requirements and their sequencing through the production process. Standard labor times and costs are also contained in the labor-operations file.

The production-planning application program integrates data from the production authorization record, bill-of-materials record, and labor-operations record and generates the necessary production order documents—a detailed production order, materials-requisition forms, and routing cards to guide the flow of production. Figure 12.4 illustrates a computer-generated production-order and materials-requisition form. These documents are distributed to the factory departments along with up-to-date production schedules. The production-planning application program also updates the production-status file. This file contains information found on the production order and establishes a production-status (WIP) record for each production order. This file is an essential input to the production-scheduling and cost-accounting applications discussed below.

Production Scheduling

As Figure 12.3 illustrates, the production-status file is updated by the production-planning application. The production-status file contains a record for each open production order. The production-status file is also used to accumulate both cost and operational data pertinent to production status. It integrates the typically distinct clerical functions

FIGURE 12.4. Computer-Generated Production Order and Materials-Parts Requisition

Production Order

PART NUMBER	PRODUCTION ORDER			
5A15654	5200037			

PART NAME	QUANTITY	CUSTOMER NUMBER	ISSUE DATE
ARM ASSEMBLY	1000	432761	9-10-7-

ENG DR & FILE REF	REVISION DATE	ACCOUNT TO CHARGE	SCHEDULE START DATE
5A15654	10-12-7-		7--171

MATERIAL NUMBER	USE UNIT	UNIT OF MEASURE	MATERIAL	SCHEDULE COMPLETION DATE 7--177

MATERIAL DESCRIPTION

OPN SEQ.	DEPT WK/CTR	OPN CODE	SET-UP TIME	OPERATION STANDARD	EXTENDED OPN TIME	OPERATION DESCRIPTION	SCHEDULE FINISH	QUANTITY COMPLETED
0010						DRAW DETAIL STOCK		
0011						5A15656		
0012						5A12458		
0013						5A12455		
0014						5A12457		
0015						5A12456		
0100	049-020	HH01	.50	.29000	3.40	RIVET 5A12458-5A15656	7--174	
0110						USE RIVET ANVIL #1430		
0200			.50	.23700	2.87	RIVET 5A12457-5A12455	7--174	
0210	049-020	HH01				USE RIVET ANVIL #22622		
0300	049-020	HH01	.20	.27700	2.97	STAKE 5A12456-5A12455	7--175	
0310						USE FIXTURE PF-48555		
0320						USE TIP PT-41632		
0330						USE ADAPTER PA-58072		
0400	049-020	HH01	.10	.25300	2.63	STAKE 5A15656-5A12455	7--175	
0410						USE FIXTURE #1342494		
0420						USE TIP PT-41632		
0500	049-020	N				INSPECT	7--175	
0600	049-020	N				BRAZE	7--175	
0700	051-018	N				NEUTRAL SALTS HARDENING	7--176	
0800	051-018	N				BARREL COPPER BRAZE STRIP	7--176	
0900	051-018	N				INSPECT	7--176	
1000	048-17A	N				LAP	7--176	
1100	049-032	HH01	.80	.10500	1.85	DRILL DEBURR	7--177	
1200	049-032	HH01	.30	.11000	1.40	REAM .5937 + .001, -.000	7--177	
1210						USE FLUTE REAMER #28533360		
1220						USE .5937- .5947 GAGE #3451 5682		
1300	010-011	N				INSPECT	7--177	
1400	010-005	N				STOCK	7--177	

MATERIAL-PARTS REQUISITION

☐ STANDARD COST   DATE FILLED _____

☐ CHARGE ACCOUNT NO. _____   FILLED BY _____

SIGNED _____

DATE	SHORTAGE NO.	QUANTITY	PART NUMBER	PART DESCRIPTION	ORDER REF.	PAGE
9-10-7-	5200029	1000	5A15654	ARM ASSEMBLY	432761	1

PART NUMBER	PART DESCRIPTION	STOCK LOCATION	DELIVER TO	QUANTITY	USE U/M	DATE NEEDED
5A15656	ARM	FF	49-020	1000	EA	9-19-7-
5A12458	STUD	FA	49-020	1000	EA	9-19-7-
5A12455	ARM	FG	49-020	1000	EA	9-19-7-
5A12457	STUD	FB	49-020	1000	EA	9-19-7-
5A12456	HUB	FC	49-020	1000	EA	9-19-7-

Courtesy NCR Corporation.

relating to production-order status and cost accounting found in a manual system. This integration results from the use of the production-status file in both the scheduling and cost-accounting applications.

The scheduling application is detailed in Figure 12.5. Production-status information is forwarded from the factory departments to the computer department for processing. At the end of each day, batches of routing cards are received from the factory departments. Routing cards, which are generated by the production-planning application, are filled in by the factory departments as work progresses on specific production orders. Each card contains a production order number and a format for specifying the work completed on an order. A routing card might be generated for each specific labor operation required on a production order. As the operations are completed, the corresponding routing card is completed by adding such information as units produced, scrap count, and actual time required. The cards are then forwarded to the computer department for processing.

Batches of routing cards received from the factory department are keypunched, key verified, and sorted into sequence on production order number, as shown in Figure 12.5. These data are used to update the production-status file in a sequential file-processing application that posts detail from the routing cards to the corresponding production-order record. Outputs of this operation include a summary and control report, the updated production-status file, and a production-loading file that details the production requirements associated with open production orders.

The production-loading file is the major input to the production-scheduling application. This file is sorted into sequence by department or work center number and processed by the scheduling application program to produce production schedules. The scheduling application program may serve simply to accumulate and print reports showing total labor operation requirements for each department. The application program might be expanded to include the use of linear programming or some other management-science technique to relate resource availabilities within each department or work center to overall production requirements to generate a schedule that represents an optimal assignment of available resources to production.

Cost Accounting

Figure 12.6 presents a systems flowchart of the cost-accounting application within a computerized production-control system. The central feature of the cost-accounting application is the updating of the production-status (WIP) file.

FIGURE 12.5. Production Scheduling Application

From Factory Operations

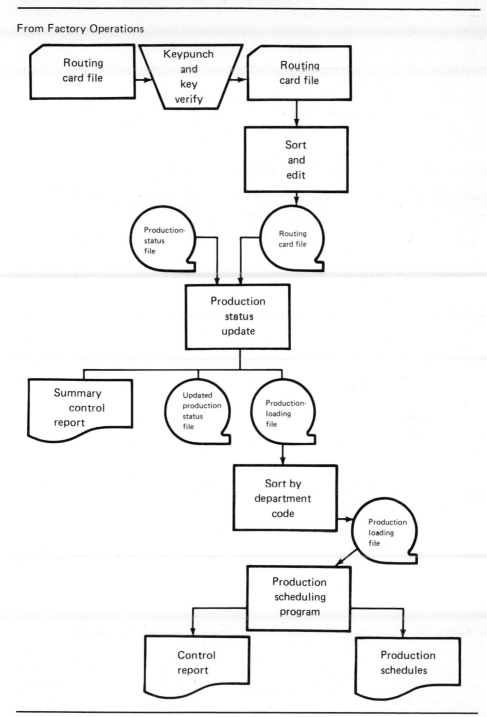

FIGURE 12.6. Cost Accounting Application

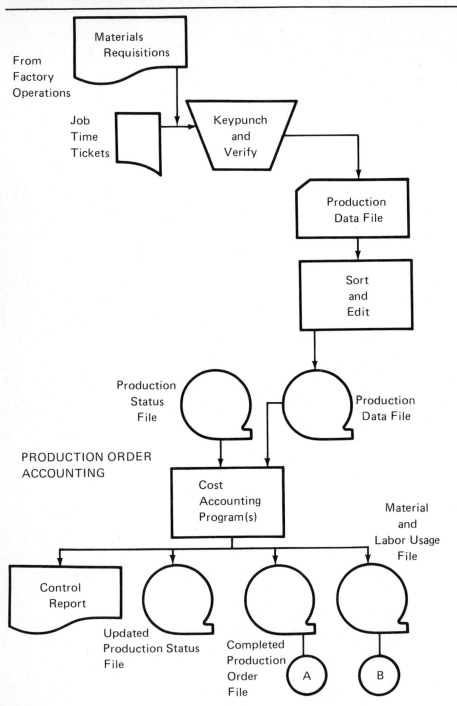

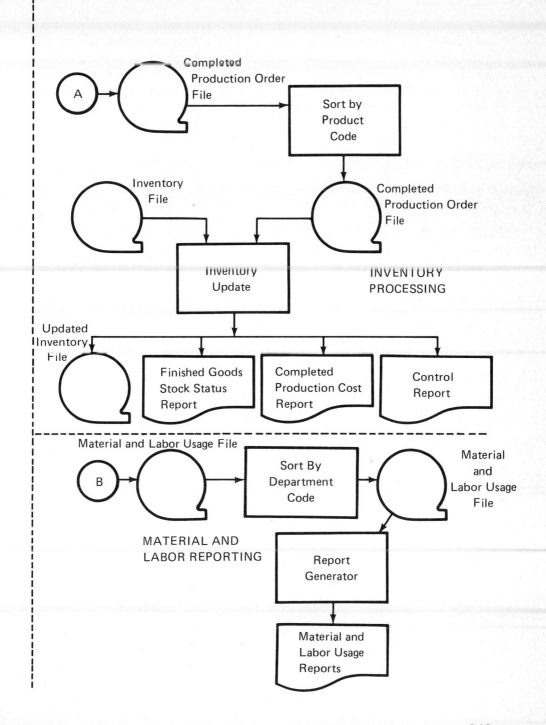

Completed
Production Order
File

Sort by
Product
Code

Inventory
File

Completed
Production Order
File

Inventory
Update

INVENTORY
PROCESSING

Updated
Inventory
File

Finished Goods
Stock Status
Report

Completed
Production Cost
Report

Control
Report

Material and Labor Usage File

Sort By
Department
Code

Material
and
Labor Usage
File

MATERIAL AND
LABOR REPORTING

Report
Generator

Material and
Labor Usage
Reports

Material-requisitions data are forwarded in batches from the inventory department to the computer department for processing. These requisitions document the issuance of materials to specific production orders. Job time tickets are forwarded in batches from the production departments to the computer department. The time tickets show the distribution of labor time to various production orders within a production department. Both material-requisitions data and time tickets are keypunched, key verified, and sorted into sequence by production order number. The resultant transaction file is fed into the cost-accounting application program along with the production-status file. This sequential file-processing application accumulates material and labor usage shown on material-requisition forms and time tickets and posts them to the WIP record maintained for each open production order. Overhead is applied to WIP on the basis of burden rates maintained in the cost-accounting program. The program monitors the status of each production order and also prepares a file that summarizes the variances between standard cost and operational data maintained in the WIP record and the actual cost and operational data posted to each production order. As orders are completed, the related WIP record is closed and a record is created to update the finished inventory file. The outputs of the cost accounting program include the following items:

1. an updated production-status file,
2. a completed production-order file,
3. a material and labor usage file, and
4. a control and summary report.

Each of these outputs is discussed in turn. The updated production-status file contains current information on the status of all open production orders. This file is used in the next cycle of the production planning and scheduling applications.

The completed production-order file lists all cost data for completed production orders. This file is sorted by product number and used to update the finished goods inventory file, as shown in Figure 12.6. Outputs of this sequential file-processing application include an updated finished-goods inventory file, a finished-goods stock status report, a completed production-order cost summary, and a summary and control report that includes batch and application control information as well as the summary journal-entry data debiting finished goods and crediting WIP for the standard cost of goods completed.

The material and labor usage file that is output from the cost-accounting application contains both the actual and standard material and labor costs for work completed, as shown on the material-requisitions and time ticket input. The standard quantities, times, and costs are copied to this file from the production-status file. This file is sorted into sequence by department or work center code and input to a computer application program that accumulates material and labor costs by department or work center and prints material and labor usage reports; these reports detail variances between standard and actual cost data. Material and labor usage reports are distributed to department foremen to assist in the overall production-control function.

The control and summary report that is the output from the cost-accounting application program includes batch and application control information as well as the summary journal-entry data debiting WIP for standard material, labor, and overhead costs, crediting stores, accrued payroll, and applied overhead, and debiting or crediting the necessary variance accounts.

AN ON-LINE CASH RECEIPTS APPLICATION

This section describes an on-line cash receipts application. Customer remittances on account are posted directly via video display terminals to the accounts-receivable file, rather than being batched, keypunched, and processed via traditional computer batch processing techniques. All files are necessary direct-access or indexed-sequential in organization and reside on DASDs. Direct-access and indexed-sequential file-processing techniques were detailed in Chapter 9.

Figure 12.7 presents a system flowchart of the on-line cash receipts application. The application maintains an open-item accounts-receivable file. New invoices are periodically posted to the open-item accounts-receivable file in a batch processing application (new invoice application). A control file is updated to reflect the addition of the new batch of invoices to the accounts-receivable file. The control file is a summary of the accounts-receivable file by type of account (such as installment or net 30 days). A file-control summary report is generated, reviewed, and approved by management prior to the processing of daily cash remittances. This procedure insures that the accounts receivable file and control file are in balance after the addition of the new billing data.

Cash Remittance Processing

Customer payments are remitted to a special post office box number. This approach separates the checks from other mail received by the organization, thereby eliminating manual sorting of the checks and reducing the number of individuals handling the checks when they are received.

FIGURE 12.7. Cash Receipts Application

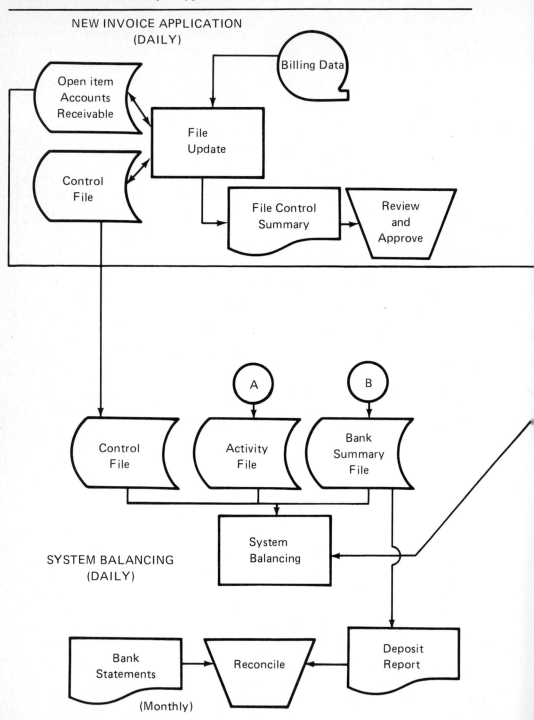

NEW INVOICE APPLICATION
(DAILY)

SYSTEM BALANCING
(DAILY)

(Monthly)

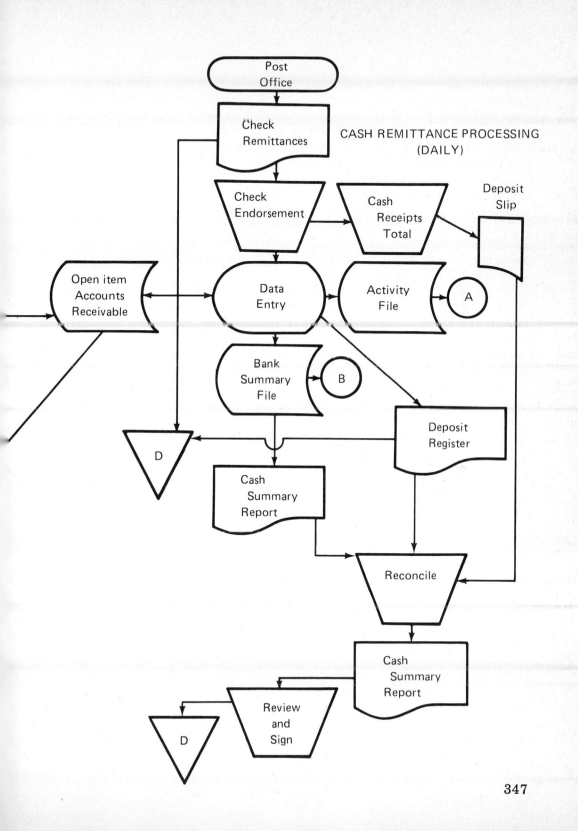

Post
Office

Check
Remittances

CASH REMITTANCE PROCESSING
(DAILY)

Check
Endorsement

Cash
Receipts
Total

Deposit
Slip

Open item
Accounts
Receivable

Data
Entry

Activity
File

A

Bank
Summary
File

B

Deposit
Register

D

Cash
Summary
Report

Reconcile

Cash
Summary
Report

D

Review
and
Sign

When the checks are brought from the post office, they are given to a control desk, where a clerk restrictively endorses them. This stamped endorsement prevents the deposit of the remittance to any unauthorized bank account. The clerk then totals all checks by adding machine and prepares a deposit slip. Doing this insures the accountability of checks received and their subsequent disposition. When the checks are deposited, the receipted deposit slip and adding machine tape are filed to be later reconciled to a cash summary report.

For ease of handling, controlling, and reconciling, the payments are batched into groups of fifty or fewer checks. When the checks are ready to be processed, a terminal operator requests access to the accounts-receivable system through a display terminal. The operator keys into the terminal a unique security code and employee number and identifies the type of transaction to be processed.

A security application, which controls access to all applications within the total system, verifies that the operator is an authorized user of the system and that his personal profile of clearances includes the transaction he has requested. Accounts-receivable management may delegate or remove authority to process transactions, but the security application limits management to the delegation of transactions within the scope of its authority (as defined by a similar type of manager's security profile) and to transactions that will not compromise good separation of duties when processed in combination with existing transaction authorities.

The terminal operator enters from the remittance advice the invoice number and check amount as an individual line item for as many lines as the terminal is capable of displaying. The accounts-receivable system then compares the individual line items against the records in the accounts-receivable file. For those line items where an invoice number and check amount match a corresponding record in the file, the check amount is applied. If there are line items that do not have a complete match on invoice number and check amount, or if the accounts-receivable system notes that an entered invoice number was previously cleared, an error message is immediately transmitted back to the input terminal, indicating the line item in error and the reason for rejection (for example, no unpaid invoice number on file; check amount entered is under or over invoice amount on file).

As payments are applied against the unpaid invoice records on the accounts-receivable file, the invoice records are updated to reflect the payment date, activity code (for example, check payment, invoice adjustment), and a sequential check number generated by the system. The paid customer invoice records are retained on-line for one year and are available for inquiries.

The terminal operator is restricted by application controls within the system to applying cash remittances to a single customer account. The terminal can access only one customer account for each check remittance. The entire check remittance amount must be applied to that customer account. The terminal operator cannot apply the remaining check amount of one customer's payment to another customer's account. If a terminal operator is unable to apply a customer remittance because the customer's account is not on the file (usually the result of a check misrouted by the customer), then accounts-receivable management follows up with the customer. If it is appropriate to do so, the check amount is subtracted from the batch total and the check is returned to the customer.

All check remittances within a batch must be applied unless the check remittance was erroneously sent to the company. If a check remittance for some reason is not entered into the system and not subtracted from the batch control totals, the discrepancy will be highlighted by the cash balancing procedure employed at the end of the daily application of remittances.

System Balancing

All cash remittance activity is logged on an activity file to provide an audit trail of all cash transactions processed. The activity file is used in the daily balancing of the accounts-receivable system and for preparing, upon request, listings that assist data processing personnel in tracing any lost activity that may have resulted from a system error.

After a batch of checks has been applied, the system updates a bank summary file for the dollar amount of the batch of checks. Also, a deposit register, detailing and totaling the invoice numbers and invoice amounts in the batch, is printed.

Daily, upon completion of the application of cash remittance, the accounts-receivable system prints a cash summary report from the bank summary file. This report lists the total number of checks and total dollars applied during that day. The deposit register is compared to the cash summary report to insure that the cash applied to the system is in balance. In addition, the bank-receipted deposit slip is reconciled to the cash summary report. This reconciliation insures that the cash deposited was applied by the accounts-receivable system. After balancing the deposit register and the cash summary report, the cash summary report is given to management for review and signature and is filed for future reference. The deposit register is filed with the day's customer remittance advices for future reference or reconciliation.

Daily, the activity file is summarized and compared to the totals in the bank summary file. Also, the activity file totals by type of accounts receivable are subtracted from the control file totals, which reflect the previous day's accounts-receivable file data by type of accounts. Finally, the current accounts-receivable file is accumulated by type of accounts. These accounts-receivable system processing steps are made daily before the accounts-receivable file is updated with new billing data or invoice adjustment data.

The comparison of the activity file and the bank summary file insures that all cash that has been deposited has been applied and recorded on the activity file. The total derived from subtracting the activity file from the control file should equal the sum of the totals by type of the current accounts-receivable file. This system balancing imposes a three-way check to insure that each file within the accounts-receivable system is in balance. As a result, any out-of-balance condition is readily identified and appropriate corrective action initiated prior to proceeding with the next day's accounts-receivable processing procedures.

Bank statements are received each month and reconciled to reports prepared from the bank summary file. Also, at the end of each month, the total amount of cash activity on the activity file is summarized and forwarded to the general ledger application system.

A POINT OF SALE AIS

A retailing situation such as a department store illustrates the close relationship between accounting data and other useful managerial information that emerges through the application of current computer technology to transaction processing systems. A consideration of the type of information useful to the management of a retail store would include numerous summaries of sales transactional data, such as total sales, total cash sales, total sales on credit, sales returns, total purchases, and current inventory status. Such summary data may take a considerable length of time to develop by manual methods. In a large retailing firm, it would be impossible to provide timely summary information pertaining to sales and other transactions with only a manual system. Further consideration of a retailing firm would indicate that a large percentage of transactions originates at the cash registers—the point of sale in the merchandising cycle. Modification of the traditional cash register to allow it to function as a source data entry (SDA) device for sales transactions is the heart of a computer-based AIS for a retail store.

A system that collects data on retail sales in this fashion is referred to as a point-of-sale (POS) system, since data are collected at the point where the sale is completed. The specially designed cash registers are called point-of-sale retail terminals, an example of which is shown in Figure 12.8.

FIGURE 12.8.   Point-of-Sale Cash Register with Point-of-Sale Recorder

Courtesy NCR Corporation.

POS terminals are used to record both cash and charge sales. Data relating to either type of sale will be transmitted, via the terminal, directly to a computer system, where it may immediately be processed. Data may be entered manually through a keying operation by the sales clerk, or automatically, through the use of special codes and sensing devices.

In a cash sale the customer pays cash and receives the goods. In addition, a sales slip is printed by the terminal. Data relating to the transaction —such as the inventory codes for the items purchased, the number of items purchased, the cost of each item, the date, the total sales amount, and any sales taxes—are recorded via the terminal and made available to the store's computer system for immediate processing. For example, the number of items on inventory of the goods purchased by the customer will be reduced by the units sold. The sales tax, cost of the items sold, and total sales price will be posted to daily sales records.

Sales on account require that a customer's charge account number and credit standing be verified prior to releasing goods. The customer's charge number is input to the POS terminal, allowing the computer system to access the customer's record, examine it, and determine the status of the account. If the charge sale is authorized, the system automatically completes the transaction. The sale on credit will be automatically posted against the appropriate records in the same manner as a cash sale. The status of the customer's charge account will also be updated to a new charge balance, an update on the credit available to the customer, and a record of the items purchased.

While a large percentage of a retail firm's transactions originate at the sales counter, many transactions do not. The purchase and receipt of goods for sale, payroll processing for employees, and the payment of vendors and creditors are examples of important transactions that do not originate at the cash registers of a retail store. These normal and routine accounting functions must also be supported by an AIS.

In addition to supporting the on-line activities associated with POS terminals, a computer-based AIS must be capable of handling other data processing requirements. Terminals and data entry sources are provided for entering transactional data that does not originate at a cash register. Payroll data, for example, may be entered through a terminal located in a store office (Figure 12.9).

The variety of data input and processing configurations that are possible, as well as the increase in the volume of information that is provided by a POS system as just discussed, will be illustrated with a brief description of an actual retail system.

The NCR 255 retail system (made by National Cash Register) consists of point-of-service terminals on-line to an in-store control processor. Sales, merchandise, and accounting information are recorded and transmitted to the computer. The data is processed, updated, and stored for instant access when needed for reporting purposes. Terminals may be located wherever customer sales or services occur, or where accounting entries are posted, such as at checkout lanes, in selected selling departments, at the customer service desk, and in the store office.

A retail store with several branch locations can upgrade the system to include telecommunication capabilities. In a multistore system, selective or summary data from each store's processor can be transmitted to a central processor. Data is collected at each store during the day and transmitted after-hours to a central processing facility. Data is transmitted over regular dial-up telephone lines.

POS terminals are used to record both cash and charge sales. Interactive communication between the point-of-service terminal and the in-store computer system takes place at electronic speed. The ability to verify

FIGURE 12.9.   Data Flow in a Point-of-Sale System

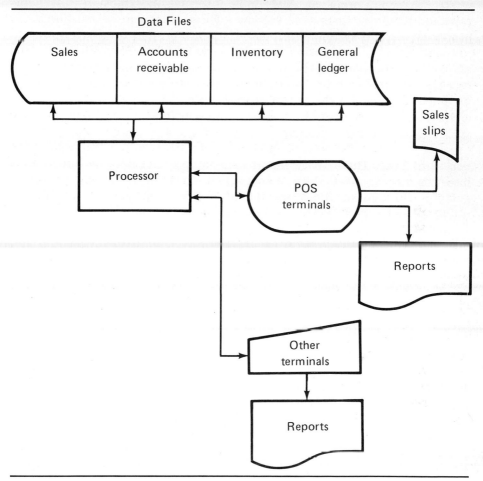

data as it is recorded plus automatic calculating functions significantly increase efficiency and productivity. Additional benefits may be realized by adding a coin dispenser, remote display unit, and tag reader.

Transaction data is transmitted from terminals and is processed, updated, summarized, and retained in computer memory for access by means of terminal inquiry. Transaction and accounting data may be collected by the system in four ways: in processor memory, on tape cassette, computer-compatible magnetic tape, or magnetic disc. The modular design built into the NCR 255 retail system permits a store to start with a basic system and later expand its capability by adding hardware and software modules.

One major aspect of most such systems is the wide variety of timely reports that may prepared. A veritable information explosion is available as a result of the increased volume of data that can be captured and processed by the system. Various reports are printed by the terminal to pinpoint areas of responsibility and accountability. Following are some of the reports that may be obtained: checker settlement, deposits and receipts, checker cash list, department sales, store dollars, hourly activity, price lookup file, and check authorization file.

Note the hourly activity report, which offers management detailed statistics concerning customer activity, average sale per customer, average number of items sold per customer, and total items sold within a specified period of time. The activity report summarizes sales data by hourly time intervals and enables store management to monitor customer traffic patterns throughout the store and at checkout lanes. It would be impossible to prepare this information in a manual system.

REVIEW QUESTIONS

1. Identify the major differences between the transaction flow in a manual production-control application system and a computer batch processing system for production control.

2. Identify several master files utilized in a computer batch processing production-control system.

3. What is a routing card? Is a routing card a "turnaround document"? Explain.

4. Identify the journal entries necessary to summarize the production process in a manufacturing system *and* their source in a batch processing production application.

5. What processing steps are necessary to account for completed production orders in a batch processing application?

6. Why is it necessary to assign security codes ("passwords") to the users of on-line systems?

7. Identify several uses of security codes in on-line accounting application systems.

8. Detail the uses of the activity (audit) file in the cash receipts application illustrated in this chapter.

9. What is meant by the term *system balancing?*

10. What are the major features of a point-of-sale (POS) system?

DISCUSSION QUESTIONS AND PROBLEMS

11. How might the following employees in a large retail store be affected by the installation of a point-of-sale system?
   a. checkout clerk
   b. inventory clerk
   c. sales manager
   d. staff analysts for the financial vice-president
   e. president of the store
   f. customer making a purchase on credit

12. The production control application detailed in this chapter made exclusive use of magnetic tape storage. Discuss several changes in processing procedures that might result from the use of magnetic disk instead of tape storage for the master files.

13. Many large manufacturing firms utilize a variety of source data automation devices to speed the processing of manufacturing data. Assume that a company installs data terminals in its production departments. Data on completed operations are entered by factory employees using the data terminals.
   a. What data might be entered by the employees?
   b. What edit checks might be made on this data?
   c. Assume that all necessary files are direct-access in organization and reside on DASDs. What on-line processing might result from an employee's entering data on a completed operation?

14. Discuss the potential advantages of utilizing on-line processing techniques for the production-control, production-scheduling, and cost-accounting applications in a manufacturing firm. What benefits might exist in having the various master files reflect current status as opposed to "last batch" status?

15. Identify application controls that might be utilized in a POS accounting application system, as discussed in this chapter. Limit your comments to the POS terminal devices, excluding other input sources.

16. Consider the on-line cash receipts application discussed in this chapter. Modify the cash application procedure to allow the operator to process customer remittances with multiple payments or no payments (invoice numbers) referenced on them. Your comments should specify in detail the options which your procedure gives to the terminal operator.

17. Consider the system flowchart in Figure 12.3. Indicate application controls that you would include in the design of the illustrated production-control application.

18. A fixed-asset application system processes fixed-asset transactions —such as the purchase and sale of an asset, revisions in useful life or cost due to repairs, and other such adjustments—against a fixed-asset master file on a monthly basis. This monthly computer run also generates depreciation charges and other transactions, which are collected as a file for processing by the general ledger application system.

Provide a systems flowchart for a fixed-asset accounting application system. Assume that all transactions will be keypunched from source documents and that the fixed-asset master file is stored on magnetic tape. Include appropriate application controls in your flowchart.

19.* Until recently, Consolidated Electricity Company employed a batch processing system for recording the receipt of customer payments. The following narrative and the flowchart presented on the next page describe the procedures involved in this system.

The customer's payment and the remittance advice (a punched card) are received in the treasurer's office. An accounts-receivable clerk in the treasurer's office keypunches the cash receipt into the remittance advice and forwards the card to the EDP department. The cash receipt is added to a control tape listing and then filed for deposit later in the day. When the deposit slips are received from EDP later in the day (approximately 2:30 *pm* each day), the cash receipts are removed from the file and deposited with the original deposit slip. The second copy of the deposit slip and the control tape are compared for accuracy before the deposit is made and then filed together.

In the EDP department, the remittance advices received from the treasurer's office are held until 2:00 *pm* daily. At that time the customer payments are processed to update the records on magnetic tape and to prepare a deposit slip in triplicate. During the update process, data are read, nondestructively, from the master accounts-receivable tape, processed, and then recorded on a new master tape. The original and second copy of the deposit slip are forwarded to the treasurer's office. The old master tape (former accounts-receivable file), the remittance advices (in customer number order), and the third copy of the deposit slip are stored and filed in a secure place. The updated accounts-receivable master tape is maintained in the system for processing the next day.

Consolidated Electricity Company has revised and redesigned its computer system so that it has on-line capabilities. The new cash receipts procedures, described below, are designed to take advantage of the new system.

The customer's payment and remittance advice are received in the treasurer's office as before. A cathode ray tube terminal is located in the

*Adapted from C.M.A. Examination.

treasurer's office to enter the cash receipts. An operator keys in the customer's number and payment from the remittance advice and checks. The cash receipt is entered into the system once the operator has confirmed that the proper account and amount are displayed on the screen. The payment is then processed on-line against the accounts-receivable file maintained on magnetic disc. The cash receipts are filed for deposit later in the day. The remittance advices are filed in the order in which they are processed; these cards will be kept until the next working day and then destroyed. The computer prints out a deposit slip in duplicate at 2:00 *pm* for all cash receipts since the last deposit. The deposit slips are forwarded to the treasurer's office. The cash receipts are removed from the file and deposited with the original deposit slip; the duplicate deposit slip is filed for further reference. At the close of business hours (5:00 *pm*) each day, the EDP department prepares a record of the current day's cash receipts activity on a magnetic tape. This tape is then stored in a secure place in the event of a systems malfunction; after ten working days the tape is released for further use.

Required:

a. Prepare a systems flow chart of Consolidated Electricity Company's new on-line cash receipt procedures.

b. Have the new cash receipt procedures as designed and implemented by Consolidated Electricity Company created any internal and systems control problems for the company? Explain your answer.

20. The Watt Widget Company manufactures two principal types of widgets and purchases some products that are directly resold without further processing. The production processes are relatively straightforward, with low technology processing and many manually controlled operations.

The purchasing agent uses various sources of information to determine when and how much to order. Three-part requisition forms are received from the various foremen and other supervisory personnel, indicating when specific supplies are needed and how much of them.

Weekly open sales order and finished goods reports are used to evaluate current and future production plans in conjunction with a review of the raw materials on hand. The purchasing agent reviews the card file of stock on hand to ascertain use history and vendor lead times contained on the card files. When large and unusual orders are received by the sales manager, he notifies the purchasing agent so that she can evaluate the related raw materials requirements.

The purchasing agent prepares a three-part purchase order, reviews it with the office manager, and obtains his signature before distributing it. The purchasing agent distributes copies (1) to the vendor, (2) to the warehouse foremen, and (3) retains a copy in alphabetical sequence by

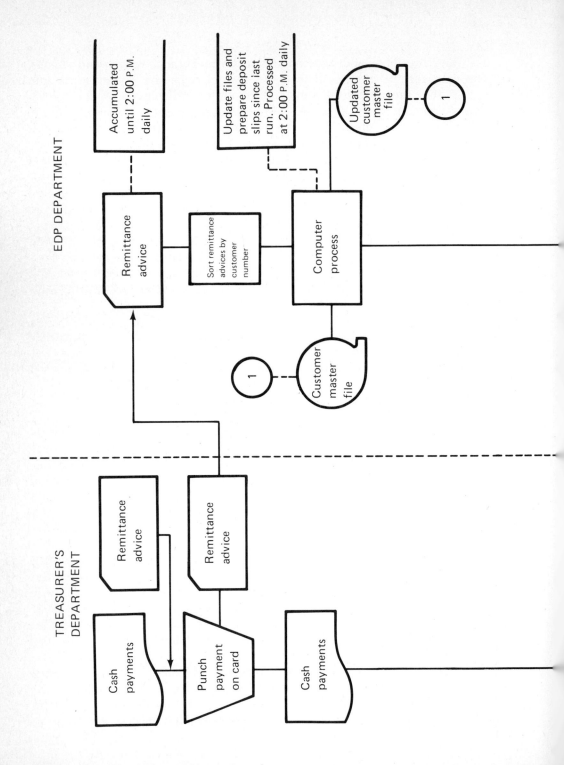

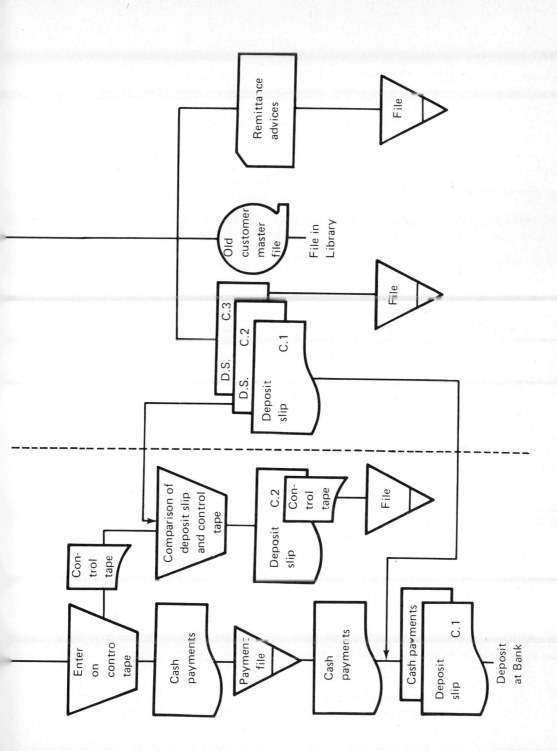

359

vendor. The purchasing agent also prepares a purchase order log to control numerically all orders issued and to assure that they are subsequently received and reported on receiving reports.

When the material is received, the receiving dock personnel count the material and prepare a three-part prenumbered receiving form. They distribute copies (1) to the purchasing agent and (2) to the cost accountant, and (3) retain and file a copy in numerical sequence. If the material received is a finished product, the receiving personnel sends the first copy of the receiving report to the sales manager, who makes a photo copy for updating the finished goods inventory records and then forwards the original copy to the purchasing agent. If the order is complete, the receiving personnel also send their copy of the purchase order to the purchasing agent, who will use it to denote the receipt of the material on her purchase order log. The cost accountant uses his copy of the receiving report to post the quantities received to the raw material card records. He then files the reports in numerical sequence, accounting for all numbers.

Production scheduling and control is based on a review of the weekly report of finished goods on hand and on order and on a "walk-through" review of work in process. There are no formal systems for evaluating the shop load or for tracking the flow of orders through the shop.

Following determination of production quantities required, the production supervisor verifies the availability of necessary raw materials with the warehouse supervisor.

While no formal priority system is established for releasing build orders to the shop floor, the production supervisor considers order requirements and releases items for production on the basis of his judgment of priorities.

Raw materials are issued from stock upon the request of the production supervisor and signatures are obtained from production personnel on material transfer forms. The forms are used to update raw material inventory files. Upon receipt of the raw materials, production on the required item begins. Occasionally, quantity checks are made at various work stations in the production process to verify piece counts; however, there is no formal production control over work in process.

The quantities and descriptions of raw materials transferred from the warehouse to the production area are recorded onto prenumbered transfer sheets. At the same time that these transfer sheets are posted to the perpetual inventory files, the actual unit cost of materials is obtained from the card records. The transfer sheets are extended and summarized for recording the monthly journal entry to credit raw materials and charge work in process.

Piecework quantities produced and payment rates per one hundred units are recorded onto time sheets by the production workers. These amounts are extended and summarized for entry into the payroll system. The total of piecework dollars is charged to work in process. Wages paid on a day-rate basis for jobs that have no piece rate or for makeup pay (that is, the per-job amount in excess of the piecework amount, in order that the individual earns a specified hourly rate) are included as part of factory overhead. Factory burden is charged to work in process at a standard rate of 200 percent of piecework dollars. There are no production order details or perpetual record controls maintained over the raw material, labor, or burden charged to work in process.

As work is completed and packaged for transfer into finished goods or for direct shipment, the quantities and descriptions are recorded onto prenumbered merchandise transfer sheets. Shipping department personnel are responsible for the accuracy of these sheets; they initial each line item as verification of the entries. Separate numerical series of transfer sheets are prepared by each production department. After obtaining shipping department approvals, transfer sheets are forwarded to the sales manager. The sales manager accounts for numerical control over all transfer sheets and enters the catalogue numbers and quantities into a computer terminal for updating the finished goods stock on-hand file. At month end, an inventory summary report is prepared, containing the quantities and extended standard cost values of all transfers from work in process to finished goods. In order to compensate for unreasonably low unit standard costs, the standard value is increased by 30 percent for making the journal entry to relieve work in process and charge finished goods.

Hourly production employees are paid on a piece-rate basis with a guaranteed minimum hourly day rate for each job and for certain unrated jobs. Each employee is responsible for accounting for his units of production and hours worked on each job, recording the information onto weekly time sheets, and obtaining the approval of the department foremen. Recently, individuals were assigned within several departments to verify the reported quantities on a test basis.

Both the clock cards and the time sheets are sent to the payroll clerk, who verifies the extensions of piece time rates, calculates makeup hours and pay, and calculates daywork hours and pay. The clerk reviews the clock cards to determine whether any time sheets are missing, but does not verify clock card hours with time sheet hours. The time sheets are then sent to a computer service bureau for preparation of checks and payroll journals. The transmittal sheets forwarded with the time sheets to the service bureau contain spaces for indicating batch totals of the gross wages within specified earnings categories. At present these batch totals are not being calculated.

The checks prepared by the bank are forwarded to the office manager, who separates them by department. The checks and journals are then given to the controller for his review. If any errors are found, the check is canceled, a new check is typed for the corrected amount, and the payroll records are corrected in the following period. The office manager distributes the checks to the employees.

The payroll journal provides subtotals of piecework, daywork, overtime, vacation, sick and bonus pay. At present, the totals of each of these breakdowns are recorded in the general ledger but with no details by department other than a separation between warehouse, shipping, and other wages. The payroll journal does not provide any product or job reporting.

The cost accountant has recently started to develop a computer program to accumulate and print product cost sheets using a time-sharing system. The program design has not been finished. The company is planning to mechanize the cost-sheet accumulation and printing process in order to expedite the revision of standard costs. Consideration is being given to merchandizing the raw-material perpetual inventory records and using this file in the standard cost program. However, before this can be done, the raw-material items must be numbered and procedures and programs for updating these records must be designed and implemented.

Watt Company relies on an annual physical count of items to determine on-hand quantities. These counts are not directly reconciled to the perpetual inventory records, because of difficulties in locating specific items. The current layout of the warehouse contains no logical organization as to part storage, bin space, or production work area. In addition, generally poor standards of orderliness (split and broken cartons, etcetera) are prevalent. These factors create difficulties in locating desired items, and contribute to inaccuracies in physical counts.

Required:

Analyze the procedures relating to production and inventory control in effect at the Watt Widget Co. Your analysis should include recommendations pertinent to the development of a formal production control system.

SOFTWARE SYSTEMS

13

From a user's point of view, most computer software may be considered as some type of programming language. Software provides the means of communication between a person with a problem and the computer he or she wishes to use to solve the problem. Software systems consist of organized sets of instructions with which a user may specify a desired operating sequence to a computer system. The process of providing instructions to a computer is called programming.

There are several levels of software systems; these software levels form a hierarchy. Each successively higher-level software system has well-defined interactions with some other software system lower in the hierarchy. Individual software levels consist of one or more programming languages. Programming languages form a hierarchy, because individual languages are largely designed to facilitate efficient processing of data at one or more specific levels in the data hierarchy.

A HIERARCHY OF SOFTWARE SYSTEMS

The software hierarchy and the data grouping most directly relevant to each software level is as follows:

1. Machine languages   (bit)
2. Assembly languages   (byte/character)
3. Higher-level languages   (fields and records)
4. Data base languages   (files and data bases)

Each of these levels is discussed in turn.

Machine Language

Machine language is a coding system based primarily on individual bit values. The instructions that computers execute *must* at some point be coded in machine language, since machine language is directly interpretable by a computer. Each computer line has its own, unique machine language.

Instructions in machine language code are essentially strings of 0's and 1's, symbolically representing either of the two digital states necessary to operate a digital computer. Coding in machine language, as was necessary with initial computer systems, is very tedious for humans. The first software advance was a higher-level software system designed to decouple the human user from the necessity to code in absolute machine language. Doing this is accomplished by providing the computer with a set of instructions which are designed to instruct the computer itself to assist in the process of developing machine level code.

Assembly Language

Assembly language is a software system designed to allow a user to code programs (sets of instructions) through the use of mnemonic (memory) codes. Assembly languages also utilize macroinstructions to further facilitate programming effort. The advantage of a mnemonic code can be illustrated by contrasting the mnemonic "Add" with "10001001." Computers are designed to carry out certain basic instructions—such as "add," "divide," "move data." These basic instruction sets are provided by the vendor of the computer. In our illustration, "Add" would be coded in an assembly-language program, whereas "10001001" would have to be coded in a machine-language program, to have the computer perform the identical standard instruction. When one considers trying to remember codes for ten or more operations, the advantage of mnemonics over strings of 0's and 1's becomes evident.

In assembly language, the user encodes most instructions through the use of defined sets of mnemonic character codes (such as "add," "move," "store") rather than symbolic strings of bits. Through a special program called the assembler, the computer translates assembly language code by code into its binary equivalents: that is, the predefined set of machine language instructions corresponding to each mnemonic code. This conversion is straightforward, and it greatly facilitates programming efforts.

Macroinstructions provide a further decoupling for the user. Consider the operation of an input-output device such as a card reader. Many programs use the same system card reader for input. Prior to the development of assembly languages, each user had to code roughly the same set of instructions to access data from a card reader. The advantages of decoupling the user from such repetitive, fairly standardized programming requirements include a saving of programming time and thus cost, and a reduction of potential errors in the programming process itself. The decoupling is effected through having the system define and provide standardized macroinstructions. A routine or procedure is factored out of a larger system, efficiently coded, stored, and made available to all users through some software system. Standard input and output routines, such as accessing data from a card reader, are accessed in assembly languages by using the proper code. The assembler program then translates macroinstructions into machine language code by searching a table file for the proper macro, and then copying the standard system program from the table file into the user's program. The concept of a macroinstruction is basic to computer systems. Software progress consists largely of developing a hierarchy of broader and more effective macroinstructions for the user of computer systems.

Because it is designed to maintain a close relationship with a particular machine language, assembly language is highly machine-oriented. Machine language and assembly language software systems are in general unique and restricted to a particular line of computers. Machine or assembly language programs coded on an IBM (International Business Machines) computer will not operate on an NCR (National Cash Register) computer without substantial modification.

The next software advance was the development of procedural or problem-oriented software systems that are largely independent of individual computer systems.

Higher-Level Languages

Higher-level languages, the next software level, provide a further decoupling from coding at the level of machine-oriented instructions. These languages are more mnemonic, more oriented toward ease of use by people than they are toward efficient translation into machine language. Such languages aim to be machine-independent in the sense that programs coded in higher-level languages may be translated into any machine language. This software attribute is called machine-independence; it is approximated in several languages but rarely completely achieved.

A higher-level language, like assembly language, is accomplished through the design of a translator program, which is used by the computer itself to translate instructions coded in the user-oriented language into binary machine instructions. Such programs, called compilers, are more complex systems than assembler programs because of the greater use of macro-type instructions to facilitate further the coding process. The translation from assembly code is directly replaced by its binary equivalent. In translating higher-level language into machine language, each higher-level code (essentially a macroinstruction) is translated into several machine instructions. Clearly, different compilers are needed to produce machine language for different computers. Even though a language may be machine-independent, its compiler is not. It is important to note that programs written in a higher-level language must be converted, through the compiler program, to machine code (sometimes called object code) in order actually to control the operation of the computer.

A higher-level language is said to be problem-oriented when the vocabulary of the language (its rules and syntax) is similar to the vocabulary of a particular subject area for which it was designed. Cobol (an abbreviation of Common Business Oriented Language) is a higher-level language oriented toward business file processing problems. Procedure-oriented languages are designed to facilitate specific procedures, such as searching a certain file structure or operating an automatic machine tool. Procedure-oriented languages tend to be more restricted in scope than problem-oriented languages.

The more logical steps or processes that can be described or defined per program statement, the more powerful the programming system is said to be. Higher-level languages facilitate working with data at the field and record level by allowing the user to manipulate these data items through the use of symbolic names. In assembly languages, the user must refer to data items by storage location numbers, keeping track of these numbers throughout coding his or her program. In higher-level languages, the user need merely to refer to a data element by a symbolic name; the machine (through the compiler program) translates the symbolic name into the required storage address. This feature is typically not available in assembly languages. In assembly language, the user must also instruct the machine explicitly how and in what form to extract desired data from a record. Higher-level languages relieve the programmer of this task by incorporating standard data description or data representation features into the language. Different programming languages provide different data representation capabilities; thus some languages are not suitable for some applications. Cobol, for example, has data representation capabilities well suited for business file processing, but Cobol is not well suited for mathematical calculations. In assembly languages, the user has more options as to the forms that data items may take; this advantage must be offset against the programming effort necessary to specify data items. Higher-level languages restrict a user's options as to data representation capabilities. For example, working with "bit" data is not possible in most higher-level languages. However, for the capabilities provided, programming effort is greatly reduced.

Data Base Languages

As noted in Chapter 8, the term *data base* is somewhat vague because of its common use. "Data base languages" as used here are distinguishable from higher-level languages in that data base languages are directed at facilitating the processing of entire files and/or sets of files from the user's viewpoint. Data base languages take several forms and differ widely in their capabilities. The essential idea is to decouple further the user from the data storage and data description responsibilities that he maintains using higher-level languages. This decoupling is achieved through the design of software translating programs that are more complex than compilers. Many data base language programs are initially translated into a higher-level language code such as Cobol and subsequently converted to machine or object code through the use of a compiler. Data base languages are discussed later in this chapter.

Summary

As one moves up the software hierarchy, there is more machine assistance and therefore more standardization in the coding process. This process involves a basic trade-off between two major resources in a computer system: machine time and programming personnel time. In general, higher-level languages are easier to learn and utilize than machine-oriented languages, with a corresponding savings in personnel time and cost. However, programs coded in machine-oriented languages tend to be more efficient from the viewpoint of actual machine operation. That is, a program coded in machine language will generally run more efficiently (that is, take less time) than the same program coded in a higher-level language. In addition, compiler programs are large compared to assembler programs (they occupy more storage resources), and it takes more time to compile a higher-level language program than it does to assemble an assembly language program. These two points are disadvantages relative to machine-oriented languages. Many higher-level languages are not available on minicomputers simply because the necessary compiler is too large to be stored on a minimachine.

However, with the continuing dramatic decrease in computer hardware and software costs and a contrary dramatic increase in personnel costs, there is a clear and definite trend toward the use of higher-level languages. Data base languages amplify the same advantages and disadvantages that higher-level languages have in relation to machine-oriented languages. In short, machine time is becoming relatively inexpensive vis-à-vis personnel time. Although the resultant programs tend to be somewhat inefficient with respect to machine resources, the corresponding savings in personnel costs and resources typically outweigh this disadvantage of higher-level languages.

PROGRAMMING CONCEPTS IN HIGHER-LEVEL LANGUAGES

Basic Concepts

This section provides an overview of some basic concepts relative to coding an accounting-related business program in a higher-level language. Such programs are typically directed at the repetitive processing of a large file of data rather than detailed, complex processing of relatively few records. Accordingly, a large percentage of a typical business program concerns data transfer—input and output statements. Unfortunately, coding data transfer statements, especially in the rigid formats demanded by business applications, is relatively the most tedious aspect of coding in most higher-level languages. This is true simply because alpha-numerical character data must be coded and keyed letter-for-letter, and a typical business application uses a large percentage and volume of alpha-numerical data.

Programming in a higher-level language initially involves developing a block or program flowchart of the problem or application to be coded for machine operation. Figure 13.1 illustrates a program flowchart for a simple billing program. The detail in Figure 13.1 is somewhat abbreviated —typically the symbols in a program flowchart should have roughly a one-to-one relationship with the equivalent programming statements specified in the higher-level language. The symbols in Figure 13.1 are condensed to show only the points that will be detailed in this discussion.

As Figure 13.1 indicates, there are three major sections of a program. These sections are analogous to the three phases of the data processing cycle. In the input, or "housekeeping," stage of a program, initial values are read and verified, and parameters that will be used in the program logic—such as dates, check numbers, counters, or tax rates—are set at their initial program values. The program statements in this section of the program will be executed only once, as the flowchart logic indicates. The processing, or "looping," stage of a program contains the program statements that will be executed repetitively—once for each record in the file (other than the header record). In the output, or "end-of-job," section, summary statistics are processed and control reports are printed. The statements in the end-of-job section of a program are executed only once, as the logic of Figure 13.1 indicates.

From the user's point of view, there are essentially two types of pro-

FIGURE 13.1. **Program Flowchart**

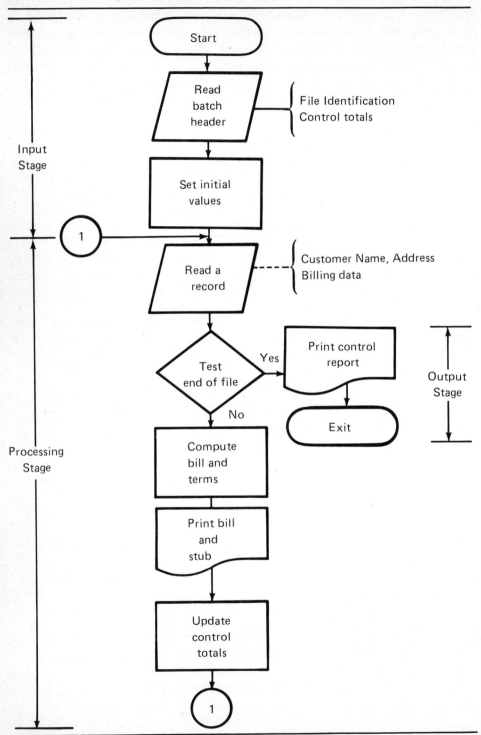

gramming statements provided in higher-level languages. These two statement types we shall label *declaratives* and *commands*. Declarative statements provide instructions that are necessary to enable a translating program to structure the user's program in a form suitable for its purpose. Declarative statements are not executed by the user program during its operation, but rather provide input to the compiler program. Declarative statements are used to set storage space requirements, identify the types of data a program will utilize, and often specify the I/O devices that will be used in the program. Declarative statements may also be used to initialize program variables. Declarative statements are largely concerned with the data representation capabilities of a language, and they differ from command statements, which are concerned with data manipulation —such operations as addition, comparison, input, and output commands.

Declarative statements are necessary to define the environment in which program command statements operate. From the user's point of view, declarative statements are not directly a part of his problem solution logic. They are unnecessary to the logic, but not to the machine. Thus, the fewer declarative statements needed in a program, the more user-oriented the language.

Figure 13.1 illustrates several basic programming concepts in a typical file-oriented business program. Declarative statements are generally not shown in a program flowchart, as they do not affect the logic of a program. Many of the symbols in Figure 13.1 illustrate control rather than processing steps. These control steps, discussed in detail in Chapter 10, are essential in a business program to insure that data have been properly processed. The first symbol—"read batch header"—refers to inputing the name or number of the file and batch control totals. The second symbol—a processing symbol titled "set initial values"—indicates the processing of information on the batch header as well as the setting of initial values. This processing might include verifying the name of the file, setting program-generated control total variables to an initial value of zero, as well as setting initial values for check numbers, document numbers, tax rates, and other such items. Such tasks are referred to as housekeeping, as they are necessary before a file can actually be processed.

The third statement—"read a record"—begins the looping section of the program. Note the flow arrow above this statement. Coding this statement causes an input of a block of records contained in the file. The next statement—"test end of file"—indicates that logically, each input operation must be checked to insure that data has been input; that is, that one has not yet processed the entire file. This symbol is coded as a question with two possible answers: yes and no. The flow of logic is dictated by the answer to this question. The "end of file" statement illustrates a major programming concept—the ability to alter instruction execution sequence on the basis of program values. No human intervention is required to stop the program and change the processing sequence. Such tasks may be accomplished automatically under machine control.

Assuming that there is data to be processed, the processing block "compute bill and terms" should indicate the necessary processing steps. In a real program flowchart, the single flowchart symbol in Figure 13.1 would be replaced by a sequence of symbols illustrating detailed processing operations and their sequence. After the bill has been computed, the bill is output, as shown by the "print bill" symbol. The last processing symbol in the loop—"update control totals"—should be more detailed to indicate the logic needed to accumulate batch control and processing totals—such as number of records processed, total amount billed, etcetera. Notice the looping from this step back to the initial statement in the loop: "read a record." This branching is accomplished under machine control and is the main feature in the program.

When the file has been processed, the program logic branches to the end-of-job or output section of a program. This section may be used to compute summary statistics, such as the average bill, which can be computed only after the entire file has been processed. Such statistics, along with input and program-generated batch control totals, are output, as shown by the symbol "print control report." After this step, the program is complete.

Note the logical independence of Figure 13.1 from the number of records (that is, the size of the file) to be processed. The ability to alter the sequence of execution allows this program logic to process one or 10,000 records—indeed, any number. Note also the necessity to specify absolutely the detailed logic of operation. The end-of-file test and initialization of control total variables to zero illustrate the level of detail that must be considered in programming in a higher-level language.

There are well over one hundred higher-level programming languages; however, for a variety of reasons only a few such languages are widely used. Languages differ in the types and numbers of declarative and command statements that they offer. The following sections will briefly contrast two widely used languages—Fortran and Cobol.

Fortran

Fortran (FORmula TRANslator) was the first widely accepted higher-level language. It was originally developed in 1957 to reduce the task of preparing scientific problems for the IBM 704 computer. At that time—and still today—most of the cost and nearly all of the human time in solving scientific or engineering problems on computers were and are usually spent on planning, writing, and "debugging" programs. Fortran was developed to facilitate the programming of numerical procedures. Fortran has been updated, expanded, and improved since it was originally issued, but it is still primarily used as a mathematically oriented language. Mathematics problems usually involve little input or output but require a high volume of computation.

The data-descriptive capabilities of Fortran are directed at the data variable, which corresponds to an individual field in a record. Fortran is designed to allow convenient manipulation of arrays of data. This is essential to mathematical work. The traditional Fortran language, however, was designed for processing strictly sequential file structures. Although some newer versions of Fortran support direct-access files as well as sequential files, ISAM (indexed sequential access method) files are generally not supported by the Fortran language.

The data manipulation abilities of Fortran are extensive; however, these abilities are largely directed at numerical data and numerical variables. Fortran is not designed to process alpha-numerical (character) data efficiently. While Fortran's mathematical and computational abilities are extensive, most business applications require relatively little mathematical computation, but do require extensive manipulation of alpha-numerical data.

As this brief discussion indicates, Fortran is not ideal for data processing applications. It is, however, capable of handling traditional business data processing problems.

Figure 13.2 illustrates a Fortran program. This program reads payroll data (employee number, name, hours worked, and pay rate) and calculates normal and overtime pay. The statements that begin with a "C" are comments: these statements are provided for documentation and are not part of the program that will be executed by the computer. Data description is provided in the format statements. The overall logic of this program is quite similar to that presented in Figure 13.1.

Cobol

Cobol (an acronym for *CO*mmon *B*usiness *O*riented *L*anguage) was developed in the early 1960s to provide a higher-level language especially suited for business data processing, and it is the language most frequently used in business data processing. Cobol's objective is to facilitate file processing, accurate arithmetic, efficient data editing and I/O capabilities, and self-documentation. Cobol was designed to facilitate the typical business data processing problem involving large volumes of input and output with repeated references to files and their component records and fields.

Whereas the data-descriptive ability of Fortran is directed at the data

---

FIGURE 13.2. A Fortran Program

```
C       PROGRAM CALCULATES GROSS PAY FROM HOUR AND WAGE DATA
C       INITIALIZE ACCUMULATING VARIABLES FOR TOTAL PAY
C       AND RECORD COUNT
        TOTPAY = 0.0
        NCARD  = 0
C       INPUT AN EMPLOYEE RECORD
    1   READ (5,10) NUM, NAME, HOURS, RATE
   10   FORMAT (I5,A10,F5.2,F5.2)
C       TEST FOR END OF FILE
        IF (NUM - 99999) 25,100,25
C       HOUR TEST FOR OVERTIME PAY
   25   IF (HOURS - 40.) 20,20,30
C       RATE TEST FOR OVERTIME PAY
   30   IF (RATE - 10.) 40,40,20
C       NORMAL PAY CALCULATION
   20   PAY = HOURS * RATE
        GO TO 50
C       OVERTIME PAY CALCULATION
   40   PAY = HOURS * RATE + (HOURS - 40.) * .5 * RATE
C       OUTPUT AN EMPLOYEE RECORD
   50   WRITE (6,11) NUM, NAME, HOURS, RATE, PAY
   11   FORMAT (3X,I5,3X,A10,2F5.2,5X,F10.2)
C       UPDATE ACCUMULATORS
        NCARD = NCARD +1
        TOTPAY = TOTPAY + PAY
        GO TO 1
C       END OF JOB PROCESSING
  100   WRITE (6,12) TOTPAY, NCARD
   12   FORMAT (F12.2,I10)
        STOP
        END
```

---

variable, the data-descriptive abilities of Cobol are directed at the data record, which is a collection of data variables. Thus Cobol is directed at processing files; the file structures available to Cobol include sequential, ISAM, and direct access. ISAM files are often attractive for business applications.

Cobol was designed to provide "accurate arithmetic" in the sense that Cobol arithmetic is usually done in binary code rather than binary numbers. Binary code arithmetic mimics decimal arithmetic. Arithmetic in Fortran is performed in a different number system—the binary system. This difference is entirely consistent with the objectives of these languages. Fortran is designed for extensive computation—binary-system arithmetic facilitates this objective. Cobol, on the other hand, is not designed to accommodate extensive computation. Binary-code decimal arithmetic is inefficient from a computational point of view, though it yields results consistent with decimal arithmetic. The practical implication from the user's point of view is that instructions concerning round-off errors are specifically provided in Cobol; whereas in Fortran, the user must consider and code his own rounding procedures because they are not specifically supplied. This "data editing" feature is more crucial to business programs (to insure penny accuracy or equality of debits and credits, for example) than it is to scientific programs.

The data-manipulation capability of Cobol is directed at alpha-numerical data. Mathematical computations are much more restricted in Cobol than in Fortran. Cobol is a language very like English, whereas Fortran is algebraic. The English-like Cobol instructions are essentially self-documenting. However, Cobol programs typically require more coding time than Fortran programs do, because instructions are English-like (that is, many characters) rather than concise algebraic statements.

Figure 13.3 illustrates a short Cobol program. Each Cobol program is

---

FIGURE 13.3.   Sample Cobol Program

```
IDENTIFICATION DIVISION.
PROGRAM-ID. SLS01.

ENVIRONMENT DIVISION.
CONFIGURATION SECTION.
SOURCE-COMPUTER. XYZ-1.
OBJECT-COMPUTER.  XYZ-1.
INPUT-OUTPUT SECTION.
FILE-CONTROL.
     SELECT SALES-PERSON-FILE
         ASSIGN TO CARD-READER.
     SELECT REPORT-FILE
         ASSIGN TO PRINTER.

DATA DIVISION.
FILE SECTION.
FD    SALES-PERSON-FILE,
      LABEL RECORDS ARE OMITTED,
```

FIGURE 13.3. continued

```
        RECORD CONTAINS 80 CHARACTERS,
        DATA RECORD IS SALES-PERSON-RECORD.
01      SALES-PERSON-RECORD.
        02    FILLER                          PICTURE XX.
        02    SP-NUMBER                       PICTURE XXXX.
        02    SP-NAME                         PICTURE X(18).
        02    FILLER                          PICTURE X(21).
        02    SP-CURRENT-SALES                PICTURE 9(5)V99.
        02    SP-CURRENT-RETURNS              PICTURE 9(4)V99.
        02    FILLER                          PICTURE X(22).
FD      REPORT-FILE,
        LABEL RECORDS ARE OMITTED,
        RECORD CONTAINS 132 CHARACTERS,
        DATA RECORD IS REPORT-RECORD.
01      REPORT-RECORD.
        02    FILLER                          PICTURE X(10).
        02    RT-NUMBER                       PICTURE XXXX.
        02    FILLER                          PICTURE X(6).
        02    RT-NAME                         PICTURE X(18).
        02    FILLER                          PICTURE X(6).
        02    RT-CURRENT-SALES                PICTURE ZZ,ZZZ.99.
        02    FILLER                          PICTURE X(6).
        02    RT-CURRENT-RETURNS              PICTURE Z,ZZZ.99.
        02    FILLER                          PICTURE X(65).

PROCEDURE DIVISION.
OPEN-FILES.
        OPEN INPUT SALES-PERSON-FILE,
            OUTPUT REPORT-FILE.
MAIN-ROUTINE.
        READ SALES-PERSON-FILE,
            AT END
                CLOSE SALES-PERSON-FILE, REPORT-FILE
                STOP RUN.
        MOVE SPACES TO REPORT-RECORD.
        MOVE SP-NUMBER TO RT-NUMBER.
        MOVE SP-NAME TO RT-NAME.
        MOVE SP-CURRENT-SALES TO RT-CURRENT-SALES.
        MOVE SP-CURRENT-RETURNS TO RT-CURRENT-RETURNS.
        WRITE REPORT-RECORD.
        GO TO MAIN-ROUTINE.
```

Robert C. Nickerson, *Cobol Programming* © 1977. Reprinted by permission of Winthrop Publishers, Inc., Cambridge, Massachusetts.

composed of four divisions: identification, environment, data, and procedure. In the identification division, the programmer assigns a name to the program. He may also specify other information, such as the date, to be incorporated into the program listings. The environment division tells the computer what input and output devices will be used in the program. The data division describes the layout of each file and any work areas that may be needed. The procedure division contains the actual instructions for processing and input and output. The four divisions are always written in the same order as shown in Figure 13.3. This requirement is one of the self-documenting features of the Cobol language. For contrast, note that in the Fortran illustration in Figure 13.2, input and output device and data format specifications are scattered throughout the program in the several format statements.

DATA BASE LANGUAGES

The general characteristics of the data base approach to data processing were discussed in Chapter 9. The data base approach involves the use of data management systems (DMS) to control the physical storage of data within a computer system. DMS are computer programs; this section views DMS as programming languages of a higher level than languages such as Fortran or Cobol.

The primary objective of DMS is to decouple further the user from data storage and data description responsibilities that he maintains in using higher-level programming languages. As programming languages, DMS decouple the user from the necessity to describe data representation instructions (that is, code declarative statements) in his programs.

Historically, programming languages have evolved to facilitate the programming function and to decrease the amount of user effort necessary to implement computer programs. The development of data management systems (DMS) extends this trend by allowing a more complete separation of physical and logical data management functions from programs that use a data base. Under a DMS, a programmer works with a logical data structure; the DMS accepts requests for logical data elements, retrieves the appropriate elements from the physical storage media, and delivers these elements to the program as if they had actually been stored as indicated by the logical data structure.

The CODASYL DMS Model

The CODASYL Data Base Task Group (DBTG) Report (1971) proposed the adoption of a standard data definition language (DDL). This standard is an extension of the data definition capabilities of the Cobol programming language. The terms *schema* and *subschema*, defined in Chapter 9, refer to the structuring of the data base. The DBTG proposed the use of the term *schema* for a set of DDL statements that describes the entire data base. A user program would contain a series of subschema of DDL statements that describe that part of the schema that is of interest to a particular application program in a logical structure suited to the particular program's function.

The DBTG also proposed that the programmer be furnished as well with a data manipulation language (DML), which would be used to effect transfers of data between the program and the data base. Transfers of data from physical storage (where it is stored in the structure defined by the schema) to the program (where it is delivered in the structure defined by the subschema) are accomplished by the DMS. The actual physical transfers occur between secondary storage and a user working storage area in main memory.

The interactions between the data management system, physical storage, and the user program that were proposed by the DBTG report are detailed in Figure 13.4 (this figure appeared in the DBTG report). The numbered arrows in Figure 13.4 trace a request for data by user program 1, and are explained below. Calls for data by other user programs are handled concurrently by the DMS, but this is not shown in the diagram.

1. The user program requests data. All calls for services of the DMS are made in the DML.
2. The DMS analyzes the request. This requires the interpretation of the logical data structure defined in the subschema in terms of the schema—the characteristics of the data base as it appears in disk or tape storage.
3. The DMS requests as required physical input and output operations from the computer's operating system.
4. The operating system accesses physical storage.
5. The operating system transfers data between secondary storage and the system buffers (storage areas within main memory).
6. The DMS transfers data, as required to fulfill the request, between the system buffers and the user working area of the program that requested the data. Any required data transformations between the description of the data as it appears in secondary storage and the description of the data used in the program's user working area are handled by the DMS using the schema (physical layout) and subschema (logical layout) data definitions.

FIGURE 13.4.   Conceptual Data Base Management System

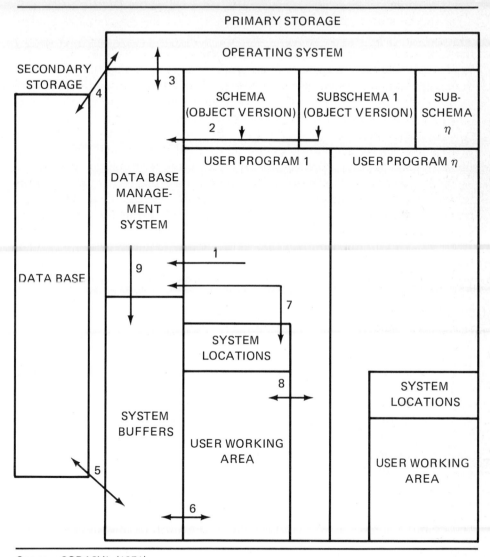

Courtesy CODASYL (1971).

7. The DMS communicates the status of the data request to the user program.
8. Data in the program's user working area is processed as required.
9. The DMS administers the system buffers. User programs interact

with the system buffers entirely through the DMS. The system buffers are shared by all programs serviced by the DMS.

An Illustration of a Data Management System

Many existing data management systems differ from the model proposed by the CODASYL DBTG—particularly in its relationship to the Cobol language. The significant difference between programming in a DMS and a higher-level language is that a DMS handles the interfaces between a program and the computer's operating system; in a higher-level language the user program must directly interact with the operating system.

DMS are generally classified as either "host language" or "self-contained" systems, although this distinction is not always clear-cut. A host-language DMS is one that supplies a unique data-definition language, but this language must be used in conjunction with some other programming language, commonly Cobol, PL/I, or assembly language. File processing functions are programmed in the host language. The necessity to program in another procedural language confines the use of host-language DMS to expert programmers.

Self-contained DMS usually have no direct connection with another programming language and generally supply capabilities for the non-programmer as well as the programmer. File processing functions are generalized in the self-contained DMS: that is, programmed once within the system and made available to users through some form of pseudo-language. This class of data management systems may be viewed primarily as user-oriented languages in which the parameters provided to the system by the user are equivalent to instructions coded in a higher-level language and the DBS itself functions as a translator program, converting user code into machine code either directly or indirectly through the use of another language translator system.

ASAP, a proprietary software package of Compuvisor, Inc., is an English-like programming language designed to facilitate certain types of file processing. Like most self-contained DMS, ASAP cannot be used to accomplish all of the functions that may be performed by using a general-purpose language such as Fortran or Cobol. However, for a certain range of file processing applications, ASAP is far easier to use than a general-purpose language such as Cobol. ASAP, like all data base languages, is designed to be highly efficient in performing certain tasks. Other tasks may not be possible to accomplish at all. Languages such as ASAP simply are not designed to be general-purpose.

As a software system, ASAP possesses several of the DMS features just discussed. ASAP maintains a single data base that is logically independent of individual user programs. This data base, however, is accessible only through the ASAP software system. ASAP maintains a single data base, which is a file in sequential order. Several user requests (tasks) are collected and are serviced against a single pass of the data base. This reduces overall processing time, because one is not passing the entire file against each request. In servicing multiple requests against a single pass of the sequential data base, ASAP, through the use of a coding system, may restrict the portion of the data base available to each user. Thus each user in effect accesses a logical file, a subset of the overall data base maintained by the system.

Although the data-descriptive and file-management capabilities of ASAP will not be further detailed here, some of ASAP's data-manipulation abilities are illustrated in Figure 13.5. Figure 13.5 is a sequential file processing program; actually there are three separate programs (also called tasks) contained in the illustration! The ASAP language is very English-like and highly user-oriented. Section 1 of the program illustrates a user-defined manipulation routine. The program defines form "Two up" and report "Filecard." These routines could be catalogued by the ASAP system, allowing subsequent programs to access these routines by name, without having to redefine them to the ASAP system. Section 2 defines working storage requirements. "Working storage" refers to program data items that are not a part of the data base maintained by the system. That is, these data items are temporary and unique to a user program. At the end of a program's execution, working storage data values are lost. Section 3 illustrates the program code itself. Note the complete lack of data description or specification statements (for example, how or where to read or write data) other than name, and the simplicity of the command statements. The "ordered by broker-name" statement, for example, will have ASAP sort a file of records on basis of the broker-name field value. The simplicity and power of the program illustrated can be fully appreciated only if one has undertaken to code a sequential file processing program in a language such as Cobol or Fortran.

Systems Design Considerations

There is a clear trend toward increased machine assistance in programming efforts. This trend involves a basic trade-off between machine and human resources in a computer system that continues to evolve as hardware costs decline and personnel costs increase. The design features of specific languages such as Fortran and Cobol necessitate basic trade-offs between various aspects of computer capabilities. Some other languages, notably PL/1 (an acronym for Programming Language 1), support a broader range

FIGURE 13.5. An ASAP Program

```
ASAP 'PASSW'

       .. ASAP DEFINITIONS

DEFINE FORM TWO_UP . . .              A SPECIAL FORM FOR CREATING CLIENT CARDS
         PAGE 66 BY 132              . SIZE IN MARK POSITIONS OF OUTPUT PAGE
         LINE   1 TO 50              . VERTICAL SIZE OF THE FILECARD
         COLS 1 TO 66                . WIDTH OF THE FORM
         COLS 67 TO 132              . WIDTH OF THE FORM

DEFINE REPORT FILECARD              . A FORMATTED TEXT FOR FORM TWO_UP
  LINE 1    COL 1 =  NAME            . .    LINE & COLUMN POSITIONS
            COL 40 = CUSTNO          . .    SPECIFY THE PRINT POSITIONS
  LINE 2    COL 3 =  ADDRESS         . .    OF THE RECORD FIELD ON
  LINE 3    COL 3 =  CITY            . .    REPORT FILECARD
            COL 20 = STATE
            COL 25 = ZIP
  LINE 4    COL 3 =  'PHONE'
            COL 10 = PHONE
  LINE 5    COL 3 =  'BROKER'
            COL 11 = REVERSE OF BROKER_NAME
  LINE 6    COL 3 =  'BROKER_NO'
            COL 15 = BROKER_NO
            COL 25 = 'BRANCH ID'
            COL 35 = BRANCH
  LINE 8    COL 3 =  'EQUITY'
            COL 15 = DOLLAR OF EQUITY
  LINE 9    COL 3 =  'TOTAL_MV'
            COL 15 = DOLLAR OF TOTAL_MV
  LINE 10   COL 3 =  'MARGIN_AMT'
            COL 15 = DOLLAR OF MARGIN_AMT
                .. DEFINITION OF VARIABLES USED IN THIS PROGRAM
```

Section 1

```
DEFINE WORKING STORAGE
  BUY_POWER 9 COMPUTE $          ..BUYING POWER FOR A CLIENT
  AVAIL_MARGIN 9 COMPUTE S       ..AVAILABLE MARGIN OF A CLIENT
                                 ..DEFINED LATTER ON IN THE PROGRAM
                                 ..ASSUMES A 65 PER CENT MARGIN

  ..TASK 1     PRINT THE DAILY LIST OF CUSTOMER ACCOUNTS FOR
               EACH BROKER WITH THE SPECIFIED INFORMATION

FOR ALL CUSTOMERS               ..SCOPE INCLUDES ENTIRE FILE
SET BUY_POWER = ( (.35 * TOTAL_MV) - MARGIN_AMT ) / .65
SET AVAIL_MARGIN = ( .35 * TOTAL_MV ) - MARGIN_AMT
    ..EXECUTE TASK 1
PRINT A LIST     NAME
                 PHONE
                 EQUITY
                 TOTAL_MV
                 MARGIN_AMT
                 AVAIL_MARGIN
                 BUY_POWER
ORDERED BY BROKER_NAME
WITH HEADING 'DAILY LIST FOR' VALUE
ORDERED BY NAME

  ..TASK 2     PRINT A LIST FOR BRANCH MANAGERS WITH CLIENT
               ..INFORMATION SUBTOTALED BY BROKER

    ..EXECUTE TASK 2
PRINT A LIST     NAME
                 PHONE
                 EQUITY
                 TOTAL_MV
                 MARGIN_AMT
```

Section 2

Section 3

FIGURE 13.5. continued

```
                    AVAIL_MARGIN
                    BUY_POWER
TOTALED      ORDERED BY BRANCH
WITH HEADING 'BRANCH ID' VALUE
SUBTOTALED   ORDERED BY BROKER_NAME
WITH SUBHEADING VALUE
ORDERED BY NAME
..TASK 3       PREPARE A SET OF CLIENT FILECARDS USING
               ..THE REPORT FORMAT FILECARD & FORM TWO_UP
         ..EXECUTE TASK 3
PRINT REPORT FILECARD          ..FILECARD IS A DEFINED REPORT FORMAT
ORDERED BY NAME
ON FORM TWO_UP

ASAP END
ASAP END RUN
```

Note: All words to the right of double period marks (..) are comments, not program statements.

of capabilities than are provided for in either Fortran or Cobol. However, as the power of a language increases, so does its complexity and size. PL/1, for example, is more difficult to learn than Fortran or Cobol. Its translator program is very large, and programs generally take longer to compile into machine code.

Data management systems are a logical continuation of the trend toward machine assistance. DMS, as we have seen, are computer programs designed to provide an intermediary role between user-written programs and the computer operating system. An operating system itself is a set of stored programs designed to manage the allocation and assignment of computer resources. Operating systems are essential to support modern technology, performing such tasks as input-output control, managing the translation of programs into machine code, and loading machine-ready programs into the CPU for processing. The operating system maintains a library of utility routines that users may request to perform standard functions such as sorting, accessing I/O devices, and card-to-tape data transfers.

Users working with non-DMS software (such as Fortran or Cobol) must deal directly with a computer's operating system. An application coded in a non-DMS language generally consists of a file and a particular set of programs designed to process that file. Some other user wishing to utilize such a file must code a program consistent with the particular file's structure. That is, the other user needs to be able to specify to the operating system the data representation details of the application file in order for the system to be able to extract the desired data in the proper format. DMS software mitigates this problem but in doing so creates a new set of system problems, which stem directly from the advantages such software is capable of providing.

DMS facilitates user programming efforts by standardizing data and delegating the management of the resultant data base to a sophisticated software system. The "system" assumes more responsibility and becomes more efficient through the integration of data previously scattered and redundant throughout several application files.

This elimination of redundancy through integration of data raises important questions concerning data and system integrity. Redundancy and control are closely related. A single data base cannot stand alone: periodically, copies must be made and stored off-line to provide system back-up capability. DMS software may operate in either a batch or real-time environment. The problem of back-up exists in both cases, but is more severe in a real-time environment because of the increased frequency of changes to the data base.

From the viewpoint of internal control, the design and operation of DBS systems must be carefully scrutinized. Conventional internal control theory suggests that access to data files that potentially represent the recording of both sides of an entire transaction should not normally be granted to any single person. In a data base environment with integrated data files, the software system must be designed with internal control features designed to insure organizational independence. The privacy and security codes utilized in DMS ("password" systems) are the only major preventive controls available, as the only "thing" between a person and the data base is the DMS system itself. Copying each transaction to a separate transactions log (file) provides an audit trail that may also be used for back-up. The point is simply that the internal control functions assigned to duly segregated persons may be neutralized by allowing some other individual to have access to a complete set of books. The DMS system itself must provide these features unless the data base does not possess all of the accounts necessary to record a complete transaction.

All data processing systems require controls in the areas of organization plan, documentation, back-up policies, security measures, and hardware features. Additional controls that are required in a data base system include the following considerations (Reneau, 1977):

1. Program modifications for data base systems are more critical be-cause of possible impact the modifications may have on several applications. Changes to a file system would only impact on the one user of the file. Programming changes in a data base system must be reviewed by an individual familiar with all application programs in order to determine the impact on each of the various applications.
2. Access to the data base requires specific controls. In a file system, individual files are usually available only to a specific user; whereas in a data base system many different users will require access to the same data. Security information is built into the data base management system to determine who has access to what data.
3. The data base system requires centralized management by an in-dividual responsible for the organization, protection, efficiency, and control of the data base. Because of his responsibilities, this individual should not be allowed to operate the equipment or initiate transactions into the data base.
4. Controls that are applicable to file systems as well as data base systems can be more critical to the data base system. Documenta-tion standards, back-up and recovery procedures, and program testing standards are more critical because of the impact on the various applications using the data base.

There are other potential drawbacks to a data base environment. An incorrect entry that is posted to a data base is potentially more serious than an error posted to an independent application file. DMS software itself is complex; almost all DMS software is purchased from a vendor, as doing so is generally more cost-effective than trying to develop such software in-house. This software technology is relatively new and untested, and some users have experienced major disappointments and difficulties in converting to DMS software. Nevertheless, DMS software is clearly on its way to being widely accepted as a continuation of the overall software trend toward machine assistance.

REVIEW QUESTIONS

1. Define the terms *software* and *programming*.

2. Contrast "machine" language and "assembly" language.

3. What is a macroinstruction? How do macroinstructions facilitate programming a computer?

4. Higher level languages are said to be "machine-independent." Discuss.

5. Distinguish between "problem-oriented" and "procedure-oriented" higher level languages.

6. What factors have and are contributing to the trend toward more machine assistance in the programming of computers?

7. Identify the three major sections of a computer program. What tasks typically occur in each of these sections in a business file processing application?

8. Distinguish between declarative statements and command statements in a higher-level language.

9. Contrast Fortran and Cobol.

10. Define the terms *data base* and *data base software*.

11. What are some problems associated with the "traditional" approach to file processing?

12. What are essential characteristics of data base software systems?

13. What are some systems problems associated with the design and use of data base software systems?

14. Define the following terms:
    a. assembler
    b. data base dictionary

    c. compiler
    d. working storage
    e. object code
    f. operating system

15. Identify the four divisions in a Cobol program.

16. Distinguish between a "host-language" and a "self-contained" DMS.

DISCUSSION QUESTIONS AND PROBLEMS

17.* Contrast the principal characteristic of an "assembly" computer programming language with that of a "higher-level" computer programming language. Name two "higher level" computer programming languages.

18. Discuss the nature and objectives of data base software systems. Identify factors that are contributing to the trend toward more and more machine assistance in programming efforts.

19.† The Ultimate Life Insurance Company recently established a data base management system. The company is now planning to provide its branch offices with terminals that have on-line access to the central computer facility.
Required:
    a. Define a "data base."
    b. Give one fundamental advantage of a data base.
    c. Briefly describe three security steps to safeguard the data base from improper access through the terminals.
    d. Briefly describe four steps to control the *completeness* and *accuracy of data* transmitted through the terminals to the data base.

20. Prepare a program flowchart for the following application. This application calculates straight-line depreciation for a file of fixed assets. The fixed asset file consists of the following record types:
    a. a header record, which contains the file ID number and a hash total of all of the record ID (key) values;
    b. a record for each fixed asset. Each record contains the following fields: ID number, a location code, original cost, useful life in months, depreciation taken to date, and salvage value.

---

*Reprinted by permission of The Institute of Internal Auditors, Inc., from the Certified Internal Auditor Examination (September, 1976).

†Reprinted by permission of The Institute of Internal Auditors, Inc., from the Certified Internal Auditor Examination (May, 1978).

The program should read each fixed-asset record, compute the amount of depreciation for the year (twelve months), update the necessary fields, and write the updated record. End-of-job processing should print the number of assets processed, print the total depreciation computed, and verify the hash total for this run.

21. Modify the above problem to compute depreciation by the double-declining balance method.

22. Discuss the objective(s) of the following questions, which are found on an EDP internal control questionnaire.
   a. Are duplicate programs (tapes or cards) maintained in another location?
   b. Are program revisions made only on the basis of written requests properly approved by user department management personnel?
   c. Do these written requests describe the nature of and reasons for the proposed changes?
   d. Are system and programming documentation updated after each change?
   e. Is a log of program changes maintained, indicating the date on which the change went into operation, in such manner as to provide an accurate chronological record of the system?
   f. Are there provisions for testing program revisions and reviewing the results with supervisory personnel before the revisions become effective?
       1) Is all testing done on a basis such that programmers do not have access to current data files or production programs?
   g. Is there a procedure to prevent superseded programs from being used by mistake? (Describe.)
       1) Are such programs ultimately destroyed?
   h. Are all changes to programs developed and programmed by persons other than those assigned to computer operations?
   i. Are operators denied access to the detailed program documentation both during and after the testing phase?

23. The data base administrator (DBA) is not necessarily a single individual. In a large organization, several individuals may share overall responsibility for the data base administration function. Discuss each of the following:
   a. Why is the DBA function crucial to the concept of data management?
   b. What administrative responsibilities should be vested in the DBA?
   c. What responsibilities and duties should *not* be vested in or permitted to the DBA function?

d. Where should the DBA function be placed in the organizational structure of a firm?

24. Consider a large data base environment with several users sharing the same physical data base. What types of problems might arise in having two or more users sharing and updating the same data element?

REFERENCES

American Institute of Certified Public Accountants, Computer Auditing Subcommittee, "Advanced EDP Systems and the Auditor's Concern," *Journal of Accountancy* (January 1975).

Cardenas, A., *Data Base Management Systems* (Boston: Allyn and Bacon, 1979).

CODASYL, "A Survey of Generalized Data Base Management Systems." New York: Association for Computing Machinery (May 1969).

—— "Data Base Task Group (DBTG) Report, 1971." New York: Association for Computing Machinery (April 1971).

Haseman, W.D., and A.B. Whinston, *Introduction to Data Management* (Homewood, Ill.: Irwin, 1977).

Nickerson, R.C., *COBOL Programming* (Cambridge: Winthrop Publishers, 1977).

Reneau, J.H., "Auditing in a Data Base Environment," *Journal of Accountancy* (December 1977).

MINICOMPUTERS AND DISTRIBUTIVE PROCESSING CONSIDERATIONS

14

Increasingly, the term *computer* has little direct meaning. There is in existence a wide spectrum of electronic equipment oriented toward "symbol processing"; whether these symbols represent accounts payable data, a patient's heartbeat in a hospital, words and punctuation in a business letter, or elevator control information, the difference is mainly application, not technology. The term *minicomputer* captures the dramatic cost reductions and technological advances of the later 1960s and early 1970s in computing equipment: today a $2,000 minicomputer is more powerful, more reliable, and easier to use than $100,000 "second-generation" machines of a decade ago. Minicomputers are permeating every aspect of our society, from control of traffic signals on city streets to checking the validity of credit cards and authorizing their use for purchases. As the prices of minicomputers continue to decline, the number of applications that it becomes economical to computerize continues to increase dramatically.

CENTRALIZATION OF COMPUTING RESOURCES

Over the decades of the 1950s and 1960s, a trend toward centralization and complexity of computing resources was evident. The impetus for this trend was economics. A relationship known as Grosch's Law postulated that a computer system's performance in terms of speed, and hence its productive potential or "throughput", is proportional to the square of the system's cost. This "law" appeared to be valid. Under Grosch's Law, the average cost per computation decreases as system size increases. This was a strong impetus toward centralization of computer resources; economies of scale with respect to hardware, personnel specialization, and software development were expected and often realized in centralized data processing facilities. Relative shortages of computer specialists, programmers, and other personnel contributed to this trend, as did the emergence of data base software systems, which promised further economies in large-scale data storage and integration. Data base management systems gave new impetus to the concept of a centralized management-information system. In many large organizations, the computer resources are highly centralized, even if the organization follows a decentralization philosophy in its other operations. In short, many things were possible only in large centralized systems because of the cost and complexity of computer technology.

The benefits of centralized data processing were and are significant; however, some important caveats increasingly became apparent as the size and complexity of large "host" processing systems (a centralized computer system) continued to increase. Large centralized data processing centers are faced with the problem of digesting tremendous volumes of incoming data and disseminating similar volumes of outputs to users. To control the simultaneous operation of many tasks within a centralized system, complex operating systems have been developed and implemented. Overhead costs become significant: communications cost increase as bulk data is transferred to and from remote locations; operating systems and other system-support software occupy more and more of a computer's facilities, requiring increasing expenditures in human and technological resources. The complex problems and risks inherent in backing up and recovering massive data bases and complex on-line systems in a single, large-scale facility are "costs" not explicitly considered in Grosch's Law.

The next two decades may well witness a reversal of this trend toward centralization of computer resources. The cost-effectiveness of large computers relative to smaller ones is shifting rapidly. Minicomputers, at first oriented toward and used almost exclusively by scientific users, are making inroads into commercial data processing.

MINICOMPUTERS: DEFINITIONS AND CHARACTERISTICS

Although the term *minicomputer* has been used extensively by the data processing community, the term defies a precise definition. Defining *small-business computer* is a little easier, as the word *business* denotes a minicomputer dedicated to processing standard business applications: payroll, accounts receivable, inventory, and so on. In price and performance, small-business computers offer an attractive alternative to larger computers, and span a wide range between medium and large computers on one end and conventional bookkeeping or accounting machines (now electronic) at the other. We shall consider a small-business computer to be a commercially oriented minicomputer: that is, a mini whose equipment configuration and major marketing effort is directed at business data processing problems.

Minicomputers differ in their architecture, data formats, peripheral equipment, and software; there are, however, several characteristics that distinguish commercially oriented minicomputers from larger general-purpose computers; these are discussed briefly in turn.

1. Environmental requirements: large computers require special environments, such as air conditioning, special floors, and complicated electrical installations. Minis do not require special environments; many minis simply plug in like any common electrical equipment.

2. Price: the most notable distinction is price. Minis are generally categorized as having a purchase price of $100,000 or less. This cutoff point is arbitrary; however, large computers may easily rent for as much as $100,000 a month. Complete mini systems, including software, may be purchased for $15,000 to $20,000. A few years ago it would not have been possible to rent a complete computer system for this price per month. The comparison by price can be misleading, however; larger computers are much more powerful than minis. (Nevertheless, for many dedicated applications, such as payroll, minis are very cost-effective.) A mini's price may also exclude products or services that are typically included in the price or rental of a larger general-purpose computer.

3. Physical characteristics: technical features of minis—such as memory, word size, and instruction sets—are either smaller or simpler than those of large computers. A mini's processing time is generally longer, although this depends on the type of processing and may not be a significant difference. There may, as we've said, be fewer technical features.

4. Software: manufacturers' libraries of systems software—programs, procedures, and related documentation—are generally limited. Fortran or Cobol compilers, for example, are too large to be utilized on some minicomputers. The practical implication is that programming by the owner or user of a mini is either very difficult or very restricted compared to what is possible with larger computers. But since many small businesses do not desire or frequently cannot support programming capabilities, this difference may not be significant. There is a strong trend toward the marketing of complete transaction processing systems software in the small-business market; in fact, it was largely the lack of such software systems that kept minis out of the commercial market until the

early 1970s. The first commercially available minicomputer was introduced in 1963, but up until the early 1970s most applications were scientifically oriented. This orientation was largely due to very limited software support, which placed extensive technical requirements on the user or owner.

It is difficult to estimate the number of minicomputers installed in operation, because there are differences of opinion over the definition of a minicomputer. There is also the possibility of some double-counting, as many centralized data processing installations utilize minicomputers for such tasks as communication control and input/output control in conjunction with a large host central processor. However, by any definition there are over 300,000 minicomputers in use, and the number is growing rapidly.

Small-business computers are a subset of minicomputers; the distinction rests on a strong orientation, in both equipment and software, toward conventional business data processing applications. The small-business computer market is served by four distinct types of vendors. The first is large, established companies such as Burroughs, NCR, and IBM, all of which market large computers and have long-established product lines and large marketing resources. A second group consists of "traditional" minicomputer manufacturers such as Hewlett-Packard, Data General, and Digital Equipment Corporation. This group was active in the 1960s, serving primarily a scientific market. As the small-business market has grown, this group of manufacturers has repackaged its equipment with new software aimed at the small-business market. A third group of "turn-key" vendors purchases minicomputers and/or peripherals from manufacturers, supply software packages, and market the resulting configuration. This group tends to offer more software support and/or customized software than minicomputer manufacturers, although the gap is being closed by the larger manufacturers. A fourth group consists of semiconductor and microcomputer companies that have begun to offer small-business systems aimed primarily at the lower end of the small-business market. Complete microcomputer-based business systems may be purchased from a new breed of consumer-oriented "computer stores" for less than $5,000 apiece. The bulk of business is captured by the first group of established computer companies, who are also leading suppliers of office equipment and business paper.

DISTRIBUTIVE DATA PROCESSING

From a systems point of view, the significance of minicomputers lies in the inroads they offer into the economics of centralized data processing.

Before the advent of the minicomputer, computer economics clearly favored centralized data processing with large central data files. This type tended to create bureaucratic data processing departments that users had to interface with, and, perhaps more significant, centralized control over data files with which users often felt uncomfortable. The compact size and low cost of minis permits the development of cost-effective systems that are dedicated to a single application; that is, a single minicomputer can handle a typical business application at a cost comparable to putting the same application on a larger centralized system. And in doing so, a minicomputer alleviates many of the user problems that have come to be associated with large, centralized data processing systems.

The data base concept, relatively recent in its software implementations, is an important concept—the complete separation of physical data files from the logical processing requirements of any particular application. Through the decoupling mechanism of a data base software system.

FIGURE 14.1. **Distributive Processing with Centralized Data Base**

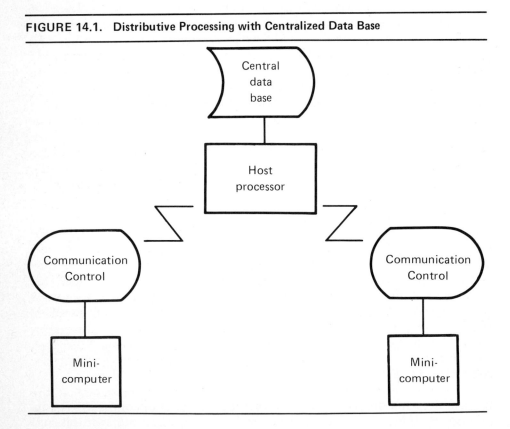

the processing of the data base is separated or distributed from the processing of user applications.

Under distributive processing, computing activity is decentralized among a network of interconnected processors. Figure 14.1 represents distributive processing with a centralized data base. The host system controls the physical data base and contains the logical data base software system. Logical user applications are processed in independent minicomputer systems that have the capability of communicating with the data base processing system. The advantages of such a configuration are many. First, one does not require a complex operating system to distribute processing time among multiple logical tasks. Each local processing system is operating on its own. One does not face the problem of restarting many logical systems because the host computer has failed. If the system that is processing the accounts-receivable application fails, the failure has no effect on the systems that are processing order entries. Distributive processing distributes the problems of the scheduling, control, and operation of the user applications formerly managed by a single host processor.

As minis become more powerful and cost-effective, the cost relationship between decentralized processing (distributive processing) and centralized processing becomes narrower. And with the advent and almost certain continued development and availability of logical data base systems and higher-level programming languages for minis, the concept of distributive data bases becomes increasingly feasible.

Consider an example. A warehouse has a minisystem with its own physical and logical data base, including the inventory file. Each sales office has its own logical and physical computer system, including files on customers served by the particular office. When the sales office system is processing a customer's order, it will access the customer file locally and the inventory file at the warehouse through a communications network. The organization's central processing center would have the capacity to standardize the design of the logical data bases, which are physically distributed to the users of the specific data base subsets. Under distributive processing with distributed data bases (Figure 14.2), two-way communication would be possible because of the standardized data base structure. The central computer could access data from the distributed data bases, and remote centers would be able to access selected portions of the central, corporate data base. This would entail some duplication of data but would likely reduce overall communication requirements, which are extensive under distributive processing with a single centralized data base. In addition, problems of back up and recovery would be reduced.

Such a system represents the technological implementation of the information requirements of decentralized management in a large orga-

FIGURE 14.2. Distributive Processing with Distributed Data Base

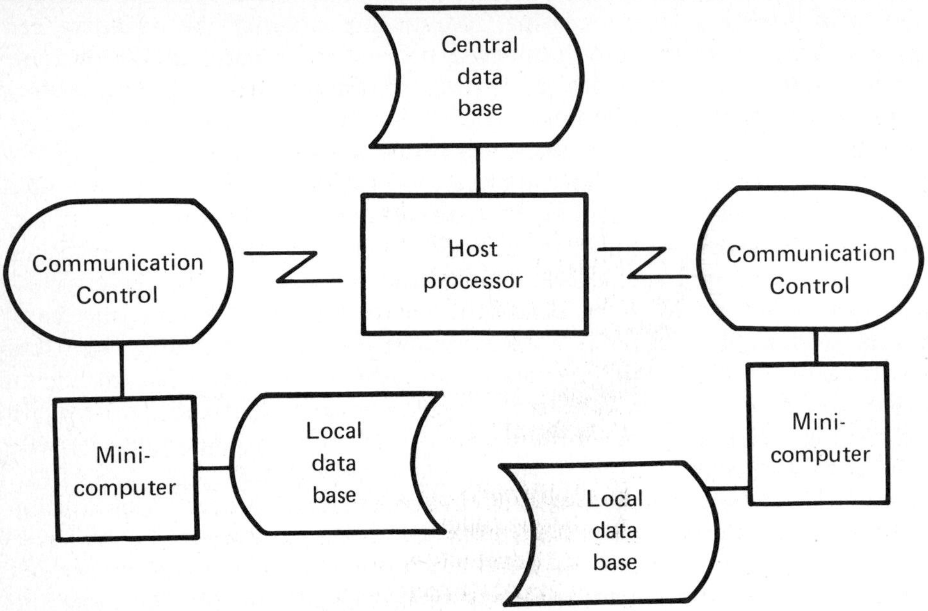

nization. Information resources are totally decentralized, with selective integration at the corporate level. Ironically, the result is similar to the way data bases were processed in a small organization before automation. In the manual era, the warehouse maintained the inventory file, the payables department the payables file, and so on. Automation offered cost reduction through centralized processing of large volumes of data. Files of data were moved to and subsequently processed at central facilities. Users, who previously had access to and managed their own data files, had to rely on another organizational unit to supply them with data. Remote terminals have somewhat mitigated this aspect. But now computer technology is on the threshold of giving data files and their management back to the user, where they were originally—with one major difference: instant communication over vast distances. In the time it took to carry inventory information from one department to another, the same information could be transferred by electronics over hundreds of miles.

Distributive Processing Concepts

Distributed systems can be distributive in four ways: processing logic, functions, data, and control (Infotech, 1977, p. 13). "Processing logic" refers to the physical distribution of processors (and possibly storage) to the points at which transactions occur. Closely related to the distribution of processing logic is the distribution of function, which, for example, may range from distributing an order-entry activity among several processors to the use of a single processor dedicated to the performance of that specific job alone. The storage of data may also be distributed, but doing this is less common among distributed systems, which often rely on a central data base or upon replicated portions of a central base. Finally, a fully distributed system is characterized by a decentralization of control. Decentralization distinguishes such a system from the numerous multiprocessor and parallel processor systems that currently exist. The distribution of control is regarded by many authorities to be *the* distinguishing feature of a distributive system. This discussion illustrates that the concept of distributive processing is subject to various differences in interpretation. A survey of the literature reveals definitions ranging from remote data-entry capabilities to completely independent minicomputer applications.

Large computer systems are usually batch-oriented; they are most efficient when processing large amounts of data, doing high-speed computations, and working on one task at a time without much interruption. Minicomputers, on the other hand, are best at handling smaller amounts of data with a high degree of interaction from the person who is using the computer. Minis are useful in data entry applications, in handling a rapidly changing data base, in editing and word-processing applications, and in situations where undetected errors pose a serious problem.

Some types of situation where a distributed system may be more efficient than a centralized system are as follows. First, large volumes of data are generated at many locations, fast access is required, and summaries of the data are needed promptly at a central site. An example would be a chain of retail stores requiring the current status of operations.

A second situation exists where a large amount of data is generated centrally, but fast access is required at remote locations. Either the central or remote site can update the information. An example is the production scheduling of manufacturing plants.

A third situation exists where remote locations generate large volumes of data for fast response to immediate inquiry. Most of the inquiries may be local, but fast response may sometimes be needed from a remote location. An example of this is interairline passenger-reservation processing (Champine, 1977).

This is not to say that these situations could not be served by a centralized system, but rather that distributed processing should be considered.

Distributive data processing (DDP) does not necessarily require a sophisticated computer network with computers constantly exchanging information via telecommunication lines. DDP does require some communication between systems to insure a degree of central planning and control. One problem associated with DDP is the potential for a random mushrooming of computer systems within an organization—a piecemeal approach to system design. DDP—as opposed to decentralized data processing—requires some form of communication between systems. This communication does not have to involve telecommunication: computers can communicate by other means, such as punched cards, disk packs, or reels of magnetic tape. If a system does include telecommunication lines, DDP implies that some kind of processing can continue without a communication link between computers.

DDP is a system design concept that consists of placing one computer system or more at user departments or divisions. Each computer performs a specific group of applications oriented to the particular user, and while direct physical interconnection is not essential, often telecommunications facilities are employed to communicate with a larger computer. DDP is a concept offering a large number of choices as to hardware, software, and data communications, which may be arranged in the form best suited to an organization's needs. A DDP system is typically comprised of many components, most of which complement or interchange with one another. They are designed as modules so that additional devices may be added, whether they are terminals for keyboarding, storage, or printing. Since the needs and requirements of business change, certain components may no longer be required at a node. Having a modular DDP site makes it relatively easy to reassign components to locations where higher priorities exist.

Technological developments in both hardware and software have contributed to this stage of evolution in the computer industry. The advances in integrated circuitry enable tremendous processing power to be packaged in small computers at relatively low cost.

Historically, as business organizations grew larger, management has tended to centralize control, especially in accounting for profit and loss. The concept of management by objectives has resulted in more autonomy at all levels of many organizations. As profit centers are created and managers of separate operations are given more control over their own operations, they require more control over the information resources that they need in order to function effectively. DDP offers this control, especially in areas where information is time-critical, such as order entry, inventory, production, customer services, and cash management.

Although most computer systems are still highly centralized, there is a clear trend toward distributive data processing. The major advantages of this approach are summarized below:

1. The compact size, increasing power, and low cost of minicomputers permits greater cost-efficiency.

2. A greater throughput is possible by enabling different types of work to be dedicated to specialized processors.

3. Broader range of function is possible, because additional functions can be provided that were not possible or economical using a single large computer.

4. Greater flexibility and economy are possible because of the ease with which distributed systems can be reconfigured and enhanced to meet evolving application requirements.

5. The reliability of the entire system is increased as the failure of one processor will not disturb other processing subsystems.

6. Data communication costs can be lowered as node processors become increasingly independent and there is less reliance on a main-frame computer for continual control and data base access.

7. A final benefit to be derived from DDP—one of the most important —is that processing power can be located where it is needed. By the placement of the network computers at local sites, the needs of the final user can be better served. The critical element of management philosophy is the determining factor here, as the concept of distributive data processing can permit greater decentralization of organizational structure if management so desires.

Control Considerations in Minicomputer Systems

Minicomputers may be utilized in a distributive data processing system or they may be the only computer facility in a small business. In either situation, minis pose several unique control problems.

In a distributive processing network, a major control problem is insuring compatibility and communication capability among the various nodes of the system. If node processing sites utilize different computer systems, communication capabilities may be impaired because of different equipment design features.

Besides the above type of problem, minis pose similar control problems in both DDP and small-business situations. These problems stem from the nature of minis themselves and the environment in which they are implemented. New installations of minicomputers are most often system upgrades from the use of manual systems, posting machines, or a service bureau; less frequent are installations that are downgrades from larger main-frames because of reevaluations of needs or spinoffs of an operating unit that had formerly relied on the parent's computer installation. Accordingly, it appears that most users of minicomputer installations will have had limited or no experience with their own computer system.

The small size of a company using a minicomputer and/or the dedicated nature of the application in a DDP system tends to make the segregation of computer-related duties difficult or impossible. Under these circumstances it is extremely important that the basic control concept of segregation of custody of assets from the record-keeping function be rigidly enforced. One of the aspects of minicomputers that differentiate them from large main-frame installations is a great potential for use by nonspecialized personnel. In some ways the smaller minicomputers begin to resemble superposting machines in that they may be dedicated to a single application and are operated directly by the user. Under circumstances where the minicomputer serves somewhat like an electronic one-write system, traditional internal controls such as separation of custody from record-keeping and adequate general ledger controls become much more important than EDP control concepts. Some EDP control concepts, such as restricting the user from the automated files and equipment, do not apply. However, the existence of a strong audit trail must be insured.

One of the major internal controls over application systems, a separate path for summary control totals from the detail data, is just as important in minicomputer applications as in larger installations. Further, the use of predetermined manual control totals over the input data and the subsequent processing cycles is also equally necessary.

Adequate software controls for the validation of processing totals, and so on, are just as valid for minicomputer installations. However, because of limited budgets, smaller minicomputer installations may attempt to minimize software costs by omitting desirable internal control features. The budgetary restraints on some minicomputer installations may also prevent the development of adequate summary and exceptions reports for management review.

In brief, many of the control problems unique to minicomputer installations are caused by limitations imposed by the size of the company and/or dedicated nature of the application. Generally, a small number of personnel makes adequate segregation and specialization difficult. Most small companies do not maintain internal audit staffs capable of reviewing and evaluating computer systems. Since the smaller volumes frequently associated with minicomputers do not permit high economies of scale, there is a potential for omitting internal control functions during the system development process and operations.

In addition, the lower level of experience with computers on the part of management personnel in smaller companies increases the possibility of omissions or errors in establishing internal control procedures. Rapidly increasing use of minicomputers in smaller, less sophisticated companies will intensify this problem. One of the major advantages of minicomputers, flexibility of location, can increase the difficulty of establishing adequate control over access to the equipment. Another concern with respect to minicomputer installations is that management's lack of experience may permit systems development on a haphazard "in the analyst's head" basis. The solutions to these problems seem to be the same as those proffered for larger EDP installations—better-informed and more involved management.

SMALL-BUSINESS COMPUTER TECHNOLOGY

Any computer system must have certain basic components: a logic unit, memory or storage, and input and output device(s). A typical small-business computer is made up of a processor with an integral main storage unit for data and programs, a keyboard device for data entry, a printer to record the results produced, and a magnetic disk or cassette unit for secondary (that is, low-cost and relatively large-capacity) data storage. These four elements constitute the input (keyboard data entry), the logic (processor), the memory (main storage and disk or cassette) and the output (printer), which are the four classic elements of every computer. Technologically, small-business computers are similar to larger machines, but there are several features that are unique or more common to smaller systems. This section provides an overview of some of these features, contrasting them with those typically found on larger systems.

Central Processing Unit and Memory

Most minicomputer systems are based on an eight-bit byte as the basic unit of memory, sometimes organized into sixteen-bit words. A variety of memory speeds is available from most manufacturers with an average of perhaps 1.0 microsecond typical. An 8-bit processor can handle a character in one byte; can hold two binary-coded decimal (BCD) digits; or represent a number in the range 0 to 255 (decimal). Most large systems (for example, the IBM 360/370) have 32-bit words. Processors that handle larger word sizes are more expensive and are particularly useful in scientific applications or simulations that require a lot of mathematical computation. Typical business applications do not require this.

Typically, a large system is faster than a smaller system, but speed is an elusive concept in computers. A large number of factors affect the "speed" of a processor. First, the basic clock rate establishes the cycle time of the processor. Then the number of machine cycles needed to perform each instruction causes differences in speed. The number of instructions required to be executed for a particular program adds its effect. For many applications, the "speed" is either not important or is determined by something other than the processor.

Overlapped processing (discussed in Chapter 8) is not standard in many small systems. In the typical disk-based system, more time may be spent waiting for the disk to access the data than is spent actually processing the data. This problem is solved in large systems by delegating input and output operations to a channel. To do this, there must be a method for suspending the central processing unit's operation. Such a device is called an interrupt system and is usually associated with multiprogramming capabilities for the processor. A multiprogramming system timeshares the processor and its resources between concurrent programs. These programs can be segregated into batch, on-line/real-time, and in any combination. This capability facilitates and enhances the economics of large file processing. Many small-business computers are operator-/rather than file-oriented: basic inputs are keyed in for "line-by-line" processing. For example, payroll data for an employee is entered; the machine processes the related forms and files and signals for the next entry. In such systems the speed of processing is almost always determined by the keying speed of the human operator, not by the computer. For machines of this type, CPU power is not a significant factor in overall performance.

Memory sizes are usually expandable to 64,000 (64K) bytes on smaller systems and much more on larger systems. Main memory is typically random-access, but small-business systems tend to make more use of read-only memory (ROM). Any ROM is nonvolatile: that is, it keeps its memory contents even when power is shut off. This makes it extremely valuable as a bootstrap for getting a system started after a power failure. The user may not change the contents of the ROM. Operating systems, programs, and monitors may be provided to the user in ROM. A computer always needs some memory that it can alter in order to maintain data. For certain applications, the amount of such memory may be extremely small, perhaps only a dozen or so bytes for a dedicated instrument or simple process control system. Other applications may need tremendous amounts of read-and-write memory, thousands of bytes, to hold both programs and data. Read-and-write memory can be modified by the computer. It can hold data and programs. It is more expensive than the ROM memory, since it requires "write" circuitry as well as "read" circuitry, and it is volatile: that is, it loses its contents when power is turned off or when power is seriously interrupted for a brief time.

The major technological differences in memory and logic between small-business computers and larger machines are appropriate to the tasks envisioned for the machines. The hardware of larger machines is designed to be efficient for large data processing demands in a multiprogramming environment. This is just the reverse of small-business machines: they are designed to be efficient in dedicated task environments, with upward compatibility to multiprogramming functions available for future growth (at a cost, of course) on most lines of equipment. More software options (higher-level languages, data base systems) are available on larger equipment, but they are not significant unless one envisions running one's small-business computer like a larger computer. To summarize, there are considerable differences, but it is just these differences, and their related costs features, that have made minis and small-business computers an exciting development.

Input/Output and Secondary Storage Devices

There are practical limits to the amount of main memory a system can afford, and there are often requirements for data to be stored for long periods of time and for it to be able simply to be moved from system to system. Various forms of magnetic tape recording can be used to meet these requirements. The two basic forms of magnetic tape recording available are industry-standard magtape and the cassette tape.

Magtapes are the high-quality units common to large computer systems. They are large, use reel-to-reel techniques, are capable of high-speed operation, and can be obtained with a large number of "standard" interfaces. They use a digital recording technique, which makes them highly reliable. The computer industry has developed a number of standards that make the transfer of data from one computer system to another via magtape fairly simple. The main drawbacks for the small computer system are the cost and size of these units.

A solution to the size and cost problems has been the development of the cassette tape as a computer storage medium. Some of these units use digital recording techniques; others use audio recording. The digital ones are of generally higher quality and more reliable, but they are considerably more expensive. The speed and capacity of cassette tapes is much lower than that of magtapes. Standards have not yet been accepted for cassette tape. Different systems record with different basic frequencies, speeds, record formats, and so forth, so that it is virtually impossible to use on one system tapes recorded on another system. Cassette tapes are used extensively in small-business computers. Cassette tapes store approximately 120,000 bytes on a standard Phillips cassette. The transfer rate is approximately 350 bytes per second.

Although some tape units are capable of sophisticated stop-and-start and/or search techniques, magnetic tape is inherently a sequential-access device. The diskette, or "floppy disk," is a major technological advance: a low-cost random-access storage device. Diskettes originally came into public view in 1972 as an IBM device used to load microprograms into the control memories on some models of the System/370 computers.

The floppy disk is a smaller unit, which uses an inexpensive recording medium. These units are normally removable, although some have a fixed disk. The disk is magnetically coated Mylar, which rotates within its own protective case. The magnetic head actually comes into contact with the magnetic medium. This is a drawback, since the friction induces wear and limits the life of the disk. However, with a little bit of bookkeeping, this does not have to be a serious problem. The advantages of the floppy disk are cost, size, and ease of operation and handling. The disk controller, which is the interface to the computer plus logic that services the disk unit, is coming down in price rapidly. Diskettes store approximately 250,000 bytes on an easily stored, cheap ($6 to $8 per diskette) random-access medium. The average time for a direct access is about 500 milliseconds, with a data transfer rate of 31,250 bytes per second.

The floppy disk (diskette) is utilized more and more as a basic system component in small-business computers. It allows rapid, direct access to systems programs and data files, and is a significant improvement in processing potential, as it allows the simultaneous updating of several related files. Low-cost direct-access storage devices have added significant strength to the small-business computer alternative and remove a major technological constraint on decentralized or distributed data processing.

Almost all computers utilize human oriented I/O devices—keyboards, printers, or video terminals. Such devices for small computers are generally scaled-down versions of larger equipment. The major I/O consideration is whether a "hard" copy (that is, paper printing) is necessary. Most business applications demand hard copy, and printing devices (largely mechanical) are still relatively expensive.

A terminal is a means by which a user gets information into and out of a computer. It has some kind of keyboard and a display that usually immediately echoes the operator's input. There are several basic types of terminal. Each has certain advantages and disadvantages.

The most common printing terminal is the Teletype (TTY) or a similar slow-speed keyboard-printer device. Its traditional advantage has been low cost. With the advent of inexpensive cathode-ray-tube-based displays, this advantage has largely disappeared. Such devices do provide a hard copy. Many such terminals include a paper tape reader or punch. The data rate is between 10 and 30 characters per second. This is more than adequate for most operator input requirements, but it is often very slow for output. There are two major subcategories of printing terminals: impact and thermal. The impact printer tends to be noisy but can use a variety of cheap papers. The thermal printer is quiet but requires special papers, which can add to operating cost.

Printer terminals contain a medium- to high-quality printing mechanism and a keyboard. These are primarily hard-character printers. The data rate is generally 15 to 45 characters per second. The advantage over the TTY terminal is in quality of output.

If hardcopy is not required, then a cathode-ray-tube-based terminal has definite advantages over the hard-copy terminals. It is much faster, is absolutely noiseless, and it permits dynamic interaction with the data for such operations as correcting a character, deleting and/or inserting a character, and moving data around the display. The price of CRT terminals has dropped dramatically. The major drawback to this type is the lack of hard copy. This lack might be solved by the addition of an inexpensive printer, a single printer that is shared by several users, a service that prints from cassette tapes or floppy disks, and so forth.

In larger systems, the devices just discussed are typically used to support remote time-sharing. They are typically connected to the computer over telephone lines by use of *modems*. Modems are little boxes of electronic equipment used to convert data from digital form into an analog form for transmission over the phone lines, and then to convert from transmission form at the other end back into digital data. In small-business systems, the devices just discussed serve as the basic I/O devices. This is particularly true for the operator-oriented "line-by-line" processing equipment.

High-volume printers are relatively the most expensive feature of small-business systems. Some of the considerations and features of high-speed printers are:

1. Quality of printing: there are two basic techniques: engraved or cast characters such as are found on a typewriter, and dot matrix characters, which are formed of separately controlled small dots. The advantage of the cast character is the fine detail and quality. The advantage of the dot matrix is primarily cost.
2. Size of character set: the more characters, the more flexibility and the higher the cost.
3. Paper width: printers are available that have as few as 40 columns or as many as 132, the common size on larger systems.
4. Special papers: some printers, especially the lower-speed ones, can work with regular paper. Most printers require paper with holes along one or both edges of the paper. This pin-feed paper comes in many preprinted forms. Thermal printers require specially treated papers, which cost more than regular paper.
5. Speed: there is tremendous variation in printer speed. Some printers are as slow as 10 or 15 characters per second, about the same as a Teletype. Others may print in excess of 1,200 lines per minute, a typical speed on larger systems.

6. Forms-handling device: a continuous forms handler is a device designed to retain and space a continuous set of forms such as payroll checks, invoices, and statements on a printer. A forms-handling device is essential for the use of continuous forms, which provide a means of increasing system throughput by reducing the time required for forms handling. Machines with a split-platen feature may utilize twin forms-handling devices to manipulate two different sets of continuous forms simultaneously.

Operator-oriented Systems

Minicomputer systems designed for business data processing are either operator-oriented or file-oriented. In basic form, operator-oriented small-business computers are the direct descendants of earlier electromechanical accounting and posting machines. Although based on computer technology, operator-oriented systems are programmed to operate much like older posting machines. They are, however, much more powerful than the earlier electromechanical machines and are also much more reliable, so that overall maintenance costs are reduced. "Operator-oriented" means that the system's processing capabilities are designed for data that are manually entered record-by-record through the use of a keyboard. The processing of each record is completed prior to the entry of the next record by the human keyboard operator. This system is in contrast to a file-oriented one, in which a file of data is fed in under machine control (a deck of cards read into a card reader, for example). In basic form, operator-oriented systems are intended for low-volume applications. This equipment is adequate for small businesses or offices whose number of accounts, customers, and so on, is not large. These machines can perform the operations previously handled by electromechanical systems, plus many other desirable operations that were not possible with solely electromechanical devices.

Several significant attributes of operator-oriented systems deserve mention. First is the general trend toward "turnkey systems." A turnkey system is intended to be one that a user simply turns on and begins using with very little implementation time or cost. New and established vendors of small-business equipment are marketing the machine, necessary software, and documentation in one complete package. Generally the equipment is not intended to be programmed by the user. To the typical small business that does not have an EDP staff, this is the only practical way to purchase computer equipment. Second is the general ability to upgrade this equipment to include limited file-processing capabilities. In most cases this is accomplished by purchasing more sophisticated I/O devices and software packages. This step significantly increases both the capabilities and costs of operator-oriented systems. Last, many operator-oriented systems are capable of functioning as "intelligent data entry terminals." That is, they are capable of both independent processing and communicating (transferring data) with other, typically larger, computer systems. Thus, these machines may be used to achieve distributive processing in an overall information system.

File-Oriented Systems

For all practical purposes, small-business computers that are file-oriented in their base system structure (that is, minimum configuration) function very much like larger computers. The differences lie in reduced capacity—such as less storage, slower processing times, fewer software options, and less overall versatility—for reduced costs. However, these minis have made third-generation computer technology and its associated information-processing capabilities significantly less expensive. That is, minis offer powerful computer processing capabilities to a segment of the overall market that previously could not afford third-generation technology. Minis also make distributive, as opposed to centralized, data processing a viable economic alternative. The effects of both of these dramatic changes have only begun to be understood and felt by the business community.

File-oriented systems, unlike the operator-oriented models discussed in the previous section, support multiprogramming capabilities and features. File-oriented systems are generally larger than the operator-oriented ones, in base system form they include one or more direct-access storage devices, and they support at least one higher-level programming language. Some data base software is available on file-oriented systems, and the availability and power of data base software for minis is almost certain to increase over time. Accordingly, file processing systems are general-purpose computers, capable of basic data processing capabilities as well as other types of processing not possible on operator-oriented systems. The remainder of this chapter provides a brief description of several file-oriented minicomputer systems.

Burroughs B-80

The B-80, introduced in 1976, is a small-business computer based on the large-scale integrated-circuit technology of the 1970s. The features of the computer include a sophisticated operating system, a powerful processor, and a wide variety of options, both hardware devices and application software packages. A typical entry-level configuration includes a console with keyboard and printer, two minidisks, a visual display unit, and a cassette tape station. A sophisticated operating system gives the B-80 multiprogramming capabilities. Virtual memory is available as an operating system optional feature.

"Virtual memory" is a sophisticated software technique now common to large computers. A virtual memory software system divides a program into physical segments called pages. Program pages are stored on a direct-access storage device that has more storage capacity than main memory. Under the control of the software system, individual pages are brought into the main memory as needed. With virtual memory, only those program segments currently needed for execution of a program reside in the main memory. Virtual memory decouples *physical* memory (now called "real" memory) from *logical* memory, thereby enabling a programmer to write and a computer to execute a program whose physical size is larger than the computer's main memory.

The B-80 supports Cobol as well as several other higher-level languages. Methods of access to files include sequential, random, and indexed-sequential capabilities. The Burroughs B-80 superminidisk system has a one-million-byte capacity on each disk and an average access time of 266 milliseconds. Two disks in a basic B-80 system can store system software, application programs, and approximately 5,500 account records. Up to six disks can be used on a B-80 system. Disk cartridges, available as options, may be used to increase system capacity to over 25 million bytes.

In a data communications environment, the B-80 can control its own network of terminals, communicate with other B-80 systems, or serve as a very intelligent remote terminal in a distributive processing system.

The B-80 has a base price of less than $25,000.

IBM System/32

The IBM System/32, introduced in early 1975, is an entry-level business computer system that may be purchased for less than $40,000. Introduced a year earlier than the B-80, it possesses similar features and options. IBM's entry into the small-business computer market greatly stimulated interest and efforts in this area. Since 1975, numerous manufacturers have begun to market file-oriented small-business computers; each new system seems to be more powerful yet less expensive than its recent predecessors. In basic configuration, a System/32 includes a keyboard, display unit, printer, a nonremovable disk drive, a diskette drive, and 16K (16 bytes) of main memory. Numerous business-accounting-application software packages are available, as well as a higher-level business-oriented language known as RPG II.

REVIEW QUESTIONS

1.   Identify several factors that have contributed to a historical trend toward large centralized computer processing installations.

2.   What is Grosch's Law? Is this "law" still a correct generalization in the area of computer processing?

3.   What is a "minicomputer"? How does it differ from a "small-business computer"?

4.   Why is software an important consideration in an evaluation of small-business computers?

5.   What types of vendors market small-business computers?

6.   What is a "turnkey" system?

7.   What are several "user-related problems" that have become associated with large centralized data processing facilities?

8.   Distinguish between "distributive processing" and "decentralized data processing."

9.   For each of the following areas, identify several characteristics that are unique or more common to small-business computers:
    a.   Central processor unit and main memory
    b.   Input/output devices
    c.   Secondary storage devices

10.   Distinguish between an "operator-oriented" and a "file-oriented" system.

11.   Is the speed of the central processing unit a major consideration in the selection of an operator-oriented system? Why or why not?

12.   Define the following terms:
    a.   macroinstruction
    b.   intelligent data entry terminal
    c.   virtual memory
    d.   floppy disk or diskette
    e.   ROM

13.   Identify several similiarities and differences between small-business computers that are file-oriented in their basic configuration and large general-purpose computers.

14.   Identify several methods that may be used to provide communication between separate processors in a distributed network. What factors would you consider in choosing a means of communication?

DISCUSSION QUESTIONS AND PROBLEMS

15.   A client of yours is considering the replacement of a mechanical bookkeeping and posting machine with a minicomputer system. He asks you for your advice concerning the following extra-cost options. Identify and then briefly discuss the general desirability of each of the following:
   a.   check digit verification
   b.   cassette tape unit
   c.   parity checking
   d.   magnetic ledger cards
   e.   floppy disk unit
   f.   user programming capability

16.   What are some possible disadvantages to a distributive processing approach to systems design?

17.*   Are control concepts different for minicomputer applications from those for "ordinary" computers? Discuss several control problems you see associated with the use of minicomputers. Identify the source(s) of the problem and suggest solutions.

18.   Your company has procured a number of minicomputers for use in various locations and applications. One of these has been installed in the stores department, which has the responsibility for disbursing stock items and for maintaining stores records. In your audit you find, among other things, that a competent employee, trained in computer applications, receives the requisitions for stores, reviews them for completeness and for the propriety of approvals, disburses the stock, maintains the records, operates the computer, and authorizes adjustments to the total amounts of stock accumulated by the computer.

When you discuss the applicable controls with the department manager, you are told that the minicomputer is assigned exclusively to that department and that it therefore does not require the same types of control applicable to the large computer systems.

*Reprinted by permission of The Institute of Internal Auditors, Inc., from the Certified Internal Auditor Examination (September, 1976).

Required:

Comment on the manager's contentions, discussing briefly five types of control that would apply to this minicomputer application.

19. The KEND Co. has recently purchased a minicomputer system for its order-entry function. The system makes use of the following master and data files:

customer master file: 6-digit customer number

finished goods master file: 5-digit catalogue number

open order file: 5-digit primary order number with 1-digit suffix for backorders.

When orders are received, the sales manager edits the order, assigns customer number and order number, verifies catalog number, and indicates discount percentage. These data are typed directly into the computer system. Each day, three-part order forms are printed and distributed as follows:

sales manager: open order file

factory: shipping copy

factory: packing slip.

Sales returns and allowances are initiated by the salesmen. Upon notification of details from the salesmen, the sales manager prepares a three-part credit memorandum. This form is prenumbered and manually prepared. If a return of merchandise is involved, the entire form is kept pending notification of the receipt of the returned goods from the receiving department. Upon receipt of a returned goods form from receiving, the credit memorandum is approved in writing by the sales manager. One part of the form is filed by the sales manager, one copy is sent to the customer, and the third copy is sent to the office manager to relieve the customer's account. The sales manager uses his copy of the returned goods form to update the finished goods inventory file, and then files the form numerically. No adjustment is made to the sales commission file for sales returns and other sales adjustments. A weekly report is printed in sequence by catalogue number, showing the description and the on-order and on-hand quantities for use by the production supervisor in scheduling shop production. Another weekly report lists open sales orders sequenced by order number.

All shipments are made F.O.B. by truck. Prenumbered bills of lading are prepared, which are signed by the truck drivers to indicate their receipt of the goods. The bills of lading are three-part forms: two copies are retained by the driver and one copy is filed in the shipping department.

When products are shipped, the factory shipping copy of the order is marked with quantities shipped and then forwarded to the sales manager. He adjusts the open-order file when shipping quantities do not equal original order quantities; back-order data is then entered into the computer, adding a suffix digit to the original order number. Customer invoices are prepared by entering the order number, quantity discount percentage, terms code, and routing description. After the invoices have been prepared, the finished goods-on-hand quantities are relieved and a shipments file is created. Copies of three-part invoice forms are (1) mailed to the customer, (2) forwarded to the office manager, and (3) retained by the sales manager.

At month end, the computer system is used to print the following reports:

Inventory summary: quantities and standard cost of monthly finished production and inventory on hand.

Backlog summary: quantities and list price value of new orders for the month and open orders.

Shipment summary: quantities shipped and amounts extended times the standard costs and times the list prices.

Sales commission reports for each sales representative: invoice dates, order number, customer names, invoice amounts, and commission percentage and amounts.

The sales commission report is manually adjusted, using a typewriter, to adjust commissions payable when the sales representative has not reached his monthly quota or when he has earned bonus commissions related to monthly promotion quotas. Worksheets are maintained to control the accrued, but unpaid, amounts and sales-quota amounts.

Required:

   a. Flowchart the above procedure.

   b. Identify potential internal control weaknesses in the order entry application.

   20. Consider the following questions from an EDP control checklist. Discuss the appropriateness of each question to the review of a minicomputer application system.

   a. Are check digits used where appropriate?

   b. Do the operating instructions for each program clearly identify output files and storage requirements?

   c. Is the control over the file storage area sufficient to reduce the unauthorized access to, or inappropriate use of, programs and data files?

   d. Is there provision for retaining and/or copying master and transaction files as a practical means of reconstructing a damaged or destroyed file?

   e. Are all data files stored under conditions that provide reasonable protection against accidental damage or destruction by fire or other hazards?

f.   Are the completeness and accuracy of random access files verified by periodic balancing?
  (i) By computer developed totals?
 (ii) By externally developed totals?
g.   Are changes to master files, such as pay or commission rates, and price changes, properly authorized and is their posting to the file verified and reviewed by the originating department?
h.   Are output totals and record counts balanced to the control totals generated prior to or during input processing?
i.   What procedures are followed in order to avoid the processing of source documents twice?

21.   The Watt Widget Company was a small family-held corporation until its purchase by Acme Corporation early in 197X. After its acquisition, Acme continued to operate the company under the former management. In July, 197X, the president, purchasing agent, and the controller were terminated. In August, 197X, a physical inventory was taken and a large shortage was discovered. Significant effort was expended to determine the cause of the shortage, including the taking of an additional physical inventory. The amount of the adjustment was identified, and financial and inventory records were adjusted accordingly. The current organization structure of the company is given below.

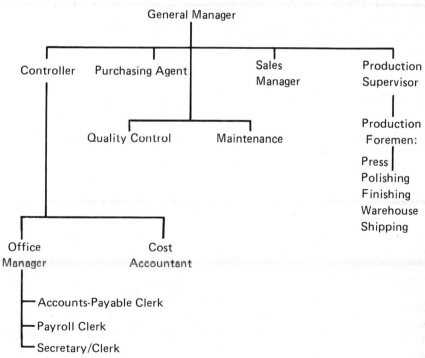

The accounting system is composed of a number of interrelated subsystems, including:

Order entry,

Purchasing and receiving,

Accounts payable and cash disbursements,

Payroll,

Inventory,

Billing,

Accounts receivable and collection,

General accounting.

Most of these systems are relatively new and have been implemented in response to an immediate need.

There are several methods being used to process each of the individual systems, certain of them integrated while others are completely separate.

A brief summary of the various methods being used to process information follows.

a.   The XYZ Company Computer

The general ledger system is processed on the XYZ Company computer. This is the only Watt Company application being processed by XYZ. All transaction input is based on manually prepared journal vouchers. A general ledger summary is the only report being produced. Financial statements are manually prepared from the general ledger report.

The XYZ Company initially offered to process Watt Company's general ledger for a small fee because of excess capacity in a new computer system.

The XYZ Company has indicated that they are not in a position to continue to provide data processing services to Watt Company. The company is currently looking for a new processing source and is considering a time-sharing financial reporting package. Standard preprinted journal entries are being used to expedite the processing of general ledger entries.

b.   Computer time-sharing service

A series of 28 related computer programs were especially written for the Watt Company by a local computer time-sharing service bureau. These programs are integrated to the extent that they update and access common files such as the open-sales-order file, finished-goods file, customer master file, monthly order entry file, and the monthly shipments file.

The system provides the following outputs:

customer order forms (3-part form including packing slip),

customer invoices (3-part form),

weekly report—quantities of finished goods on hand and on order for each product, monthly inventory summary—quantities and standard value of finished goods produced and on hand,

monthly backlog summary—quantities and list-price value of new orders and open orders of each product

monthly shipment summary—quantities of each product shipped, valued at the standard cost and list price.

Programs to update an accounts-receivable file and related report programs were also written but never implemented. In addition, systems and operating procedures and other documentation for the programs being used were never written, or at least never provided to the Watt Company. This has not been a problem, however, as the sales manager was extensively involved in the design and implementation of the order-entry system.

c. Computer service

Both the hourly and salaries payrolls are being processed by a local computer service bureau. The summaries contained on the hourly time sheets serve as the input to the system. The weekly payroll reports provide breakdowns of piecework, makeup, and other pay by department, but do not provide any product or job reporting. The weekly reports are manually summarized for preparing monthly journal vouchers.

d. Bookkeeping machine

Copies of the sales invoices printed on the computer time-sharing terminal are used as the source for posting sales to accounts-receivable cards and sales journal, using a bookkeeping machine. The cards are also updated, using this machine, from manually typed credit memos and photocopies of customer checks and remittance advices. As a by-product of posting to the cards, credit memo and cash receipt journals are also produced. The journal summaries are used as the basis for preparing journal vouchers at month end. An accounts-receivable aging report is manually prepared from the customer account cards.

e. One-write system

The accounts-payable and cash-disbursements functions are accomplished using standard one-write systems. For accounts-payable credits, the transactions are recorded simultaneously on vendor ledger cards and a purchase journal. For cash disbursements, the check is written and the vendor ledger card and the cash-disbursements journal are posted simultaneously. At month end, the purchases and the cash-disbursements journals are summarized for preparing monthly journal vouchers.

f. Manually operated systems

Raw-material perpetual inventory records are maintained on cardfile trays. The quantity records are updated with the receiving reports and material transfer sheets. The unit costs are posted from the vendor invoices. These cards are currently being used by purchasing and are not integrated with or reconciled to the raw material control account in the general ledger.

Product cost sheets are manually prepared. For each finished product, the product structure, bill of material, piece-rate labor operations, and the burden factors are recorded, calculated, and summarized. When specific factors change, such as a raw-material cost, the cost sheet for each product using that raw material must be manually changed.

Production scheduling and control is based on a review of the weekly report of finished goods on hand and on order and on a "walk-through" review of work in process. There are no formal systems for evaluating the shop load or for tracking the flow of orders through the shop.

Required:

Analyze the status of Watt Widget Co.'s accounting information system. Discuss some possible applications of minicomputers in Watt's accounting operations.

REFERENCES

Champine, G.A., "Six Approaches to Distributed Data Bases," *Datamation* (May, 1977).

Digital Equipment Corporation, *Distributed Data Processing: A Management Guide* (1977).

Infotech International, Ltd., *Distributed Processing* (1977).

THE DEVELOPMENT OF COMPUTER-BASED ACCOUNTING INFORMATION SYSTEMS

15

The basic advantages of mechanization are increased speed and processing capabilities, which stem from the integrated data-use capabilities inherent in computers. Electronic data processing systems allow multiple use of the same data item. Once data has been keyed into an EDP system, the data can be used as many times as is necessary to produce a variety of reports without further human intervention. These advantages are gained through the increased formalization that accompanies mechanization. When data are processed by a computer, formal programs must be prepared and implemented *before* any data are actually processed. Lengthy coding is fundamental to EDP systems. The advantages of integrated data use can be realized only if the coding system that is used supports the desired outputs. In other words, coding systems must be designed and programmed into the machine before operation.

Although this is still basically true, the amount of planning and development time can be reduced through the purchase of a wide variety of application software packages. In addition, third-generation technology is now over a decade old. First-time users now have a history of computer use to look back and reflect upon. Software in particular is much improved and much more widely available than it was in the 1960s. It becomes more and more economical to purchase software that has a reliable history of use rather than to develop similar software in-house and to bear all the attendant developmental risks. This is true even for large organizations. In addition to the software, there is an incredible variety of hardware available to the potential EDP user.

In the 1960s, only large organizations could realistically consider computer-based systems, because the only cost-effective EDP systems available were large general-purpose systems. Thus a change to EDP was a major organizational commitment, involving the expenditures of large amounts of capital and human resources and subsequently undertaking huge risks. In the sense that an EDP system, like any other capital investment, should earn a return on investment, there were many failures.

The above characterization is no longer true. Today's technology and marketplace make EDP an option for all but the very smallest business organizations. Large organizations as well as small have available to them an increased variety of EDP options. Users may gradually introduce their organizations to small systems; subsequently they may upgrade with relative ease to larger systems, or, alternatively, connect several small systems in a distributive network.

The point is that today a business of almost any size can realistically consider in-house computerization at the level of *individual applications*. The reduced level of risk is apparent; this option is in marked contrast to having to formalize and implement an organization's entire information system in one great big step to EDP. While this option still exists, so do a wide variety of other options. The material in this chapter is directed at providing an overview of computer-based systems development and some related considerations.

COMPUTER PROCESSING ALTERNATIVES

Prior to the advent of mini and small-business computers, an organization wishing to computerize only selected applications could do so only by obtaining the use of someone else's large computer. Numerous vendors have offered "computer processing for hire" since the early 1960s. These vendors have developed into an important segment in the overall technological environment. A company with little interest or capability to support an in-house machine can obtain the use of increasingly sophisticated services from vendors who operate large computer systems with the sole intent of marketing their services. Historically there has been a trend from service bureaus, which operate on a batch processing basis, to time-sharing bureaus, which offer on-line processing.

Service Bureaus

Service bureaus are completely remote from the user. Data is sent to the bureau for processing, and the output is returned in a few days. The bureau will write programs or will adapt less expensive packaged programs to a company's needs. Service bureaus look for routine, high-volume, easily programmed jobs. The relative advantages are simplicity and low cost from the user's viewpoint. No computer knowledge or expertise is needed. Note that the processing interval is several days from input to output. Assuming an honest and professional vendor, the only relative disadvantage is that most service bureau contracts are of a fixed-cost nature. For payroll and other such periodic processing applications where short processing intervals are not crucial and volume is relatively stable, service bureaus are a viable computer-based option.

Time-sharing Bureaus

A time-sharing bureau installs one or more computer terminals in a company's office. Terminals are usually connected to the bureau's computer via telephone wires. There are many other terminals in offices of other customers, but since the computer is so powerful, the company is unaware that others are using the same system.

Data communications technology is essential to time-sharing. The terms *data communication*, *teleprocessing*, and *telecommunication* refer to the increasingly sophisticated capabilities of computer data transmission over longer and longer distances. Such communication may be computer-to-computer or computer-to-I/O-device. Increasingly, I/O devices are "intelligent" themselves: that is, capable of independent processing. Business data communications take place most frequently through telephone lines. The cost of data communications equipment has constantly decreased, while at the same time its reliability has constantly increased. Ordinary telephone lines may be used or special lines may be leased.

The services offered by time-sharing bureaus are varied because of the extensive capabilities of modern technology. Users may enter input data interactively for on-line processing or in a batch for off-line processing. Depending on the type and sophistication of the terminal that is used, output may be printed on-site or, as is typical for large-volume applications, printed at the service bureau and delivered or mailed by the vendor. The user's files may be on-line or off-line. If on-line, then the user may perform real-time updating of his files and receive immediate processing results via the terminal.

Time-sharing bureaus are capable of providing most of the services available from modern computer technology. To the small business, the major advantages over service bureaus are the decrease in overall processing turnaround time and the broader range of processing options. The cost is typically a little higher, and there is a need to gain at least some computer knowledge sufficient to run the terminal. Large companies frequently utilize time-sharing bureaus for work that they do not want to do in-house, such as special statistical or mathematical work that would necessitate the purchase and maintenance of specialized, expensive software.

In-House Computer Systems

Most large organizations process data on their own in-house computer systems. This option is now, with minicomputers, available to a wider group of businesses than before. The two basic methods of acquiring an in-house computer are buying and leasing. Outright purchase requires a large initial investment, but if the company plans to use the computer for a long time, it may be cheaper to buy than to lease it. The company also gains the tax advantages of depreciation and the investment tax credit. Leasing a computer is more popular for small businesses because the capital investment is less extensive, and leases often include maintenance contracts. Businesses that lease computers are also protected against technological obsolescence, since they can trade in the computer for the latest model.

No matter how it is obtained, an in-house computer is an expensive proposition. There are not only the initial costs of the equipment and facilities, but also the costs of hiring and training personnel, programming, supplies, etcetera. A successful installation requires extensive knowledge of computers as well as of the company's applications. Even when the computer itself is running smoothly, managing it can be difficult. Most small companies will have little need of a large, general-purpose computer installation in-house. Use of minicomputers for specialized systems may be a viable solution to a company's needs. When evaluating alternatives for obtaining computer services, a company should consider a combination of methods. Peak needs should not necessarily define the size of a computer system. Perhaps a minicomputer can handle day-to-day needs, and the company can run periodic reports at a service bureau.

As the size of the computer system planned to be purchased increases, the amount of preplanning and design work necessary will correspondingly increase quite rapidly. More workload will be put on a larger machine, it will integrate more functions, it will cost more, it will require more maintenance, special personnel will be required, and the number of options to choose from (software, peripherals) will be large.

Other Options and Services

In addition to the three basic options just discussed, computer services may be purchased or obtained in a variety of other ways. Some companies rent computer time from other companies who are themselves not vendors. A company may allow another to rent its computer during the evening hours, when it would not be using the machine. Alternatively, one company may simply process applications for another company for a fee. Cooperative centers are sometimes formed by groups of similar businesses, who buy or lease a computer and use it jointly. These centers, as well as companies that have their own machine, may purchase the services of facilities management vendors. A facilities management vendor is an organization that contracts to manage the computer system (facility) of a user for a fee. Hospitals and banks frequently purchase such services. This service eliminates the need to manage the computer system directly.

Numerous EDP consultation services are available from private firms that specialize in this practice, including most larger public accounting firms. For the first-time user, such services are invaluable if in-house expertise is not available. The viewpoint of an EDP consultant is a useful contrast to the advice of an EDP salesman. The services available from consultants include advice on vendor selection procedures. Consultants are frequently used to assist in evaluating vendor proposals and bids to a company, especially a company making an initial acquisition.

In addition to EDP consultation services, numerous software vendors have carried the general software trend of standardization into the applications area. Increasingly these services are used to avoid "reinventing the software wheel." A "proprietary software package" is a program or application developed by a company and sold or leased to several users. If such a package fits the particular needs of an organization, its price is almost certain to be less than the overall cost of developing an equivalent program in-house. The history of operation and available documentation are the major considerations in the purchase of such software. It is also possible to hire the services of some outside agency to perform contract programming. In this case, consultants are hired to develop specialized software for in-house use by the client. In some instances, companies that have developed software either in-house or through contract programming have subsequently marketed their systems to other users. Good software is a valuable resource, and proprietary software packages are copyrighted. A company should always inquire into the legal rights it obtains with any software, particularly applications software, that it purchases.

In summary, two points should be noted. First, the options just discussed are now all mature industries. In the late 1960s and early 1970s, EDP service vendors sprouted into existence like mushrooms. Software service in particular requires very little startup cost—an office, a programmer or two, and not much more. Not all of these vendors were reliable or "good." Although this is still true today, it is true to a much smaller degree. These industries have matured: there are now well-established vendors with long histories of service able to supply the above options. Numerous other services, such as data preparation, programmer or personnel training and recruitment, and others too varied to mention have been available for more than a decade in the EDP marketplace as well.

Second, the acquisition of any computer services is a business decision, with financial, tax, perhaps legal, and certainly organizational implications. Each of these dimensions is important, and should be carefully and systematically evaluated.

AN OVERVIEW OF THE COMPUTER ACQUISITION PROCESS

General principles and detailed tools of systems analysis and design have been presented throughout this text; accordingly, the following discussion is directed at the overall context of the computer acquisition process. The discussion is general in order to be relevant to the acquisition of both large systems, which may involve a million-dollar-or-more commitment, and small systems, which cost much less. In overall tone the discussion is directed at minisystems. Thus, such factors as site selection and preparation, personnel training and recruitment, data base design, and other topics more relevant to large-scale information system design and development are not discussed. Likewise, financial implications, such as the tax consequences of leasing versus buying or the capital budgeting aspects of the computer acquisition decision, are not detailed here.

The Feasibility Study

Any decision to acquire a computer-based in-house system should be the result of a systematic process, such as the "systems approach" outlined in Chapter 2. A structured approach is essential because of the numerous considerations involved in the design and implementation of computer-based systems. Computer systems require hardware, software, personnel, procedures, and data in order to operate. All of these elements must be considered in the design of a system. Each step in the computer acquisition process should consider all of these factors, although at a level of detail appropriate to the particular step.

The computer acquisition process typically begins with a feasibility study. A feasibility study is an analysis undertaken to determine whether or not an organization should computerize all or part of its information system. Because of the integrative nature of computer-based systems, most organizations create special committees consisting of representatives from several organizational subunits to serve as members of the feasibility committee. While technical factors are important, they are not the only consideration in installing a computer system. The feasibility study serves to formalize the statement of system objectives.

The general objectives of the feasibility study are to answer overall questions concerning technical, economic, and operational feasibility. Technical feasibility involves determining whether or not a proposed system is possible, given current technology. Economic feasibility involves whether or not a proposed system will yield benefits that exceed its costs. Operational feasibility is concerned with whether or not a proposed system will work when it is installed. "Work," in this sense, means more than economic or technical feasibility: will the system be used and accepted by the ultimate users?

The length of time taken and the complexity of the feasibility study will depend on the size of the system considered as well as the number of alternatives considered. There are no hard-and-fast rules. The level of detail considered in the feasibility study will generally vary according to the application considered. The feasibility study should consider the use of outside EDP services or consultants, as appropriate to the organization's interests.

Vendor Selection

Assuming that the feasibility study justifies the acquisition of an in-house computer, the next major step is the selection of a vendor. Before negotiations with a vendor begin, however, some form of application study will generally be undertaken to specify the physical characteristics of the proposed system at a level of detail sufficient to evaluate alternatives that the vendors will present. The application study may have been part of the feasibility study. The level of detail necessary to deal effectively with vendors is generally more than what is required to determine overall feasibility, but usually less than what is needed actually to implement a system. In fact, the final level of detail will depend somewhat, or perhaps completely, on the actual vendor(s) selected.

The vendor selection process actually begins with the determination of which vendors will be invited to submit proposals and/or bids. If the project is complex, a company may wish to have several vendors present proposals, and then, based on an analysis of these presentations, it may ask for final bids from one or more of these vendors. This overall process is "purchasing," as discussed in Chapter 4, and should be subject to the same overall policies and controls.

A request for a proposal or bid sent to a vendor should contain a specific statement of system requirements, with detail sufficient to allow the vendor to match his equipment to the company's needs and to plan his overall presentation or bid. In addition to general requirements and some background information on the company itself, information on particular applications should be provided. The following items should be specified:

1. Input requirements: the source documents to be used, the means of preparing and transmitting documents, the frequency of preparation, and the volume figures expected should be detailed.
2. Processing specifications: the new procedures must be defined. How the inputs will be used to prepare the desired outputs should be indicated. All files and records to be used and maintained should be identified, frequency of file use must be known, and processing volumes (both current and expected) associated with the files should be specified.
3. Output requirements: output specifications should include the form, content, and frequency of reports.
4. Control provisions: the steps to be taken to provide the necessary internal control should be specified.
5. Cost estimates: preliminary estimates of conversion costs and annual operating costs using the new system should be developed.

Typically a vendor will contact a company after being notified, to insure that it fully understands their request, before submitting a proposal or bid. This process is generally useful to both parties. The vendors may suggest additional applications, alternative designs, or other considerations. The vendor negotiation process usually provides a company with a fuller understanding of the features of its proposed system.

The role of a vendor may be quite large. This is particularly true for the acquisition of small-business computers, where in-house EDP expertise is typically not great. Furthermore, with small-business computers one is likely to be buying a "complete package," which one expects simply to turn on and begin processing data with. Thus little if any postpurchase planning and development tasks exist; it's all included in the package. Many small-business-computer vendors include some personnel training, program preparation and debugging, and site preparation (if needed) in the services they offer. Plans and assistance in file conversion are also typically offered.

The evaluation of vendors' bids is a crucial task in both large and small systems. In large systems, sizable amounts of money and future commitments are at risk. In small systems, less may be at risk if the company is large; but for a small company, the overall financial risk to the organization may be significant. Basic methods of evaluation include examining a vendor's history, contacting other users of a vendor's services, or having the vendor perform some benchmark tests for the potential customer. Benchmark testing involves sample runs of a vendor's equipment and programs, using a potential client's data. Care must be exercised to insure that benchmark tests are representative of a company's overall processing requirements. For the evaluation of large systems, several system-evaluation software packages are available on the market. System-evaluation software is loaded on a machine and run in a benchmark test. During its operation, the software accumulates numerous statistics on the performance of the computer system. These statistics may be used to evaluate in detail the relative merits of the hardware being considered.

With respect to small systems, the evaluation problem may be particularly acute. Implementing the sophisticated evaluation techniques relevant to large systems involves substantial costs. Such costs are prohibitive in the consideration of minisystems. It makes little sense to spend $50,000 to evaluate the purchase of a $50,000 machine. It might make more sense to choose a system at random (or perhaps solely on the basis of vendor reputation) and spend whatever money it takes to get the system working *after* it is purchased—rather than to spend the same money on prepurchase evaluation. While this approach may also be used in the purchase of large systems (and it sometimes is), it seems particularly appropriate to the acquisition of small systems.

Although hardware costs have become relatively cheap, people time has not. Feasibility and application studies, programming, and evaluation consume vast amounts of human time and thus cost sizable sums of money. Although such costs for large systems may be many times greater than for small systems (for example, $150,000 compared to $10,000), *proportionately* such human costs are larger for small systems (for example, $150,000 to $3,000,000 compared to $10,000 to $50,000). These basic relationships are true for vendors as well. In marketing small systems, vendors have to reduce correspondingly the services and effort put into selling systems. Thus, a potential purchaser cannot ignore the low cost of minisystems in its acquisition process. A company should neither overplan nor overevaluate, nor should it expect excessive demonstrations or consulting from potential vendors. Adherence to basic procurement principles, in particular competitive bidding practices, is the best strategy.

System Design and Implementation Factors

Once a system has been selected, the system conversion process begins. Programs and procedures must be designed in detail. Data files may have to be converted from manual to machine form. Data file conversion almost always involves key transcription; this may be an expensive process. Careful attention to control standards, such as documentation and organizational independence considerations, is necessary. It is usually desirable to have a pilot test or parallel operation period during which both the old and new systems operate. Doing this allows a check against the capabilities and performance of the new system and an opportunity to debug any deficiencies that could potentially be disastrous if the new system immediately replaced the old system in daily operation.

The major differences between acquiring large and minisystems stem from the fact that large systems are general-purpose, whereas most minis are specifically-dedicated systems. Large systems are intended to do more than process transactional data, while small-business systems are directed largely at transactional data processing. Thus minisystems pose less of an organizational shock: they affect perhaps only one segment of an organization (for example, payroll processing), whereas a large, centralized system may touch upon all organizational subunits. Thus a "committee approach" is essential to the acquisition of a large system. As we have said, most companies acquiring large systems delegate control of the overall project to a committee that consists of representatives from various organizational subunits. The committee approach brings several organizational viewpoints to bear on the solution of the technical, organizational, and project management problems that are associated with implementing large, multipurpose systems.

AUDIT AND CONTROL CONSIDERATIONS IN THE SYSTEM DEVELOPMENT PROCESS

Computer-based information systems are becoming more sophisticated and pervasive. The industry is continually developing technological achievements in the areas of acquisition, transmission, processing, storage, and retrieval of data. Executive management, as well as regulatory agencies and the general public, have tended to rely on the auditor and the audit community to help protect organizations against the hazards of inadequate control in electronic data processing systems. However, traditional audit techniques, first developed to audit manual systems, have been affected by the increased use and technological development of electronic data processing systems. Innovations such as data base software and distributive processing systems are significantly changing the audit environment and correspondingly affecting both the internal and external audit functions. Audit considerations in advanced computer systems necessitate both external and internal auditor involvement in the system development process.

Traditional EDP Audit Techniques

During the early years of EDP development, the use of EDP accounting systems provided auditors with very little need to significantly alter audit approaches and techniques used in manual systems. Batch processing was the dominant method used in computers, and an "around the computer" approach provided for an adequate audit.

In general terms, an accounting system is comprised of input, processing, and output. In the *"around the computer"* approach, the processing portion is ignored. Instead, source documents supplying the input to the system were selected and summarized manually so that they could be compared to the output. As batches were processed through the system, totals were accumulated for accepted and rejected records. Auditors would emphasize control over rejected transactions, their correction, and then resubmission.

Given EDP advances, the "around the computer" approach is no longer widely utilized. This approach implicitly assumes that the computer does not exist. Assumptions about the system are drawn by examining the source documents and the output, comprised of error listings, reports, and so on. This approach also assumes that a computer could not be utilized to falsify records without being detected by manual procedures.

The first form of auditing using the computer to verify the processes and controls in a processing system was the *test deck*. A test deck is made up of punched cards (now magnetic tape or other input media), containing both valid and invalid data. Prior to running the test deck, the input is manually processed to determine what the output should look like. The auditor then compares the test output with the manual results. If the results are not as expected, the auditor attempts to determine the cause of the discrepancy.

This technique represented the first attempt to audit *"through the computer."* While it is impractical for an auditor to be able to understand the detailed logic of a computer program, he can understand the general specifications of a system and use this knowledge to determine whether or not a system works.

In spite of the simplicity of a test deck and its benefits over earlier techniques, it still has several limitations. A test can be run only on a specific program at a specific point in time. The test deck is subject to rapid obsolescence because of program changes. An auditor cannot always insure that the program being tested is the one used regularly. Finally, test decks cannot cover all combinations of conditions.

An extension of the test deck is the *integrated test facility* (ITF). ITF involves creating a pseudocompany on a company's master files and extracting selected transactions from normal processing and applying them to the pseudocompany. The auditor can then check the pseudo-company's results against predetermined figures. By using live files and being part of the normal processing cycle, the system can be audited on a continuous basis. ITF is a valuable tool, especially in auditing on-line systems, but it does require the maintenance of a separate system and the removal of test transactions that were mixed with the regular transactions.

The most common technique in use today is *generalized audit software*. This software has the capability to perform audit tests on the operation of the computer system and procedural internal controls. It can also test the validity of large amounts of data contained in computer files. Audit software provides the advantage of using the computer as an auditing tool. Its use allows auditors to increase audit samples and utilize the speed and accuracy of the computer without increasing audit time.

Audit software are models of manual auditing procedures adapted to computer systems. Some of its design features are: (1) the selection of items and comparison with the standard; (2) the performance of mathematical functions; (3) the resorting of files; (4) statistical sampling; (5) summarizing files; and (6) the selection and printing of detailed reports.

Audit and Control in Advanced Computer Systems

Data base software has significantly altered the effectiveness of the traditional EDP audit techniques discussed above. Auditing and systems controls of data base management systems are significantly more entailed than in conventional file-oriented systems. A data base system maintains a common data base for several applications and is organized in a hierarchical structure that complicates all aspects of entering and retrieving data for audit.

The complex data structure of a data base system affects the use of audit software packages. Most audit software packages have not been able to interface with data base systems. These packages have been developed for use on a file type of system and have to be revised for use on a data base system. A revised audit software package could access data either via the data base software or direct from the data base. Using an audit software package in combination with the data base software presents a problem of not providing record interrelationships because of restructuring data to a one-level file in order for the audit software package to function (Wilkinson, 1978, p. 54). In addition, constantly changing technology would require frequent changes to the audit software packages. The development of a revised audit software package may be cost-prohibitive because of the lack of standardization among the many data base systems in existence.

An alternative approach to data base auditing is to dump the data base, using the client's software. The data would have to be reformatted prior to using an audit software package. This is the process most frequently used for data base auditing (Wilkinson, 1978).

The audit function can be incorporated into the data base software. This alternative may be the most cost-effective for auditing a data base; but the independence of the auditor can be compromised. Several approaches are available to test the integrity of the client's software so as to assure the independence of the audit. They include the auditor's review of the manufacturer's blueprint of the software and comparison to the software in use; the auditor's verification of the hash total of the object code of the client's software to detect modifications to the software; or the auditor's developing test data for critical modules in the software and testing the modules during each audit (Jenkins and Weber, 1976, p. 68).

Another proposed alternative to the auditing difficulties of a data base system is software standardization. Under this concept, uniform examination and evaluation procedures could be instituted (Cash *et al.*, 1977, p. 895). However, standardization may be difficult because of the various hardware and software combinations that a client may install. Also, consistency of implementation would be difficult to enforce among manufacturers of data base systems.

Other techniques are being developed to audit data base systems. They include the integrated test facility, the on-line audit monitor, and the audit evaluation model (Wilkinson, 1978).

1. The integrated test facility provides continuous testing of the system and assures that the programs tested are the same as those used to process actual data by allowing test data to be entered into the system together with actual transactions.
2. On-line audit monitors are various software packages that can be incorporated into the data base system to perform on a continuous basis. The monitoring would provide information to the auditors on the functioning of the programmed controls.
3. The audit evaluation model would incorporate programmed controls that process data to determine exceptions or deviations from preestablished standards.

The evaluation and verification of controls in a data base system is a major concern of auditors in order to provide assurance of a reliable and error-free information system. These controls are more involved than those in a file system. In a data base system, the software programs perform many of the checks and verifications for accuracy and completeness of data and records. The controls are, or should be, prepared simultaneously with the design and development of application programs to assure that adequate systems of internal control are developed and implemented before the system becomes operational. The independence and objectivity of the auditor could be questioned when the auditor participates in the system development. However, it is important that the auditor review and test the control decisions made by others to insure accuracy and completeness. If they are in the software, the controls cannot be reviewed or verified through direct observation; therefore the auditor can no longer audit around the computer, but must audit through the computer.

Audit Involvement in System Development

In 1975 the Institute of Internal Auditors initiated a research project to study and document internal auditing in a computerized environment. The *Systems Auditability and Control* study, published in 1977, suggests that although data processing systems and internal auditing techniques have been evolving, there has been a lack of coordination between the two areas. From the standpoint of those managing the EDP facility, the internal auditors' mandate and their range of activities is not clear. On the other hand, internal auditors are faced with the task of investigating an environment in which many of them have very little expertise or ability. Making matters worse is the fact that top management in many organizations has not been sufficiently informed to give adequate attention to the repercussions of inadequate EDP audit and control procedures.

The outcome of the study was a series of recommendations designed to insure that computer-based information systems are developed with adequate controls, are auditable, and operate reliably. Several of the recommendations contained in the *Systems Auditability and Control Study* are:

As a result of the growth in complexity and use of computer based information systems, needs exist for greater internal audit involvement relative to auditing in the data processing environment.

There is an important need for EDP audit staff development because few internal audit staffs have enough data processing knowledge and experience to audit effectively in the EDP environment.

Very few EDP audit tools and techniques meet the needs of the EDP auditors as they approach the task of verifying the accuracy and completeness of data processing activities and results. New tools and techniques are needed.

Internal auditors must participate in the system development process to ensure that appropriate audit and control features are designed into new computer-based information systems.

Another important observation made by the study is that the responsibility for internal control in data processing systems tends to be fragmented. Internal controls governing the manual phases of transaction processing and record keeping tend to be the responsibility of line management in charge of specific organization units. Users can be viewed as being responsible for establishing the requirements for controls within the computer-processing phase of an application system. Data processing management typically is responsible for designing and implementing the controls governing automated phases of computer application systems and other phases of data processing activities. In some situations, controls in these two areas reflect accounting and financial reporting objectives. However, controls are often established to meet the needs of various stages of manual and computer processing without being evaluated within the context of the total application system and its associated control objectives.

In view of this situation, the auditors should be involved in the establishment of adequate controls in new systems, and they should also evaluate the adequacy of controls in existing systems. As for system design, auditors should be concerned with the environment in which the system is developed. To construct an information system for management purposes, the management functions need to be defined and those activities that require information or produce information or both must be delineated. This can be one of the auditor's responsibilities, and it has several possible implications. It involves project management and adherence to a comprehensive set of standards pertaining to user involvement, design checkpoints and approvals, systems design and programming techniques, testing, conversion, and procedures for implementation. Once a system has been implemented, there should be adequate controls over future program changes, in order to prevent unauthorized or improperly tested changes. If established procedures and standards exist, auditors should periodically review adherence to the standards and test the adequacy of the control mechanisms.

COMPUTERS, ORGANIZATIONS, AND PEOPLE

This section provides a discussion of some of the organizational and management factors associated with the implementation of large, general-purpose systems. These same factors may exist in the implementation of minisystems, especially as one moves up the minisystem spectrum from operator-oriented to file-oriented systems.

Organizational Structure Considerations

The acquisition of large, general-purpose computers has created numerous organization problems, which were largely unique to third-generation technology. Second-generation computers by design were largely dedicated to either business or scientific processing. It was not uncommon for a large organization to have one machine for accounting purposes and perhaps another machine for scientific calculations: for example, in a factory or research and planning facility. Third-generation technology was general-purpose and much more powerful at the same time. A single computer was now capable of doing, expected to do, and indeed it had to do more than simple bookkeeping to justify its acquisition.

Clerical-cost savings (transaction processing) has been and continues to be the most common initial application of computers in organizations. Bookkeeping applications show the most tangible and direct benefits of automation. Because of the primacy of this task, many organizations initially placed (and still do place) computers under the organizational authority of the controller or vice-president of finance. This seems to be the logical organizational location for systems that are primarily oriented toward bookkeeping functions. However, to the extent that other organization subunits—such as marketing, production, or planning—are to share a computer's resources, this organizational placement may not be entirely satisfactory. In the first place, a large general-purpose computer is a complex management problem in and of itself. Sophisticated technology demands some understanding by the person organizationally responsible for its management. A controller may well lack such expertise. More important, however, is the change in organizational power relationships that results in a centralized system serving multiple users. The unit that controls computing resources controls access to information. In our white-collar, information-oriented society, information is a good measure of power. There are important scheduling and production problems in large systems relating to both the operation and development of applications. If control over these aspects is in the hands of only one of several users, conflicts of interest and charges of bias may be expected. Historically, these factors have led many organizations to establish new organizational positions at the vice-president level, such as "vice-president of information systems," to oversee directly the information-system function. Under this organization structure, which is common to banking, insurance, and other "information-heavy" companies, the accounting department simply becomes one of several users, albeit an important one.

The organizational placement of a computer should be fitted to the needs of a particular organization. Minisystems, much like second-generation equipment, pose relatively few problems because of their dedicated and limited nature and purpose. A mini purchased to do nothing but accounting is best placed in the accounting department; a mini purchased to control inventory is best placed in the factory, warehouse, or storeroom. As a system grows in size and begins to serve multiple users, special organizational structures, such as the vice-president of information systems mentioned above, should be considered as alternatives to placing the system under the control of only one of several user units. As a system grows in size and complexity, it also requires more management. A large system cannot effectively be managed by a person who is responsible for some other major function at the same time.

Organizational Personnel Considerations

Organizations consist of decision-making positions. The authorities and responsibilities of these positions increasingly require and depend on information for successful execution. The three general levels of personnel —top, middle, and operational—are each affected by their interactions with large general-purpose computer systems.

Top-level management personnel have overall responsibility for computer operations and are probably the principal beneficiaries of EDP systems. Any overall improvements in organizational operations resultant from EDP, such as more reliable information at lower cost, accrue to and further the interests of top-level direction and control. However, top-level personnel usually have little day-to-day contact with a computerized information system.

It is a common fallacy to equate the technical sophistication of a system directly with the sophistication or level of the decisions supported. Real-time systems in business (an airline reservation system, for example) most often support relatively low-level, operational decisions, where response time to information must be low to facilitate quick action. Top-level decisions are usually long-term in nature rather than immediate and are often based on summary data and other information that lies outside the scope of a transaction-processing system. Such information is more often produced off-line and reaches the desks of top executives via paper rather than "direct access" via an on-line terminal device.

Middle-level management personnel are responsible for the daily direction of computer-related activities. They direct the operations—sales, production, etcetera—that provide input and/or receive output from the system on a routine basis. This level of personnel has experienced changes in job content and work relationships. Generally they have a narrower set of decisions to make than before as some tasks have been assumed by the system. However, due to the centralized systems' capabilities, the decisions made by persons on this level have a broader impact on the overall organization.

Operating personnel are at the level of constant interaction with a computer system. This is obviously true for clerks who receive, check, and distribute inputs or outputs and for other system operating personnel, but also for people such as salesmen, who depend on the system to process information relevant to their tasks. Salesmen, stock clerks, and numerous other employees who used to deal with other people directly for information must now deal either with the machine directly via a terminal or indirectly via some printed output. A large-scale general-purpose information system relates yet separates operating personnel through centralization of data processing. Operating personnel experience the greatest change in job content and work relationships. At the same time, it is the continuing cooperation of operating personnel that is essential to smooth operation of an EDP facility.

"Successful" Computer Systems

While it is difficult to define a "successful" computer system rigidly, several factors that contribute toward success have been identified by surveys and studies that have been published over the last few years. Central among these factors is the role of management in overall computer activity. The key factor to success is not technical but managerial. Top-management involvement is essential, as is active participation by all levels of operating management personnel. The design and implementation of a general-purpose system cannot fruitfully be delegated to a small group of computer experts. Human factors, as was discussed in Chapter 1, are essential to systems analysis and design.

Other factors relevant to successful implementation of large-scale systems pertain to the management information system (MIS) concept. MIS, as originally conceived and popularized, is a totally computerized information system that gathers and processes information on a wide variety of company activities in a form that expedites executive decision making. The results are lower costs and higher managerial efficiency. However, studies have shown that in many companies a large computer is used to work solely on clerical and operational tasks such as billing, payroll, and maintaining mailing lists. In these cases, the enormous costs of large-scale technology are hardly ever fully recovered through clerical-cost savings. Such systems are failures under conventional managerial criteria such as return on investment. To realize fully the benefits of large-scale technology, a system must support a broad range of applications other than accounting. While technical factors are important, the main overall problems are managerial. This is simply because management makes the decisions that guide organizations, and decisions require information. Information requirements must be realistically identified prior to the implementation of a system. Although computers can capture and process information in a wide variety of forms, computers cannot identify any particular information as being relevant or irrelevant to the successful operation and management of an organization. This task is up to management itself.

REVIEW QUESTIONS

1.   What major change has occurred in the computer processing environment?

2.   Distinguish between service bureaus and time-sharing bureaus.

3.   Outline the major stages of the computer acquisition process.

4.   What role do vendors play in the computer acquisition process?

5.   Identify several computer-related services that may be purchased from a vendor rather than performed by an organization's own personnel.

6.   Why is a "committee approach" essential to the acquisition of a general-purpose computer system?

7.   Describe the following EDP audit techniques: (a) around-the-computer; (b) test deck; (c) integrated test facility; (d) generalized audit software.

8.   What factors are contributing to increased auditor involvement in the system-development process?

9.   What differences exist between the acquisition of large general-purpose computers and minicomputers?

10.   What factors contribute to the "success" of a computer system?

11.   What effects do computer systems have on the various levels of personnel in an organization?

12.   Discuss the statement "Information is power" in the context of locating a computer system within an organization.

DISCUSSION QUESTIONS AND PROBLEMS

13.   Discuss the trend toward increased audit involvement in the system development cycle. Identify factors that are contributing to

this trend. What effects does increased involvement have on auditor independence?

14.* You are performing an audit of the EDP function of a chemical company with about $150 million in annual sales. Your initial survey discloses the following points:

a. The EDP manager reports to the director of accounting, who, in turn, reports to the controller. The controller reports to the treasurer, who is one of several vice-presidents in the company. The EDP manager has made several unsuccessful requests to the director of accounting for another printer.

b. There is no written charter for the EDP function, but the EDP manager tells you that the primary objective is to get the accounting reports out on time.

c. Transaction tapes are used daily to update the master file and are then retired to the scratch tape area.

d. A third-generation computer with large disk capacity was installed three years ago. The EDP activity previously used a second-generation computer, and many of the programs written for that computer are used on the present equipment by means of an emulator.

e. You observe that the output from the computer runs is written on tape for printing at a later time. Some output tapes from several days' runs are waiting to be printed.

f. The EDP manager states that the CPU could handle at least twice the work currently being processed.

Required:

a. Identify the defect inherent in *each* of the *six* conditions shown above.

b. Briefly describe the probable effect if the condition is permitted to continue.

15. Discuss the objectives of the following questions from an EDP checklist. Each of the questions concerns the use of service bureaus for data processing.

a. Is a record maintained by the client of source records forwarded to the service bureau for processing?

b. When source records are returned from the service bureau, are they and the service bureau output checked with the client's controls?

c. Do the client's internal auditors or other representatives periodically review processing at the service bureau?

*Reprinted by permission of The Institute of Internal Auditors, Inc., from the Certified Internal Auditor Examination (May, 1977).

d. Is the outside application a "time-shared system"? If so, how is the security of the client's data assured?

e. What steps are taken to determine that the service bureau charges are proper?

16.* Your internal auditing department has not performed any audits of the EDP function in your company, nor has it utilized EDP for auditing. In a recent management letter, the external auditors expressed concern over this situation. The letter was referred to the audit committee of the board of directors. The chairman of the audit committee asked you, as the director of internal auditing, to meet with the committee and present a plan to audit the EDP function.

The company has a single major computer center, with some divisions doing their own processing through remote job entry (RJE). All major financial systems are computer-based.

You have identified the major areas of audit concern as follows:

a. computer operations
b. systems under development
c. systems in operation
d. disaster recovery
e. security
f. postimplementation review.

Required:

State *two* reasons why each of the major areas above should be an area of audit concern.

17.† Linder Company is completing the implementation of its new computerized inventory-control and purchase-order system. Linder's controller wants the controls incorporated into the programs of the new system to be reviewed and evaluated. This is to insure that all necessary computer controls are included and functioning properly. He respects and has confidence in the system department's work and evaluation procedures, but he would like a separate appraisal of the control procedures by the internal audit department. It is hoped that such a review would reveal any weaknesses or omissions in control procedures and lead to their immediate correction before the system becomes operational.

The internal audit department carefully reviews the input, processing, and output controls when evaluating a new system. When assessing the processing controls incorporated into the programs of new systems applications, the internal auditors regularly employ the technique commonly referred to as "auditing through the computer."

*Reprinted by permission of The Institute of Internal Auditors, Inc., from the Certified Internal Auditor Examination (May, 1978).
† Adapted from CMA Examination.

Required:

a. Identify the types of controls that should be incorporated in the programs of the new system.

b. Explain how the existence of the computer controls and their proper functioning are verified by the "auditing through the computer" technique.

18.* Curtis Company operates in a five-county industrial area. The company employs a manual system for all its record keeping except payroll; the payroll is processed by a local service bureau. Other applications have not been computerized because they could not be cost-justified previously.

The company's sales have grown over the past five years. With this substantial growth rate, a computer-based system seemed more practical. Consequently, Curtis Company engaged the management consulting department of their public accounting firm to conduct a feasibility study for converting their record-keeping systems to a computer-based system. The accounting firm reported that a computer-based system would improve the company's record-keeping system and still provide material cost savings.

Therefore, Curtis Company decided to develop a computer-based system for their records. Curtis hired a person with experience in systems development as manager of system data processing. Her responsibilities are to oversee the systems operation, with special emphasis on the development of the new system.

Required:

Describe the major steps that will be undertaken to develop and implement Curtis Company's new computer-based system.

19.† Bonn Company recently reorganized its computer and data processing activities. The small installations located within the accounting departments at its plants and subsidiaries have been replaced with a single data processing department at corporate headquarters, responsible for the operations of a newly acquired large-scale computer system. The new department has been in operation for two years and has been regularly producing reliable and timely data for the past twelve months.

Because the department has focused its activities on converting applications to the new system and producing reports for the plant and subsidiary managements, little attention has been devoted to the costs of the department. Now that the department's activities are operating relatively smoothly, company management has requested that the departmental

*Adapted from CMA Examination.
†Adapted from CMA Examination.

manager recommend a cost-accumulation system to facilitate cost control and the development of suitable rates to charge users for service.

For the past two years, the departmental costs have been recorded in one account. The costs have then been allocated to user departments on the basis of computer time used. The schedule below reports the costs and charging rate for 1975.

Data Processing Department
Costs for the Year Ended December 31, 1975

(1)	Salaries and benefits	$ 622,600
(2)	Supplies	40,000
(3)	Equipment maintenance contract	15,000
(4)	Insurance	25,000
(5)	Heat and air conditioning	36,000
(6)	Electricity	50,000
(7)	Equipment and furniture depreciation	285,400
(8)	Building improvements depreciation	10,000
(9)	Building occupancy and security	39,300
(10)	Corporate administrative charges	52,700
	Total costs	$1,176,000
	Computer hours for user processing*	2,750
	Hourly rate ($1,176,000 ÷ 2,750)	$ 428

*Use of available computer hours

Testing and debugging programs	250
Setup of jobs	500
Processing jobs	2,750
Down-time for maintenance	750
Idle time	742
	4,992

The department manager recommends that the department costs be accumulated by five activity centers within the department: systems analysis, programming, data preparation, computer operations (processing), and administration. He then suggests that the costs of the administration activity should be allocated to the other four activity centers before a separate rate for charging users is developed for each of the first four activities.

The manager made the following observations regarding the charges to the several subsidiary accounts within the department after reviewing the details of the accounts:

a. Salaries and benefits—records the salary and benefit costs of all employees in the department.

b. Supplies—records punch-card costs, paper costs for printers, and a small amount for miscellaneous other costs.
c. Equipment maintenance contracts—records charges for maintenance contracts; all equipment is covered by maintenance contracts.
d. Insurance—records costs of insurance covering the equipment and the furniture.
e. Heat and air conditioning—records a charge from the corporate heating and air-conditioning department estimated to be the incremental costs to meet the special needs of the computer department.
f. Electricity—records the charge for electricity based upon a separate meter within the department.
g. Equipment and furniture depreciation—records the depreciation charges for all owned equipment and furniture within the department.
h. Building improvements—records the amortization charges for the building changes required to provide proper environmental control and electrical service for the computer equipment.
i. Building occupancy and security—records the computer department's share of the depreciation, maintenance, heat, and security costs of the building; these costs are allocated to the department on the basis of square feet occupied.
j. Corporate administrative charges—records the computer department's share of the corporate administrative costs. They are allocated to the department on the basis of number of employees in the department.

Required:

a. For each of the ten cost items, state whether or not it should be distributed to the five activity centers, and for each cost item that should be distributed, recommend the basis upon which it should be distributed. Justify your conclusion in each case.

b. Assume that the costs of the computer operations (processing) activity will be charged to the user departments on the basis of computer hours. Using the analysis of computer utilization shown as a footnote to the department cost schedule presented in the problem, determine the total number of hours that should be employed to determine the charging rate for computer operations (processing). Justify your answer.

REFERENCES

Burch, John G., and J. Sardinas, *Computer Control and Audit: A Total Systems Approach* (New York: Wiley, 1978).
Cash, James I., Jr., Andrew D. Bailey, Jr., and Andrew B. Whinston, "A Survey of

Techniques for Auditing EDP-Based Accounting Information Systems," *Accounting Review* (October 1977).

Institute of Internal Auditors, Inc., *Systems Auditability and Control Study* (Attamonte Springs, Fla., 1977).

Jenkins, A. Milton, and Ron Weber, "Using DBMS Software as an Audit Tool: The Issue of Independence," *Journal of Accountancy* (April 1976).

Wilkinson, Joseph W., "Evaluating Controls in Advanced Computer Systems," *Internal Auditor* (October 1978).

VALUE OF INFORMATION AND PROJECT SCHEDULING CONSIDERATIONS

16

This final chapter addresses two separate and important aspects of the system development process. The first aspect concerns relationships between information and decisions—the theoretical basis for the design of accounting information systems (AIS). Contemporary AIS are capable of supplying a vast quantity of information to decision makers in an organization. Contemporary organization theory is concerned with the value of information provided to decision makers and the role information occupies in decision-making processes.

The second aspect of systems development addressed in this chapter is scheduling. Scheduling is an important factor in the success of any system project. Scheduling techniques are particularly appropriate in the development of computer-based AIS.

THE VALUE AND RELEVANCE OF INFORMATION
IN DECISION MAKING

Classical organization theory is rooted in economics and scientific management. In contrast, contemporary organization theory has its roots in psychology and other social sciences. What is known as behavioral science is the application of psychology and social science to the study of formal organizations. Contemporary organization theory is concerned with how people behave in organizational environments.

A major difference between classical and contemporary theories of organization lies in the object of interest. Classical theory is primarily oriented toward principles of structure; modern theory is more concerned with factors that influence behavior, such as leadership style, interpersonal relationships, and the motivational effects of budget and other control techniques. Organizations, in essence—groups of people—exist to attain objectives. All organizations face resource-allocation problems. Resource-allocation problems are "solved" by managerial decision making.

In contemporary organization theory, the basic element of organizational study is the decision. The objective of managerial decisionmaking is to secure and coordinate the contribution of other participants. "This is accomplished by influencing, to the extent possible, their perception of alternatives and consequences of choice and their value structures so that the resulting decisions are consistent with current objectives . . ." (Caplan, 1971, p. 29).

The power to make decisions is essentially what is delegated to managers within an organization. Management is decentralized to the extent that decisions are made on a low organizational level and centralized to the extent that decisions are made at a high organizational level. Decentralization and centralization are concepts; no organization can be either completely decentralized or completely centralized. Organizations are usually characterized as being decentralized or centralized according to the relative degree of decisionmaking authority delegated to the lower management levels within the organization.

Most larger firms are decentralized. The reasons for and claimed benefits of decentralization include the following:

1. Better decisions are likely because the manager of the subunit can react quickly to local conditions.
2. The burden of processing a massive volume of decisions is distributed so that all the decisions are collectively optimized. Moreover, top managers are more likely to have time for strategic planning.
3. Greater freedom heightens incentives because managers have more control over the factors that affect the measures of their performance.
4. Greater freedom induces more frequent checks on outside market forces. This built-in check is more likely to spot opportunities and uneconomic activities sooner rather than later.
5. More decisionmaking over a wide spectrum provides better training for executives as they rise in the organization.
6. Greater freedom bestows higher status and a more desirable motivational effect.

(Horngren, 1977, pp. 674–675.)

These reasons and advantages are postulated to yield greater profits (the benefits) than in centralized organizations. To date, these claims have not been substantiated in any manner sufficient to close the centralization-decentralization issue. Considering that decentralization is a matter of degree, it is unlikely that this issue will ever be totally resolved.

The Relevance of Contemporary Organization Theory

Classical organization theory, which preceded modern theories, evolved with the blue-collar worker as its primary objective and the manufacturing

FIGURE 16.1.   A Generalized Decision Model

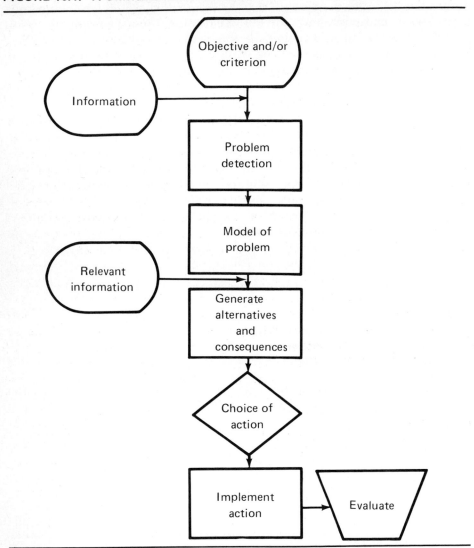

firm as its major consideration. Even the blue-collar worker is changing substantially in education, economic status, attitudes, and competence.[1]

---

[1] Recent changes in the historic pay relationships between white-collar, blue-collar, and skilled-craft employees are noted in a recent study:

Beginning in the early 1960s, the basic pay hierarchy which placed office workers on top, skilled tradesmen next, and unskilled plant workers on the bottom began

But classical theory is simply inappropriate to the task of directing and controlling the efforts of a professional work force, which is an increasing percentage of our total work force. Professional work cannot be "programmed" in the same way as factory work. Contemporary organization theory stresses "management by objectives" rather than management by direct control. The management of professional (that is, creative) work consists chiefly in establishing objectives and obtaining the professional's commitment to these objectives.

Contemporary theories of organization suggest a role for management that is significantly different from its role in classical theory. Whereas in classical theory, management is expected to control actions, in contemporary organization theory, management should control decisions. In a production setting, actions are controlled by issuing instructions and comparing results to plan; operations are relatively quantifiable. A worker is told to operate a given machine and is expected to produce so many units per time period. In a professional setting, one is typically (perhaps necessarily) held more responsible for outcomes than for actions. In a professional setting, a manager is still expected to control, although the object of his or her control is fundamentally different. The control of decisions requires an analysis of decision processes and the role information plays in decisions.

Figure 16.1 presents a generalized decision model. The steps are somewhat arbitrary, but the model is indicative of the types of decision models found in the literature. The first stage of a decision is the recognition that a problem exists: that is, a gap exists between a desired state of affairs and the actual existing state of affairs. Step 2, problem detection, requires information concerning actual affairs and desired affairs (the objective). Steps 3 and 4 concern the analytical phase of problem-solving: a formulation (model)[2] of the problem, which may be explicit or implicit; the generation of alternative courses of action; and measurement of outcomes for each of the alternatives considered. Step 5, choice or problem resolution, is the actual selection of a course of action. Choice may be made on

---

to change significantly. . . . The plant group has kept up with living costs best. Their pay shows them to be almost 10 percent better off than office workers, although only 3 percent better off than the craft workers.

If the trend continues, the real pay differential among the three groups will decrease substantially and the gains in standard of living among factory workers will become evident to the other two groups. [D. Weeks, "Compensating Employees: Lessons of the 1970's." The Conference Board, Washington, D.C., 1977]

[2] A model is a representation of one system by another. A model normally represents certain attributes of the original system and ignores others. A toy model airplane, for instance, represents the spatial attributes of an airplane. A mathematical model of an airplane may represent its flight characteristics in the form of equations, which, however, do not look like the airplane.

moral, logical, or other grounds. Steps 6 and 7, implementation and evaluation, are conceptually straightforward but frequently difficult matters in practice.

The Value of Information

Information derives value from its effect on decisions. It requires data storage, preparation, and presentation. Information is typically obtained at a cost; if this information does not improve or affect a decision, it has negative value.

The *quality* of information generally improves with

1. accuracy: information's "correctness" in reflecting reality,
2. timeliness: being current or up-to-date,
3. response time: the speed of retrieval,
4. completeness: the percentage of representation, and
5. relevance: the desired information.

The astute reader will observe that the above definitions are circular. Qualitative discussions of information are necessarily ambiguous. For example, information should always be relevant. Who would want or use irrelevant information?

Quantitatively, a model of information value exists in terms of incremental expected payoff from the decision-theory literature. Payoff is the benefit derived from a decision. An incremental increase in payoff is the value of information that yielded this increase. Payoffs are usually measured monetarily.

FIGURE 16.2.   Hypothetical Payoff Matrix

		State of Nature	
		Good item	Defective item
Action	Sell	$5	$-18
	Reject	$-10	$-10

FIGURE 16.3. **Hypothetical Accuracy Characteristics of an Imperfect Information System**

| | | State of Nature | |
		Good item	Defective item
Reported Information	Good	.94	0
	Defective	.06	1

Consider an example.[3] A product costs $10 to make and sells for $15. Historically it is known that the production process generates a 10 percent defective rate. If the product is sold and returned as defective, the producer incurs an additional $8 per unit handling cost, for a total loss on the defective unit of $18 (10 + 8). Figure 16.2 illustrates the payoff matrix for the decision either to scrap or sell an item as it is produced. At this point there is no information concerning individual items (that is, no quality control). The expected profit of selling each item as it is produced may be computed as follows:

E (selling) = Probability (Good item) (Profit/good item)
+ Probability (defect) (Cost/defective item)
= (.9) ($5) + (.1) (–$18)
= $2.70

To reject each item would cost $10 per item.

"Perfect" information about individual items would allow the sale of only nondefective production and the scrapping of all defective production. The expected value of perfect information may be computed as:

E (Perfect information) = (.90) ($5) + (.10) (–$10)
= $3.50

Comparing this to the expected value obtained with no information about individual items, we get:

$3.50 – $2.70 = 80¢/unit

[3] This example is adapted with permission from Mader, *Information Systems*, 2nd ed. (Science Research Associates, 1979).

The value of perfect information would be 80¢ per unit, *less* the unit cost of obtaining perfect information.

But information is rarely perfect. Suppose our manufacturer installed an electronic quality-control system to inspect each item prior to sale. Figure 16.3 illustrates the accuracy characteristics of this imperfect information system. Note that the system catches all of the defects, but classifies some good items as defective. If this system is utilized, the expected profit from selling only the items that pass inspection is:

$$E\,(\text{Quality control}) = .9[.94(\$5) + .06\,(-\$10)]$$
$$+ .1\,[0\,(-\$18) + 1\,(-\$10)]$$
$$= \$2.69$$

The expected profit is *less* than operating the system with no information on individual items. This information system is useless, regardless of cost.

The illustration is obviously contrived. However, it shows that it is all too easy to overvalue information. It also illustrates the problem of qualitatively discussing information. The information system in the example is highly accurate and timely, has an instantaneous response time, is obviously relevant, and is 100 percent complete. However, these qualities are not necessarily of economic value.

Computing the value of information requires the construction of alternatives and payoffs. Generally these can only be approximated; nevertheless, a careful estimate is desirable. Knowledge concerning outcomes ranges from complete certainty to risk to complete uncertainty. Risk is characterized by some amount of previous information concerning outcomes. The example was a risk situation; we had prior knowledge of outcomes (that is, 10 percent are defective). As one moves up in the organization hierarchy, uncertainty typically becomes the prevalent state of affairs concerning outcomes.

Decision theory formally addresses the numerous considerations raised in this example. Typically, decision theory seeks to maximize economic value. However, economic decisions themselves are often extremely complicated because economic values are, in the final analysis, subjective. Churchman (1971) discusses a situation in which an airport is to be built, and the problem is whether or not to raze a very old church to make room for a runway. Decision theory requires an estimate of the church's "value" to compare to the value of the proposed runway. One estimate of the church's economic value was the fire insurance carried on the church. This amount was quite low. Another estimate of the church's value was the compounded initial cost of erecting the church. Because of the age of the church, this amount was extremely large. The only decision required was how to value the church, because the method of valuation dominated the decision. Many would probably feel that neither value is appropriate, which is the point being made. In many decision situations, people agree on the ends or objectives (for example, maximize profit) but not on the means of measurement or implementation.

Relevance of Information

In a hierarchical organization, a decision maker is typically dependent on other individuals (or machines) to supply him with data. As a decision maker gets farther removed from the original source of data, a problem becomes apparent. It concerns the articulation between the user and the source of data. How can the user insure that only relevant information is passed on to him? And how can the source assure itself that it is collecting only relevant information?

This is an important question to be considered in the design of an information system. The question of relevance is complex; the intent of this section is to provide an awareness of this topic.

User Considerations in the Design of Information Systems

In recent years, discussion and research on the relevance of accounting data have centered on the ability of the data to permit predictions that are of interest to decision makers. Most decisions concern future events, and thus require predictions.

In 1972, a committee charged with the study of accounting information systems proposed that descriptive prediction models be used as a framework for determining internal accounting data to be supplied to decision makers (American Accounting Association, 1972). The model proposed by the committee as a framework for the formulation of prediction models is the Lens Model, developed by Egon Brunswik (1952) and so named because it is analogous to a bundle of light rays scattering from a light source through a double-convex lens and converging at another point. Brunswik, in exploring the role of probability in the life of the individual, theorized that people often use probabilistic information in making judgments or predictions about some part of an uncertain environment. The Lens Model, represented in Figure 16.4, is conceptualized in terms of probabilistic relationships. The left side of the model represents the uncertain environment, with Y_e being the part of the environment that is to be predicted by an individual, and the right side represents the individual's predictive system, with Y_s being the individual's prediction of the event of interest. The cues (X_i) are the data available to be used in predicting; they are susceptible to observation and

FIGURE 16.4. Brunswik's Lens Model

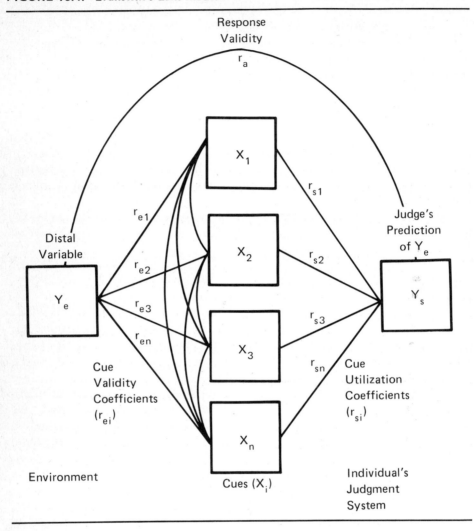

coding. The relationships (r_{ei}) between the distal variable and each cue are called validity coefficients and are weights that indicate the extent to which each cue is associated (correlated) with the distal variable. The relationships (r_{si}) between the cues and the individual's prediction are called utilization coefficients; they are weights that indicate the extent to which the individual is using each cue to predict the environmental event. The response validity (r_a), the relationship between the event and the individual's prediction of it, represents the accuracy of the individual's predictions.

There is substantial evidence in the psychology literature to support the use of multiple linear regression equations to describe the relationships depicted in the Lens Model. In numerous studies, the cue-weighting scheme of an individual has been captured by treating the predictions as dependent variables and the cues as independent variables in a multiple regression. The equation

$$Y_s = b_{s1}X_1 + b_{s2}X_2 + b_{s3}X_3 + \ldots + b_{sn}X_n \qquad (1)$$

where b_{si} is a multiple regression beta weight (an optimal weight determined by the validities of the cues), describes the linear relationship between the cues and the individual's prediction of the environmental event (the criterion).

The other side of the model, the environmental side, can be expressed in a similar equation:

$$Y_e = b_{e1}X_1 + b_{e2}X_2 + b_{e3}X_3 + \ldots + b_{en}X_n \qquad (2)$$

which represents the optimal prediction based on pure correlations between the cues and the event of interest.

The Lens Model framework formally structures an interesting problem in systems design: should a user be supplied with information he needs in a normative sense (that is, information someone else deems he should logically use), or with information he wants and will actually use (a positive approach)? It is quite possible that these information sets differ. In different words, there are at least two concepts of the relevance of accounting data to decisions. Predictive ability (represented by Equation 2) measures the usefulness of accounting data if the user is replaced with a statistical model or educated to process information in the same fashion as the model. Predictive achievement (Equation 1) measures the usefulness of the data if the user is not replaced: that is, if the user is allowed to process the information in his or her own manner.

The role of the human decision maker must be considered by the systems analyst. Accounting data with perfect environmental predictive ability is *useless if* it is not or cannot be utilized effectively by a human decision maker. If incorrect utilization causes prediction achievement to be significantly lower than the environmental predictability, some characteristic of the information set should be changed and/or users should be educated to use the information more effectively. The point is that information properties (predictive ability) and information use (predictive achievement) may differ. Data deemed relevant by the designer of an information system is not necessarily deemed relevant or utilized effectively by the ultimate user.

SCHEDULING TECHNIQUES

A final topic to be considered is scheduling. To a large extent, the success of a system project depends on the planning and scheduling that is done at the project's outset and the control exercised during its conduct. In simplest terms, planning may be defined as listing the steps in the project, scheduling means applying a time requirement to the performance of the steps, and control is the administration of the project after it is begun.

Probably the most common scheduling technique is the Gantt or bar chart. In the Gantt chart (Figure 16.5) equal divisions of space on a single horizontal line represent at the same time: (1) equal time divisions; (2) varying amount of work scheduled; and (3) varying amount of work accomplished. In Figure 16.5 the numbers on the top of the chart represent: (1) daily production schedules on the left; and (2) total production scheduled to date on the right. The light lines represent work accomplished each day; and the heavy line (bottom line) represents cumulative work done. For example, the light line (upper line) shows that on Friday, out of 150 work units scheduled, only 50 percent, or 75 work units, are accomplished. The cumulative line (bottom line) shows that by Friday night, the work is two-thirds of a day behind schedule.

The Gantt chart is a good graphic method for illustrating progress. However, it has some serious limitations:

1. the inability of the chart to show interdependencies which exist between the efforts represented by the bars;
2. the inflexibility of a bar chart plotted against a calendar scale, which prevents it from easily reflecting slippage or changes in plans;

FIGURE 16.5. Gantt Chart

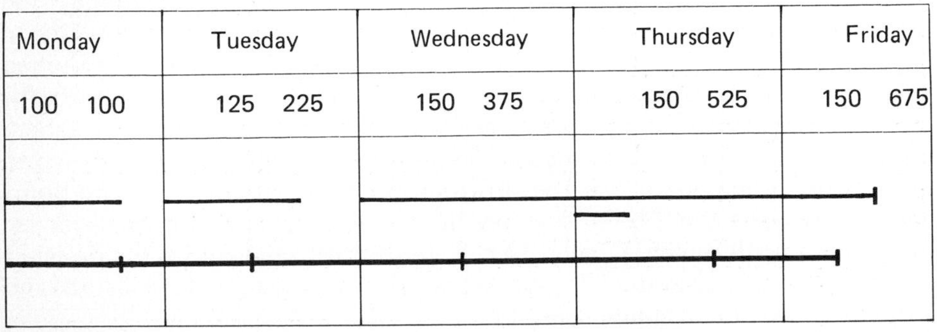

Monday	Tuesday	Wednesday	Thursday	Friday
100 100	125 225	150 375	150 525	150 675

3. the inability to reflect uncertainty or tolerances in the duration times estimated for the various activities.

The Milestone chart is an improvement over the Gantt chart. It provides a sequential list of various tasks to be accomplished in the program. Figure 16.6 illustrates such a chart of seven related activities. Work progress has been filled in and is examined at the end of the seventh week (denoted by two small arrows at the top and the bottom of the chart). The following information should be readily apparent:

1. Activities B, D, and F are two, one, and seven weeks behind schedule.
2. Activities E and G are two weeks and one week ahead of schedule.

The Milestone chart is still unable to establish clear relationships among tasks. Tasks are merely displayed in chronological, not logical, sequence. As an example of this limitation, consider a project that is complete only when three activities—C, H, and I—are complete. H cannot start until D is complete, and I cannot start until E, F, and G are complete. G cannot start till D is complete, which in turn cannot start until B is complete. E must follow B and F must follow A.

Attempting to represent this on a Milestone chart could result in a diagram as shown in Figure 16.7, upper. This does not indicate that activity I *necessarily* depends on activities E, F, and G. The same informa-

---

FIGURE 16.6. Milestone Chart

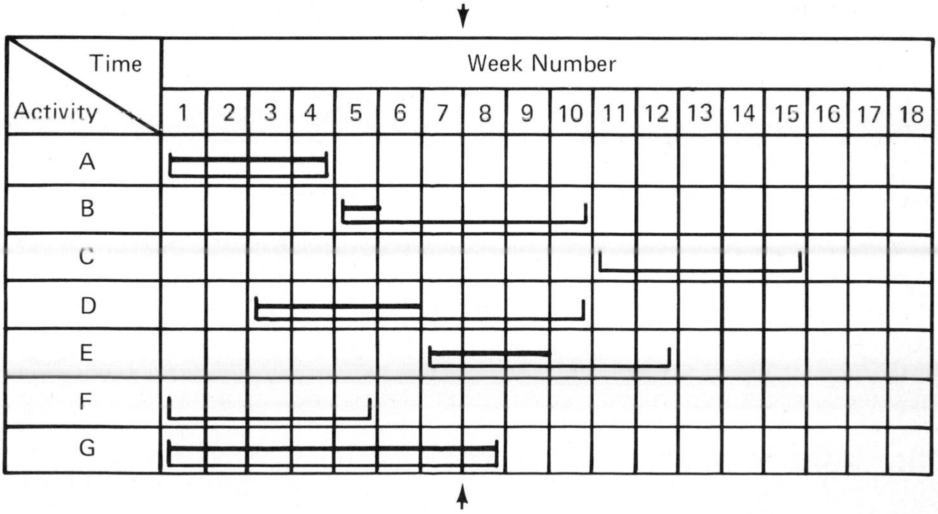

FIGURE 16.7.   Milestone Chart and Arrow Network for Nine Activities

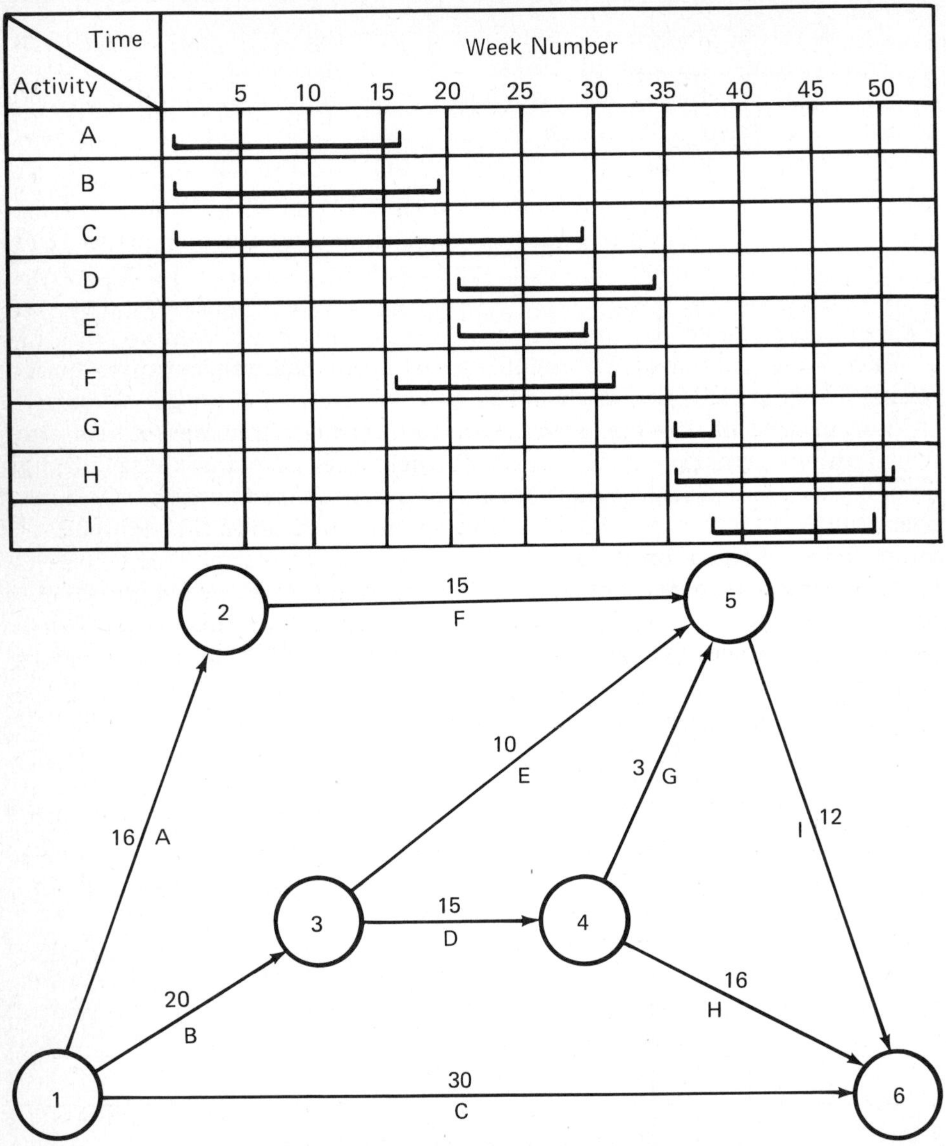

tion is displayed (Figure 16.7, lower) through the use of a simple arrow network (upon which PERT/CPM is based). A comparison of these two figures should illustrate the relative strengths of the arrow network in showing dependency and sequential relationships among activities.

PERT (Program Evaluation Review Technique) and CPM (Critical Path Method)

The limitations of the traditional methods presented above prompted the search for more effective planning and control tools. These tools were drawn from the field of operations research. PERT and CPM are examples of network analysis techniques. The present day widespread use of PERT and CPM and their derivatives stems from the growing importance of the time element in commerce, industries, public works, and defense commitments. High overheads resulting from mechanization and the need to achieve maximal utilization of expensive plant, equipment, manpower, and other resources have made it essential that the planning and control of projects are precise and provide ample warning of difficulties that may lie ahead, in sufficient time to permit any replanning that may be necessary.

PERT and CPM provide a clear picture of the relationship between the activities or operations making up the project and show how delays at any particular stage will affect the remainder of the project. In this way, resources can be reallocated well in advance and last-minute panics and delays, which could be irrevocable or costly to overcome, are avoided. In their original form, PERT and CPM closely resembled each other, although a few variations existed. At the present time, the two methods are almost completely interchangeable. CPM was developed in industry in the late 1950s. PERT was developed by the U.S. Navy Special Projects Office in 1957. PERT was used by the contractors of the Polaris program (1958) and is credited with making it possible for the Navy to obtain ballistic missiles for submarines years ahead of schedule.

Basically, PERT and CPM consist of the division of a project into clearly defined activities. An activity represents a task that has to be carried out. An event is an occurrence at a point in time marking the commencement or completion of one or more activities. An event itself takes no time. There must be continuity through the network. Every activity must be connected to the beginning and end of the project. The project is illustrated graphically as a network of arrows, with each arrow representing an activity. Activities that follow each other during the project are drawn as arrows in sequence, with the direction of the arrow indicating progress. Activities that can be carried out concurrently are drawn as arrows in parallel. There cannot be a closed loop. A closed loop represents a backward passage of time, which is not possible. Dummy arrows may be used to show that one event cannot take place until a previous event has taken place, although there may be no job or activity connecting the two. A dummy indicates logical dependence. Events are numbered for scheduling and analysis. It is desirable to leave gaps in numbering in order to facilitate later changes, if required.

A complex project will be made up of many such sequences, and the interrelationship of these sequences is illustrated by the direction of the arrows that connect the sequences. Once the network has been completed, it is possible to assign details of durations, cost, and resources to each activity. The next step involves the determination of the critical path, calculations of float, earliest and latest start, and finish time.

Earliest event time (T_E) is the earliest time or date when an event can take place. It is based on the length of time required to carry out the chain of activities that leads up to this event. Where two or more chains of activities lead up to an event, the earliest time at which that event can take place is the time of the chain taking the longest time to complete. Latest event time (T_L) is the latest time at which an event must start if the project is to be completed on time. The procedure is to start with the project and event and work backward through the network, deducting the duration of the activity from the latest event time of its end event. The critical path is that sequence of activities which determines the total project time, the project time being the earliest time by which the project can be completed. The critical path is therefore the longest path to completion of the project. Total float (F_T) is the amount of spare time that can be attributed to an activity in a noncritical path such that the duration of that activity does not delay the next activity in sequence, and the duration of the noncritical path does not exceed the duration of the critical path.

After the chart has been completed, it is possible to examine, schedule, and control the rate of progress, costs, and allocation of resources. Activity times are calculated as follows:

1. Earliest start time (E_S) is the earliest time at which an activity can start: that is, immediately when the start occurs.
2. Earliest finish time (E_F): for the earliest finish, an activity must start at the earliest start time.
3. Latest start time (L_S) is the latest time at which an activity can start without delaying the finish of a project.
4. Latest finish time (L_F): the latest time at which an activity can finish is immediately before the latest time at which the end event takes place.

Note that the difference between the two start times and between the two finish times are the same and equal to the total float of an activity. Where the difference is zero, there is zero total float, and the activity is on the critical path.

Figure 16.8 illustrates a PERT/CPM analysis for the project management of a computer information system application development. Once

FIGURE 16.8.   PERT/CPM Illustration

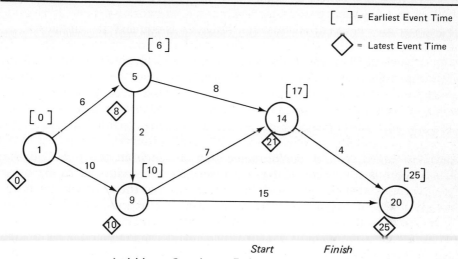

			Start		Finish			
Activities	Duration		Early	Late	Early	Late	Float	Critical
	d		Es	Ls	Ef	Lf	Fr	
Application Study	1–5	6	0	2	6	8	2	
Vendor Selection	1–9	10	0	0	10	10	0	√
Output Design	5–9	2	6	8	8	10	2	
Form Design	5–14	8	6	13	14	21	7	
Program Design	9–14	7	10	14	17	21	4	
Equipment Delivery	9–20	15	10	10	25	25	0	√
Documentation	14–20	4	17	21	21	25	4	

the chart is drawn, the statistics are calculated in two passes through the chart. In the forward pass, the earliest event time (T_E) is calculated for each event:

1. Set $T_E = 0$ for the initial event.
2. For each activity, the earliest start time (E_S) is equal to the largest of the arrow times for previous events.
3. For each activity, the earliest finish time (E_F) is equal to the earliest start time (E_S) + d, the estimate of the duration of an activity.
4. For each event other than the initial, T_E is equal to the largest E_F.

In the backward pass,

1. Put $T_L = T_E$ for the final event.

2. For each event $L_F = T_L$ of the successor event. T_L is the smallest of all arrow times, working backward.
3. For each activity, $L_S = L_F - d$.
4. For each event other than the final, T_L is equal to the smallest L_S.

In Figure 16.8, path 1-9, 9-20 is the critical path. If some of the resources being used in noncritical activities may be diverted toward activities on the critical path, it may be possible to shorten the project completion time at little or no additional cost. The preparation of a network and the processing of the time schedules enables an acceptable plan to be established. Inevitably, and regardless of the amount of effort and care taken, actual performance will differ from the plan. So that close control can be maintained, it is necessary to measure actual progress, compare this with the planned progress, gauge the effect of any deviation from the plan, and then replan to meet the new circumstances.

This will be a continuous process during the life of the project. The frequency of each cycle or review will depend on the amount of control required and the type of project. Most leading computer manufacturers provide a complete range of "canned" versions of PERT/CPM. Reviews using the computer may be a relatively simple matter, involving only amendment of some of the input data.

PERT/CPM methods have many advantages; these stem from the rigor and documentation necessary in quantifying planning information. However, planning by such methods can be time-consuming and expensive. A common estimate is that PERT/CPM costs twice as much as conventional planning methods.

The PERT/CPM distinction rests on the element of uncertainty. PERT techniques are associated with the use of three time estimates for each activity's duration—an optimistic (T_o), pessimistic (T_p), and an expected time estimate (T_m). These may be statistically analyzed to provide probability estimates concerning the duration of the project. The estimated mean time of an activity (T_E) may be calculated as follows:

$$T_E = \frac{T_o + 4\,T_m + T_p}{6}$$

This statistic approximates a common statistical distribution known as the beta distribution. The interested reader is referred to the bibliography at the end of the chapter for further discussion of the uncertainty element in PERT methods.

REVIEW QUESTIONS

1. What is meant by the term *decentralization*?

2. Why are many large firms decentralized?

3. Are the principles of management relevant to a blue-collar or factory setting the same as those relevant to the management of a CPA or law firm? If not, how and why do they differ?

4. Why must information have value? Can the value of information always be measured?

5. Distinguish among certainty, risk, and uncertainty.

6. What does the Lens Model suggest about the concept of relevant information?

7. What does the Lens Model framework suggest concerning the preparation of accounting reports for use by management?

8. Does computer technology affect the relevance of accounting information?

9. Outline the steps necessary to develop a Gantt Chart.

10. Outline the steps necessary to prepare a PERT/CPM chart. What is a "critical path"?

11. What is a "dummy activity" in a PERT/CPM network? Why is it sometimes necessary for networks to include dummy activities?

DISCUSSION QUESTIONS AND PROBLEMS

12. The chapter contained an illustration in which the value of the information provided by a quality-control system was measured using the incremental expected-payoff model of decision theory.
   a. Can relevance be determined qualitatively?
   b. Could the accuracy of the information system be improved to a point where the value of information it provided was economic? What level of accuracy is required?

13. A machine produces either 2, or 10, or 25 percent defectives. It costs $600 to check the machine each morning to guarantee that it will produce 2 percent defectives for that day. If the machine is not checked, the extra cost created by a batch containing 10 percent defectives is $500, and with a batch containing 25 percent defectives is $3,000. The probability that the machine will be in a state producing a percentage of

defectives of 2, 10, or 25 percent is .7, .2, and .1, respectively. What should the manager decide if his objective is to minimize the expected costs?

What is the expected value of perfect information concerning the true state of nature (2, 10, or 25 percent)?

14. Discuss "predictive ability" as it relates to the concept of relevance. How can predictive ability be measured?

15. Is "depreciation" always a relevant expense in an income statement? Discuss.

16. An accountant prepares an income statement for a production manager based on "direct costing," an accounting technique that the manager does not understand. Discuss this situation in the context of the Lens Model.

17.* A construction company has contracted to complete a new building and has asked for assistance in analyzing the project. Using the *program evaluation* and Review Technique (PERT), the following network has been developed.

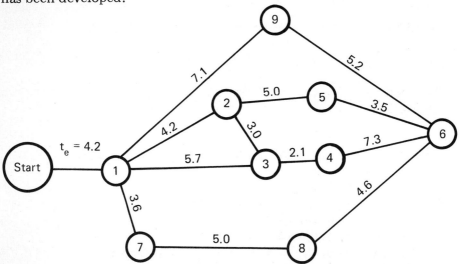

All paths from the start point to the finish point, event 6, represent activities or processes that must be completed before the entire project, the building, will be completed. The numbers above the paths or line segments represent expected completion times for the activities or processes.

*Material from the Uniform CPA Examinations and Unofficial Answers, copyright © 1971 by the American Institute of Certified Public Accountants, Inc., is reprinted (or adapted) with permission.

The expected time is based upon the commonly used 1-4-1, three-estimate method. For example, the three-estimate method gives an estimated time of 4.2 to complete event 1.

Answer the following questions:

The critical path (the path requiring the greatest amount of time) is
a.   1-2-5-6.
b.   1-2-3-4-6.
c.   1-3-4-6.
d.   1-7-8-6.
e.   1-9-6.

Slack time on path 1-9-6 equals
a.   4.3
b.   2.8
c.   .9
d.   .4
e.   0

The latest time for reaching event 6 via path 1-2-5-6 is
a.   20.8
b.   19.3
c.   17.4
d.   16.5
e.   12.7

The earliest time for reaching event 6 via path 1-2-5-6 is
a.   20.8
b.   16.9
c.   16.5
d.   12.7
e.   3.5

If all other paths are operating on schedule, but path segment 7-8 has an unfavorable time variance of 1.9,
a.   The critical path will be shortened.
b.   The critical path will be eliminated.
c.   The critical path will be unaffected.
d.   Another path will become the critical path.
e.   The critical path will have an increased time of 1.9.

18.* Wright Company employs a computer-based data processing system for maintaining all company records. The present system was developed in stages over the past five years and has been fully operational for the last twenty-four months.

When the system was being designed, all department heads were asked to specify the types of information and reports they would need for

*Adapted from C.M.A. Examination.

planning and controlling operations. The systems department attempted to meet the specifications of each department head. Company management specified that certain other reports be prepared for department heads. During the five years of systems development and operation there have been several changes in the department-head positions due to attrition and promotions. The new department heads often made requests for additional reports according to their specifications. The systems department complied with all of these requests. Reports were discontinued only upon request by a department head, and then only if it was not a standard report required by top management. As a result, few reports were in fact discontinued. Consequently, the data processing system was generating a large number of reports each reporting period.

Company management became concerned about the quantity of information that was being produced by the system. The internal audit department was asked to evaluate the effectiveness of the reports generated by the system. The audit staff determined early in the study that more information was being generated by the data processing system than could be used effectively. They noted the following reactions to this information overload.

    a. Many department heads would not act on certain reports during periods of peak activity. The department head would let these reports accumulate with the hope of catching up during a subsequent lull.

    b. Some department heads had so many reports that they did not act at all upon the information or they made incorrect decisions because of misuse of the information.

    c. Frequently, action required by the nature of the report data was not taken until the department head was reminded by someone who needed the decision. These department heads did not appear to have developed a priority system for acting on the information produced by the data processing system.

    d. Department heads often would develop the information they needed from alternative, independent sources, rather than utilizing the reports generated by the data processing system. This was often easier than trying to search among the reports for the needed data.

Required:

    a. Indicate, for each of the observed reactions, whether they are functional or dysfunctional behavioral responses. Explain your answer in each case.

    b. Assuming one or more of the above were dysfunctional, recommend procedures the company could employ to eliminate the dysfunctional behavior and to prevent its recurrence.

19.* Edwina Jones is responsible for finding a suitable building and establishing a new convenience grocery store for Thrift-Mart, Inc. Ms. Jones enumerated the specific activities that had to be completed and the estimated time to establish each activity. In addition, she prepared a network diagram, which appears below, to aid in the coordination of of the activities. The list of activities to locate a building and establish a new store is as follows:

Activity Number	Description of Activity	Estimated Time Required
1–2	Find building	4 weeks
2–3	Negotiate rental terms	2 weeks
3–4	Draft lease	4 weeks
2–5	Prepare store plans	4 weeks
5–6	Select and order fixtures	1 week
6–4	Delivery of fixtures	6 weeks
4–8	Install fixtures	3 weeks
5–7	Hire staff	5 weeks
7–8	Train staff	4 weeks
8–9	Receive inventory	2 weeks
9–10	Stock shelves	1 week

Required:
a. Identify the critical path for finding and establishing the new convenience store.
b. Edwina Jones would like to finish the store two weeks earlier than indicated by the schedule, and as a result, she is considering several alternatives. One such alternative is to convince the fixture manufacturer to deliver the fixtures in four weeks rather than in

*Adapted from C.M.A. Examination.

six weeks. Should Ms. Jones arrange for the manufacturer to deliver the fixtures in four weeks if the sole advantage of this schedule change is to open the store two weeks early? Justify your answer.

c. A program, such as the one illustrated by the network diagram for the new convenience store, cannot be implemented unless the required resources are available at the required dates. What additional information does Ms. Jones need to administer the proposed project properly?

20. Some companies operate their computer departments as "profit centers." The department earns revenue by charging users for the services they receive. Standard rates are set for the services provided by the computer department and charged to users as they receive services.

a. How might this encourage users to consider the value of information?

b. Suppose a user finds that he could have a special report prepared outside the organization for a lower cost than he would be charged for the same service by the organization's own computer department. Should the user department have the authority to take this work outside? Would the absence of this authority weaken the viability of the "profit center" as a control technique?

c. Rather than set standard usage rates for computer services, many companies charge out (allocate) the actual costs of their computer systems to users. These allocations are commonly based on relative usage of computer services. Discuss the relative merits of this approach versus that of charging users a standard rate for the services they receive. (Note that a standard rate may charge out more or less than the computer department's actual costs, depending on use.)

REFERENCES

American Accounting Association, Committee on Accounting Valuation, "Report of the Committee on Accounting Valuation Bases," *Accounting Review* (Supplement, 1972), pp. 535-573.

Ashton, R.H., "User Prediction Models in Accounting: An Alternative Use," *Accounting Review* (October 1975), pp. 710-722.

Baker, B., and R. Eris, *An Introduction to PERT-CPM* (Homewood, Ill.: Irwin, 1964).

Brunswik, E., *The Conceptual Framework of Psychology* (Chicago: University of Chicago Press, 1952).

Caplan, E., *Management Accounting and Behavioral Science* (Reading, Mass.: Addison-Wesley, 1971).

Churchman, C.W., "On the Facility, Felicity, and Morality of Measuring Social Change," *Accounting Review* (January 1971).

Horngren, Charles, *Cost Accounting: A Managerial Emphasis* 4th ed. (Englewood Cliffs, N.J.: Prentice-Hall, 1977).

Kelley, J.E., Jr., "Critical Path Planning and Scheduling: Mathematical Basis," *Operation Research*, 9 (May-June 1961):296-320.

Kleinmuntz, B., ed., *Formal Representation of Human Judgment* (New York: Wiley, 1971).

Mader, Chris, *Information Systems*, 2nd Ed. (Chicago: Science Research Associates, 1979).

Weeks, D., "Compensating Employees: Lesson of the 1970's," (Washington, D.C.: Conference Board, 1977).

SUBJECT INDEX